*Donald C. Mundinger, Ph.D.*
President since 1973

# *Sesquicentennial Papers*
## ILLINOIS COLLEGE

EDITED BY
## IVER F. YEAGER

SCARBOROUGH PROFESSOR OF
RELIGION AND PHILOSOPHY

*Illinois College*

*Foreword by William N. Clark*
*Introductory Chapter by Donald C. Mundinger*

*Published for*
ILLINOIS COLLEGE
*by*
SOUTHERN ILLINOIS UNIVERSITY PRESS
1982

Printed in the United States of America
Designed by Bob Nance, Design for Publishing
Production supervised by Kathleen Giencke

Library of Congress Cataloging in Publication data
Main entry under title:

Sesquicentennial papers, Illinois College.

Includes index.
1. Illinois College—Centennial celebrations,
etc. I. Yeager, Iver F., 1922–      II. Illinois
College.
LD2341.I549   1979        378.773'463        81–9367
ISBN 0–8093–1048–1                              AACR2

Photographs by Mary Green (pp. 10, 12, 19, 263, 278, 350), Bob Line-
baugh (pp. 68 and 334), Thomas D. Smith (p. 105), and G. R. Logsdon (all
others).

# Contents

PART 4    *Illinois College's Distinctive Heritage*

---

APPENDIXES, INDEX

---

# Illustrations

# Foreword

## By William N. Clark
### Chairman of The Trustees of Illinois College

Every year is a transitional year for an institution charged with applying the lessons of the past toward preparation for the future. Each new year soon becomes another year of "past," with its own unique events and experiences contending for berths in educational curricula.

This suggests there can be nothing static about courses of study offered by colleges that manage to stay in operation for a very long time. Indeed, achievement of a long institutional life is of itself evidence that a college has been alert to changes in educational needs and has adjusted its offerings accordingly.

But, though there must be a certain adaptability in curriculum, some things need not change, and at Illinois College they have not changed. These are matters of mission, of church relationship, of dedication to the liberal arts and to an ongoing effort to provide a congenial atmosphere for the development of general intellectual capacities and constructive attitudes. It is around these enduring ingredients that a college's character forms and traditions are built.

The special events with which Illinois College celebrated its 150th Anniversary in 1979 and 1980 included, fittingly, salutes to the past, evaluations of the present, and appraisals of the future. Wisely and painstakingly planned by a committee chaired by Professor Iver F. Yeager, the programs told the story of how Illinois College came to be what it is, of the disciplines with which it concerns itself and how it perceives its place in the scheme of things in the years ahead.

This volume contains papers and other materials from Illinois College's Sesquicentennial observance. I commend them enthusiastically to your attention. They will inform you and entertain you and give you a deeper understanding of that combination of the best from the past, the excitement of the present, and the hope of the future that is Illinois College today.

# Preface

This volume is a record of Illinois College's Sesquicentennial observance during 1979 and early 1980. It will serve as a memento for the many persons in the College community who participated in the various events. It is also a means of sharing with alumni and friends who could not be present some of the intellectual excitement and cultural riches (and also the nostalgia) of the numerous activities, large and small, which constituted our celebration of the College's 150th Anniversary. We hope, too, that future generations of students and new faculty members will find here a useful record of Illinois College at this significant point in its history and will sense the direction it sought to take in its future development.

No apology is made for the enthusiasm and pride which are reflected in the long descriptive chapter and in the briefer introductions to later chapters. Such evidences are natural expressions of the affection I have for the people and ideas and events, past and present, which are Illinois College. My work as chairman of the 150th Anniversary Committee led me to investigate more thoroughly than before the heritage of the College, a task facilitated by the publication of Charles E. Frank's excellent *Pioneer's Progress*. The writings of Julian M. Sturtevant, along with President Rammelkamp's *Centennial History* and the anonymous *Centennial Celebration* volume, were also very helpful. Many hours were spent in reading files of College publications and the records in the Alumni Office, as well as in talking with senior faculty members and others in the large College family. My admiration for Illinois College has increased as my knowledge of its people and its history has grown and as my relationships with the present campus community have been enhanced.

I am grateful to the many persons who helped so much in planning and executing the design for the Sesquicentennial celebration. I am deeply indebted to the members of the 150th Anniversary Committee; their names and their important contributions will be noted in the proper contexts. Most of all I am grateful to President Donald C. Mundinger for his ideas, his constant support and encouragement, and his fine leadership in the proud succession of men and women who have brought Illinois College to this favored time and favorable state.

I wish to express my thanks to my wife, Natalee, for her encouragement and patience during my extended involvement in the celebration itself and in the preparation of this volume. I appreciate very much the many evenings she has spent in reading proof—a time consuming task made more pleasant because it recalled so many outstanding programs and because it was shared.

*Jacksonville, Illinois*                                                    IVER F. YEAGER
*July 1981*

# Acknowledgments

Acknowledgment is made of previously published material and of permission to publish the following:

IN CHAPTER 6. To Harcourt Brace Jovanovich, Inc.: four lines from T. S. Eliot, *Four Quartets: Little Gidding*, V, *Collected Poems, 1909–1962*. Reprinted by permission of the publisher.

IN CHAPTER 11. To Leo Sandon, for permission to use quotations from a hitherto unpublished address, "1968."

IN CHAPTER 12. The Program and Service of Worship of the Central Association and the address by Colin W. Williams were previously published in *Church and College on the Illinois Frontier, 1829–1867*, copyright © by The Trustees of Illinois College, 1980.

IN CHAPTER 14. To Judge Earl R. Hoover and the Kentucky Historical Society for permission to reprint a portion of Judge Hoover's article from *The Register* of the Kentucky Historical Society.

IN CHAPTER 15. The map of Diamond Grove Cemetery was redrawn for this volume by Roger Russell of Casler, Houser & Hutchison, Inc., of Jacksonville, Illinois.

IN CHAPTER 17. To George William Horton, Jr., for permission to publish his previously unpublished essay, "The Literary Society on the American College Campus."

IN CHAPTER 19. To Little, Brown and Company, for permission to include two poems. *From Verses from 1929 On*, by Ogden Nash. "Crossing the Border" first appeared in *The New Yorker*; Copyright © 1956 by Ogden Nash. "The Hippopotamus" first appeared in the

*Saturday Evening Post*; Copyright 1935 by The Curtis Publishing Company. Reprinted by permission of Little, Brown and Company.

Appreciation is hereby expressed to the authors and publishers for the use of these materials.

PART ONE

*Observing Illinois College's 150th Anniversary*

No society can grow, nor long live, that has not thinkers, independent thinkers, seers, and that is not governed by them. Such men must carry their own credentials with them; they must wait for the endorsement of no hierarchy; they must be sustained by no authority, but the authority of truth and righteousness and God. The function of a college is to aid in raising up such men and qualifying them to perform their high office.

Former President Julian M. Sturtevant
Fiftieth Anniversary Celebration, June 4, 1879

In the life of a college as in the career of an individual, the main question is not how long have you lived, but *to what purpose*. Age and service are not synonymous terms. We hope we are celebrating this occasion not only because Illinois College has endured for one hundred years, but also because it has made some significant contributions to the life of the nation.

President Charles Henry Rammelkamp
Centennial Celebration, October 15, 1929

I invite the College community . . . to rethink our mission as Illinois College prepares for the second half of its second century of service. . . . This year, and in the years immediately ahead, we must define and refine the liberal arts in terms of the twenty-first century. . . . The best education for today and beyond is one that calls for the critical use of intelligence and a sense of responsibility. . . . Therein lies our work for this year and for the years immediately beyond—the examination of our task, the clarification of our goals, and a lively desire to improve.

President Donald C. Mundinger
To the Class of 1979, September 1, 1975

$\mathrm{P}_{\text{art}}$ 1 of this volume is intended to present two aspects of the College's awareness of reaching its 150th year, an assessment of the College at this significant point in its history, and the actual celebration of that anniversary. President Donald C. Mundinger, in chapter 1, characterizes the social context of the College; describes important developments in its academic program; writes about the persons who are in key leadership positions; and notes the successful efforts to provide both the physical facilities and the financial support essential for fulfilling the educational mission.

In chapter 2, the chairman of the 150th Anniversary Committee—and editor of this book—gives an overall account of the Sesquicentennial celebration from the initial planning to the final consummation when the "Sesquicentennial Building" was dedicated. Every major facet of the observance is presented with enough detail, it is hoped, to convey a clear understanding of the events, but the account is necessarily selective; not every name can be included nor every detail described. Events dealt with more fully in individual chapters are described with relative brevity, while more thorough treatment is given to features of the celebration for which there were no addresses or programs to provide explicit reports.

# I

## *Illinois College at the Beginning of the 1980s*
### PRESIDENT DONALD C. MUNDINGER

Illinois College is part of the small-college culture of America. About one-sixth of America's three-thousand colleges have fewer than a thousand students and are known collectively as small colleges. They constitute a distinctive element in American higher education. They have made a significant contribution to the Republic.

Illinois College is a unique institution. Illinois College exists—no other institution can claim its identity. It performs a mission. It is alive. It has a being. There is only one Illinois College. However, I do not use the word *unique* in this precise sense. I mean more than identity. Illinois College has a long history of educating young people for service to the community and for personal enrichment and happiness. Illinois College strives to educate its students. It seeks to influence their values and ethics—humane and principled. Illinois College plants the seeds of commitment to a cause beyond self. Illinois College nurtures enthusiasm for the human quest.

Illinois College wants to be a good college—a very good college. Regional importance and recognition are important but not for their own sake. A good reputation is significant to us because we have earned it—it is the reward of our quest to be the quality "citizen's college" of Mid-America. Reputation is the means to a higher level of service. Our mission is clear: it is education that is honorable, essential, and exciting.

At the celebration of our 150th Anniversary, there was a natural desire to analyze the College and to suggest possibilities for the future. What has it been? What is it currently? How might Illinois College grow in importance in the lives of young people and in a society which will embrace both our College and its graduates in the future?

Before the state of the College after a century and a half of educating young people is assessed, one further word is in order. The last seventy-five years especially have been a period of revolution following on the heels of revolution. Rapidity of events, innocuous beginnings, and lack of awareness of the importance of certain technological discoveries—all have combined to play tricks on some of us. Let me explain. Some discoveries seemed minor, went unnoticed, were seemingly unimportant, and were almost curiosities. Revolutions were occurring and yet many people, indeed most people, were not aware of the potential inherent in these technological breakthroughs or of the rapid rate of change in our daily lives.

The automobile was more than a horseless carriage and the airplane more than a fragile toy. Together they revolutionized transportation. Distance and time shrank. Cultures merged and collided. The world and the College were different places because of the automobile and the airplane.

Television was a second revolution. Television was not just a radio with pictures. While it has not replaced the printed word, it certainly has become a major force in the education of our children, who have become accustomed to the nonprint movement of pictures across an electronic screen.

The computer, a third technological innovation, was more than an adding machine with memory. The computer has become a kind of electronic nervous system—one which has taken over many of the onerous and repetitive tasks of our daily lives.

And, during the 150th Anniversary, another revolution was occurring—the expanded use of the robot in American industry. The robot is the marriage of television and the computer to the machine. It is not simply an advance in the form of a new gadget. The robot has the potential radically to reorder our priorities and to alter how we manufacture goods and ultimately provide for contemporary society.

As we examined Illinois College at its 150th Anniversary, these thoughts and more preoccupied us on campus. The College recognized that it was important to know where it had been and where it stood in 1979. It sensed that there were revolutions within revolutions in our society and that in an earlier period the pace of change was much slower. At the 150th Anniversary, the pace was rapidly quickening. The Red Queen exhorted Alice, in a mirrored world, to run faster and faster, but such an uncritical response was not appropriate for Illinois College in 1979. The College should not react out of ignorance and fear to accept the imperatives of a new social order. With respect for the promise of the new and with an openness to change, the College was preparing itself for the education of undergraduates for life in the twenty-first century. In this way, the 150th Anniversary series was a way for the College, the faculty, and especially the students to become ready to live and to work with competence and conviction in a world that would require even more humane, principled, and competent citizens.

The College, as it began the second half of its second century of service, was a strong institution. The people who went before—faculty, students, trustees, and alumni—earned this reputation. Illinois College was recognized by many as the quality citizen's college of Mid-America.

The strength of Illinois College lay in its philosophy and in its attitude toward its mission. At Illinois College, the intellectual enterprise came first. The full development—intellectual, cultural, spiritual, and physical—of the students was what the College strove to achieve. In this mission, the intellectual came first in the College's consideration. The other goals were vibrant concerns of the campus, but in terms of the way the College worked and used its resources, the intellectual was first and the cultural, spiritual, and physical followed in close succession.

At the 150th Anniversary, the academic program was a strong one, one which was recognized by some of the leading graduate and professional schools in America and one which continued to command gifted students. The most significant advance in the period just prior to the anniversary was the interdisciplinary major in the fine arts. With the introduction of the major, the fine arts returned to occupy their rightful place in the academic curriculum of the College. This change was achieved by a number of faculty members who recognized the validity of the fine arts and strengthened the offerings in this area. In the fifteenth decade of the College, the fine arts were nurtured and provided intellectual and cultural excitement for the campus.

The interdisciplinary major was a coherent program drawing from the offerings of several academic departments and culminating in the baccalaureate degree. Theatre was combined with music or with the visual arts for the interdisciplinary major. Other combinations of these three fields were also available. In addition, a fine arts requirement for graduation was adopted.

Developments in economics and business administration were equally exciting and attracted a large number of students. In 1980, the career and vocational interests of students supported a strong program in business administration and accounting. The eclectic interest had its roots in the programs of the community colleges, the cost of education, inflation, and unemployment—all dominant themes at the time of the 150th Anniversary. The faculty wisely provided for expansion in economics and business administration. In the process, the liberal arts core was maintained; the work in the major was limited to forty-eight hours; and general education and electives totalled seventy-two hours.

In keeping with the thoughts discussed above about revolution, especially the revolution involving the computer, the College in the late 1970s expanded the use of the computer. The natural sciences and some of the social sciences purchased a microprocessor. Our students were able to study the computer and use it in their research. This also removed some of the mystery inherent in the computer.

In addition, Illinois College made arrangements to participate in the PLATO program of the University of Illinois. Many experts agree that PLATO (Programmed Logic for Automatic Teaching Operations) is the leading computer-aided instruction program in America. The agreement enabled Illinois College students to have access to the University of Illinois computer research lab on a twenty-four hour, seven-day-a-week basis and to use the highly sophisticated system of the University of Illinois.

The social sciences continued to be grounded upon strong philosophical and humane ordering principles. At the same time they also expanded the use of scientific or empirical techniques. The Psychology Department added a laboratory to its program and psychology majors had firsthand observation of psychological phenomena in both humans and low-ordered animals. Other departments in the social sciences showed an increased interest in the use of the computer as we concluded the 150th Anniversary celebration. Plans continue to be developed for the implementation of a stronger computer program for the College.

Other divisions and departments had similar plans to strengthen their offerings and to make them more competitive with other liberal arts colleges in the state. In addition, plans were well advanced for the introduction of majors in the department of music and the visual arts.

As we entered the 1980s the strength of the College was its philosophy and program. But it took people to do the work and to supervise the program. It is no overstatement to assert that it was the faculty who made the College. If the faculty is well trained and has high standards, then the students will be well educated and will meet similar standards. If the faculty along with its commitment to its several disciplines has a strong commitment to the College as college, then the College can claim to be an intellectual community and will flourish. At the 150th Anniversary, the faculty of Illinois College was a strong faculty—a faculty every bit as good as the faculties of previous periods, indeed, if this is possible, an even stronger faculty. The doctorate was held by almost two-thirds of the faculty members. The number of senior tenured faculty who had committed themselves to the institution approached 70 percent. Teaching loads were heavy because there was a desire to work with students in small groups as the fundamentals of knowledge were taught. Some colleges have historically been battlegrounds between faculty on one side and the administration and trustees on the other or have simply been battlegrounds for successive controversies. Such was not the case at Illinois College. The faculty approached its task with a strong sense of conviction and commitment to the College. Disagreements (which did, of course, occur) were handled with reason and persuasion and above all with goodwill.

The trustees of Illinois College number twenty-eight: twenty-two regular trustees, five alumni trustees, and the President of the College ex officio. The trustees play an important role in shaping the philosophy and mission of the College and establishing policy. Illinois College was blessed by having committed trustees who worked hard in selecting the right people for senior faculty positions and senior administrative posts, budgeting the resources of the College and working assiduously to raise funds for the support of the academic program. The Chairman of the Board of Trustees, William N. Clark '40, Secretary of Chicago Tribune Company and Executive Director of McCormick Charities, has been a trustee since 1957 and chairman since 1966. During the Sesquicentennial Anniversary, Mr. Clark approached fifteen years of service as Chairman of the Trustees. By any measure those fifteen years were some of the most vibrant, vital, and productive in our history. The College was a strong school because of the trustees and especially the leadership of William Clark.

In one sense, the alumni are the mirror or the reflection of the faculty. The values, the competencies, the excitement of the faculty directly reflect in the lives and work of the alumni. The alumni of Illinois College, some seven thousand strong, are active in their interest and support of the College. Along with their commitment, they made personal suggestions and recommendations; they were active in program development; and many contributed generously and sacrificially—all good omens for the future.

The administrative staff of the College is competent and dedicated. In the 1980s, a college simply is not a teacher sitting on a log meeting with a handful of students. A college of eight-hundred students requires the handling of many details, whether these matters involve student records, retirement plans, or the administration of large sums of scholarship assistance. The Dean of the College, Dr. Wallace N. Jamison, is a strong academic leader with a commitment to educational quality. He is responsible for the curriculum and has strengthened both the quality and number of offerings. The Development Staff completed successful campaigns for the Schewe Library and the McGaw Fine Arts Center. These efforts have been led by Howard M. Jarratt, Director of Development.

One area which has given faculty, students, trustees, and alumni a great deal of joy has been the admissions program. The staff is

*William N. Clark '40*
Trustee Since 1957
Chairman of Trustees, 1966–81

*Lyndle W. Hess '30*
Trustee, 1961–81; Chairman,
Long-Range Planning Committee

under the able direction of James M. Downer '66. The philosophy of
the department is to serve students. Students are best served when
the right people are selected for the right academic major at the right
college. The admissions staff works to achieve this goal. The
strategy is an intensely personal effort to locate, to inform, and finally to admit students. While the quantitative goal has remained
constant at approximately three-hundred students each academic
year, there has been an increase in the qualitative character of the
students. The College is striving for a larger number of entering
freshmen in the upper half of their high school class and with higher
scores on the American College Testing examination. This effort has
been a success; the College has made incremental gains in quality
with each new entering class. Thus the students are more able to
challenge the scholarly interests of the faculty and the academic program has become more exciting and rigorous.

Finally, the work of the College Business Office under the direction of Russell Walton '50 should be recognized. Often unheralded,
sometimes misunderstood, always working with limited budgets,
the business staff is skilled and keenly committed to the welfare of
students, faculty, and College. They have worked hard to provide

accurate and reliable records and to administer business matters to support the growth of the quality of life on campus.

Earlier mention was made of the success of recent campaigns. The 150th Challenge Fund began as the Library Campaign concluded. Karl and Louise Schewe made gifts of approximately $500,000 to the College as leadership gifts for the 150th Challenge Fund. The library was named after the Schewes and their gifts became the seeds for a major thrust into the fine arts. The Kresge Foundation, long a benefactor of the College, contributed $150,000 to the new fund. Later, Foster and Mary McGaw of Evanston contributed $1,000,000 to the College for a Fine Arts Center. With the McGaw gift, the original dreams for a Fine Arts Center could be expanded. While new plans were taking shape, L. D. Sibert and Robert F. Sibert '36 and family of Jacksonville made a gift of $525,000, an addition to the endowment for the support of the Fine Arts Center.

The early gifts or the leadership gifts, if you will, set the stage for a successful 150th Challenge Fund. Many friends and alumni came to the assistance of the College at its 150th Anniversary. The leadership of the campaign was in the hands of Carol C. Lohman '45 and William E. Wilton '39. They met regularly with the staff of the College and with a small campaign committee. They were assisted also by national vice-chairmen. (These persons are listed in Appendix A.)

The campaign was conducted over a forty-two month period and concluded on December 31, 1980. No federal or state money was included in this campaign and the amount of gifts from all sources including estates was over $5,250,000.

Indeed, at this writing during the early days of the Spring of 1981, the College has received word that it was included in the will of Alma Blum, the wife of Fred Blum '19. Mrs. Blum shared the vision of her husband for Illinois College, and she was especially persuaded of the importance of the fine arts in an undergraduate education. The trustees have named the music area in the McGaw Fine Arts Center the Blum Music Wing in appreciation for the Blums' vision and support of the College.

The College endowment is in strong condition. In the last twenty-five years it has grown to over $7,500,000. An additional $400,000

*Trustee Leadership During Sesquicentennial Plan*
William E. Wilton '39, Cochairman, 150th Anniversary Challenge Fund; Carol
Coultas Lohman '45, Cochairman, 150th Anniversary Challenge Fund; William N.
Clark '40, Chairman of The Trustees of Illinois College, 1966–81; and Paul F. Cor-
nelsen, Chairman, Trustees' Committee on the Fine Arts Center

currently resides in the Pooled Income Fund: that is, funds owned
by the College and providing lifetime incomes to beneficiaries. We
are rapidly reaching the textbook level of $10,000 of endowment for
each student. The future, however, will require a larger endowment
and the trustees have wisely announced that all undesignated bequests to the College shall be added to the general endowment. The
income from such gifts will support a growing academic program in
perpetuity. It is not crass to say that quality costs money. If Illinois
College is to reach premiership as the citizen's college in Mid-
America then the endowment must continue to grow.

In the final decade of the College's 150-year history, a number of
important buildings were added to the campus. But such a statement
does not recognize the post World War II developments that rightfully must be mentioned if proper credit for today's facilities is to be
given. President Hudson was responsible for the construction of the
Memorial Gymnasium after World War II; President Selden completed Gardner Hall; President Caine, beginning in 1956, built Ellis,
Turner, Pixley, Crispin, Rammelkamp, Caine Student Center, and a

*Memorial Gymnasium, 1951*
Named in Honor of the Illinois College Students Who Served in the Armed Forces

*Swimming Pool, 1964*
*Gustafson Gymnasium, 1977*
Named for Carl A. Gustafson '16, Donor

swimming pool addition to the gymnasium; he also renovated Sturtevant Hall.

In 1972, the trustees had adopted a Sesquicentennial Plan. An ambitious series of projects was established for the celebration of the 150th Anniversary. A new library was the top priority, followed by the renovation of Tanner, a second addition to the Memorial Gymnasium, the purchase of a pipe organ for Rammelkamp Chapel, and acoustical modification and expansion of the chancel. There was a commitment to the maintenance of the four historic buildings: Beecher, Crampton, Sturtevant, and Whipple. The south portion of the quadrangle was cleared of Jones Hall. Tennis courts were added and a new track, one of the best in west central Illinois, was built. The maintenance buildings—the last campus remnants of World War II—were razed and a new service building was constructed east of the football field. Parking lots, the result of the automobile revolution mentioned earlier, were added and expanded.

The McGaw Fine Arts Center—an important, albeit visionary part of the Sesquicentennial Plan—was dedicated April 30, 1980. The core of the Center is a small theatre for 250. Along the periphery of the Sibert Theatre are facilities for the visual arts, music studios, practice rooms, a choir and band rehearsal room, a television studio, and a large general-purpose classroom. After walking the campus one is struck with the beauty and the natural setting of the Center's hilltop location. People who loved the College—such as Courtney Crouch Wright, Helen C. Foreman '25, Alma C. Smith, and Helen W. Hackett '27—spent their time and energies in making the College a special place of beauty.

Finally, the Sesquicentennial Plan included study of the need for additional residences. Faculty and students asked for additional housing. In the late 1970s, fifty to sixty students had been assigned to the Dunlap Hotel. Small apartment-type units seemed to be the answer, each including two bedrooms, a living room, and bath, and accommodating four students. In 1979, the largest of these buildings was named to honor Miss Mabel Louise Griswold '26 of White Hall. In the last months of the Sesquicentennial celebration, ground was broken for two structures to house an additional thirty-two students. Residential capacity was increased to six hundred. Students, trustees, and faculty felt that increasing the capacity would also improve student retention. Residences for three-fourths of the students nurtured a sense of community while still permitting an option to live off campus.

To come full circle, the Sesquicentennial Plan was drafted by a trustee committee under the chairmanship of Lyndle Hess '30. It was an important document that was helpful to the presidential selection committee in 1973. It was one of the statements which meant a great deal to me, the current president, as the appointment was made. As the eleventh president of Illinois College, I have found many things impressive about Illinois College—the spirit and competence of the faculty, the vitality and ability of the students, and the commitment and support of the trustees and alumni. The Sesquicentennial Plan brought these elements together into a clear focus and was a prism for our dreams.

Let me identify some of the items about the College which immediately caught my attention and which I found attractive:
—its liberal arts curriculum
—its lively church relationship
—its talented and responsible students
—its desire to remain a small college of eight hundred
—its plans for expansion of the fine arts and political science
—its plans to strengthen the academic and student programs

The Sesquicentennial Plan was the blue print for continued growth and progress—a plan to lead to a new level of excellence and service.

The mission of Illinois College is not to grow into a large institution nor to compete with the megaversities. The challenge at Illinois College is to compete with itself—to be better this year than the previous year and to work for future progress. It is a large order, but one that is vital and that has earned the support of the faculty, students, and trustees.

The success of the Sesquicentennial Anniversary—the look to the past, the examination of the present, the hope for the future—was guided by a Sesquicentennial Committee composed of faculty, students, alumni, and trustees. This committee was chaired by Dr. Iver F. Yeager. Dr. Yeager, a graduate of a small liberal arts college in Minnesota, Macalester College, came to Illinois College in 1958. He came as a member of the faculty and Dean of the College. Currently he is Scarborough Professor of Religion and Philosophy and Chairman of the Department. He loves the College; he understands the College. The College is his life and his life is the College's life. His tenure has been a good twenty-three years for the College and also for Dr. Yeager and his family. Because of his ability, because of his experience, and because of his commitment, he was able to guide this committee along productive paths. The Sesquicentennial Celebration was a success and it accomplished its mission. Many people from all areas of the College community affirmed the richness of the Sesquicentennial Celebration. Illinois College, indeed, has a proud tradition and a promising future.

# 2

## *The Plans, the Programs, and the Participants: An Account of the Sesquicentennial Observance, 1979–1980*

### HISTORICAL PRECEDENTS FOR ANNIVERSARY CELEBRATIONS

Every quarter-century Illinois College has held special exercises in celebration of its existence and its progress. The first occasion was July 11, 1855, when John M. Ellis and four members of the original Illinois Association from Yale gathered with many other friends of the College to reminisce and to hear President Julian M. Sturtevant's "Historical Discourse" delivered at ceremonies at the First Presbyterian Church. The semi-centennial anniversary was observed at the 1879 Commencement, and remarkably five of the seven original members of the "Yale Band" still survived, although only John Brooks, Mason Grosvenor, and Sturtevant were able to attend. Former President Edward Beecher was present and also Truman Post, one of the first faculty members. In late September, 1904, the seventy-fifth anniversary brought many notable persons from American and foreign universities. The audience at the final meeting overflowed the huge tent which had been erected on the campus.

The Centennial Anniversary of the founding of Illinois College was appropriately celebrated by elaborate ceremonies during a four-day period in mid-October, 1929, during the tenure of President Charles Henry Rammelkamp; the program is fully chronicled in a two-hundred page volume, *Centennial Celebration*.[1] Once again many dignitaries responded to the invitation to honor "Old Illinois," and the nation's colleges, businesses, and professions were well represented. There were numerous speeches and banquets, a parade, and a Shakespearean production. Two thousand people attended the Sunday morning church service held in a tent on the College grounds. Tanner Library was dedicated as the Centennial Building and fourteen men and women were granted honorary master's and doctor's degrees following the "Centennial Address" by President James Angell of Yale University. Alumni and visitors expressed their gratitude to President Rammelkamp for his superb *Centennial History*[2] of the College, published in 1928 after years of research in the official College records, private letters, and other source materials.

Those familiar with the history of Illinois College, or that of most small colleges, are well aware of the recurring crises which have beset such institutions and brought an end to many of them. The 125th anniversary of the College coincided with one of the difficult periods of its existence, a time when enrollments had fallen far below the record attendance in the post World War II years and when there was uncertainty about the future. Nevertheless, four all-college events were scheduled in observance of the College's 125th birthday, beginning with the inauguration of William K. Selden as ninth president in December, 1953. That occasion also served to commemorate the first trustees' meeting (December, 1829) when the name "Illinois College" was adopted. Commencement and Homecoming in 1954 were especially oriented toward the observance. Special features of the Homecoming festivities included the awarding of Distinguished Service Citations to several alumni, the official acceptance of Gardner Hall (recently completed), and the opening of the cornerstone of the old gymnasium (constructed in 1891–92 and demolished in 1954). The final event, commemorating the first classes, was a Janu-

1. *Centennial Celebration of the Founding of Illinois College, October Twelfth, Thirteenth, Fourteenth, and Fifteenth, Nineteen Hundred and Twenty-Nine* (Jacksonville, IL [Chicago: Lakeside Press, 1930]).

2. Charles Henry Rammelkamp, *Illinois College: A Centennial History, 1829–1929* (New Haven: Published for Illinois College by Yale Univ. Press, 1928).

ary (1955) convocation at which nine honorary degrees were awarded, four of them to alumni.

It was a foregone conclusion that Illinois College, having survived and flourished because of the capable administrations of Presidents L. Vernon Caine and Donald C. Mundinger and increased national interest in higher education, would celebrate its 150th Anniversary in proper fashion. There was by now ample precedent for such an occasion, were precedent needed to justify it. But beyond marking one more quarter-century of history, there was much to celebrate. In 1979 student enrollment was at the eight hundred level and the physical plant was the largest and best equipped ever. The members of the Class of 1979 had, as freshmen, helped to move the Library's books and periodicals from Tanner into the beautiful facilities of Schewe, and they had watched the McGaw Fine Arts Center progress from bare concrete foundations to a steel skeleton to an outwardly complete building. By now the College had had a balanced budget for more than two decades, almost surely a record in its often-troubled financial history, and its endowment had been increased to seven million. The faculty during the decade of the seventies had grown to record size and was well-trained and dedicated to undergraduate teaching. The alumni list included more than seven-thousand names. In almost every respect this was one of the happiest in the series of quarter-century celebrations. That fact, and the richness of the College's proud heritage and the spirit of optimism for its promising future, set the stage for special celebrations of the 150th anniversary of its founding.

## THE APPOINTMENT OF A COMMITTEE AND PLANNING FOR THE CELEBRATION

The first phases of planning for the College's Sesquicentennial Anniversary were initiated early in the administration of Dr. Donald C. Mundinger, who became the eleventh president in 1973. There was now another half-century of history to be added to the printed record and Professor Charles E. Frank, chairman of the Department of English and senior member of the faculty, was the ideal choice for the task of bringing the record up to date. There was work to be done to complete the physical plant in accordance with the ongoing planning for the campus, including President H. Gary Hudson's Development Plan, President Caine's Forward Step program, and President Mundinger's One Hundred Fiftieth Anniversary Challenge. These improvements entailed raising money for construction and for additions to the endowment. The academic program received its decennial accreditation review from the North Central Association in 1975, but as always most of the work of investigation and evaluation was carried out by the administration and faculty committees long before the visiting team arrived on the campus. The result was the strengthening of the curriculum and revision of the course offerings, bringing the College into a better position for fulfilling its educational mission in its fourth half-century.

Thus the Sesquicentennial celebration was only one part of the College's recognition of its 150 years of service. But celebration in festive style was essential, and President Mundinger appointed students, faculty, administrators, alumni, and trustees to serve on the 150th Anniversary Committee. (The list of members and their identification can be found in Appendix A.) The first meeting was held

*Some Members of the 150th Anniversary Committee*
SEATED: John N. Langfitt, Donald R. Eldred, Iver F. Yeager (Chairman), Carole M. Ryan '59 (Secretary), George William Horton, Jr., -52. STANDING: Howard M. Jarratt, Martha S. Vache '67, Richard L. Pratt '49, Rebecca Schutz '81, Susan L. Pratt '80, Doris B. Hopper '41, President Donald C. Mundinger

in April, 1977. The freshman students who were present would be seniors and almost ready to graduate by the time the final event had taken place.

By fall the Committee had prepared a general statement of purpose and had sketched the outlines for the celebration. It was agreed that the extended three- and four-day programs of earlier occasions were not appropriate models, partly because the new modes of travel and the quickened pace of academic life now made it difficult to assemble the numbers present in 1929. Rather it was determined to arrange a series of convocations, concerts, and other events to be spread out over two academic years and extending from January, 1979, into the spring semester of 1980. It was hoped that alumni and others from a distance could come for at least one of the events and that no one would miss the entire celebration because of a single conflict. Those presently on the campus or in the local area could select the programs of special interest to them. The Committee adopted the recommendation of the alumni members that some events be scheduled in the evening so that employed persons could attend.

Correspondence was initiated with a number of colleges of similar size whose founding dates indicated they might recently have held sesquicentennial celebrations. Helpful letters, along with programs and committee reports, were received. One correspondent reported that he had mentioned our inquiry to a secretary who had said, "Tell them, don't." We surmised that an undue burden of detail and correspondence had fallen upon one person and we resolved not to make the same mistake.

An "Open Letter" was directed to the Illinois College community in October, 1977, with individual copies being sent to all campus organizations and to the members of the faculty. The general plan was to have a series of all-college events which would commemorate certain historic events or highlight features of the College's tradition of liberal learning. The hope was expressed that many individuals would participate and especially that student and other organizations would plan their regular programs with some recognition of the 150th anniversary. The Committee itself would sponsor the all-college programs and—when requested to do so and its resources permitted—would give assistance and encouragement to other groups.

A three-fold emphasis was proposed: "to recall and celebrate significant events and features of the past 150 years; to take stock of the College at present—its strengths, its problems, its opportunities; [and] to consider the direction the College should take as it begins its fourth half-century (with special attention to the next decade or two)." Distinctive features of Illinois College to be recognized included its "dedication to the liberal arts ideal within its special environment; the College's church-relatedness; and the College's major contributions to public service, including all levels of education, involvement in public affairs, and the cause of human freedom and dignity." Distinguished alumni—representative of various elements within the liberal arts tradition—and invited guests would be granted honorary degrees at the formal convocations.

The Committee members took their responsibilities seriously and worked faithfully through the extended period of planning and the celebration itself. The full membership was convened monthly during the academic year and the many subcommittees met frequently to plan special events, examine proposals for commemorative projects, and coordinate the overall plan. The informal consultations and the telephone calls are probably beyond enumeration. A complete record of all suggestions as well as formal actions and definite plans was kept by Associate Professor Carole Ryan '59, who served throughout as secretary with occasional assistance from others.

By March of 1978 the planning was well underway and a long list of proposed programs, concerts, speakers, special events, and suggested mementos had been drawn up. By December the printer's copy was ready for a brochure which would announce the Sesquicentennial celebration. The front of the leaflet was graced by a line drawing of Sturtevant Hall by Mrs. Dorothy B. Frank, and the back panel was the calendar of Sesquicentennial events for the spring semester of 1979. The three inside panels, using the motto adopted by the Committee, were headed "A Proud Heritage"; "1829–1979"; and "A Promising Future." Below these captions were three panels: a picture of Beecher Hall and a quotation from Sturtevant to symbol-

ize the College's beginnings; a list of the highlights of the College's
150 years; and a drawing of the proposed Fine Arts Center with a
statement by President Mundinger to direct attention to the future.
The brochure was distributed on campus and throughout the Jacksonville community and mailed to all alumni in early January, 1979.

## THE SERIES OF MAJOR CONVOCATIONS

The historic and continuing commitment of Illinois College to the
tradition of liberal learning was chosen as the theme for the series of
major convocations. There were eight of these, and the opening convocation of the semester on January 15, 1979—the first all-college
Sesquicentennial event—was devoted to the general theme. Successive convocations were centered upon public affairs, the dedication
of the new pipe organ, science and mathematics, the humanities, the
social sciences, the plans and prospects for the next decade, and (in
April, 1980) the dedication of the McGaw Fine Arts Center. The
particular order of these meetings was to some extent dependent
upon the availability of the desired speakers.

The convocations which were addressed by a guest speaker followed the general pattern to be described here. Most of them were
formal, with the faculty marching in academic regalia. Those faculty
and students holding the office of marshal during the Sesquicentennial celebration doubtless had the most active terms ever. Dr. Don P.
Filson, Strawn Professor of Chemistry, was faculty marshal, and Dr.
Vidyapati Singh, Professor of Economics and Business Administration, was his assistant. During 1978–79 the student marshals were
Jane Borrowman and Jayne Verticchio, both of the Class of 1979,
while Jon Mark Althoff and Ann Burford were the marshals from
the Class of 1980.

Music was provided on such occasions by the Illinois College
Concert Choir, directed during this period by Mr. Rick L. Erickson,
Instructor in Music. The Choir members in their bright blue robes
provided colorful background for the ceremonies on the platform of
Rammelkamp Chapel. At most convocations the Choir presented a
glorious anthem and led the audience in singing a hymn and the

*Alma Mater.* Mr. Erickson was also College Organist and played the processional and recessional music. The opening convocation of the Sesquicentennial observance was the first public use of the new Holt-kamp pipe organ, named in honor of Dr. Arthur C. Hart '25 and Mrs. Charlotte Engelbach Hart '26, major donors to the fund for the new instrument.

It has been customary for the Dean of the College to preside at academic convocations and Dean Wallace N. Jamison fulfilled his role with sprightly dignity. Scripture was read and prayer offered at the first convocation, and at the two dedication ceremonies, by the College Chaplain, Dr. John N. Langfitt. President Donald C. Mundinger usually made a statement, prior to introducing the guest speaker, in which he would comment upon the significance of the occasion and the particular theme. Often he made observations on the current scene, sometimes referring to public issues and frequently citing recent books or a timely article in *The New Yorker*. The guest speaker was chosen to exemplify in his office and person as well as his remarks that aspect of liberal learning which was the theme of the day. (All the speakers were men, except for the 1979 baccalaureate speaker; efforts to obtain women as speakers at some of the convocations were unsuccessful.) Following the address the speaker and selected alumni were awarded honorary degrees, each person being presented by a member of the faculty. Arrangements were made whenever possible for a reception, either immediately after the convocation or later in the day, when students and others could greet the visiting speaker and congratulate the honorees.

The printed programs for such convocations and many of the other all-college Sesquicentennial events had the same cover design, arranged by Dean of Students Donald R. Eldred. At the top, in bold type, were the words "Illinois College Sesquicentennial" and, in smaller type, the special motto. A drawing with a montage of College buildings—Beecher Hall (the old), Schewe Library (the new), and Sturtevant Hall (the most frequently used pictorial symbol for the College)—occupied the center of the cover, and below was the title of the specific convocation together with the date. On the inside pages were printed the details of the program and brief biographical sketches of the speaker and the other honorees. In appropriate instances the back page carried an essay by a faculty member (outlining the history of the disciplines given recognition that day). The names of alumni who had majored in those disciplines and who had been awarded honorary degrees by Illinois College since the last quarter-century celebration were also listed. It was intended that the printed programs would have value beyond their immediate usefulness, individually as mementos of specific occasions and, collectively, of the whole series of Sesquicentennial events.

The dedication services for the Hart Sesquicentennial Pipe Organ and the McGaw Fine Arts Center necessarily differed from the usual convocation format, and both will be described in some detail in the appropriate context. Obviously these events were of outstanding importance to the College community and had special significance for the observance of the College's 150th Anniversary. Catharine Crozier's dedicatory recital on the new pipe organ was but one of several highlights in the series of concerts; some others of special note were the Choir's performance of Handel's *Messiah*, Stephanie Smith-Jarratt's presentation of Jonathan E. Spilman's songs, and the program of all-American music played by the Jacksonville Symphony Orchestra. More information about these and other programs in the music series will be provided in chapter 5.

It is obvious that the faithful cooperation of many persons was essential in preparing for these convocations and then seeing that they proceeded in good order. In addition to the people already named special credit should be given to the student service organizations, Alpha Phi Omega and Alpha Kappa Phi, whose members were ushers. Dean Eldred arranged for floral decorations and the Library's audio-visual staff taped the proceedings on most occasions. The maintenance crew saw to the cleaning and dusting and set up the needed chairs and podia. While the appearance of a building is secondary to the event itself, an attractive setting lends much to the beauty and enjoyment of formal gatherings. The handsome organ console and pipes in their strikingly modern arrangement now look as if they were original with the building, but in those early months when the organ was new they provided an extra thrill to those long accustomed to the near-emptiness of the vast wall behind the speaker's lectern.

## SPECIAL COMMEMORATIVE EVENTS

The entire 150th Anniversary celebration was of course in commemoration of the founding of the College. However, the plan of extending the observance over a period of more than one calendar year made it possible to memorialize many other important events and developments in the College's subsequent history. The first such special event was on March 11, 1979, when Dr. Ethel Louise Seybold '29, Professor Emeritus of English, spoke on a subject of life-long interest to her and of course of great importance to all of us, "Illinois College and the Education of Women." Afterwards the audience proceeded to the David A. Smith House for a reception hosted jointly by the Women's Collegium and the Ladies' Education Society and held in honor of the founders of the Society. This organization, founded in 1833, is recognized by the General Federation of Women's Clubs as the oldest women's club in the U.S. still in existence. Although Illinois College itself did not become coeducational until 1903, when the Jacksonville Female Academy was merged with it just before the College's seventy-fifth anniversary, the founders of the College and others in Jacksonville had taken steps to provide education for women within a year of the founding of the College; the Academy's own founding date was 1830. The text of Dr. Seybold's delightful address is included in this volume.

Just a few days later (on March 14) the Caine Student Center was the scene of a birthday party for the College, sponsored by the Women's Collegium. Students, faculty, and administrators joined in the festivities and of course shared the huge cake.

More than a hundred people joined in a Remembrance March on Sunday afternoon, April 22. On behalf of the 150th Anniversary Committee Jon Althoff and Mr. George William Horton, Jr. '52, Associate Professor of Mathematics, had spent many hours checking city records and examining the names on the grave markers in Diamond Grove Cemetery. Their research was facilitated by help from city officials, alumni, members of the local genealogical society, and others. The result was a map directing various groups of marchers to the graves of about twenty persons prominent in the founding and history of Illinois College. Prior to the march, members of Alpha Phi Omega, aided by city workers and a local monument company, had repaired and straightened those grave markers which had been neglected. There were brief ceremonies at Diamond Grove and then special groups left to go to Jacksonville East and Memorial Lawn Cemeteries. Appropriate College officers and organizations placed flowers on the graves of College founders and early faculty members as well as those of recently-deceased trustees and professors (who were regarded as representative of many others who could not be recognized individually). The various groups then returned to Baxter Hall to share an outdoor meal.

The College's dedication to fine scholarship was highlighted by a banquet planned by the campus chapter of Phi Beta Kappa for Commencement Week. The Epsilon Chapter of Illinois had been chartered in 1932, largely through the efforts of President Rammelkamp. The banquet was open to everyone in the College community. The main address (reprinted in chapter 19) was given by Dr. Eleanor O. Miller, Professor Emeritus of Psychology, a member of Phi Beta Kappa at the University of Wisconsin, a charter member of the chapter at Illinois College, and long a faculty member here.

Another special event during Commencement Week, 1979, was the reunion of participants in the Model Constitutional Convention which had been held a decade before. In 1969, under the leadership of Mrs. Elizabeth R. Zeigler, then Instructor in Political Science, the College had been host to delegates (from colleges and universities throughout Illinois) who debated the major issues involved in the preparation of the state's new constitution. Mrs. Zeigler, now Associate Professor Emeritus, was honored at the reunion by alumni and present and former faculty members who had taken part in the Model Con-Con.

Special programs in the spring semester, 1980, commemorated the first classes at the College (January 4, 1830) and also the first graduates, Richard Yates and Jonathan E. Spilman, Class of 1835. These programs are described in greater detail in later chapters, where the texts of the various addresses can also be found.

## Pioneer's Progress, THE SESQUICENTENNIAL HISTORY BY PROFESSOR FRANK

The publication of *Pioneer's Progress: Illinois College, 1829–1979*,[3] by Professor Charles E. Frank, was by its very nature and its superb quality one of the most important, most widely-shared, and most enduring contributions to the College's Sesquicentennial observance. The precedent for such a volume had been established by President Rammelkamp's great *Centennial History*. The need was evident for chronicling the College's third half century: a period which included the Great Depression, the Second World War, and two other wars, all of which had great impact on the College's fortunes; and a period of the most serious crisis in decades as well as the era of the College's largest enrollment and its greatest growth in physical and financial resources. Dr. Frank had an intimate personal knowledge of the people and events of Illinois College over a period of four decades. Colleagues and alumni have been charmed by Dr. Frank's delightful prose just as they have been eager to share his insights and the information he reported. Many alumni confess to turning first to read that chapter which describes the College at the time when they were students. All agree that even the more difficult episodes of Illinois College's past have been described fairly and sensitively.

Dr. Frank's decision to abridge Rammelkamp's massive *Centennial History* and make that abridgment the first part of his own volume was an excellent solution to several problems. The Rammelkamp volume has long been out of print and the cost of reprinting it would have been prohibitive; moreover, that work is so lengthy that reading it to gain the necessary background for the College's recent history would quite possibly tire all but the most determined readers. The abridgment makes available to everyone the essential facts about the first century.

3. Charles E. Frank, *Pioneer's Progress: Illinois College, 1829–1979* (Carbondale: Published for Illinois College by Southern Illinois Univ. Press, 1979).

In preparation for writing the recent history of the College, Professor Frank examined the official records of the trustees and the faculty, the pages of the *Alumni Quarterly* (dating back to the early twenties), and student reporting in the *Rambler*. During the summer of 1975 Dr. Frank, accompanied by his wife, Mrs. Dorothy B. Frank, made an "Odyssey" of seventy-five hundred miles to visit former presidents, faculty members, alumni, and others with special knowledge of Illinois College; most of the interviews were taped and thus an oral history was created. Selecting pertinent and representative material from the vast resources available and writing the text was arduous though clearly a labor of love. Drawings of campus buildings by Mrs. Louise Boring Wood '34 and Mrs. Frank and photographs of presidential portraits by Mr. Thomas D. Smith, Assistant Professor of Economics and Business Administration and a skilled photographer, enhance the printed work. A striking color photo of Sturtevant Hall (also by Mr. Smith) adorns the attractive book jacket.

The volumes arrived on the campus, at the scheduled time, and an autographing party was held at the Caine Student Center during Commencement Week. Frequently during that same week we saw Dr. Frank kneeling on the grass or sitting on the Tanner steps to sign yet another copy of his book. Autographing parties were also held at alumni meetings around the country. This must have been one of the warmest welcomes ever given to a book and author!

The publication of *Pioneer's Progress* occurred during the final month of Professor Frank's active service at Illinois College. No more significant memorial could be planned for a career which had begun forty years earlier. The faculty honored him and Mrs. Frank on the occasion of his retirement at a dinner in the Caine Student Center. Representatives of the Department of English and of the faculty paid him tribute and President Mundinger presented a leather-bound copy of *Pioneer's Progress* to its author. Fortunately the Franks continue to make their winter home in the familiar white frame house across from Schewe Library on Park Street.

The 150th Anniversary Committee cannot claim credit for any part of the Sesquicentennial history itself. However, it did provide the bookmarks which were inserted in each copy. The bookmark,

printed in blue ink on fine white paper, has Mrs. Frank's line drawings of Beecher Hall and Schewe Library at top and bottom and in
between are dated quotations from three presidents: Julian Sturtevant (1830), Vernon Caine (1956), and Donald Mundinger (1973).

## SYMBOLS AND MEMENTOS

Very early in their deliberations the members of the 150th Anniversary Committee recognized the importance of visual symbols of
the Sesquicentennial observance, to herald the fact of our celebration
to the wider world and to provide mementos of the event both for
participants and for future generations of students and faculty. Special stationery was designed with the logo of the College and the
address at the top of the sheet and the Sesquicentennial motto at the
bottom: "1829 ● A Proud Heritage . . . A Promising Future ● 1979."
The letterhead and matching envelopes were from white stock imprinted with blue ink. The use of this stationery by the administrative offices of the College and the academic departments insured
wide-spread notice of the 150th anniversary. Numerous mailings
also carried a small adhesive sticker, blue on a silver background,
with a picture of Sturtevant Hall and the legend, "Illinois College
Sesquicentennial, 1829–1979."

The first five-year license plates used in the state of Illinois constituted a mobile and wide-ranging albeit silent witness to the College's
founding. Through the assistance of Eugene Callahan '55, Assistant
Secretary of State in Springfield, Illinois College blue was adopted
for the lettering and numerals on the white plates. The Elliott State
Bank issued the series of plates with the letters "IC" and consequently many Jacksonville automobiles bear such licenses. Appropriately President Mundinger was presented with "IC 1" and Mrs.
Mundinger with "IC 1829."

The College's gift to the graduates of the Class of 1979 was inspired by a member of the Class of 1929, Professor Emeritus Ethel
Seybold. She recalled the pleasure she and the other seniors had derived from President Rammelkamp's presentation to each graduate
of a walnut letter opener made from an original sill removed from
Beecher Hall during renovation. The 150th Anniversary Committee

determined to follow that example but no such artifact was available in 1979 to make mementos for the comparatively large class. The Committee therefore ordered commercially manufactured medallions, cast in silver-colored metal and with neck-bands of blue ribbon. The design of the medallions reproduced the College Seal, with "Illinois College 1829–1979" lettered around the circumference. The medallions were presented to the graduating seniors when they gathered on the campus lawn in preparation for the Commencement exercises. Medallions were also given, at the request of the senior class officers, to President Mundinger, Mr. William N. Clark '40 (chairman of the Board of Trustees), President Emeritus L. Vernon Caine, President Emeritus and Mrs. H. Gary Hudson, jointly to Professor and Mrs. Charles E. Frank, and to some of the faculty who had worked closely with the seniors. Two medallions were set aside for use by the student marshals at future academic processions.

The Class of 1979 presented several gifts to the College, including two unique and lasting symbols of the College and its founding. The four class officers (whose names are listed in Appendix H, with the roster of the Class of 1979), discussed a proposal for a president's chain of office. With the assistance of Dean Eldred and Professor Iver F. Yeager they met with Mrs. Dorothy B. Frank, who was then commissioned to design and craft the badge of office for the president. The finished chain has long silver links, eleven of them engraved with the names of the presidents from Beecher to Mundinger; the remaining links will suffice for as many more presidents in the future. Suspended from the chain is a large medallion of fine silver, hand-wrought by Mrs. Frank and bearing the design of the College Seal encircled by a band of deep blue enamel. The chain was presented to President Mundinger by Class President Milan Kruszynski and Vice-President Julie Skibiski at the Academic Honors Convocation just before the end of the spring semester. President Mundinger has since worn the Chain at the numerous Sesquicentennial and opening convocations and at the Commencement exercises.

The Class of 1979 also assumed the major financial responsibility for purchasing a College flag. The proposal for a flag had been made to the Committee by Jon Althoff, one of the original student members of the Committee. Jon was promptly named to membership on a new subcommittee and accepted very willingly, as did the others who were appointed: Associate Dean Doris B. Hopper '41 and Susan L. Pratt. Dean Hopper was designated chairperson. Mr. Peter Cohan, Instructor in Art, and Mrs. Mary Elizabeth Kirk, part-time Instructor in Interdisciplinary Studies, added their artistic expertise. The approved design portrays the College Seal, in simplified form, with the design and lettering in blue on a white circle imposed upon the field of blue. There was hope that the new flag, measuring five by eight feet, would be delivered by the manufacturer in time for Commencement but that expectation failed by nearly two weeks. It was first flown at the opening convocation of the fall semester and subsequently has been used for Homecoming, for the 1980 Commencement, and for other special College days, weather permitting. The formal dedication of the new ensign and its acceptance on behalf of the College by President Mundinger were part of the half-time ceremonies at the Homecoming football game in 1979.

These special gifts were part of a very sizable financial pledge made to the College by the Class of 1979. The full amount, acknowledged by a resolution of the Board of Trustees which was read at Commencement, was $6,250.

More than thirty items representative of the College and community were placed in the cornerstone of the McGaw Fine Arts Center at special ceremonies following the Homecoming football game. The large metal box was crammed to capacity—Chaplain Langfitt had practiced beforehand to make sure that everything would fit. Dr. Hugo Stierholz '54, president of the Alumni Association, inserted the computer print-out of the new alumni directory. Professor Frank contributed a copy of *Pioneer's Progress*. Various faculty members of the departments to be housed in the new building placed appropriate mementos of their disciplines, and student representatives of the Hilltoppers, the Band, and the Choir likewise put in printed programs. Each of the three faculty divisions was represented, too. Among the several trustees participating was Mr. Robert F. Sibert '36, who with his family donated the new theater; Mr. Sibert added the current College catalog to the growing contents. President Emeritus Caine put in a copy of the *Rig Veda* and Mrs. Elizabeth Caine, a collection of pictures of campus life. Mrs. Donald

C. (June) Mundinger stood in for the McGaw family with a set of building plans. The community was represented by Mayor Milton L. Hocking and two local pastors, Dr. Dale W. Robb of the First Presbyterian Church and the Reverend Robert M. Cassels of the Congregational Church. Mr. Martin Newman, president of the Jacksonville Area Chamber of Commerce, placed the special issue of the *Jacksonville Daily Courier* and a copy of the I. C. *Rambler* in the box. President Mundinger made the final contribution, copies of his own address at the beginning of the College's 151st year and of his statement delivered at the cornerstone ceremony.

The popularity of T-shirts emblazoned with slogans prompted a student suggestion to the Committee that there be a competition for selecting the best design for a Sesquicentennial version of this well-nigh universal campus garment. The design selected showed a game of Tic-Tac-Toe, with a diagonal slash marking the winning row of "X's," and the slogan, "A Winning Tradition Since 1829." The white design was stencilled on both dark and light blue shirts and was ordered in an assortment of sizes, including children's. From then on these T-shirts were the unofficial uniform for student and faculty Committee members at the less formal Sesquicentennial events.

## RECOGNITION OF ALUMNI AND SPECIAL GUESTS

One of the time-honored features of academic ceremonies is the awarding of honorary degrees at Commencement and on other special occasions. The Sesquicentennial celebration afforded the ideal opportunity for recognizing the achievements of outstanding alumni and of persons representative of the larger community. Members of the faculty submitted the names of many worthy persons active in the professions and public life. Those alumni whose College studies and distinguished careers were related to the general theme of a given convocation were invited for that occasion and awarded the appropriate honorary degrees. The speakers invited to address such convocations—recognized leaders in their fields—were likewise granted degrees and thus made honorary alumni. The names of these men and women are included in the subsequent chapters on the major convocations.

One of the most pleasant tasks of the many which fell to the Committee's chairman was telephoning alumni to invite them to the campus to receive the honors their Alma Mater proposed to bestow upon them. The initial cordial response to a call from the College was followed by surprise as the purpose of the conversation became clear and that in turn gave way to pleasure which sometimes approached ecstasy. Conversely, one of the frustrations experienced by the Committee was the impossibility of including all the worthy alumni and others who were recommended. This failure was to a degree compensated by the presentation of Presidential Citations of Merit and by the exceptionally large number of Distinguished Public Service Citations awarded by the Alumni Association. The names of these men and women are listed later in this chapter.

Near the end of the Sesquicentennial celebration the members of the 150th Anniversary Committee were themselves honored at a lovely February dinner hosted by President and Mrs. Mundinger at Barnes House. Each member was presented a Certificate of Recognition, encased in the familiar blue folder used for diplomas. The suggested parallel with graduation was not far-fetched. The Committee's work extended over four academic years, and the four students who were permanent members had begun their service in the spring semester of their freshman year and concluded it just prior to their own graduation from the College. Two other people who had vital roles throughout the year and a half of the celebration were honored also at this dinner. Mrs. June Mundinger was the College hostess at many dinners honoring the speakers and guests at the convocations; appropriately she, too, was given a Certificate of Recognition. A special citation was awarded to Professor Don P. Filson, faculty marshal, for his masterful arrangements of the details of the convocations and the academic processions.

## THE COLLEGE'S HOSPITALITY

Illinois College has long been noted for its friendly reception of visitors, whether prospective students or visiting dignitaries. The hospitality of the College lived up to that high reputation, which indeed was enhanced during the celebration. Students, faculty, and staff willingly served as chauffeurs to meet guests arriving at the Springfield and St. Louis airports. They served ably as ushers at the many special events. Participants in the major convocations and concerts were regularly invited to dinner at Barnes House; the speaker and the alumni to be honored, and their spouses or other family members, enjoyed the hospitality of President and Mrs. Mundinger. Mrs. Mary Lou Scott, secretary to the President, wrote many letters and made many phone calls and then served as campus receptionist to greet guests; her friendly, efficient efforts did much to help our guests and to facilitate the smooth functioning of the convocations. Many letters were subsequently received from visitors expressing their warm appreciation for the courtesies extended to them by everyone on campus.

On several occasions receptions were arranged so that the College community as a whole could greet the speaker and other guests. One especially memorable instance was the reception for Governor and Mrs. James R. Thompson and Secretary of State Alan J. Dixon and his assistants, following the Public Affairs Convocation. The newly appointed Gallery Lounge, in the former reading room of Tanner Library, was admirably suited for this purpose. Other receptions were held at Barnes House and Smith House or the lower level of Schewe Library.

## STUDENT ORGANIZATIONS AND ACTIVITIES, AND STUDENT PARTICIPATION

Students had a significant role in the work of the 150th Anniversary Committee, and some were among the most active of all the Committee members. Four persons from the Class of 1980 served on the Committee from its first meeting in April of 1977 through the final session just before their graduation. They were: Jon Althoff, Laura Armstrong, Lee Bracken, and Susan L. Pratt. Other students who served during part of 1978 and 1979 were Edward F. Flynn, Jr., Judy Goudy, and Rebecca Schutz of the Class of 1979. Special recognition is due to Jon Althoff, a vigorous and creative participant who contributed many ideas and many hours to various Committee projects, among them the Remembrance March, the College Flag, and the T-shirt project. In addition to an active role in extracurricular activities (mentioned below), Jon served for two years as director of Crampton Hall and was the recipient of the Student Laureate Award from the Lincoln Academy of Illinois in 1979.

The Remembrance March on April 22 (1979) drew more *active* student participation than any other all-College Sesquicentennial event. The combination of factors—the honor given to founders and persons later associated with the College, the emphasis on their connections with present-day organizations, a Sunday afternoon with good spring weather, and the group hike and picnic supper—attracted many from the campus and representatives of the larger community as well. The number of those in attendance at the major convocations was of course much greater, although for most students the role was passive. Fewer students were present at the concerts, most of which were held in the evening. Perhaps the long period when music had only a minor role in the curriculum contributed to the apparently limited level of student interest.

The Forum supported the fund drive for the McGaw Fine Arts Center and had liaison with the 150th Anniversary Committee by virtue of its student members. Jon Althoff was Vice-President of the Forum during 1978–79 and President during 1979–80, which helped to assure Forum support for the Sesquicentennial observance and coordination of efforts and activities.

Phi Alpha Literary Society had stolen the march on all other groups, including the 150th Anniversary Committee itself, by sponsoring the very first Sesquicentennial event in October, 1978, nearly two months before the celebration officially started. The Committee had gladly approved the proposal and indeed provided necessary financing for travel expenses and trophies. Phi Alpha invited Knox College to send a team of debaters to reenact one of the earliest of all intercollegiate debates in the country. That historic contest was held at Illinois College on May 5, 1881, as part of an oratorical meet. The topic in 1881 was prohibition, and the contestants were members of Phi Alpha and Knox College's Adelphi Society, which is no longer in existence. The topic for the 1978 meeting was "Resolved: That the Electoral College Should be Abolished." Sophomore Matthew Duensing and freshman Michael Taylor successfully argued the affirmative case to emulate Phi Alpha's earlier victory.

Other literary societies expressed the celebrative spirit in various ways. Most of them gave recognition to the Sesquicentennial in either regular meetings or open meetings or both. Several were officially represented at the Remembrance March, carrying banners and honoring men and women prominent in their own history or that of the College. Most of the societies made group contributions to the McGaw building fund.

Chi Beta Literary Society presented two February programs (in 1979) on "The Great American Dream" and "The American Frontier." Gamma Delta also had two programs on Sesquicentennial themes. Gamma Nu member Joseph Chapa was cochairman of Homecoming and enlisted the help of Nuer alums as well as half a dozen present society members.

The 50th anniversary of the founding of Pi Pi Rho Literary Society coincided with the College's Sesquicentennial. Among those honored at the March 3 banquet were: Mr. Paul Sheppard and Mr. Charles Williamson, both of the Class of 1929 and both founding members of the Society; Mr. William Curry '71; and Mr. Thomas L. Rowland '69, Assistant Professor of Physical Education. President Emeritus L. Vernon Caine was inducted as an honorary member in recognition of his assistance in reestablishing Pi Pi Rho in 1966 after it had been inactive for several years. Dean of Students Donald R. Eldred, honorary member and trustee of the society, was presented a special commendation and plaque for his years of help and supportive affiliation.

Sigma Phi Epsilon Literary Society devoted the entire spring semester program to "Reflections on the Past" in honor of the founders of education for men and women and of past presidents of the College. The meeting dates and topics were:

January 29, John Millot Ellis: A Mirror of Faith
February 7, Frances Brard Ellis: A Looking-glass of Love
February 19, Edward Beecher: A Crystal-clear Stream of Hope
March 5, Julian M. Sturtevant: A Sea of Anger
March 26, Charles Henry Rammelkamp: A Pool of Courage

April 9, H. Gary Hudson: A Window of Wisdom
April 30, L. Vernon Caine: The Eyes of Home

A handsome booklet, featuring the College Seal and "Illinois College Sesquicentennial" on the cover, was prepared for the members. The pages for the individual programs, listing the topics and the various writers and readers, were interspersed with color photos of the campus and with pages of apt quotations. The program at the love feast in May was focused upon Dr. Mundinger.

Mention has already been made of the faithful assistance of the service organizations at the convocations and concerts. They participated in other ways, too. Alpha Phi Omega planted a pin oak tree near McGaw Fine Arts Center to commemorate its own 30th anniversary and the College's 150th. In addition to its regular duties of raising and lowering the United States flag at the pole in the center of the campus, APO accepted responsibility for flying the College's new Sesquicentennial Flag for special occasions.

The Women's Collegium had as its main activity the sponsorship of a series of workshops, lectures, and films designed to help prepare women students for the twenty-first century. However, it also sponsored two events directly related to the Sesquicentennial. One was the March lecture by Dr. Ethel Seybold on "Illinois College and the Education of Women" (the text of which appears in Chapter 16). This address was followed by a reception at David A. Smith House cohosted by the Ladies' Education Society. The other was the "birthday party" for the College, held at Caine Student Center. The Collegium has been chaired by Associate Professor Carole M. Ryan '59, who was also secretary of the 150th Anniversary Committee. A second three-year grant for the Collegium was received in 1979 from the Helena Rubinstein Foundation which had accepted the new proposal entitled "Liberal Arts Women into the World."

Special theater seasons were planned by the Hilltoppers, under the direction of Miss Geraldine Staley, Associate Professor of Speech and Director of Drama. The plays presented during 1979 and 1980 exemplified the development of theater in America, beginning with Royall Tyler's *The Contrast*. Tyler was a graduate of Yale College who had entered the legal profession but was keenly interested in

*Caine Student Center, 1967*
Named for L. Vernon Caine, President, 1956–73

drama and wrote the first American comedy. His play was first performed in 1787 and emphasized the contrast between English and American social values. The heroine is at first attracted to the pompous Britisher who exhibits the mannerisms of an English gentleman and who pretends to be wealthy but is in fact hoping to marry well so as to improve his fortunes. The Yankee who has served in the American army is obviously less polished, but he is of sterling character and in the end it is he who wins the heroine. The play was itself a "revolution" in drama in that the author sought to replace the dominant British influence in theater by native works. The leading roles in the campus production were played by Cynthia Graunke, David Kwiecinski, and Eric Runkel; Ann Bishop was student director. Also in the commemorative series were the Commencement play, William Gillette's dramatic adaptation of A. Conan Doyle's *Sherlock Holmes*; Eugene O'Neill's *The Great God Brown*; Arthur Miller's *The Death of a Salesman* (which was the last production scheduled for Jones Memorial Theatre); and Neil Simon's *Plaza Suite*.

The Student Religious Life Committee, chaired by Dr. John N. Langfitt, College Chaplain, had responsibility for the campus arrangements for a visitor from India, Mr. Devasahayam Yesudhas, whose stay of several months at Illinois College during early 1979 was timed to coincide with the Sesquicentennial. (More details about him and his presence on the campus will be given in chapter 12.) The same committee also presented a "birthday gift" to the College by engaging Mr. Robert Short, well-known authority on the "Peanuts" comic strip and its creator, Mr. Charles Schultz. Using color slides to present selected frames, Mr. Short gave his theological interpretation entitled "The Gospel According to Peanuts." Mr. Short's appearance in Jacksonville was sponsored jointly with MacMurray College.

Homecoming in 1979 was in many respects the climax of student participation in the Sesquicentennial observance. The committee of some twenty students was chaired by senior Ann Burford and junior Joseph Chapa, while senior Michael Blackmer was parade marshal and float chairman. The theme for 1979, "If They Could See Us Now . . . IC Into the Past," provided both unity and inspiration for the many activities of the long weekend. The football-shaped Homecoming buttons were imprinted with the first phrase of the motto, followed by "1829–1979" and "Homecoming 1979" and had pictures of Sturtevant Hall and Schewe Library.

The extra-page Homecoming edition of the *Rambler* for October 19 printed "Welcome Back Alums" in bold red letters at the top of page one. Reporting on the first event in the busy schedule, the lead story began with these paragraphs:

Over 500 cheering students, faculty, administration, and friends of the College witnessed the crowning of vivacious Sherry Lynn Baumgarte as the 1979 Sesquicentennial Homecoming Queen at the close of Thursday morning's Homecoming convocation. 1978 Homecoming Queen Kathy Kinscherff placed the tiara upon Miss Baumgarte's head.

Sharing honors in the Homecoming court with Miss Baumgarte are LeeAnn Taylor, 1st attendant, from Springfield, and Seena Larkins, Joliet, 2nd attendant. . . .

Miss Baumgarte, a biology major from Freeburg, has served as president of the IC band, she has been actively involved in Hilltoppers theater group, and she is a member of Chi Beta Literary Society. She will reign over all Homecoming activities for the weekend.

A later writer might also have mentioned that Sherry is outstanding in academic work and has been awarded numerous honors, including the Walter Bellatti, Sr., Honor Scholarship, and selection as student marshal of the Class of 1981. She was the 1980 recipient of the Student Laureate Award from the Lincoln Academy of Illinois, an honor presented by the Governor in special ceremonies in the Old State Capitol.

Thursday evening activities at Homecoming included a pork roast and dance at the Morgan County Fairgrounds. Friday activities included the now-traditional Powder Puff football game between freshman and sophomore women, the tug of war between freshman and sophomore men, the Homecoming Follies (a variety show), and of course the bonfire and pep rally on the practice field followed by a spectacular display of fireworks and then by the customary refreshments served at Baxter Hall.

Saturday's activities began bright and early, with President Mundinger entertaining members of the Century Club (donors of $100 or more) at breakfast in Baxter. Meanwhile the Board of Directors of the Alumni Association was meeting. At 10:30 the Homecoming Parade set out from the corner of College Avenue and Westminster Street to make its way downtown and then return to the campus. In addition to the floats which had been built by the literary societies and other organizations, various community groups were represented and fourteen high school bands marched and played. Professor Charles E. Frank, recently retired, and Mrs. Frank were the honorary parade marshals.

That afternoon the I.C. Blueboys defeated the St. Ambrose Bees of Davenport, Iowa, by a score of 22 to 14. Members of the 1929 football team were special guests. During half-time ceremonies, the Homecoming Queen and her court were presented and trophies were awarded for the best floats and dormitory decorations, with first prize for the latter going to Pixley Hall. Gamma Delta won the first place trophy and consequently the prize for the best women's society float, Sigma Phi Epsilon took second, and third place Phi Alpha was awarded the trophy for the best men's society entry. The floats were constructed of a profusion of colored tissue paper tufted into wire netting over wooden framing. The Delts' float depicted a Blueboy looking through a window at a "building" with the names of Beecher Hall and McGaw Center on opposing sides and large numerals "1829" and "1979" on the other sides. This structure was made to rotate and the legend on the skirting of the float proclaimed "IC ALWAYS ON THE MOVE." The Sig Phips portrayed an enormous face, representing our collegiate forebears, with elderly eyes peering through spectacles far down on a very long nose at a book with the I.C. logo on the covers. Beneath on either side was the invitation, "LOOK AT US NOW." Phi Alpha's entry, "SAVE OUR STUMP," recalled the day some years earlier when student protests stopped the machine which had been demolishing a large stump in the middle of the campus—a stump which frequently served as the platform for candidates for student offices.

Probably for the first time in our history the football game was started with the firing of a cannon, manned by senior Connor Haynes and his Civil War gun crew dressed in Confederate gray. A shot was fired every time the Blueboys scored a touchdown, and at half-time the crew put on a special demonstration at midfield.

Following the game, coffee and cider were served on the lawn north of the Caine Student Center. The women's literary societies' Cozies were held at Smith House, and the men's societies met in their halls. The Homecoming dance that evening was at the Elks' Club.

A unique feature of the 1979 Homecoming was the laying of the cornerstone of the McGaw Fine Arts Center, a ceremony which has been described previously. This took place soon after the conclusion of the football game.

Much of the year-to-year functioning of student organizations and activities continued without special reference to the 150th Anniversary observance. Brief mention will be made of certain highlights of these activities in order to round out the picture of campus life during the Sesquicentennial year. For example, the debate squad necessarily focused its attention on the nationally selected topic. Arguing the case both for and against allowing greater freedom to law enforcement agencies, the 1978–79 squad hada winning season. John Black, a junior, and three sophomores, Bradley Bartholomew, Dennis Graber, and Michael ("Mike") Taylor, traveled to a dozen tournaments. Mike was named "outstanding debater" at the Rose Bowl

Debate Tournament at the University of Southern California in Los Angeles; Mike had competed in a field of more than 150 debaters from schools in 25 states. The team posted some impressive wins the following year, debating the question: "Resolved: that the Federal Government Should Significantly Control Mass Media Communications." Brad and Mike won the second-place trophy in the field of 50 colleges and universities at the UCLA meet that year. They continued to excel in their senior year, placing first as a team and winning both the first and second place individual awards at the Western Kentucky University "Kentucky Colonel Classic." As a consequence Debate Coach Raymond Ford, Associate Professor of Speech, was commissioned a Kentucky Colonel. The College's long tradition as a leader in forensics proudly continues.

The year 1978–79 witnessed continued participation by women's teams in intercollegiate basketball, softball, tennis, track, and volleyball. Women's teams had first engaged in such competition in 1975, in basketball. The College swimming team has included both men and women since 1975. The men's sports schedule included baseball, golf, tennis, track, and wrestling, in addition to football and basketball. The basketball team's record was 14 and 12 for a fifth consecutive winning season, while the all-time record of 8 and 1 was achieved in football in the fall of 1978 and was nearly matched by the 7 and 2 record of 1979. The 1979 football campaign was the twenty-fourth season for the Blueboys under Coach E. Joseph Brooks, Director of Athletics and Associate Professor of Physical Education. A highlight of that season was the game with the University of Aztlan in Mexico City. The game was arranged by the National Association of Intercollegiate Athletics, and the travel expenses were paid by the Mexican National Institute of Sport. The *Rambler* report characterized the game, which I.C. won 72 to 34, as "wild and woolly." Despite the lop-sided final tally, the score was tied twice in the first half. In the second half the Blueboys dominated, "reeling off five unanswered touchdowns." Halfback Jay Wessler broke all school records with his 272-yard performance and consequently led "the NAIA Division II with 161.2 yards per game and 18.2 scoring per game."

Illinois College had withdrawn from the Prairie College Conference in 1978, largely because of the difficulty of finding appropriate football competition. The College was to be independent for two years until joining the College Athletic Conference in 1980. The CAC affiliation puts I.C. into competition with Centre College of Kentucky, Principia College near Alton, Rose-Hulman Institute of Technology in Indiana, and two Tennessee schools, Southwestern at Memphis and the University of the South at Sewanee.

## CAMPUS PUBLICITY AND STUDENT PUBLICATIONS

On a small campus much of the news circulates quickly by word-of-mouth, but more formal means were utilized to insure full reporting on Sesquicentennial events. The "Illinois College Preview" is published by the Deans' Office each week during the school year and lists all campus activities along with official announcements. The Illinois College *Rambler*, however, was the major medium for news items and feature stories regarding the 150th Anniversary celebration. The first official communication of the Committee to students and faculty was the "Open Letter," which was printed in the *Rambler* for November 3, 1977. This described the general plan of the celebration and invited organizations and individuals to participate. A special issue was published at the beginning of classes in January, 1979, to announce the Convocation on Liberal Learning and the afternoon seminar on the church-related college, both scheduled for Monday, January 15.

The April 4, 1979, issue was typical of several which carried numerous stories and photographs relating to Sesquicentennial programs. Among the events featured were the dedication of the Hart Sesquicentennial Pipe Organ in Rammelkamp Chapel and the recital by Catharine Crozier, the plans for a College flag, and the publication of Professor Frank's history of the College. The October 19 *Rambler* was the Homecoming issue and in addition to the story on the Queen and court, already mentioned, the full schedule of weekend activities was listed. Other stories told of the laying of the cornerstone of McGaw and the forthcoming Humanities Convocation. Also included was a capsule history of "Star Events in IC History" (which included quotations from Rammelkamp and earlier volumes of the *Rambler*). Feature articles provided background information for the varsity game and a tongue-in-cheek account of the strengths and weaknesses of the teams to be fielded by the freshman and sophomore women in the Powder Puff football game. The Pompon squad was the subject of still another story. The first issue published after Homecoming carried several pages of pictures of activities and personalities and also announced the John Walker concert. The April 18, 1980, *Rambler* headlined a story on the new Fine Arts Center: "McGaw Ready." It also included a story on the program of addresses and songs honoring the College's first two graduates.

Some of the students serving as editors of the *Rambler* during this period were Diane Bogosian, Leslie Conklin, Robin Gee, Steve Loos, Michael Taylor, and Randall Wirsing. Feature stories were written by Jon Althoff, Amy Duensing, Ronald Schaulat, and Michael Tanzer, among others. Photographers were Jon Althoff, Bruce Anderson, Leslie Conklin, Barbara Kiebel, Joseph Kozma, Howard Sizek, and Kathy Windhorst.

The 1979 *Rig Veda* was not only the largest ever published (over three hundred pages) but certainly one of the finest. Coeditors Rebecca (Becky) Schutz and Sheila Wyatt presented the College with a superb record of the year 1978–79. The *Rig* was appropriately dedicated to Dr. Charles E. Frank, and close to the front there is a double-page spread with color photographs of Dr. Frank and a summary of his career at I.C. which notes that he is "More Than a Scholar," an apt phrase which recognizes "his many years of outstanding service to both the college and the community." The yearbook includes the usual coverage of student organizations and activities, Homecoming and Commencement, individual members of the four classes, and the faculty, administration, and staff. In addition there is a fourteen-page section on the Sesquicentennial, edited by Becky Schutz. This includes a summary history of the beginnings of Illinois College and its development, photographs of old and new buildings, a map of the campus from an aerial perspective (showing the buildings in three dimensions), and full photo coverage of the Public Affairs Convocation and the Remembrance March. The volume is all the more attractive because of the many pages of color photographs of familiar campus scenes and candid shots of students in thoughtful moods and comic poses.

The 1980 *Rig Veda* is another outstanding yearbook. Presented in a distinctive format, this volume (number eighty-one) is focused on *people* and includes many candid comments by students. The large number of superb photographs (many of them in color), the carefully prepared captions, and the extensive descriptions of major events combine to make the book an especially meaningful record of the persons, the events, and the traditions which made up Illinois College in 1979–80. There is thorough coverage of the 1979 Homecoming and the 1980 Commencement. Several of the programs in the later months of the Sesquicentennial observance are included. Prominently featured is a photo of the poster, signed by a large number of students and headed, "We, the Student Body, with thoughts toward the future of the Arts at Illinois College, pledge [to contribute to the building fund for the Fine Arts Center]." The committee in charge of this project is also pictured; Venice Meyer was chairperson and the members were Jon Althoff, Jane Davidson, Matthew Mundinger, and Laurie Newman. The coeditors of the 1980 *Rig Veda* were Kathy Windhorst, who had charge of the Homecoming section, and Joseph Kozma who took many of the photographs and edited the Sesquicentennial pages.

The handsome exhibit case on the main floor of Schewe Library was used to display historical documents and mementos of previous celebrations. One exhibit featured the original copy of the Yale Compact, signed at Yale College in February, 1829, by Julian M. Sturtevant, Theron Baldwin, and five others when they pledged themselves to establish a college and serve churches on the Illinois frontier. Another display included pictures of the first two graduates, Jonathan E. Spilman and Richard Yates, along with photocopies of sheet music for songs composed by Spilman, such as "Flow Gently, Sweet Afton." At other times copies of the *Rambler* and *Rig Vedas* were opened out to show photos and stories of previous quarter-century celebrations. The histories by Rammelkamp and Frank were also displayed, along with catalogs and pamphlets published during the early period of the College's history.

*Forte*, the I.C. literary magazine, was published three times during the Sesquicentennial observance. The prose and poetry, by students and faculty, did not specifically mention the 150th Anniversary, but the tone of nostalgia and respect for the past is evident. The writing is sensitive and sincere, the artistic and photographic illustrations creative. Sue Horn '82 reflected awareness of the past and hope for the future in her poem, "Untouchable Memory," in the Spring, 1980, issue: "The sands flow on, now out of reach, / a new day to learn, a new day to teach." The editors of the three issues were junior John Black (Spring, 1979) and seniors David Kwiecinski and Rebecca Schutz (Fall, 1979, and Spring, 1980, respectively).

## FACULTY, ADMINISTRATION AND STAFF, AND TRUSTEES

The direct responsibility for planning and carrying out the varied programs of the Sesquicentennial Committee was to a large extent assumed by members of the faculty and administration, with strong support from the staff and from the trustees. The three academic divisions were represented by alumni: Division I by Mrs. Carole M. Ryan '59, Associate Professor of Modern Languages (French); Division II by Mr. George William Horton, Jr. -52, Associate Professor of Mathematics; and Division III by Mr. Richard L. Pratt '49, Librarian. Other faculty members were Dr. John N. Langfitt, Chaplain and Assistant Professor of Religion, and (as chairman) Dr. Iver F. Yeager, Scarborough Professor of Philosophy and Religion and chairman of the department. The three deans were also on the roster and in addition to providing direct help on many projects aided in coordinating the observance with other College functions; they are Dr. Wallace N. Jamison, Dean of the College; Dean of Students Donald R. Eldred; and Associate Dean of Students (and Registrar) Doris B. Hopper '41. Dr. Donald C. Mundinger, president of the College, was an active member of the Committee and gave his continuing and enthusiastic support. In some instances he had anticipated the needs of the Committee and had already set in motion the background arrangements for a featured aspect of the celebration.

Staff members who served during part or all of the extended period of planning and observance included Mr. Howard M. Jarratt, Director of Development; Mr. Mark J. Schwartz '74, Director of Public Information until the end of 1978, and his successor, Mrs. Mary Green '78; and Mrs. Martha S. Vache '67, then Director of Alumni Affairs.

The Board of Trustees was represented on the Committee by two of its officers, Mr. William N. Clark '40, chairman, and Dr. Robert R. Hartman '35, secretary. Special subcommittee sessions were arranged on occasions when the Board was meeting on the campus so that Mr. Clark could be present. Mr. Clark was on the Committee's mailing list and responded frequently by letter with comments and suggestions. The help and encouragement given by these and all the members of the Committee did much to make the Sesquicentennial celebration a significant observance of the College's 150 years.

The total membership of the 150th Anniversary Committee, including the two alumni representatives to be named shortly, was about twenty at any given time. The group met around the elegant cherry table in the Faculty-Trustees Room for the monthly meetings. The membership was not so large as to be unwieldy and at times seemed barely large enough to staff the numerous subcommittees which accomplished much of the day-to-day business. This Committee was indeed a working committee.

The faculty participated actively in the celebration, marching in numerous academic processions, wearing their gowns and hoods. A member of the faculty read the citation for each candidate for an honorary degree. Members of the appropriate divisions served as hosts at the receptions given for the speaker and other special guests after the various convocations.

The Faculty Senate, which includes all the full professors, arranged a reception during Commencement weekend, 1979, for all emeritus faculty. Dr. William Cross, Professor of Sociology, was chairman of the Senate that year. Dr. Wilbur Chien, Professor of Economics and Business Administration, was in charge of arrangements; assisting him were Dr. Louise Rainbolt, Professor of Biology, and Dr. Donald R. Tracey, Professor of History. Invitations were sent to all emeriti, and happily almost all of them were able to attend. Attending were President L. Vernon Caine and Mrs. Caine, Professor Charles C. Barlow '29 and Mrs. Margaret Barlow '30, Dr. Louis F. Meek and Mrs. Meek, Dr. Eleanor O. Miller, Dr. Ethel Seybold '29, Dr. Malcolm F. Stewart and Mrs. Stewart, and Professor Elizabeth R. Zeigler. Other special guests were Mrs. Ernest G. Hildner, Mrs. Joe Patterson Smith, and Mrs. John Sorenson. Sending their regrets were President H. Gary Hudson and Mrs. Hudson and Professor Leonora Tomlinson. A large number of active faculty were present to greet their former colleagues.

The Committee had suggested that the faculty might provide a mace for the faculty marshal to be a symbol of office and which would then be a memento of the Sesquicentennial. An informal questionnaire indicated that a little more than half of the faculty responding did not favor the plan and so the proposal was dropped. Some remarked that there was already more pomp and formality than a small college needed!

There is no way of knowing how many occasions there were when faculty members made reference in classes to statements by the various speakers and commented upon the concert artists. So far as is known only one course examination included a question explicitly related to the 150th anniversary. The freshman Interdisciplinary Studies course had regularly included a unit on art in the second semester. That spring, one of the test questions asked the students to draw upon their studies of art and, imagining themselves to be artists commissioned to create a piece of work for the Sesquicentennial, to describe both the form and the content of their proposed sculpture or painting.

Various faculty members charged with such responsibilities made the usual arrangements for the annual lectureships on campus and also for some special cultural events during 1978–79. The Joe Patterson Smith lecture was delivered in November by Elmer Gertz, an attorney and a delegate to the 1970 Constitutional Convention, on the subject "The Illinois Constitutional Convention—Almost a Decade Later." His assessment was that overall the Convention had done its work well. In February, Dr. David H. C. Read, appointed as the Staley Distinguished Christian Scholar, spent three days on campus. His main address was entitled "With Wings of Wonder—Beyond the World of the Wise Guys." Dr. Read is pastor of the Madison Avenue

Presbyterian Church in New York City. Another February event was "Minority Awareness Week," sponsored by the Minority Students for Cultural Advancement, a campus organization for which Dr. Lynette H. Seator, Professor of Modern Languages (Spanish), has served as faculty advisor. A student art exhibit was on display during the week, a number of special films were screened, and a lecture was given by Mrs. Velma Carey of the Springfield Urban League.

In March the campus chapter of Phi Beta Kappa presented Professor Benjamin Aaron, of the University of California at Los Angeles, who spoke on the topic, "Worker Participation in Management: A Comparative View." The April calendar was crowded with special events. The Yakshagana Dance-Drama Group from India included nearly a dozen male dancers, in elaborate and colorful costumes and some with enormous headdresses, who performed to the accompaniment of drums and cymbals. Mr. Harry Mark Petrakis, a Greek-American author from Chicago, made his second visit to the campus and this time stayed for three days as Writer-in-Residence. Mr. Petrakis charmed the large audience with his stories. Dr. Ethel Seybold gave the Claridge lecture, a keen and witty analysis of one of her favorite authors and entitled "Thoreau: Some Popular Myths Exploded."

An event of the 1979–80 academic year will also be noted here, although it was not formally a part of the Sesquicentennial observance, in order to present a reasonably complete picture of the major facets of the College's program during this period. Several times in the preceding years the opening convocation of the second semester had been made the occasion for installing a professor in one of the named chairs. This pattern had been interrupted by the Convocation on Liberal Learning, which initiated the series of special 150th anniversary events. The arrangement was resumed in January, 1980, when Dr. Donald R. Tracey was installed as the William and Charlotte Gardner Professor of History. In keeping with the tradition of several years' standing, Dr. Tracey delivered an inaugural address. His subject, "The Middle-Eastern Crisis in Historical Perspective," was of particular interest to the large audience because only two months before more than fifty Americans assigned to the United

States Embassy in Teheran had been taken hostage by militant students.

Although many of the members of the 150th Anniversary Committee were alumni who served as representatives of the faculty, staff, and trustees, two others were chosen explicitly as alumni, Mrs. Patricia B. Manker '71 and Mr. Robert E. Chipman '74. Specifically they were spokespersons for local alumni and graduates of recent years.

Every effort was made to keep the alumni and friends of the College fully informed regarding the Sesquicentennial celebration. The two brochures listing the special programs for the spring and fall (1979) semesters were mailed to all of them. The *Alumni Quarterly*, especially attractive with the recently-adopted cover photo in color, reported the major convocations and concerts through stories and pictures. Mrs. Mary Green '78, Director of Public Information, prepared for alumni a four-page tabloid report on Homecoming, 1979. The front page featured the College's beginnings ("1829") and its present status and future prospects ("1979"). The back page was filled with picture memories of past Homecomings and the inside spread was a pictorial record of 1979 Homecoming activities and personalities—the queen and queen candidates, parade floats and football action, and the cornerstone ceremonies for McGaw.

Periodic reports on the 150th Anniversary Challenge Fund were made by Mr. Howard M. Jarratt of the Development Office on behalf of the national cochairmen, Mr. William E. Wilton '39 and Mrs. Carol Coultas Lohman '45. Along with the latest figures on the fund's growth the half-dozen issues of the four-page brochure included a series of illustrated stories about the College's early history and its historic buildings as well as progress reports on the construction of the Fine Arts Center.

As noted earlier, it was decided that many of the honorary degrees awarded during the Sesquicentennial observance would be granted to alumni. Often the files in the Alumni Office provided ample documentation to support a given nomination, although in some cases the special subcommittee on honors had to make discreet inquiries to get information about an alumnus who obviously had achieved distinction in a career but who had not sent such information to the College.

Special mention of three of the alumni granted honorary degrees is appropriate here. (The others will be mentioned in other contexts.) Professor Arthur E. Hallerberg '40, for many years a member of the Mathematics Department at I.C. and then at Valparaiso University from 1960 until his untimely death in late 1979, had been chosen to represent all alumni who have demonstrated excellence in teaching. Emeritus Professors Charles C. Barlow and Ethel Seybold deserved recognition for their services to education generally and to Illinois College in particular. They also represented the Centennial Class of 1929; it seemed appropriate that each of them should receive a second diploma from the College—fifty years later!

The Alumni Association undertook numerous projects, including the computerized publication of an *Alumni Directory* in 1979; this included the names of all known living graduates and former students of Illinois College. The Association made available, by mail order and through the College Bookstore, several commemorative items, among them porcelain plates with a picture of Sturtevant Hall. Packets of note stationery with drawings of College buildings were a popular item. There were five designs, including drawings of Jones, Tanner, and Rammelkamp by Mrs. Louise Boring Wood '34 and line drawings of Schewe Library and Sturtevant by Mrs. Dorothy B. Frank. Also prized by alumni and others were six prints with Mrs. Wood's detailed drawings which were sold both singly and in sets. The prints were ten by thirteen inches and included Crampton, Sturtevant, and Whipple in addition to the buildings previously named. Mrs. Wood signed, labeled, and numbered 100 sets of her drawings. The College Bookstore had all these items for sale and also Dr. Frank's *Pioneer's Progress*. In addition College mugs, glasses embossed with the College Seal, Sesquicentennial seals, and an assortment of T-shirts with different I.C. mottoes were available for purchase. Mrs. Alice Chipman, manager of the Bookstore, reported that business was especially brisk at Homecoming.

In recognition of the importance of the 150th Anniversary, the

Alumni Association decided to award the annual Distinguished Public Service Citations to an exceptionally large group of alumni. As
usual the presentations were made at the alumni luncheon on Commencement Day. The senior alumnus to be so honored was Mr.
Charles M. Capps '20 of Wichita, Kansas, a printer (now retired) and
an accomplished etcher whose works have been purchased by the
Library of Congress and the Swedish National Museum. Dr. William R. Wood '27 had been president of the University of Alaska for
thirteen years and since retiring had been elected mayor of Fairbanks.
Mrs. Dorothy E. Brant and Mr. Ellis L. Brant, both of the Class of
1928, had had long careers in the public schools of Illinois. Mr. Philip
Bradish and Mr. Cecil Tendick were chosen from the Class of 1929.
The former was circuit clerk of Morgan county for twenty-eight
years and director of student financial aid at Illinois College for a
decade after that. The latter has held various editorial and reportorial
positions on the local newspaper, contributing for many years a column in the Sunday edition to tell humorous tales of people he has
known or heard about. Mr. Charles B. Menees '41 had also been a
reporter and columnist and currently was editing an employee newspaper for a large corporation and hosting a jazz show on St. Louis
radio station KMOX. Dr. Harvey D. Scott '42 is a highly respected
physician and surgeon in Jacksonville. Mr. Darrow Steinheimer '55,
then manager of the family's drug store, was founder of the Big
Brother-Big Sister organization in Jacksonville and has been active
in many other civic causes. The selection of these alumni was made
by a committee of alumni, faculty, and administrative staff persons.

Several area Alumni Association meetings were held during 1979.
The Carrollton Society held a March dinner meeting. The meeting
was organized by President John B. Pratt '48 and featured a talk by
basketball coach William Merris '56, Associate Professor of Physical
Education. Mr. William N. Clark '40 was the speaker at the April
meeting in Chicago; a special attraction of that meeting was the auc-
tion of some I.C. souvenirs by President Garry Barnett '68. Mr. Patrick Kennedy '67 presided at the Jacksonville meeting, also in April,
when Professor and Mrs. Charles E. Frank were honored for their
service to Illinois College over the span of four decades. Fall meetings were held in Dallas and Houston, with President Donald C.

Mundinger present at both to speak about the College. Mr. Raymond Allen Ford, Associate Professor of Speech and Director of Forensics, spoke twice at November meetings, first to the Springfield Society (Mrs. Marianne W. Stowers '64, president) and then to the St. Louis Society (Mrs. Eula G. Stierholz '56, president).

## ILLINOIS COLLEGE'S CHURCH RELATIONSHIPS

Like many other liberal arts colleges, Illinois College was founded and nurtured by people who were motivated by Christian faith and who sought to bring the blessings of Christian civilization to the frontier, and like many others it in time gained its independence from church control. However, the College has been unlike many others in neither repudiating its origins nor rejecting a continuing relationship with the churches whose heritage it shares and with which it continues to have many common concerns. Consequently the importance of religious faith and the College's ties with the United Church of Christ and the United Presbyterian Church in the U.S.A. were acknowledged on several occasions during the long observance. Representatives of the higher education agencies of the two denominations were invited to participate in the Convocation on Liberal Learning and to lead an afternoon seminar on the church-related college of the 1980s. Due to the severe weather only part of the plan was carried out at the time originally scheduled. Also during 1979 Illinois College was host to regional meetings of the two churches. Further information about these aspects of the College's Sesquicentennial will be provided in chapters 11–13.

## RECOGNITION OF ILLINOIS COLLEGE'S 150TH ANNIVERSARY BY THE LARGER COMMUNITY

Throughout the years Illinois College has received due attention because it was the first college in the state to grant baccalaureate degrees and because of other "firsts" as well. In 1974 the National Park Service listed Beecher Hall on the National Register of Historic Places. Beecher has been in continuous use since the first classes met there in January, 1830, and it is the oldest college building in Illinois.

The College's 150th Anniversary attracted the attention of prominent persons and various news media. Letters and telegrams of congratulations were received from President Jimmie Carter, Governor James R. Thompson, 20th District Congressman Paul Findley '43, the Honorable Arthur Burns, the Honorable Melvin Laird, and others. Greetings were received also from Emeritus Presidents H. Gary Hudson and L. Vernon Caine. Some of these letters have been included in Appendix C.

The *Jacksonville Daily Journal* (morning) and *Courier* (evening), the state's oldest continuously published newspaper, provided full coverage with news stories and photographs. Feature stories were printed regarding many special events relating to the Sesquicentennial, such as the new five-year Illinois license plates with Yale-blue numerals on a white background, in honor of the College. The staff of the Jacksonville daily published a very attractive supplement to the October 19 *Courier* and the October 20 *Journal* in honor of Illinois College. This was timed to coincide with the 1979 Homecoming. The banner headline on the front reads "Illinois College, 1829–1979." Mrs. Wood's drawing of Jones Memorial Hall fills most of the page. The special issue is tabloid size and has fifty-two pages of text and pictures, with some advertisements.

Only a limited survey of the contents can be included here. For example, there is Julian M. Sturtevant's 1831 account of Illinois College, the first "history" of the school, which was printed in Peck's *A Guide for Immigrants* (published in Boston). After telling of the founding of the College and the first classes, which had met in its lone building, Sturtevant described the library as including six to eight hundred volumes. The faculty was listed as "the Rev. Edward Beecher . . . President"; "the Rev. J. M. Sturtevant, Professor of Mathematics"; and "a temporary Instructor in the Latin and Greek languages."

The supplement also includes appropriate stories reprinted from earlier volumes of the *Journal* and *Courier*, some as early as 1904. Nearly three pages are given to an account of the Centennial celebration. A lengthy excerpt from *Pioneer's Progress* tells of the early years of student government. Many old photographs are reproduced, depicting presidents and faculty, football and baseball teams and various student activities of earlier years, and buildings no longer standing, such as the old gymnasium. Reminiscences of graduates of recent decades recall both humorous and poignant experiences on the hilltop. The portrayal of the College is brought up to the present by other stories and pictures: there are photographs of the Mundingers and the Caines and statements by these two presidents. Mr. John Power '73, City Editor of the newspaper, was primarily responsible for the research and writing of the special supplement, with the acknowledged help of Mrs. Mary Green who assisted him in locating many of the early photos of the College. Correctly anticipating a heavy demand by the Homecoming crowd, the newspaper printed one thousand extra copies of that issue.

There are many in the Jacksonville area who have a serious interest in history and they and others enjoy the tid-bits of the past which appear in the newspaper's daily column, "A Glance into the Past." Gleaned from the newspaper's files and presented in often-tantalizing brevity are items from issues of the corresponding date 10, 20, 50, 75, 100, and 120 years ago. Illinois College has been well-represented in all these time periods, including of course the earliest. A few examples will serve both to illustrate the contents of the column and to recall some of the highlights of the College's history. From "120 Years Ago" we learned of Abraham Lincoln's lecture, sponsored in 1859 by Phi Alpha Literary Society, on "Discoveries and Inventions." That same year there was first the disapproving acknowledgment that Illinois College manufactures abolitionist students, and then two weeks later the blunt warning that if the College's "managers persist in making it an abolition machine" their movement will be exposed. It was "100 Years Ago" that the paper reported that the Reverend Edward Beecher, first president, would attend the fiftieth anniversary celebration, and "75 Years Ago" that the Reverend Hugh Black of Scotland delivered a masterly discourse as the diamond-anniversary sermon. Then "50 Years Ago" Illinois College made plans to plant 100 elm trees along College Avenue in recognition of its centennial anniversary. At the centennial commencement that same year diplomas were awarded to seventy students in the exercises at the Westminster Presbyterian Church. Some of the recollections are humorous—for example, the report of finding a certain professor's light-colored horse painted with black stripes to resemble a zebra!

One of the items in this newspaper column led, after a few months, to an instance of history repeating itself. Mr. Power as City Editor of the paper reads the microfilmed issues of past years and selects the stories which are printed in abbreviated fashion. He recalled the account of the 100 elms which were planted in 1929 and suggested to Mrs. Helen Cleary Foreman '25, an active alumna and a member of the City Council, that the College should plant 150 trees in honor of its 150th Anniversary. The proposal was discussed with President Mundinger, who approved it as a very appropriate gesture of thanks to the community for its support through the years. This time, to avoid the possibility of a blight which had destroyed the elms, a wide variety of trees (both shade and ornamental) was purchased. Townspeople were invited to submit their requests for the kind of tree they wished to have planted along the boulevard. Responses came from every quarter of Jacksonville. Most of the trees were planted in front of individual residences, although some were placed in the public parks and in Diamond Grove Cemetery. The work of planting was done by City of Jacksonville crews during the spring and fall of 1980. The 150th tree had been reserved for the new President of MacMurray College, Dr. Bob Stephens, whose wife Sandra selected the tree for their residence after their arrival in the community.

The three local radio stations—WLDS, soon after to celebrate its own fortieth anniversary, WEAI-FM, and WJIL—aired current announcements of Sesquicentennial events. Springfield television station WICS-NBC (Channel 20) sent camera and sound technicians to report on the Public Affairs Convocation, the 1979 Commencement, and the dedication of McGaw Fine Arts Center.

The Morgan County Historical Society included in its schedule some programs on Illinois College. On November 8, 1979, Dr. Harold E. Gibson '30, retired college professor and administrator and author of *Sigma Pi Society of Illinois College*,[4] gave a detailed account

4. Harold E. Gibson, *Sigma Pi Society of Illinois College—1843–1971* (Jacksonville, IL: Sigma Pi Society, 1972).

of the College's first decade. Dr. Gibson had undertaken extensive research to ferret out little known details about "Illinois College 150 Years Ago." He declared that John M. Ellis had never received proper recognition for his role in founding the College and raising the money, in Illinois and in the East, which was needed to get it started. He explained that Ellis had written reports, published in magazines, which contained candid descriptions of the rude behavior of area residents. Presumably this was the reason that Ellis was never elected a trustee, out of fear that antagonism toward him would be harmful to the College. Turning to another subject, the speaker recalled that more than fifty years ago, as a student, he had heard President Rammelkamp comment in a chapel speech that there were certain intriguing questions about the College for which he had been unable to find answers. One of these had to do with the way Abraham Lincoln had voted on the bill to grant Illinois College (and three other colleges), a charter. Dr. Gibson discovered that the seemingly-lost minutes of the House of Representatives for 1835 were printed with the 1836 record. Lincoln had voted against the charter but, said Gibson, he could not learn the reason for his opposition. Along with copies of early maps and pictures and other records, Dr. Gibson displayed a photocopy of the earliest-known Illinois College catalog published in pamphlet form. This 1832–33 "Catalogue of the Officers and Students in Illinois College," eight pages in length, is in the archives of the American Antiquarian Society in Worcester, Massachusetts, and is a year earlier than the oldest catalog in the College's possession. Dr. Gibson's address was printed by the *Jacksonville Journal Courier* in four successive Sunday issues in January, 1980.

In March, 1980, Professor Iver F. Yeager presented a program of slides and narrative to the Morgan County Historical Society. Using the title, "Church and College on the Illinois Frontier," Professor Yeager dealt with the role of the Congregationalists and Presbyterians in founding the College and also the role of the College's staff and of the members of the Yale Band (who were trustees of the College) in organizing and serving churches in west central Illinois from 1829 to 1867. This program was also presented to several civic and church groups in the area.

Many community groups have enjoyed the numerous slide-talk programs given by Mr. Arthur Seeman -47 during the last several

years. Combining his interest in history and photography, Mr. Seeman has made hundreds of slides from early drawings, maps, and
photos depicting the history of Jacksonville from early times. His
program on "Dormitory Life at Illinois College in the 1890s" had
special appeal. The story of the source of the pictures used in this
talk is interesting. Mr. Warren Wallace -42 of Winchester had purchased a box for $1.50 at a Jacksonville auction, and in it he had
found about one hundred fifty glass plate negatives. Mr. Seeman
used prints made from these to prepare his own slides. Many of the
pictures portray students in their dormitory rooms, studying at their
desks, talking with friends, and often clowning. Other pictures were
taken in labs and classrooms, or during a tennis match, or on the
playing fields—with the athletes sometimes in action and sometimes
posing for a team picture. The cornerstone ceremonies for Jones
Memorial Hall had been recorded and also some scenes at the Jacksonville Female Academy. The photographer who had taken these
pictures was Michael H. Grassley, a senior in 1898. Most of the pictures have been well-preserved and many are excellent in composition and sharp in detail.

Another facet of the College's early history was memorialized in
an address by a local physician, Dr. Joseph Kozma, to the Central
Illinois Medical History Club. His subject was "The Illinois College
Medical School, 1843–1848: A Social-Historical Analysis."[5] Ar-
rangements were made for the Club to have its 1980 meeting in
Beecher Hall which for a time had housed the state's first medical
school. For several years Dr. Kozma has lectured on the same subject
to students enrolled in the Southern Illinois University School of
Medicine in Springfield. Dr. Kozma is the father of Joseph Kozma,
Class of 1980.

It was a coincidence that the University of Illinois had completed
the second part of a building for agricultural education and research
during Illinois College's Sesquicentennial observance and dedicated
that building in March of 1979. But there was a solid historical link
between the two events because that structure was named "Jonathan
Baldwin Turner Hall" in honor of the pioneer educator and agricul-

5. A copy of Dr. Kozma's address (typewritten) has been given by the author to the Illinois
College Library.

tural experimentalist who had been one of Illinois College's first faculty members. Turner was honored by the University for his work in agriculture and also because of his prominent role in the passage of the federal legislation which established the land-grant colleges.

## THE RECORDS OF THE SESQUICENTENNIAL OBSERVANCE

The Sesquicentennial Anniversary celebration of the founding of Illinois College was itself a historical event or, more accurately, a series of historical events. Even before the first convocation the suggestion had been made by Dr. James E. Davis (Associate Professor of History) that copies of printed programs and examples of memorabilia be collected for the College's archives and for various historical societies. This was done, and upon the conclusion of the observance more than a dozen sets of programs for Sesquicentennial activities and other major events of the period were assembled. Two sets were deposited in the archives room of Schewe Library, and other sets were placed in the President's Office, the Alumni and Development Offices, and the 150th Anniversary Committee files (eventually to be placed in Schewe). Sets were also delivered to the Jacksonville Public Library, the Illinois State Historical Library, the library of the Divinity School of Yale University, and the Congregational, Presbyterian, and United Church of Christ historical societies.

Schewe Library is the repository for special items, including examples of the medallions given to the Class of 1979, cassette tape recordings of some of the addresses, color slides, and the files of the chairman (which include copies of the addresses, newspaper clippings, and correspondence). Many photographs and some other records are in the Alumni Office, in the individual folders for alumni and in anniversary folders. The Registrar, while microfilming student academic records during 1979 and 1980, has copied some of the printed programs also.

The files of the President's Office and the Alumni Office also contain resources for that future historian who will someday chronicle the College's fourth half-century. The *Rambler*, the *Rig Veda*, and the

*Jacksonville Daily Journal* and *Courier* will be valuable to that person
as they have been to previous historians and to the present writer.
Finally, this volume itself should be a reasonably complete summary
record of this memorable period of Illinois College's history, with
enough detail (it is hoped) to interest many a future reader and sufficient clues for the researcher so that he or she will be able to pursue
that study of Illinois College's past which others have found so fascinating.

PART TWO

---

*Illinois College and Liberal Learning: The Major Convocations*

---

In the course of instruction in this college, it has been an object to maintain such a proportion between the different branches of literature and science, as to form in the student a proper *balance* of character. From the pure mathematics, he learns the art of demonstrative reasoning. In attending to the physical sciences, he becomes familiar with facts, with the process of induction, and the varieties of probable evidence. In ancient literature, he finds some of the most finished models of taste. By English reading, he learns the powers of the language in which he is to speak and write. By logic and mental philosophy, he is taught the art of thinking; by rhetoric and oratory, the art of speaking. By frequent exercise on written composition, he acquires copiousness and accuracy of expression. By extemporaneous discussion, he becomes prompt, and fluent, and animated.

The Yale Report of 1828

Seven young gentlemen, then members of the Theological Department of Yale college, had associated themselves together, with the view of devoting their lives to the cause of education and religion in some of the new settlements of our rapidly extending country. Their plan [was to establish] a literary Institution on the most enlarged and liberal principles. . . .

Sketch of Illinois College (1831),
Rev. J. M. Sturtevant, Professor of Mathematics

The liberal arts curriculum is still the basic program of the College. . . . A liberally educated person is one who is making significant progress toward several goals: an understanding of the most significant areas of human knowledge; the development of certain habits of reflective thought, considered value judgment, and informed action; and the attainment of a satisfactory capacity for effective communication.

Illinois College Catalog, 1979–81

The series of major convocations extending from January, 1979, through April, 1980, constituted the basic framework of the College's observance of the 150th Anniversary of its founding. These events properly directed the attention of the campus community toward liberal learning, the core of the mission and curriculum of Illinois College throughout its history. The College has sometimes added new programs, as in agriculture (during the nineteenth century), and it has often had experimental and subsidiary programs, but it always maintained the liberal purpose of its founders. In recent decades this has been manifest in the solid core of distribution requirements in literature, mathematics and science, and the social sciences for all graduates and its insistence on foreign language as a requisite for the bachelor of arts degree and thus for students majoring in most departments.

These convocations provided the opportunity for a look at the past in the faculty essays surveying the history of the given branch of liberal education at Illinois College. Sometimes the President in his remarks made references to previous eras. The main emphasis, however, was always upon present expressions of such study, as manifested both in the address by a distinguished speaker and by honoring presently active scholars and professional people. We wished to make it unmistakably clear to students that the liberal arts are alive and vigorous and constitute an excellent base for the thrust into the eighties. This aim was stated well by Dean Donald R. Eldred's statement, printed on the January 15 program, in which he sketched broadly the purpose and program plans for the Sesquicentennial observance. The first paragraph of his essay follows:

Beginning today and throughout the coming year the Illinois College family on campus and spread widely throughout the land will celebrate the College's 150 years. Few of the approximately three-thousand colleges and universities in America have attained this hall-mark of distinction. This celebration recalls the heroic efforts of men and women who had hardly settled in this frontier community before they set about establishing the hilltop college; it celebrates 150 years of liberal learning and providing distinctive leadership for every segment of society; it celebrates the prospects of moving into the 1980s and beyond, confidently, and meeting yet new challenges open to higher education in America.

In planning for the Sesquicentennial the 150th Anniversary Committee had deliberately adopted a format different from the intensive four-day schedule of the Centennial observance. Yet many of the same topics were included in the recent celebration, not because the present Committee sought to imitate the earlier one but because the College's educational philosophy and mission were maintained with remarkable consistency. Consequently the emphases of both observances were largely congruent. For example, in both 1929 and 1979–80 there were major addresses on educational leadership, public service, and the humanities, and both times special attention was given to the education of women and to the College's church relationships. Although the earlier observance included an address on "The College Man and Business," the recent one did not focus specifically on that topic. Had there been a similar address, the subject would have been something like "College Men and Women in the Field of Business"—to reflect the great increase in the number of women students entering that profession! The 1979 program was on a more inclusive topic, the social sciences, and directed attention to broad themes of social and political policy.

One advantage of the Sesquicentennial schedule was that on a given occasion undivided attention could be directed to one aspect of liberal learning instead of having (as in 1929) three major addresses in one morning followed by two more that same afternoon. The Committee had doubts whether the endurance of contemporary audiences would be equal to that of a generation ago. The extended schedule also made it possible to include numerous concerts and a number of special programs which could hardly have been incorporated into a few consecutive days.

A letter from President Mundinger went to each member of the student body, faculty, and staff, inviting all to share in the historic observance. Dr. Mundinger's letter (dated January 5, 1979) stated, in part:

As each class now in attendance at the College was welcomed, the Sesquicentennial Anniversary was highlighted. This was especially true for the Class of 1979. In a sense, the events of the next twelve months have been planned for over four years. The celebration, after all of these months of planning and waiting, is about to begin. The opening convocation of the spring semester . . . marks the official beginning of the jubilee year. I invite you to this special event and to participate fully in the Sesquicentennial Program. Your personal involvement will benefit both you and your College. . . .

It is my hunch that future historians will identify our present period as a pivotal moment in history. The release of human energy in the Pacific Basin and the developing world will make the remaining years of this century critically important. Our work, as professors, students, and staff, in defining liberal learning, will be important as we prepare for these years. I urge you to see the immensity of the challenge facing us and to use the 150th Anniversary as a special opportunity for personal growth.

Special notice was given in the letter about the first convocation and the guest speaker. Following his well-established custom, Dr. Mundinger suggested some reading—the article on the Club of Rome in the current issue of *Atlas*.

Alumni were informed of the beginning of the observance by a special mailing which included the Sesquicentennial brochure. The people of the Jacksonville area were reached through the local media.

The Sesquicentennial celebration was now underway.

# 3

## *The Convocation on Liberal Learning*
## *January 15, 1979*

The affirmation of liberal learning as the central element of Illinois College was considered by the 150th Anniversary Committee to be the most appropriate theme for the very first event in the Sesquicentennial celebration. We wished to recognize its importance not only at the College but on the national scene as well. Accordingly arrangements were made for a special program on Liberal Learning for the opening convocation of the spring semester, and the speaker and other guests were invited to join with us.

Jacksonville had already experienced two severe winters, and despite the weather prophets who intoned "never three in a row," the winter of 1978–79 easily matched its predecessors. Monday, January 15, 1979, was a genuinely wintry day; early that morning the temperature had dipped to about 15° below zero and about a foot of snow blanketed the campus. Those familiar with Sturtevant's vivid descriptions of the harsh winters he and his family experienced in the 1830s were grateful for the much more adequate shelter our generation enjoys. This was one time when the faculty appreciated the added warmth of academic robes. The conditions of the region's highways made it more difficult to bring our out-of-town guests from the St. Louis airport to Jacksonville. The most serious interference with our plans caused by the weather was that one of the seminar leaders could not come because the Philadelphia airport (near his home) had been closed.

The excitement of the College's 150th birthday was expressed in the joyous music of the processional anthem, sung by the Concert

Choir with accompaniment on the new pipe organ played by Mr. Rick L. Erickson. The selection was entitled, "I Was Glad When They Said Unto Me." The words, taken from Psalm 122, were set to music by C. Hubert H. Parry. Mr. Erickson, who also served as director of the choir, had adapted one line so that the Choir sang in Latin the proclamation, "Long live Illinois College!"

The academic procession in Rammelkamp Chapel (where all the convocations were held) was led by Professor Don P. Filson, faculty marshal, and Professor Vidyapati Singh, assistant marshal. They were followed by the student marshals of the Class of 1979, Jane Borrowman and Jayne Verticchio, and then the faculty and the platform party. Dr. Wallace N. Jamison, Dean of the College, presided at the convocation and gave a warm welcome on behalf of the College to the assembled group.

The Scripture was read and the Prayer of Invocation given by Dr. John N. Langfitt, Chaplain to the College and Assistant Professor of Religion. Chaplain Langfitt read passages from Exodus 19 (verses 2–6) and Hebrews 3 (verses 1–6) to express the themes of wandering and sojourn, thus recalling not only the experiences of the ancient Israelites and the early Christians but also those of our own forebears who in so many ways consciously shared similar hardships and eventual triumph. Following is the prayer offered by Dr. Langfitt:

> O God, all praise and glory be unto you on this our day of jubilee! Great and wonderful are your words, O mighty Yahweh, the causative agent in our history.
> Just and true are your words, O sustaining Yahweh, the support and foundation of all true response to your causation.
> Glorious is our faith and our hope, O coming Yahweh, the true goal of life and living.
> We praise you, O God;
> We affirm that you are God;
> We gather in your name and by your grace.
> One hundred fifty years is a long time and we give thanks for it, and for those who, having lived by your name, have created that history that we here celebrate.
>
> Being true to those who responded to your impetus and followed your guidance to this place, we also turn our

*Rammelkamp Chapel, 1962*
Remodeled, 1979
Named for Charles Henry Rammelkamp, President, 1905–32

thoughts from the past, for they have taught us that remembering our heritage, we answer your sovereign call by living each day and moving out into our own future. Thank you for such a challenge.

Grant us your Spirit of responsible living.
Grant us your Spirit of creative teaching.
Grant us your Spirit of affirmative scholarship.
Grant us your Spirit of chastening dialogue.
Grant us your Spirit of exciting challenge—for the time being, which is for us the most trying time of all.

We pray in the name of Jesus, our model for authentic human life. Amen.

President Donald C. Mundinger then declared his own welcome to the students, faculty, and guests. He commented on the nature and purpose of the small liberal arts college, defining it as "an institution dedicated to the education of citizens in basic knowledge, in critical thought, in the development of an ethical sense of service." The full text of the President's remarks follows this introductory section.

The convocation address was delivered by Dr. Mark H. Curtis, recently installed as president of the Association of American Colleges. The Association is comprised of about six-hundred member colleges and universities and has as its purpose the fostering of liberal education. Dr. Curtis's education and professional experience make him a fine example of that tradition in his own person and well-qualified to speak on "Frontiers in Space, Time, Society, and Education." He had earned his baccalaureate, master's, and doctoral degrees in history at Yale University, where he had specialized in the history of Renaissance and Reformation England. Subsequent to teaching and administrative experience at several higher institutions he was appointed president of Scripps College, a post he held for twelve years. Dr. Curtis's address is printed in full in this chapter.

Following the address, the audience stood to sing a hymn, "O God, Our Help in Ages Past." Dr. Mundinger then conferred the honorary degree of Doctor of Humane Letters upon the chosen candidates. President Curtis was presented by Dean Jamison. It was necessary to award the degree to the Reverend A. Myrvin DeLapp *in absentia* because the severe weather had prevented him from leaving home, let alone reaching Jacksonville. The Reverend Mr. DeLapp's career has been closely identified with higher education. He has served as college chaplain, dean of men, Presbyterian university pastor, and for some years as a leader in the Presbyterian church on the national level. His current title is Associate for Ministries in Education of the United Presbyterian Church in the U.S.A. Dr. DeLapp's subsequent visit to Jacksonville will be noted in another context, and the texts of his seminar paper and sermon will be included in chapters 11 and 13. The citation for Dr. DeLapp was read by Dr. Malcolm F. Stewart, Scarborough Professor Emeritus of Religion and Philosophy and himself an ordained minister of the Presbyterian Church.

Dean Doris B. Hopper presented the Reverend Wesley A. Hotchkiss, who had been awarded the Ph.D. degree in geography by the University of Chicago and had earlier been engaged in research projects for his denomination. Since 1959 he has directed the work of the United Church of Christ in the field of higher education. More than thirty colleges and other schools are involved in that work, including Illinois College and others like it which have their roots in the Congregational heritage or in various other denominations now also part of the United Church of Christ. Among these other colleges are six which were originally developed by the American Missionary Association for black students. Dr. Hotchkiss was especially interested in visiting the David A. Smith House on campus because of Smith's stand against slavery. Dr. Hotchkiss's paper read before the afternoon seminar will be included in chapter 11.

The awarding of the fourth honorary degree on this otherwise very happy occasion was for many in the audience as sad as it was appropriate. Several months before Professor Arthur E. Hallerberg of Valparaiso University had been invited to return to his Alma Mater on this day to be recognized for his own great achievements as a college teacher and author and to represent the many Illinois College alumni who have served in higher education. Regrettably his untimely death in November deprived him of receiving the honor during his lifetime. College officials and Committee members concurred in the decision to grant the degree *post obitum* (an honor accorded once before by the College, to President Charles Henry Rammelkamp). Professor Charles E. Frank, a long-time friend and for many years a colleague of Dr. Hallerberg, described the latter's brilliant career in the presentation statement. Dr. Hallerberg had been outstanding as an undergraduate at Illinois College and had been elected to Phi Beta Kappa. He was a campus leader, serving on the *Rig Veda* and *Rambler* staffs and being active in Sigma Pi Literary Society. He later earned the doctorate in mathematics at the University of Michigan and had taught in that department at Illinois College for fourteen years before joining the Valparaiso faculty in 1960. The printed program for the convocation carried this notice in recognition of him: "*In Memoriam*: Arthur E. Hallerberg, 1918–1978; Alumnus . . Professor . . Author . . Active Churchman."

After this solemn ceremony the audience sang the Illinois College *Alma Mater* and the faculty recessed to the music of Bach's "Toccata in F Major." All who were free from fourth-hour classes were invited to a reception in Schewe Library so that they might meet and congratulate the honored guests. Afterwards the participants in the program and other special guests braved the wind and snow in their walk to Barnes House, where Dr. and Mrs. Mundinger were hosts and luncheon was served. Even then the day's celebration was not concluded, and early in the afternoon a seminar was convened in Smith House to discuss "The Church-Related College in the 1980s." The seminar is described, and the two papers prepared for presentation are printed, in chapter 11.

The remarks of President Mundinger at the morning Convocation, and the address by Dr. Mark H. Curtis, are included here and have been printed in full.

---

### WELCOMING STATEMENT AND INTRODUCTION
### PRESIDENT DONALD C. MUNDINGER

Welcome to the Opening Convocation of the 150th Anniversary Year!

If not mocking, then at least haunting, best describes a paragraph in Don Harrison Doyle's book, *The Social Order of a Frontier Community, Jacksonville, Illinois, 1825–70*. "Boosterism provided powererful energy to a rising young town, but what happened when the prophecies of future greatness clearly failed? How did towns like Jacksonville justify their failures? In the end, the boosters retreated to nurture the image of a quiet, genteel midwestern town, the home of two small private colleges and a constellation of state charitable institutions. Jacksonville's apologists smugly pretended they had never wanted any other destiny."[1] Doyle writes about a Jacksonville which was defeated and of little consequence.

The paragraph is harsh and the judgment unwarranted, but let me use it to make a point.

The lesson I seek to draw is the contrast with Illinois College. We began in a modest way, a frontier college in an antiintellectual period and region. We were small and remained small. We always worked at becoming better, larger if you will, in quality.

In 1929, at the Centennial, President Rammelkamp announced a goal of six-hundred students. After World War II, the goal was reached, but then the slide began to a level of less than three-hundred students. We have in our recent history, in 1969, been over nine-hundred students. But, by any standard, that is not large. We have always been a liberal arts college and a small one. That has seemed appropriate for us. It was a goal that we desired, that we defined, and not one which we backed into through defeat or resignation.

America strives to be a social democracy. We believe in pluralism. One of the things deeply important to me is the idea of institutional pluralism, or, if you will, educational pluralism. I am committed to both private and public education and I believe in the importance, or the appropriateness, if you will, of a variety of educational institutions—professional schools, graduate schools, vocational institutions, universities, and liberal arts colleges.

Our goal is to remain a small liberal arts college—an institution dedicated to the education of citizens in basic knowledge, in critical thought, in the development of an ethical sense of service. While our currency has been devalued by vocationalism and social engineering, our mission, in my judgment, has never been more important. We are needed most when we appear to be wanted least.

What is important for us as we look at our own 150 years of life

1. Don Harrison Doyle, *The Social Order of a Frontier Community: Jacksonville, Illinois, 1825–70* (Urbana: Univ. of Illinois Press, 1978), p. 6.

and to the decades before us, is that we understand what we have been and what we are today. We must not default or resign. That is, we must not fall prey to the "Doyle thesis." Let us redouble our efforts to serve youth, to define and redefine liberal education, to meet the needs of mankind as we race to meet the twenty-first century. We must enhance the intellectual power of this College and not seek to do the most education, but strive only to do the best. Camelot may never be attained. But, it is worth a try and the try is its own reward!

We will do this best if there is confidence in our intellectual strength and confidence in our mission. For students, it is rejecting the faddish, and for faculty, it is the courage to follow the right.

Barbara Tuchman, in the Foreword of her book, *A Distant Mirror*, combines a few Anglo-Saxon words into a short but powerful sentence. "I like finding my own way," writes Tuchman.[2] These words meant much to me. They are relevant today to Illinois College and for our next decades. The great challenge that we face is "finding our own way."

The words *college* and *colleague* come from the same root. A college is nothing more or nothing less than a group of colleagues— faculty and students learning together as partners. This is the most fundamental and basic definition of the college. Our future will be secure if we honor this tradition, if we continue as colleagues—as partners—and work together to reach our goal—the life of the mind in service to man.

Now, it is my privilege to introduce a distinguished historian, college president, and organizational executive. Dr. Mark Curtis will help us begin.

---

FRONTIERS IN SPACE, TIME, SOCIETY, AND
EDUCATION
DR. MARK H. CURTIS
PRESIDENT, ASSOCIATION OF AMERICAN COLLEGES

President Mundinger, trustees, faculty, students, and honored guests of Illinois College: I consider it a great privilege to be with

2. Barbara Tuchman, *A Distant Mirror: The Calamitous 14th Century* (New York: Knopf, 1978), p. xv.

you today. My heritage is similar to yours. I am by birth and rearing a Midwesterner. Soon after the founding of Illinois College, my greatgrandfather was breaking the deep sod of the virgin Iowa prairie to plant corn and wheat. I myself grew up in Iowa and lived as a boy near enough to the Mississippi to be captivated by the romance of that great river. Later I received my undergraduate and graduate education at Yale, from whence had come more than a hundred years earlier a few committed men to help found this college.

In reading the history of your College the sense of my own frontier heritage was quickened and I was deeply stirred by both the vision and dauntless spirit which characterized the founders of this College. Many illustrations of these attributes can be found in the early annals of the College but I shall share only one that contains the essence of them all. It is an account of the opening of the College and the beginning of instruction on January 4, 1830, written by Julian M. Sturtevant who was the first instructor appointed to the faculty and the second president of the College. He wrote:

I repaired to the building and found the floors completed, and the building quite enclosed, but no lathing or plastering, no stove, no teacher's desk and only a part of the seats for pupils completed. But we were pledged to commence instruction at that time. . . . I was accompanied and assisted by Wm. C. Posey, Esq. [a trustee], to whose active efforts to nurse its infancy, the college owes much. Our first business was to put up a stove, which occupied us about two hours, carpenters and teacher, and trustee and students cooperating in the work. Pupils were then called to order. I addressed them a few words and among other things told them . . . what my heart felt and believed, that we had come there that morning to open a fountain for future generations to drink at. We then commended ourselves and the whole great enterprise to God in prayer. It was to me a season never to be forgotten, whatever the fate of the college may be.[3]

The vivid account of the courage and vision that attended the founding of this college provides a basemark for my remarks today,

3. Quoted in Charles Henry Rammelkamp, *Illinois College: A Centennial History, 1829–1929* (New Haven: Published for Illinois College by Yale Univ. Press, 1928), p. 39.

for I wish to reflect on the meaning of our frontier heritage by thinking about the frontiers of the present as well as those of the past.

In one sense, the frontier is a geographical and social reality in an area of new settlement. In another sense, it is an idea or concept that captures the imagination and challenges the prophetic and creative powers of a people. In our nation it has been both. As the account of the opening day of Illinois College indicates, both senses of the word *frontier* have been a part of the life of this institution since its inception. The College has been a new institution, located on the geographic frontier of the nation, and it has been, since the first class was called to order, a concept or ideal that challenged the prophetic and creative powers of those who have taught and studied here.

In our age the frontier as a geographical phenomenon has largely disappeared in the United States, except perhaps for Alaska. It still exists as a concept with continuing significance for the social and intellectual life of our country. To appreciate this point, we need only think of the frontiers of space which the scientists and astronauts have been daringly exploring or the social frontiers in race relations and women's rights which challenge us. Such frontiers call for unflagging commitment of the best our wills and minds can bring to them, but there is another, almost more basic frontier to which I wish to direct our attention this morning. It is one on which Illinois College and all institutions dedicated to liberal learning exist. It is a frontier in time—the present when a wilderness of attitudes impedes the full development of liberal learning.

I do not wish to use this occasion to elaborate on the virtues of liberal learning. Illinois College and this audience are familar—indeed, well-versed—in the teachings of such persons as Plato, Cicero, John of Salisbury, Erasmus, Milton, Newman, Arnold, Ortega y Gasset, and Whitehead who have each in his generation over the last twenty-five-hundred years set forth the case for liberal learning more eloquently than I can. I take for granted, and I assume you do also, that liberal learning has been and is justified. I deem it more important at this time to attempt to overcome misconceptions outside the academic world and illusions within the academic world that make the present-day frontier so hazardous to liberal learning.

Over the centuries liberal learning has been in jeopardy on many occasions. The term "Dark Ages" calls to mind the long period of barbarism and ignorance between the fall of Rome and the revival of learning in the twelfth century, relieved only by sporadic and tenuous flashes of enlightenment in Charlemagne's court or among Irish monks. Even after learning began once more to flourish in the newly founded medieval universities, faculties in the liberal arts had constantly to contend with pressure from career-minded students and the prestige of professional faculties to maintain the status of the liberal arts as the fountainhead of all other learning. Even during the Renaissance, when humanism with its emphasis on liberal learning seemed dominant, practical men like Sir Humphrey Gilbert, explorer and Elizabethan courtier, disdaining study of the liberal arts, made vigorous attempts to establish special professional academies for young aristocrats at the expense of Oxford and Cambridge. We can, therefore, conclude that though the present-day attacks on liberal learning are not as serious as those that plunged Europe into the Dark Ages, they are akin to those of other centuries. As those were overcome, so may we take heart to resist the adverse influences of our own time.

The attitudes that threaten liberal learning and weaken its role in higher education are prevalent not only outside the walls of colleges and universities but within them. Study of the liberal arts is therefore in a particularly precarious condition because its natural defenders have not maintained the strength to repel the attacks from the outside. Four attitudes appear to me to be especially inimical to liberal learning: two of these are shared widely among the general public, including students, and two are prevalent within colleges and universities. They are: first, a desire for immediate gratification or satisfaction of practical goals, both individual and collective; second, an overevaluation, almost to the point of idolatry, of experts and their expertise; third, and closely related to the second, an overemphasis on the value of narrow specialized studies and research; and fourth, a long-standing and perverse misunderstanding of the purposes of liberal learning.

The first two are found widely among students and the general public. They seem to underlie the large-scale shift in majors in the early seventies when the proportion of students majoring in professional fields mounted from 38 percent to 58 percent in the course of five years. They were reinforced, to be sure, by a number of influences prevailing among both young people and society at large. Those of us who are veterans in dealing with the protests and demonstrations were astounded to see how fast student disillusionment—even disenchantment—with the causes and activities of the 1960s grew after 1970 and even before the onset of a deep recession in 1973–74. When the recession did come and jobs became scarce amid the complications of double-digit inflation, it only accelerated the trend towards practical interests and studies which had already begun. (Parenthetically, I have begun to wonder whether the demand for relevance in the 1960s did not have a strong subconscious root in yearnings for the practical more than in strivings for the ideal with which we credited most students.)

Whatever the causes, a desire for immediate gratification of one's personal practical goals and a corporate demand for immediate productivity from new employees, have combined to disparage the value of liberal education. Both attitudes result in the sacrifice of long-term goods for short-term gains. For the individual immediate gratification through pursuit of a narrow professional education means limiting one's chances for future career advancement, to say nothing of curtailing one's opportunities for development as a human being, in return only for improved prospects of gaining an entry level job. For the employer, it means reducing the chances of finding within one's organization persons with the breadth of understanding and the imaginative, intelligent grasp of problems needed for promotion to executive positions. It's questionable whether either the individual, the corporation, or society as a whole is well served in the long run by such attitudes and practices.

Closely allied to this first attitude is our proclivity these days to overvalue the expert and his expertise. In making this assertion, I do not wish to be misunderstood. I am neither a primitivist nor a twentieth-century Luddite protesting the advancement of knowledge or the improvement of technology and technical competence. I appreciate the grasp on many of our problems that technical skill in engineering, the health sciences, and social services has provided us. We cannot do without the work of experts in those and other fields.

What I deplore is excessive respect for the expert that leads us too easily and blindly to place reliance in his expertise alone. Offsetting the benefits that we derive from experts are the confusion and dislocation that arise from decisions made only on the basis of the narrow range of factors relevant to his special field. Such decisions rarely take into account the far-reaching impact or consequences that may flow from them. What we need is not to abolish experts or not to deny them positions of responsibility, but to insist that experts undergird their professional training with the breadth of vision and sensitivity of understanding that results from liberal learning. Then they will be able to perceive how the parts relate to the whole and how decisions that appear good in a narrow sense may have widespread ramifications that are perverse.

If external social attitudes inimical to liberal learning can be challenged as easily as I have suggested in the last few minutes, why has liberal learning fallen into such disrepute? The answer to this question, I respectfully submit, lies within the colleges and universities of our nation and particularly within the academic programs or curricula that are intended to provide liberal learning to our students. The Carnegie Council on Policy Studies in Higher Education has recently described general education, one aspect of liberal learning, as a "disaster area." I believe a close reading of that report will also confirm my opinion that the major, another fundamental part of liberal education, is disoriented if not dysfunctional. Furthermore, the blame for these dismaying conditions cannot be laid at the doorstep of the student disorders of the 1960s and the abject surrender of college faculties and administrators to student demonstrators. A close reading of Frederick Rudolph's book on the curriculum will show that by the early 1960s, in all but a few colleges and universities, the ills afflicting liberal learning were already far advanced. So far as the disruptions of the 1960s had anything to do with the curriculum, they either highlighted existing weaknesses or delivered the coup de grâce to end a long and lingering illness.

The primary causes of the sad state of liberal learning are to be found in the two attitudes mentioned above and described as being prevalent in the community of higher education. Briefly restated they are overemphasis on specialization, both in scholarship and educational programs, and a widespread misunderstanding of the purposes of liberal learning. Let me explain these points further.

A recent article by William D. Schaefer, who was until last summer Executive Director of the Modern Language Association, is a devastating criticism of the discipline of literature as it is currently taught and studied. Perhaps the gravity of his charges can best be appreciated by noticing in particular one of his assertions. It is a *cri de coeur*: "We have got to liberalize our graduate and undergraduate programs."[4] I concur. The deep irony of the situation is that liberal learning as practiced in most institutions of higher education is not liberal. I first became aware of this fifteen years ago. In a conference with some faculty members from a prestigious liberal arts college, I was astounded to hear one of them say: "Mark, you are laboring under the misapprehension that we provide a liberal education at our institution. We are not a liberal arts college. What we are in fact is one of the best prep schools in the country for graduate and professional training. Many of our departments use the Graduate Record Examination for their fields as their senior comprehensive examination."

William Schaefer understands this situation and discusses in his article seven sins, though he refrains from calling them deadly sins, besetting the study of literature. Most of them are sins affecting not only literature but also the other disciplines within the liberal arts. All of them can be categorized under the two headings I have mentioned earlier. Under the heading "Overemphasis on Specialization" can be listed the sin of "Perpetuating the image of 'Herr Professor,'" the sin of "Isolating the profession from the public." Under the heading of "Misunderstanding the Purposes of Liberal Learning" can be listed the sin of "Ignoring teaching and teacher training," the sin of "Ignoring the curriculum," the sin of "Ignoring basic skills," and the sin of "Failing to understand the students."[5]

I cannot take the time to comment on these one by one, but the mere listing of them does indicate that something is seriously wrong

---

4. William D. Schaefer, "Still Crazy After All These Years," *Profession 78: Selected Articles from the Bulletins* of the *Association of Departments of English* and *Association of Departments of Foreign Languages* (New York: Modern Language Association, 1978), p. 6.

5. Ibid., pp. 2–4.

in the "groves of academe." On the other hand, the fact that they have been so perceptively analyzed by a distinguished professor of the humanities gives promise that the situation can be rectified.

One point I must make before turning to my final remarks. Schaefer's analysis does confirm the point that the problem concerns attitudes among those who profess the liberal arts. Being a problem of attitude can, of course, make its solution difficult if members of the profession out of a mixture of pride, complacency, and fear get their backs up and resist change. Yet a matter of attitude is a human-sized problem, not one involving imponderable shadowy forces beyond the reach of human will and intelligence.

Perhaps the principal key to changing attitudes within the academic profession is to get a fix for our day on the guide star for liberal learning, namely the end it should serve. Here I return in my thinking to the concept of the frontier. Liberal learning has been since time out of mind denominated "liberal" because it is intended to do two things: first, *to free* men and women from the bonds of superstition, ignorance, and parochialism and secondly, as much as humanly possible, to set them above the vicissitudes of time and circumstance. In each generation there is a unique frontier characterized by that generation's brand of ignorance and superstition and by its special set of circumstances and perplexities. Hence each generation confronts men and women pragmatically with its own intellectual, spiritual, and social frontier. If learning is to be liberal in any generation, it must provide them with the practical means to live on that generation's frontier and to be active, effective, responsible persons in what they do and say. In a very real sense, therefore, liberal learning is the most pragmatic and practical of all kinds of education. When it has thrived, its practical nature has been clearly understood. Milton stated it succinctly and cogently not only for his age but for all time when he wrote: "I call therefore a compleat and generous Education that which fits a man to perform justly, skilfully and magnanimously all the offices both private and publick of Peace and War."[6]

Over the last fifty years, the academic profession has lost sight of

6. John Milton, "Of Education," *Complete Poetry and Selected Prose of John Milton* (New York: Modern Library, 1942), p. 667.

the traditional purpose of liberal learning. Members of the profession have substituted for it purposes of their own, some of which have been proclaimed in plausible but yet delusive ways. More often than not these purposes served the ends of professional study of the several disciplines but not the humane and liberating goals of the students engaged in them. In the study of literature for its own sake, scholars lost sight of the importance of literature in fashioning the imaginative understanding and sensitive perceptions of students, to say nothing of its capacity to add to their power to express themselves clearly and cogently. In its baser form, the pursuit of studies for their own sake led to the education of students to be replicas of their masters, not generously educated persons who could play a responsible role in affairs both public and private.

There are those who justify such purposes on the grounds that they are essential for the ultimate goal of learning and scholarship—the pursuit of truth. They seem to say that to teach or to fashion studies for the sake of the student and not for the pursuit of truth is to betray their calling and to subordinate truth to human needs. But are they not making a false dichotomy? Do truth and human needs really stand in such an opposed relationship to one another? Is it not possible that truth and human needs are compatible? Indeed, I would suggest that human needs justify the pursuit of truth more than the study of a discipline for its own sake. Learning that provides a student with anything less than the best insight into truth afforded to a conscientious scholar-teacher is not liberal and in fact offers the student a stone instead of bread. It will not fit a person to act realistically within a real world.

To address these remarks to an audience containing the administrators, faculty, and students of Illinois College may seem like carrying coals to Newcastle. This College has fulfilled 150 years of faithful service to liberal learning. It started with a curriculum patterned after the Yale example of education in the liberal arts. In its subsequent developments, it kept the fundamental purpose of liberal learning as the lodestar of its reforms. Today it is once again searching for ways to translate the ideal of liberal learning into programs of teaching and learning that meet the needs of students in the last quarter of the twentieth century. True to its frontier heritage, it is hard at work on the intellectual and social frontiers of our day. Furthermore, throughout its history it has educated men and women generously and liberally so that they could serve their generations justly, skillfully, and magnanimously.

Yet if this College needs the warning of my remarks less than many others, I am sure that you are as concerned as I that the cause you espouse remain strong and flourishing for at least another century and a half. With this point in mind I urge you and challenge you, as you review your accomplishments and renew your commitment through this Sesquicentennial year, to take up the baton of leadership and help all of higher education redirect its attitudes and find once again effective ways to prepare young people to be free of the superstitions and fears of our day and the vicissitudes of time and circumstance. Only then can their energies and ideals be released to serve our country and the world responsibly in specialized vocations and professions as well as in the difficult task of advancing the general welfare in a time of perplexity and confusion.

# 4

## *The Convocation on Public Affairs February 20, 1979*

Many of the men who founded Illinois College and served as its staff and trustees during the early decades had been reared and educated in New England. They shared the common conviction that people are responsible for establishing a society in which public order is maintained and essential services such as education are provided. Many of the College's presidents and faculty members, in addition to their service in higher education, fulfilled their public duties by working for humanitarian causes and by serving on local and state commissions. Even more important in the long run was their teaching of civic responsibility to their students with subsequent encouragement to those elected to public office. The College's first graduate, Richard Yates (Class of 1835), was governor of Illinois during the Civil War and then was elected to the United States Senate. Julian M. Sturtevant, professor and president, declared that the College deserved credit for Yates' interest in public service. The commitment to serve the common good, in government and in many public service professions, has been characteristic of alumni throughout the College's history. The most famous alumni name is doubtless that of William Jennings Bryan, Class of 1881, who was a candidate for the presidency three times.

The Public Affairs Convocation on February 20 (1979) was planned as a celebration of the College's past contributions to the public good and its continuing concern for the commonwealth. It was intended also to be itself a contribution to that cause by bringing to the campus the two highest elected officials of the State of Illinois, men who were also the leaders of the two major political parties: Governor James R. Thompson, a Republican, and Secretary of State Alan J. Dixon, a Democrat. These officials were asked to discuss, in dialogue fashion, the "Issues and Opportunities Facing Illinois in the Next Decade."

The format of the convocation was very similar to that of the first one. The faculty and platform party wore academic regalia and participated in the customary processional and recessional. The Concert Choir led the audience in the singing of two appropriate hymns, "God of Our Fathers, Whose Almighty Hand" and "America the Beautiful." This program was set for 8:00 P.M., the evening hour being necessary to accommodate the schedules of two busy state officials and also to enable other public officials and the many interested local citizens to attend. Governor Thompson had had an afternoon speaking engagement in Chicago and reached the campus just in time for the academic procession. Arrangements for both speakers were facilitated by three alumni who were members of their staffs, Gregory Baise '74 in the Office of the Governor and Robert Merris '53 and Eugene Callahan '55 in the Office of the Secretary of State.

The audience filled Rammelkamp Chapel to capacity and the mood was one of eager, even festive, anticipation. In addition to the faculty and several trustees and a good turnout of students, there were many people from the Jacksonville area who were in attendance. Special invitations had been sent to civic leaders, elected officials, and area leaders of the major political parties. Among those present were Mayor Milton Hocking of Jacksonville and members of the City Council (several of them alumni), Mayor Richard Godfrey and trustees of South Jacksonville, Representative James Reilly '67, and State Senator Vincent Demuzio.

The honorary Doctor of Laws degree was awarded to each of the two speakers and to two alumni prominent in public affairs and in the legal profession. President Emeritus L. Vernon Caine presented Governor Thompson, noting in the citation his service in several positions: as Prosecutor in the Cook County State's Attorney's Office, as a law professor at Northwestern University School of Law (where he had earlier won his law degree), and as United States Attorney. Governor Thompson was elected and then reelected to his gubernatorial position by the largest margins ever recorded for that office in Illinois history. Associate Professor Raymond Allen Ford read the citation for the Secretary of State. The Honorable Alan J. Dixon, after a long tenure in the Illinois General Assembly, where he had served in both the House and the Senate, was State Treasurer for six years before he became Secretary of State—an office he had won by the largest plurality ever given a Democratic candidate for state office.

The two alumni who were honored were Mrs. Helen Cleary Foreman '25, presented by Professor Charles E. Frank (a colleague on the City Council at that time), and Mr. John C. Shepherd -49, presented by Professor Donald R. Tracey. As an undergraduate, Mrs. Foreman had joined Gamma Delta Literary Society, edited the *Rig Veda*, won the Bryan Prize in Political Science, and qualified for Department Honors. Mrs. Foreman was for more than two decades a member of various state commissions on human rights and fair employment practices. She has held offices in the League of Women Voters at all levels, including the national. In 1975 she was named one of the six outstanding women in Illinois. Mrs. Foreman was currently serving her second term on the City Council (and subsequently has been reelected).

Mr. Shepherd was one of the many World War II veterans to enroll in Illinois College after the end of that conflict. He was a member of Phi Alpha Literary Society. Earning a law degree from the St. Louis University School of Law, he became a partner in a St. Louis law firm and later was elected president of the bar association in that city. Currently Mr. Shepherd was chairperson of the House of Delegates, the policy-making body of the American Bar Association. Mr. Shepherd has been active in numerous professional associations and several civic organizations and is in demand as a lecturer on advocacy proceedings.

The reception for the honorees and other distinguished guests was held in Tanner Hall's Gallery Lounge, the central portion of the Mason Grosvenor Room on the second floor. This afforded many students and of course people from the community the opportunity to meet and congratulate those granted honorary degrees and to greet the members of their families. Some of the special guests stayed on long after their announced time of departure; they were obviously enjoying the warmth and friendliness of the College's hospitality.

The introductory statement by President Mundinger, delivered in the early part of the evening program, is printed in full below. The remarks by Governor Thompson and Secretary of State Dixon are printed in substantially complete form. The dialogue form of their presentation made it necessary to transcribe their statements from a tape recording. Occasionally one of the speakers would step away from the microphone with the result that a few words here and there were not recorded clearly. The informal style of the dialogue has been retained although some editing has been done to eliminate the repetition of phrases which frequently occurs in public speaking and to provide for proper punctuation of the printed text. The good humor of the exchange between men who, though rivals in certain respects, consider themselves to be colleagues in state governance will be evident from their words, although explicit notations have been made to indicate the occasions of spontaneous laughter. There is a break in the tape recording near the end of the discussion and a few sentences have been reconstructed from the editor's notes and from the feature story in the *Jacksonville Daily Courier* (February 21, 1979). These passages are enclosed within square brackets [ ]. The omission of more than a brief phrase is indicated by ellipsis points.

## STATEMENT BY PRESIDENT MUNDINGER

Today we pause to examine a very special facet of the life and work of Illinois College. For a small college—somewhat larger than the Rammelkamp norm of six hundred—this College has contributed an inordinately high number of people to the public life—six governors, two U.S. Senators, twenty U.S. Congressmen, one presidential candidate, a vice-presidential candidate, a secretary of state, and a commissioner of a federal regulatory agency. In addition, hundreds of other sons and daughters have served as leaders in state and local government, the professions, industry, and public service organizations. Our contribution to the public weal has become a distinguishing trait of Illinois College.

There is an Illinois College Pantheon of Great Teachers. Whom would you select? The names of John Ames, Stella Cole, Willis DeRyke, Ernest G. Hildner, R. H. Lacey, Earle B. Miller, Eleanor O. Miller, F. B. Oxtoby, Isabel Smith, Joe Patterson Smith, and Mary L. Strong along with Jonathan B. Turner, Edward A. Tanner, Julian M. Sturtevant, and Charles Henry Rammelkamp would be on everyone's list. These stand symbolically for the scores of gifted professors who have shaped the lives of students for some 150 years.

Russell Kirk, in his book, *Decadence and Renewal in the Higher Learning*, details a mission for the liberal arts to which Illinois College has always aspired. "Certain things a college can do very well. It can give the student the tools for educating himself throughout his life. It can present to him certain general principles for the governance of personality and community. It can help him to see what makes life worth living. It can teach him basic disciplines which will be of infinite value in professional specialization at a graduate school or in his subsequent apprenticeship to any commercial or industrial occupation."[1] Illinois College has had its finest hours when it has wrestled with this imperative, when the College has sought to nurture both wisdom and virtue within its students.

At our inception, our faculty sensed the importance of what they were about. They possessed a vision of harnessing one of the driving forces of history. Napoleon once remarked that it is imagination that governs the human race. The hearts of our students were inflamed with the desire to serve the Republic. Our students captured the imagination of the faculty as they sought to serve.

This philosophy of service also influenced this College in another way. Competence, moderation, and the common good were values which left an imprint upon each of our students. Our College shared this value and encouraged a new generation to savor the durable pleasures of the life of the public man and the public woman.

Woodrow Wilson, a personal hero and perhaps the hero of many of you, called for leaders who would boldly interpret the national conscience and lift a whole people out of their everyday selves. Would that we might rise, with imagination and with generous

1. Russell Kirk, *Decadence and Renewal in the Higher Learning: An Episodic History of American University and College since 1953* (South Bend, IN: Gateway Editions, Limited, 1978), p. 298.

spirit, to this challenge in a deliberate and purposeful way to educate that new generation of leaders who will lift our people out of their everyday selves.

T. S. Eliot once wrote about the desirability of frequent exchange of views among men of public affairs and men of learning. This is our purpose tonight. As this dialogue unfolds, we practice our historic mission and celebrate 150 years of being the Citizens' College of Illinois.

---

DIALOGUE DISCUSSION:
ISSUES AND OPPORTUNITIES FACING ILLINOIS IN THE NEXT DECADE
*The Honorable James R. Thompson, Governor of Illinois*
*The Honorable Alan J. Dixon, Secretary of State of Illinois*
*President Donald C. Mundinger, Presiding*

President Mundinger: Ladies and Gentlemen: The Governor of the State of Illinois. [Applause]

Governor Thompson: Mr. President, members of the faculty, Mr. Secretary, distinguished guests and friends of Illinois College. I bring to you tonight the greetings and the best wishes of the more than eleven million people of the State of Illinois for a most successful and most productive Sesquicentennial. We in Illinois are proud of the contributions of Illinois College, not only to the greater learning of our people but especially, as the President has indicated, to the government of Illinois and indeed to the government of this land.

I was thinking as we crossed the campus tonight what would be said by the Secretary and me about the future of Illinois in our dialoguing on this broad topic tonight. If we were truly to deal with that we would preempt the work, for example, of the Illinois Futures Commission that promises in a few short months to tell us what life in Illinois will be like in the year 2000. I would also preempt my State of the State address and both the Secretary and I would preempt all the speeches we are going to make in the next four years.

But I thought of four things we can be certain of. I will just mention them briefly in the order of ascending importance. By the year 2000 Illinois will have 1.7 million more people than it has now. At current levels there will not be enough snow to go around [laughter], therefore God will see to it that there is sufficient snow to share with 1.7 million more people. Thirdly, God's timetable is out of whack—He has sent it all in 1979 and we must find some way to conserve it until the year 2000 and at the rate the weather is going it looks like we may make it. [Laughter] Most importantly in the year 2000 there will still be an Illinois College and it will still be making the unique liberal arts contributions the President has spoken of this day and it will be even more important. [Extended applause]

President Mundinger: Ladies and Gentlemen: The Secretary of State. [Applause]

Secretary of State Dixon: Thank you very much. Dr. Mundinger, Your Excellency [laughter], members of the faculty, and those who love Illinois College: I am delighted, of course, and deeply honored to have this opportunity to be with you tonight and to share this glorious evening with all of you who are friends of Illinois College. I don't need to tell you about your grand history, about the fact that this was the first college in Illinois to grant the bachelor's degree. The President has referred to some of the distinguished alumni of this College, those who have gone on to great heights in public life— the governors, the United States Senators, who have known and loved Illinois College. I had the privilege of serving in the General Assembly for a period of years. As a matter of fact, I was there with one of your distinguished alumni who rose to the heights of Speaker of the Illinois House and went on to the Senate of the United States—a man from my own part of the state, Ralph Tyler Smith from Madison County, who served the same geographical area that I served in the legislature some years ago.

It is true that you have a grand tradition at this school and I am very proud to share this evening with the Governor and the rest of you on the occasion of the celebration of your 150th anniversary. I am particularly indebted to Illinois College for two things in my own political career that I want to call to your attention. Professor Raymond Allen Ford brought to my attention when I was a candidate some years ago an idea that he thought had some significance. And believe it or not we incorporated it into the 1976 campaign, made it a reality in my first term as Secretary of State, and talked about it in my reelection campaign in 1978. It was here in Jacksonville that Allen gave me the idea to put medical information on the driver's license, so the germ of that idea came from Illinois College. Then, too, I have to thank you for the five-year license plate. Some time ago we were having a meeting in the office of the committee that was going to pick the colors. I said, "There is one thing that I want to make very clear at the outset—there has to be very strong contrast," and one of your alums, Gene Callahan, who is here in the audience tonight, said "Yes, Mr. Secretary, we have black on white right now." I said "That's very true, and it's a perfect contrast." Then he said, "What would you think of blue on white?" and I said, "I think that would be a marvelous idea." And so of course after that he and Dr. Mundinger and all the rest met and introduced into that discussion the idea of Illinois College blue on white. I hope for the next five years the folks of this state will enjoy that color because they will certainly be looking at it a good deal. [Laughter and applause]

The Governor called me today before he came down to the city of Springfield and he said, "You know, you and I are going to carry on a dialogue at Illinois College tonight. What shall we talk about?" and I said, "I don't know, Governor, let's fly it." So whatever you hear tonight comes from the heart of the Governor and myself—we haven't rehearsed a word of it! Thank you. [Extended applause]

President Mundinger: Now, Ladies and Gentlemen, I invite the Governor and the Secretary of State to participate in an exchange of views.

Secretary of State Dixon: Okay, Gov, let's fly it! [Laughter]

Governor Thompson: Mr. Secretary, Ladies and Gentlemen: This debate is indeed not to deny that the Secretary and I see eye-to-eye on many of the critical issues which face the people of this State. The issues and the opportunities facing Illinois are the subject of the dialogue this evening. I would like to begin, I think, by at least a quick reference to the framework of politics and government within the State of Illinois today, making some observations to see if the Secretary agrees or disagrees. He is much more of a political scientist than I—he has practiced the trade for more years than I.

The first issue is not just an Illinois phenomenon though—it is a nation-wide phenomenon. How do we bring government to deci-sive—incisive—action when the strength and unity and indeed sometimes the purpose of the vehicles that we have relied upon for many of the years that we have existed as a nation seem to be declin-ing? A number of writers in the popular literature, and certainly in the journals of political science, decry the declining strength of the political party. America's government and the government of Illinois are based upon the assumption that we have two strong and conflict-ing political parties, Republicans and Democrats. And that the par-ties are the vehicles by which philosophies are shaped, urged upon the electorate, acted upon by the electorate, and then used to carry out the voters' perceived wishes in both the executive branch of gov-ernment and in the legislative branch of government.

The political phenomena of the last several decades would seem to indicate that more and more of our people decline now to identify themselves as Democrats or Republicans. They not only refuse to participate in the political process by working in campaigns, but they stay away from party primaries because of their refusal to iden-tify their political affiliations. And, as we know, in general elections where political affiliations cannot be known behind the curtain of the polling place, the voter has the opportunity of splitting his ballot and Illinois citizens are doing that in greater and greater numbers. I was very proud in 1976 when I won office with the largest majority in the history of the State of Illinois. The Secretary of State, on the other side of the ballot, was elected with the second largest majority in the history of the State of Illinois. In 1978 the Secretary of State was reelected with the new largest-majority in the history of the State of Illinois. Back and forth on the ballot the voters went, pick-ing their choices of Republicans and Democrats so that we have myriad split delegations in our state offices and a very close balance in the House of the Illinois General Assembly. Clearly adherence to political parties in terms of straight ballot voting, and the willingness of voters to identify with and work with parties, and party discipline in the legislative branch of government, have declined.

A new phenomenon is the fact of the special interest group. Indeed there are some candidates and managers at work in this nation who are cynical enough to conclude (I must believe this because they write about it) that if you can find twenty-six groups of people who care about only one idea in government then each needs to constitute no more than 2 percent of the population. In fact, they need consti-stitute no more than 2 percent each of those who will vote in the next election. If you can find twenty-six groups like that whose numbers equal at least 2 percent of the expected vote in the next election you will have a majority. It makes no difference what the idea is, it makes no difference how important the idea is, it may not even make any difference if one of the twenty-six ideas conflicts with another of the twenty-six ideas—given the adroitness of politicians today for advocating both during the heat of the campaign. Is this not one of the challenges facing us in the next several decades, aside from all the substantive issues that I assume we will at least touch upon tonight? Our declining reliance on the two-party system and the declining strength of political parties, the emergence of very tiny minorities which when put together become at least an electoral majority. Perhaps not a majority which is good for running the government. I see that as a danger. Perhaps the Secretary who, as I say, has been in this business far longer than I, would have some comment on that.

Secretary of State Dixon: Certainly I think there is a lot of truth in what the Governor says about the declining importance of the political parties. When I came to the House in 1951, the elections at that time demonstrated the fact that we pretty religiously voted strictly the Democratic or the Republican party in this State. As a young member of the House in the years when the Republican party was the large majority party in this state I observed that people voted pretty much the straight Republican ticket or, in the case of some of the counties, the straight Democratic ticket. I think clearly the strength of the political parties has declined, but I think interestingly enough the importance of the two political parties in the structured type of political society that we have in this country is still important to us.

I am not one of those who thinks that because a great many people exercise independence of judgment now—that they may vote, for instance, for a Republican for Governor and a Democrat for Secretary of State and be a little choosy and picky as they go down the ticket—that we ought to say that the two-party system is no longer important to this country. Unfortunately I think some of those suggestions are beginning to receive some credence now around the country by virtue of the declining importance of the two political parties in the thought processes of the individual voter. But I think the two-party system is still fundamentally important to our country.

Although people sometimes say to me, "You know, we ought to seek out another solution. Inflation is rampant in the country. We have a lot of problems, and no solutions to those problems," I don't see in any other society in the world a better solution to problems than the one we have found in this country. I don't think the multiparty system in other countries is a solution to the problem. Clearly all those other countries with multiparty systems have higher inflation and more problems than America. I think, Governor, that while your thesis is correct that the strength of the two political parties is declining, the two-party system is one of the fundamentally important things that makes this country a great country.

I might even take that a step further and say this, Governor, relating to what I understand about this history. All the great leaders of this country, all the great governors, all the great presidents, all the great United States Senators (with one or two exceptions who established their reputation as mavericks in the Senate of the United States), have been great and strong political leaders within their parties as well. Clearly the great leaders are also fundamentally great leaders within the province of their own political parties.

One of the problems that we have, Governor, is that too often nowadays people think that if you are of differing political opinion or even of differing political philosophies within the framework of your own party (because we all understand that within your party and within mine the extremes are quite large) that you ought to dislike someone or you ought to hate someone. I think that we can get along. I think that a Republican and a Democrat can sit down and achieve compromise, or arrive at an accord to make government work. I think people can get along and like one another and differ honestly on their basic philosophy, and I think that that's one of the things we ought to stress in these great universities and other public places—that we can differ, that we can belong to different political parties, that we can have a different political philosophy and we can still get along and be friends while we agitate for our own point of view.

Finally along these lines, Governor, I would say that the final and most important single thing this country needs in its political institutions and its thought among people, so far as politics is concerned, is a greater optimism once again. The kind of optimism our country had when it was younger, the kind of optimism that made our people in this country think that there was always a new frontier and always new opportunities. I get so sick and tired of going around this state, around this country, and having people say, "There isn't any hope anymore. Inflation is too high. There isn't a chance any more to get ahead. There aren't any real opportunities anymore—no chance for success." All of that is untrue. There are greater opportunities, greater opportunities for success and achievement and greater opportunities to get ahead in this country right now than there ever were in the history of this country. More people ought to be talking about that, instead of being prophets of doom and gloom and telling everybody what's the matter with this country.

Governor Thompson: I might carry the procedural framework one step further, before turning to a substantive issue, [to discuss] the issue of trusting government and government institutions and government leaders and political leaders. We find this as we go on the campaign trail and we find this in noncampaign years when we encounter members of the public, and I saw it illustrated the other day in a kind of paradox, I suppose. You made reference to the founding fathers. There is currently abroad in the land a drive to petition the Congress of the United States to call a constitutional convention for the purpose of amending the Constitution to require a balanced budget at the federal level, and over twenty states, I guess, have now passed such resolutions. In the early days they whizzed through state legislatures because they belonged to the category of motherhood and apple-pie resolutions, and probably some of them were sandwiched in between congratulatory resolutions and birthday resolutions and the like.

We have not yet faced that resolution in Illinois and I predict that if we do we will face it with a great deal more seriousness and thought than perhaps has been given it by some of the ratifying states. But here we have a strange thing, aided and abetted by leaders themselves, congressmen, senators, potential candidates for president of the United States, declared candidates for president of the United States, who do not want to have a constitutional convention called because they do not trust those whom they believe will be elected delegates with the process of amending our Constitution.

Senator Baker visited Springfield a week ago to deliver a Lincoln Day address. He was one of the few dissenting voices from this popular opinion of political leaders today that the people can't be trusted to amend their own Constitution. He said he did not believe that all the wisdom in this nation died at the end of the eighteenth century, that there was as much or more alive in the United States today, and that he for one, though he preferred the process of constitutional enactment, would not fear a constitutional convention and in fact would hope to be a part of it.

I was thinking about the fact that so many of our political leaders have echoed the opposite sentiment. I have myself. What does that say about what we think of ourselves as leaders in government and politics? What does that say concerning what we think of our people and how they will behave some two-hundred years after the ratification of our Constitution? Or is the context different? Did the men who drafted the Constitution two hundred years ago have a greater appreciation for what kind of document that should be, and have we lost that sense today? Would we be inclined in a new constitutional convention to stuff all sorts of notions and ideas which have come upon us in the last few years into the most fundamental charter of our land? Would we be courting danger by calling together the great minds in political science and government of this nation and taking a look at a document two-hundred-years old? How do you see that? Secretary of State Dixon: I think it's worked pretty well, Governor, for two hundred years. I think there's a probability, quite frankly, that people do trust us less than they trusted the leaders two hundred years ago. I read an article not too long ago that suggested that over 90 percent of the parents in American families would not want to raise one of their children to go into public service. A rather sad commentary on our democratic institutions when only a few centuries ago in the mother country of England parents expected that one of their sons would serve in public life. . . .

[Governor, I think that the primary concern of the electorate is obviously to hold the line on taxes and government spending. The people now realize that you don't solve all the problems by spending money on them.]

Governor Thompson: [I want to know how you can reconcile the desire for a limit on taxes with the desire for increased governmental services. In the General Assembly some five-hundred bills to hold the line have been introduced—and several-thousand bills to spend money. And many legislators will in good conscience vote for all of them.

[There is a long list of imperative requests for increased funding: education, higher education, care for the handicapped. The public schools illustrate the difficulty of this situation with their fervent plea for more money even though school officials acknowledge there will be a reduction in enrollment of] fifty-thousand kids next year. Somewhat akin to the cry I suppose if the president of a corporation suddenly woke up and found out that in the next fiscal year he was going to lose fifty-thousand customers. Now if we were in the business world I daresay the board members would not let that corporate president raise prices in the face of the loss of fifty-thousand customers. Rather the board would seek to cut costs in an effort to keep the corporation afloat. And yet if we look to what may or may not be a proper analogy in the governmental sector we do not seem to take account of a statistic like fifty-thousand down next year in the number of children served normally by the Secretary of Education in this state but instead look frantically for new ways to spend the money, in fact for increased ways to spend the money.

How does a governor or a member of the General Assembly like the Senator who sits out in the audience tonight, or you as another leader of the executive branch with enormous influence and power in politics and government in Illinios—how do we set our priorities? Whom do we listen to? Whose voice is the loudest? Is it the combined voices of some thirty-thousand abused and neglected children whose names will be brought to the attention of the government this year, of whom at least fifteen-thousand will become actual cases? Or is it the voices of thousands of men and women confined in Illinois penitentiaries, some quite medieval in appearance and condition, for having committed crimes of such magnitude that we have decided as a society that they shouldn't be among us, not be free tonight to enter this hall and listen to this discussion or to celebrate this Sesquicentennial? Or is it the thousands upon thousands, far outweighing the number of children who will be entering elementary and secondary education this year, of the students in higher education in Illinois in both the public and private sector? Or is it the sometimes strangled cries of those who are mentally ill or developmentally disabled, children and adults whose level of development is so low that they cannot form human words, who stand behind fences in institutions, who shriek instead of speaking? Or is it the tax-payers who, not being able to see all of these things directly, focus more upon services in terms of concrete, steel, buildings, roads, mail deliveries—whose voices number in the millions and upon whom we rely to provide the resources to fund the imperative cries of just a few that I have illustrated?

How do we put all that together in the next decade? How do we reconcile all these competing forces? How much wasted fat is there? Every politician wants to cut out waste and fat, and both of us do that to the best of our abilities. But after you cut through all that fat and get into the meat and then you get into the nerve and then you get down to the bone and there is nothing left, can we really answer all those cries here at home or in Washington and still hope to satisfy what seems to me to be not a temporary phenomenon? I think some people in government are misguided when they believe that the so-called Proposition 13 on the ballot is a temporary phenomenon. The notion of Proposition 13, to cut spending like this, may be temporary and may fade and may lower in volume, but the yearning of the average person—the one who wants to get ahead, the one who wants to answer your notion of the American dream—the yearning of that person and his chance to get ahead says to many of us in government, "You can put your hand into my pocket so far, but no farther before you'll take it out." How do we balance this?

Secretary of State Dixon: Let me briefly respond to that, Governor.

I think really in the end that, as most successful men and women in the public service do, we listen to the people. From them we really hear a message from which we draw our conclusions. Let me just give you one example, something that faces you now, that I am aware will be a thing that will require your attention. I have heard you speak of it. My colleagues, Senator Demuzio and others, are talking about this subject matter now. It is the question of roads and road work. You have said—and we have not yet seen your figures, your bottom line—you have said that the road fund is depleted. I am inclined to take your word for that, although being a member of the wild opposition I want to see those figures first, but you have said the road fund is depleted.

Governor Thompson: You noticed on the way over here tonight that the temporary patching we did this winter in filling in every pothole in the State of Illinois with ice isn't going to last much longer. [Laughter]

Secretary of State Dixon: That is exactly correct, Mr. Governor. All of us would have to recognize that the roads are pretty bad. I just came from Springfield to Jacksonville and we almost lost a wheel and one hub cap on the ride. Just to the west of us lies a place called Forgottonia where, they say, the roads have never been adequate and those of us who have gone there would have to support what they have said. Somewhere, sometime soon each of us, you as Governor, Senator Demuzio and every member of the General Assembly, has to weigh the feelings of the taxpayers who want no additional taxes against the condition of those roads and the needs for those roads and come to a decision. I suspect, knowing how these democratic institutions have worked all these decades and through these centuries, that in the end most of the men and women in government who have been successful will listen very, very carefully and respond correctly. So I think the answer is that in each case we listen to the people and make our decision on the basis of what they have said. And now, Governor, I yield, sir, to you for the close.

Governor Thompson: We still don't know whether he is for or against the gas tax. [Laughter]

Alan, with your permission, I think you will probably agree with this—

Secretary of State Dixon [interrupting]: May I hear it first? [Laughter]

Governor Thompson: Well, I'll tell you. I'll give it to you on a tentative basis, and then you can say aye or nay. Edward Everett Hale said something many years ago that I think is particularly appropriate to the position that the Secretary and I find ourselves in every day in the exercise of our duties, in the exercise of the confidence and trust the people reposed in us in the last election. . . . I will close with a paraphrase of something Hale said that I think describes not only our duties but describes the duty of everyone here in both public and private life. We are only two, but still we are two. We cannot do everything, but still we can do something. Because we cannot do everything, we will not refuse to do some things that we can do. I think that is the most appropriate moral for public and for private life.

Will the Secretary say aye or nay to that, now that he has heard it? I suspect that he will say aye.

Secretary of State Dixon: Governor, it is my pleasure to agree with you on this occasion. [Prolonged applause]

President Mundinger: Mr. Secretary, Mr. Governor, thank you for a very humane and enlightening exchange of your views. We are in your debt.

# 5

## The Dedication of the Hart Sesquicentennial Pipe Organ, March 30, 1979, and the Series of Concerts

The dedication of the Hart Sesquicentennial Pipe Organ in Rammelkamp Chapel in March, 1979, marked the beginning of a renaissance in music instruction and performance on the Illinois College campus. The years 1979 and 1980 presented a rich fare of vocal and instrumental concerts, and the greatly improved facilities and equipment paved the way for a more adequate curriculum. The use of the term *renaissance* is appropriate because the new sounds of music represented the revival of a once prominent feature of the College's program which for various reasons had lapsed nearly to the vanishing point.

Illinois College had already observed its fiftieth anniversary before the first organized music group—a glee club—was established on the campus in 1883, during President Tanner's administration. The glee club (all men, of course, at that time) sometimes accompanied the athletic teams and orators when they traveled to other towns for intercollegiate competition. One such trip was a four-day outing in 1887 to Champaign, where the singers presented a concert described by the *Rambler* as a great success. Several of the men also gave solo performances. The glee club frequently performed on the campus, too, as for example on Osage Orange Day. There were concerts in many towns in central Illinois and even in Chicago. Ten years after the establishment of the glee club a band was organized and flourished for two or three seasons before being discontinued.

Music instruction became a part of the formal curriculum with the 1903 merger of Illinois College and the Jacksonville Female Academy with its Conservatory of Music. The Conservatory had its origins in schools founded by the Reverend William D. Sanders, who had joined the Illinois College faculty in 1854 as Professor of Rhetoric and Elocution. While still teaching at the College Sanders had founded the "Young Ladies' Athenaeum," which from the beginning offered instruction in music. The music program was subsequently expanded and reorganized as a separate school, the Illinois Conservatory of Music, which opened in 1872. In 1885 the Conservatory became affiliated with the Jacksonville Female Academy and so eventually became a part of I.C. In 1928, after experiencing several years of deficits in the operation of the music program, Illinois College agreed to the merger of its Conservatory with that of Illinois Woman's College (MacMurray), which assumed control of the union program. The provisions of the agreement restricted Illinois College from offering any courses in music for twenty-five years. Moreover the glee clubs and band at I.C. were to be directed by instructors from MacMurray's Conservatory, which would also have responsibility for any community choruses and orchestras. The formal "curriculum" in music at Illinois College for many years thereafter was a single course in music appreciation, although both band and chorus continued and students were permitted to take music courses at MacMurray. President Rammelkamp, who summarized this story in his *Centennial History*, acknowledged near the end of the volume that he had "said nothing" about the glee club and band during his administration. Music would continue to be relatively unimportant for a considerable time.

In the last twenty-five years there have been heroic efforts to strengthen the music program, and these efforts found expression in modest improvements. At first instruction was provided by a part-time member of the faculty. Mrs. Ruth M. Bellatti directed the Chapel Choir from 1955 to 1961 and also offered course work in music theory. The music program continued to be under the direction of part-time instructors until Mr. R. John Specht joined the faculty in 1964 but his services were shared with the English Department. Similarly his successor in 1970, Mr. John P. Sorenson, was on the staff of the Interdisciplinary Studies program along with teaching some classroom courses in music and directing the performing groups. The energy and dedication of all these people did much to provide a quality program, however limited, and thus contributed to the long process of rebuilding the music department. The first full-time faculty member to serve exclusively in music (in recent years) was Mr. Rick L. Erickson, who came to the College in early 1977 following Mr. Sorenson's untimely death.

The 1979 dedication of the new pipe organ was significant in itself but it also was the dramatic symbol of the College's renewed commitment to providing a more adequate program in music. Little wonder then that this achievement and other important improvements have met with such rejoicing.

## THE DEDICATION CEREMONIES AND THE RECITAL BY CATHARINE CROZIER

### The College's New Pipe Organ

The special convocation held on March 30, 1979, for the dedication of the Hart Sesquicentennial Pipe Organ and the Dedicatory Recital by Catharine Crozier represented the culmination of several years of effort and the fulfillment of dreams dating back even more years. There were many who had long hoped for a larger place for music both in the curriculum and in performance, recognizing that this would require far more adequate facilities and instruments than the College then had. The realization of these hopes had its beginning in early 1977 when the Board of Trustees appointed a committee to select an organ company and draw up the specifications for an organ suitable for installation in Rammelkamp Chapel. Dr. Arthur C. Hart '25, an emeritus trustee and long active in the community both as a musician and as one who regularly attended concerts, was made chairman. Others named to the Committee were Mrs. Ruth M. Bellatti (Mrs. Walter R. Bellatti); Mr. Rick L. Erickson, Instructor in Music, College Organist, and Director of Choral Music; Mr. Howard Jarratt, who after a long career as a professional musician was now Director of Development at Illinois College; and two outstanding music students, John Goldsborough[1] and Otis Thompson,

---

1. John Goldsborough died on May 30, 1980, in a swimming pool accident in Austin, Texas. He was a student at the University of Texas and a candidate for the master's degree in philosophy.

both of the Class of 1978. President Mundinger gave strong encouragement to the Committee.

The Committee also engaged as consultant for this project a distinguished musician and organist, Dr. James Moeser, Dean of the Department of Fine Arts at the University of Kansas. The Committee members made numerous trips to various cities in Illinois and surrounding states to listen to and examine organ installations. The decisive step was taken when the Committee selected the Holtkamp Company of Cleveland, Ohio, to build the organ. The firm is noted not only for the excellence of its craftsmanship but also for leading the return to the classic principles of organ manufacture, producing instruments characterized by clarity, color, warmth, and brilliance of performance. Holtkamp organs are in use for teaching and concert purposes at the Juilliard School, the Eastman School of Music, Yale University, and numerous other fine music schools.

The process of designing and building the organ required about a year. After fully testing the instrument at the factory the builders shipped the organ to Jacksonville and carefully assembled it in Rammelkamp Chapel. The organ has thirty stops, thirty-nine ranks, and more than two thousand pipes. The mechanical key action gives the artist direct control over the air valves and thus of the sounds produced by the pipes. It is a truly modern organ, yet capable of interpreting the music of traditional and classical composers as well as that of our contemporaries.

Dr. Moeser has stated that the case which houses the organ is the most important single feature of the instrument. Illinois College is fortunate because the Holtkamp Company succeeded in designing a case which gives full expression to the tonal qualities and power of the organ and at the same time is handsome in appearance. The organ stands in the center of the chancel and thus the sound is focused directly into the auditorium. The exposed pipes of spotted metal and burnished zinc are set in a frame of solid red oak, with some parts in natural color and other parts stained. The top of the frame is angled downward from the sides of the chancel toward the center so as not to obscure the College Seal in the upper part of the wall behind the organ. Surmounting the central section, which is thrust forward somewhat, are forty-eight horizontal trumpets of polished copper.

Upon the recommendation of Dr. Moeser, the Chapel building

## THE HART SESQUICENTENNIAL PIPE ORGAN
### BUILT BY THE HOLTKAMP COMPANY, CLEVELAND, OHIO

### Great Organ

| | | |
|---|---|---|
| 16' | Pommer | 61 pipes |
| 8' | Principal | 61 pipes |
| 8' | Rohr Gedackt | 61 pipes |
| 4' | Octave | 61 pipes |
| 4' | Spitz flöte | 61 pipes |
| 2' | Super Octave | 61 pipes |
| IV | Mixture | 244 pipes |
| 8' | Trumpet | 61 pipes |

### Swell Organ

| | | |
|---|---|---|
| 8' | Geigen | 61 pipes |
| 8' | Voix Celeste | 56 pipes |
| 8' | Hohl flöte | 61 pipes |
| 4' | Principal | 61 pipes |
| 4' | Holtz Gedackt | 61 pipes |
| 2' | Bock flöte | 61 pipes |
| 1⅓' | Larigot | 61 pipes |
| III | Scharf | 183 pipes |
| 16' | Cromorne | 61 pipes |
| 8' | Oboe | 61 pipes |

Mechanical Key Action
Electric Stop Action

### Solo Organ

| | | |
|---|---|---|
| 8' | Copula Major | 61 pipes |
| 4' | Copula Minor | 61 pipes |
| III | Cornet | 183 pipes |
| 8' | Fanfara | 49 pipes |
| | (en chamade) | |

### Pedal Organ

| | | |
|---|---|---|
| 16' | Principal | 32 pipes |
| 16' | Pommer | (Great) |
| 8' | Octave | 32 pipes |
| 8' | Flute | 32 pipes |
| 4' | Choralbass | 32 pipes |
| IV | Rausch Bass | 128 pipes |
| 16' | Posaune | 32 pipes |
| 8' | Trumpet | 32 pipes |

### Couplers

Great to Pedal
Swell to Pedal
Solo to Pedal
Swell to Great
Solo to Great

*The Hart Sesquicentennial Pipe Organ, 1979*
Named for Dr. A. C. Hart '25 and Mrs. Charlotte Engelbach Hart '26, Major
Donors

was acoustically renovated prior to the installation of the organ to achieve an appropriate reverberation time for music performances. Several bays of the ceiling were covered with birch plywood, the old organ lofts at the sides of the chancel were covered with walnut board, and the cinderblock walls were covered with bridging paint to make them less absorbent. Another change was the extension of the stage twelve feet, more than compensating for the floor space taken up by the organ case and thus providing additional room for choral and orchestral groups.

This magnificent instrument has been named by the Board of Trustees as the "Dr. Arthur C. Hart '25, and Mrs. Charlotte Engelbach Hart '26 Sesquicentennial Organ." The Harts have long been enthusiastic supporters of Illinois College and of its music program, and it was their major contribution to the 150th Anniversary Challenge Fund which made the acquisition of the organ possible. The new pipe organ is a joy to hear and behold; in the words of a member of the science faculty, it is a great treasure. Many will agree with that.

### The Dedication Ceremonies and the Dedicatory Recital

The Committee arranged for Catharine Crozier, a noted concert organist with an international reputation, to play the Dedicatory Recital on the new Hart Sesquicentennial Pipe Organ. This was scheduled for Friday evening, March 30, 1979; the weekend date made it easier for out-of-town guests to attend. Miss Crozier herself arrived three days earlier to allow ample time for practice. She was accompanied by her husband, Dr. Harold Gleason, also an accomplished organist and widely known as a teacher and an author. They, the Harts, Mr. and Mrs. Walter R. Bellatti, members of the Organ Committee, and others were guests of President and Mrs. Mundinger at a dinner in Barnes House on March 28.

The large audience at the convocation on Friday evening was warmly welcomed by President Mundinger. Many faculty members were present but, unlike the preceding special occasions, there was no academic procession. Mr. Rick L. Erickson opened the dedication service, leading the audience in the responsive reading of Psalm 150, a most appropriate passage for the occasion, and then he read the New Testament Lesson, Phil. 4:4–9. President Mundinger's "Words of Dedication" are printed here in full.

In 1962, this building was dedicated to honor the work and memory of President Charles Henry Rammelkamp. The Chapel was, and is, a place for the College, as community, to meet for worship, instruction, and recreation.

As President Caine and his colleagues planned this Chapel, they were mindful of Winston Churchill's admonition that we shape our buildings and thereafter they shape us. The Rammelkamp Chapel has shaped the spirits and the minds of students for almost two decades. When the book, the lecture, and the experiment stop, the Chapel begins to work its marvelous discipline and mystery.

For fifty years, there has been a hunger and longing for a return to an earlier day, to a time when a tradition of music was an inspirational part of College life. In 1962, this Chapel was the first step in that return. Tonight we take a second step. We dedicate the Sesquicentennial Organ crafted by Walter Holtkamp.

Tonight is important, for it marks a return to an earlier tradition and, symbolically, it is a commitment to reach a higher level of excellence and culture. It is a new beginning in the fine arts. Dr. Frank, in his history of Illinois College, *Pioneer's Progress*, expressed this commitment in the words: "There is no intention of creating a professional music school here, only a demonstration that music is an essential part of the human experience, of the liberating arts."[2]

The pipe organ expresses the humanity of Walter Holtkamp—his competence, his spirit, and his aesthetics; it is the work of his head, hands, and heart. This brilliant instrument will shape and nurture faculty and students for generation upon generation.

As the steel skeleton of the Fine Arts Center rises at the west edge of the campus, the new organ will have provided the foretaste of a fuller cultural life to the campus. Tonight is, indeed, the second important step.

As this pipe organ is dedicated, it is dedicated to the glory of God and the enrichment of the cultural life of our community.

We are blessed as we receive this gift. May we have the courage and the vision to let this instrument inspire us so that we will grow and mature in the liberating arts.

2. Charles E. Frank, *Pioneer's Progress: Illinois College, 1829–1979* (Carbondale: Published for Illinois College by Southern Illinois Univ. Press, 1979), p. 333.

As this instrument is a testimony to human genius, so Catharine Crozier, our organist, attests to artistic genius—renowned, yet humble; disciplined, yet creative; the master, yet the student. We are privileged to have her with us on this proud occasion and our anticipation grows as her performance nears.

The poet, Heine, once wrote that when the words leave off, the music begins. Our education at this place will be more complete in the future because as the words leave off, the music can begin.

Following the President's remarks, Chaplain John N. Langfitt offered the dedicatory prayer—a prayer of celebration and thanksgiving for the fine new instrument to be used "for leading the worship of God, teaching in the language of music, and singing God's praises through concert and recital." Thanks were expressed also for "the people who conceived this organ, the organ builders who have crafted it with care, and the artist who now introduces it to us." Dr. Langfitt concluded the prayer with these words:

> O God, let this organ now be dedicated
>> to Your glory
>> to inspiration in the service of song
>> to thanksgiving in seasons of celebration
>> to healing discord
>> to revealing harmony
>> to ministry to the disheartened
>> to comforting the sorrowing
>> to humbling our hearts before You
>> to blessing those who seek to bless You;
>
> We dedicate this organ in the name of
>> the Father,
>> the Son,
>> and the Holy Spirit. Amen.

President Mundinger then introduced Catharine Crozier to the enthusiastic audience. For the first part of her recital Miss Crozier had chosen works from seventeenth and eighteenth century composers— chorales by Bach and Buxtehude and "The Mass for the Convents" by Couperin. The second part of the program was comprised of music by four twentieth-century composers. (The titles of the selections are included in the following section of this chapter.) Many music lovers from the College and the Jacksonville area were present and in addition there were about one hundred teachers and students from university schools of music in Illinois and five near-by states. Some in the audience had come from as far as California and Massachusetts.

Miss Crozier's mastery of the music and the superb quality of the instrument produced a truly beautiful evening for all who were present. The excellent choice of compositions displayed the versatility of the new organ and demonstrated its capabilities for dynamic variety and a wide range of tonal colors. Of special interest was the "Pastorale and Roundelay" by David Isele, which had been commissioned by Mr. Walter Holtkamp especially for this occasion.

Following the intermission, and before Miss Crozier resumed playing, she and Mrs. Ruth M. Bellatti were each awarded the honorary degree of Doctor of Humane Letters by President Mundinger. Miss Crozier's distinguished career had an early beginning—she gave her first recital as a pianist when only six years old. She studied organ with Harold Gleason at the Eastman School of Music in Rochester, New York, graduating with the Bachelor of Music degree and earning the Performer's Certificate. Graduate studies brought her the Master of Music degree and the Artist's Diploma, the highest award for performance. She also did special work with the distinguished French organist and teacher, Joseph Bonnet. Miss Crozier has performed throughout the United States, Canada, and Europe and has been featured on radio and television programs. She has appeared with numerous civic orchestras and was one of three organists chosen to play the inaugural organ recital at Lincoln Center's Philharmonic Hall in 1962. Miss Crozier's citation was read by Dean Wallace N. Jamison; the hood was placed upon her shoulders by Dr. Don P. Filson, faculty marshal.

Mrs. Ruth Melville Bellatti is very well known in the Jacksonville area for her active leadership in music—both as a performer and as a devoted promoter of music concerts. She too received Bachelor's and Master's degrees in music at the Eastman School of Music, where she also studied with Harold Gleason and was awarded the

Performer's Certificate. This achievement was followed by studies
in France with Marcel Dupré and Nadia Boulanger at the American
Conservatory of Music in Fontainebleau, where she earned diplomas
in Solfeggio and Organ Pedagogy and Performance. Coming to
Jacksonville in 1937, Mrs. Bellatti taught organ and music theory at
the Illinois Conservatory of Music at MacMurray College from then
until 1947. During that time she guided the early planning for the
large pipe organ in MacMurray's Annie Merner Chapel. Mrs. Bellatti began her long tenure as organist and choir director at Trinity
Episcopal Church in 1938 and greatly aided in securing a fine new
organ for Trinity. As Director of Chapel Music at Illinois College
from 1955 to 1961, she introduced course work in music theory and
arranged for credit to be given students participating in the Chapel
Choir. She has been prominent in arranging music programs on the
campus as well as in the community and has been one of the key
leaders in arranging for the Sesquicentennial Organ. Her contributions to the community have not been restricted to music, although
that has been her primary interest; she is a life-member of the Ladies'
Education Society and has served on the Board of Directors of the
Sherwood Eddy Memorial YMCA. Mrs. Bellatti was presented for
the L.H.D. degree by Professor Iver F. Yeager, and Dr. Hart, at his
request, had the honor of bestowing the hood.

*The Program*

Chorale ......................Harmonized by Johann Sebastian Bach
    "Wie schön leuchtet der Morgenstern"
Chorale Fantasia ...................................... Dietrich Buxtehude
    "Wie schön leuchtet der Morgenstern"    1637–1707
Messe pour les Couvents ............................François Couperin
                                   1668–1773
Variations on a Chorale .........................Johann Sebastian Bach
    "Sei gegrüsset, Jesu gutig"    1685–1750
Intermission
Partita ...................................................... Hugo Distler
    "Wachet auf, ruft uns die Stimme"    1908–1942
Pastorale and Roundelay ...................................... David Isele
                                   1946-

The Despair and Agony of Dachau ..........................Paul Sifler
                                                                        1911–
Prelude and Fugue in g minor ........................... Marcel Dupré
                                                                    1886–1971

### The Lecture-Demonstration

On Saturday, the day following the Dedicatory Recital, Miss Crozier and Dr. Gleason conducted a lecture-demonstration on "Performance Practice and Organ Instruction in the Seventeenth Century." A large number of the visitors from a distance who had come for the recital had arranged to stay overnight so that they could participate in the workshop. College students and faculty members and their families were also encouraged to attend, as well as interested persons from the community. Miss Crozier and Dr. Gleason have often served as visiting professors in similar demonstrations across the country. Dr. Gleason was formerly head of the organ department and director of graduate studies at the Eastman School of Music and had been private organist for Mr. George Eastman. He has published several books on music, and the sixth edition of his *Method of Organ Playing* appeared shortly after the Jacksonville visit.

## THE SERIES OF CONCERTS

### Performances by College Music Organizations

The Illinois College Concert Choir of fifty-five voices enhanced the formal convocations of the Sesquicentennial celebration with their anthems and sometimes with special processional music, as was reported in preceding chapters. There were other occasions when the Choir itself provided the program. For example, on April 29, 1979, the Choir, under Mr. Erickson's direction, presented Handel's *Messiah* in complete form, thus including the Christmas and Easter portions familiar to so many in shorter versions. The Choir performed magnificently, as did the four professional soloists, of whom the most outstanding was John Walker.

The Madrigal Choir, consisting of sixteen select voices from the larger group, had made its spring debut on March 10, appearing by invitation at the Governor's Mansion in Springfield. For their spring concerts the Madrigal Choir prepared a program of sacred and secular music by composers from the fifteenth to the twentieth centuries. In addition to performing for several local churches and a number of community organizations in the area, the group traveled to Missouri, Kansas, and Texas on concert tour. In the spring of 1980, the Madrigal Choir made a trip to the eastern United States, singing a number of concerts—the most important of which were in Washington, D.C., and Charleston, South Carolina.

The Choir's Christmas concert on December 9, 1979, was a special treat, both musically and visually. Called "A Festival of Lessons and Carols," the service began with the lovely choral introit, "Let All Mortal Flesh Keep Silence." Singing by the Choir was alternated with carols by the Madrigals and hymns by the congregation. The Christmas story was told in nine Scripture readings by men and women representing every part of the campus community. The chancel of Rammelkamp Chapel was beautifully decorated with large evergreen wreaths and a lighted tree and gleamed with the candles of nearly a dozen seven-branched candelabra. The service concluded with people and Choir singing the joyful carol, "O Come, All Ye Faithful," while the Choir recessed.

There were occasional student recitals, sometimes during the Monday convocation period, when half a dozen vocal and instrumental solos were presented by those with special skill and experience. Some of these students had received individual instruction from Mr. Erickson.

The College Band has been under the direction of Mr. Leslie Fonza, part-time Instructor in Music, since 1978. The spring concerts by the Band have been given out-of-doors, wind and weather permitting. The pleasant Courtney Crouch Wright Patio just east of Schewe Library now provides an ideal place for such performances. A smaller pep band, under the direction of Mr. Fonza, has been faithful in giving encouragement to the football and basketball teams at home games as well as providing entertainment for the spectators.

*Concerts by Guest Artists*

The Jacksonville Symphony Society devoted its fall concert to works by American composers in celebration of Illinois College's

Sesquicentennial Anniversary. The performance was in Rammel-kamp Chapel on October 21, 1979, with the orchestra under Music Director Phillip Paeltz. The first part of the program included a wide variety of music: the "Chorale Prelude for Organ and Bass" by the Colonial composer, William Billings; an arrangement of Richard Rodgers' "The Sound of Music"; and a new work, "Ann Rutledge." Mr. Paeltz had composed this music in 1979 using Harold E. Wolfe's poem about Abraham Lincoln's first love. The world premiere took place at Illinois College with Stephanie Smith-Jarratt, Soprano—to whom the work is dedicated—as soloist. Following the intermission the Orchestra played Ferde Grofé's "Grand Canyon Suite," which has been described as a "travelogue in tones." The review of the concert printed in the *Jacksonville Daily Courier* (October 23, 1979) described it as "well-planned and superbly executed" and noted that "the concert was the final event in the College's successful homecoming weekend." The final sentence gave due praise to the Orchestra, declaring that "Sunday night's concert . . . would convince music lovers everywhere that Jacksonville has an orchestra that can hold its own with orchestras from much larger cities. It is a civic asset of magnitude."

Illinois College faculty and staff are active both as officers and financial supporters of the Jacksonville Symphony Society, and usually they provide two or three players for the Orchestra as well. Sometimes students are also members of the Orchestra.

Smaller music groups and individual artists presented several evenings of beautiful music during the period of the 150th Anniversary celebration. In the spring semester (in February, 1979), the Fresk String Quartet from Sweden played music by Schubert and Beethoven. The autumn series featured John Walker, lyric tenor, on November 3 and an organ-trumpet duo, David Hickman and William Neill, in a program of baroque music on November 28. John Walker, an alumnus of Illinois College, is always popular with students and the community. Mr. Walker sang groups of songs by German, English, and American composers. A special hit was his beautiful rendition of "Flow Gently, Sweet Afton," the poem by Robert Burns set to music by Jonathan E. Spilman, an 1835 graduate of Illinois College. The spring semester of 1980 included an organ concert by

James Moeser and a piano concert by Daniel Barber. Mr. Barber played the new Steinway concert piano which had been selected by the international artist, Van Cliburn. A substantial part of the funds for the purchase of this fine instrument was given by the members of the Class of 1977 as their class gift to the College.

The students and faculty of the College have for many years enjoyed the regular concerts given by the Band and Choir and, on occasion, by visiting artists. The Jacksonville Symphony Orchestra has played some of its concerts in Rammelkamp Chapel each season since the Society was organized in 1968. Also, students have been able to obtain through the College free tickets for the programs of the Jacksonville-MacMurray Music Association, and many faculty members have regularly purchased memberships. Nevertheless the new facilities which Illinois College has now acquired through the Sesquicentennial effort have made possible a much richer music program on the campus. Gratitude is due the many alumni, students, faculty and staff, and friends of the College who have contributed so generously. The music curriculum and the opportunities for music enjoyment are already far greater than appeared likely even five years ago and further development is anticipated. The names of many of those who have been the leaders in this significant achievement have been mentioned, but one other group deserves explicit mention in this context—the Convocation Committee, chaired by Dean Donald R. Eldred. This Committee has been responsible for arranging several special concerts as well as those which have been part of the regular weekly Convocation program. Also, brief mention will be made of the McGaw Fine Arts Series of the 1980–81 academic year. This was not a part of the Sesquicentennial observance as such but the programs could not have been presented without the facilities and instruments provided as part of the 150th Anniversary Challenge project. The McGaw Fine Arts Series has been established in order to "showcase the Hart Organ, the Sibert Theatre, and the music, television, and visual arts facilities of the McGaw Fine Arts Center," as President Mundinger has stated. The series included Organist Wolfgang Oehms (West Germany), the Missouri Concert Ballet, Pianist Ralph Robbins (Professor Emeritus, MacMurray College), Pi-

anist David Bar-Illan (Israel), the Audubon String Quartet, Broadway star Pat Carroll in *Gertrude Stein/Gertrude Stein* . . . , and a
special exhibition of alumni art. These arrangements were made by
Dean Eldred and a committee composed of faculty, alumni, and
friends of the College.

# 6

## *The Convocation on Science and Mathematics September 24, 1979*

A brief statement about the opening convocation of the fall semester is in order before describing the Science and Mathematics Convocation. When the College community assembled for the first time at the beginning of fall semester classes, President Mundinger welcomed new and returning students and faculty and reminded his audience of the continuing Sesquicentennial observance. In his address, entitled "New Beginnings," the President commented on the status of the liberal arts college in a time when many students (and their parents) are more concerned with achieving credentials with which to enter the job market than with the content of education. He reaffirmed Illinois College's commitment to education which not only aids the student in fulfilling individual goals but which enables—and motivates—graduates to make this world a better place in which to live. Western culture, he said, has always experienced a tension between achievement of the common good and the welfare of the individual. Dr. Mundinger declared that liberal learning must assist the student in achieving mastery of a given discipline and in acquiring a critical acquaintance with the spectrum of knowledge. These in turn must serve both the student and others. "This is a college which serves you," he said, "and which asks you, in turn, to serve." In his closing remarks President Mundinger declared that this, the 151st academic year of Illinois College, provided the opportunity for "new beginnings as individuals, . . . for the College, . . . and for the larger society. As we strive to master our craft, let us strive for a fuller and better life—a more humane and civilized community."

During the fall semester three special convocations were arranged by the 150th Anniversary Committee as occasions for recognizing those curricular divisions of the College which together represent the spectrum of knowledge and which serve to organize the individual disciplines in one of which each graduating senior must demonstrate a suitable level of mastery. The graduation requirements of the College have been designed to fulfill both these purposes.

The first of this series of academic convocations was devoted to science and mathematics and was held on September 24, 1979. The order of events and the format of the printed program established the pattern for the other two. The College community assembled in Rammelkamp Chapel and precisely at 10:00 A.M. the faculty began its procession. The faculty marshals of the previous year continued with their duties but the student marshals had been newly elected just prior to Commencement. They were Jon Mark Althoff and Ann Burford, both of the Class of 1980. They were to serve throughout the academic year and consequently were the student marshals for all remaining Sesquicentennial convocations.

The printed programs for these convocations provided the audience with brief sketches of the educational backgrounds and professional careers of the guest speaker and the alumni who were to be honored. Each program also included a list of the alumni who had majored in the disciplines of the given division and had been awarded honorary degrees by the College during the past twenty-five years. A faculty essay printed in the program presented a brief survey of the history of that area of studies at Illinois College.

The essay for this convocation was prepared by Associate Professor of Mathematics George William Horton, Jr. -52, who noted that the earliest catalogs prescribed more than two years of study in each of these subjects for the prospective Bachelor of Arts candidate. Dr. Mundinger's remarks prior to his introduction of the speaker warned of the danger of scientific illiteracy and stressed the continuing importance of the natural sciences and mathematics.

The guest speaker for this convocation was Dr. Kip S. Thorne, Professor of Theoretical Physics at the California Institute of Technology. He had been recommended by Associate Professor Frederick Pilcher (Physics and Astronomy). Mr. Pilcher's strong endorsement was fully matched by Professor Thorne's brilliant lecture on "The Search for a Black Hole in Space," a lucid and graphic explanation of a fascinating subject on the frontiers of scientific theory and research. The Committee in extending its invitation to the speaker had asked that he deal with science "as a human enterprise," and his descriptions of the pioneers in the study of black holes and related phenomena were beautiful illustrations of this facet of science. Afterwards a faculty member in a field quite different from the sciences acknowledged that the announcement of the topic had had no appeal whatsoever but that Professor Thorne's address had been absolutely fascinating!

Professor Thorne and three alumni were granted the honorary degree of Doctor of Science. The citation for Dr. Thorne, read by Professor Pilcher, summarized his pre- and postdoctoral studies at the California Institute of Technology and at Princeton. Dr. Thorne has held numerous prestigious fellowships, including the Danforth Fellowship (which attested not only to his ability but also to his concern for values). He has been a lecturer at the University of Chicago, at Cambridge and Moscow Universities, and also in France and Italy. He had just recently been a member of the Committee for U.S.-U.S.S.R. Cooperation in Physics. After witnessing his skill in oral communication we were not surprised that he had won an award as a science writer in physics and astronomy. Unfortunately a tape recording was not made, but with the aid of modern technology Dr. Thorne was able to dictate the substance of his address while enroute home by plane and subsequently sent a typed copy for inclusion in this chapter.

Two of the alumni presented for honorary degrees had majored in chemistry. They were Dr. David Bridgman Capps '48 and Dr. Edward William Lawless '53. Dr. Capps' professional career has been in pharmaceutical research, primarily for the discovery of drugs for the treatment of infectious tropical diseases. He has been inventor on twenty U.S. patents and has written many technical articles. His excellence in his avocation, photography, has resulted in several exhibitions of his work. At Illinois College Dr. Capps had been a member of Sigma Pi. Dr. Capps was presented by Dr. Robert J. Evans,

Professor of Chemistry, who like Dr. Capps had earned his doctorate at the University of Nebraska.

Dr. Edward William Lawless for two decades has been a member of a research institute and in recent years has headed his firm's technology assessment section. In this work he has been responsible for determining social attitudes toward new technologies as well as their technical feasibility and environmental impact. He is the author of twenty articles and two books and has participated in conferences in the U.S., Japan, Italy, and India. Professor Edgar A. Franz, chairman of the Department of Mathematics, read the citation for Dr. Lawless.

The fourth person upon whom President Mundinger conferred the honorary Doctor of Science degree was Dr. Harvey Dixon Scott, Jr., who was presented by Dr. Louise Rainbolt, Professor of Biology and Chairman of that Department. Dr. Scott had majored in Biology at Illinois College and at the time of his graduation in 1942 was elected to Phi Beta Kappa. He was a member of the football and track teams for four years and cocaptained both. A member of Gamma Nu Literary Society, he was twice elected president of his class. After service in World War II Dr. Scott earned his M.D. degree at Northwestern University and has been a surgeon in Jacksonville since 1954. He is active in numerous professional societies and community organizations.

Immediately after the convocation had ended, students, faculty, and friends greeted the honored guests at a reception in Schewe Library. The evening before President and Mrs. Mundinger were hosts to the special guests and their spouses at a dinner in Barnes House. Later that evening the faculty of the Science and Mathematics Division and a group of students had joined the guests in Baxter Lounge for an informal discussion with Professor Thorne. (Each department had invited several of the top students majoring in its field.) Professor Thorne in his opening remarks spoke about his contacts with his Russian counterparts in physics and astronomy, commented on the manner in which scientific studies transcend national boundaries, and discussed the ways in which ideological differences hamper or even thwart individual scientists and science itself.

The following pages include the faculty essay, reprinted from the convocation program, the remarks by President Mundinger, and the address by Professor Kip S. Thorne.

---

### SCIENCE AND MATHEMATICS AT ILLINOIS COLLEGE
### MR. GEORGE WILLIAM HORTON, JR. -52
### ASSOCIATE PROFESSOR OF MATHEMATICS

Ever since the founding of the colonies' first college, Harvard, in 1636, the Bachelor of Arts degree has indicated that the degree recipient was a broadly educated individual. Relative to today's convocation, it has indicated at least a conversancy with science and mathematics. It has done so at Illinois College for 150 years.

One of the College's earliest catalogs, published in 1833, shows that more than two years each of prescribed courses in science and mathematics was required for the Bachelor of Arts. The passing of the years has lessened the length of time for those requirements and offered alternative routes to meet them, but the College's commitment to science and mathematics as vital components of a liberal arts education remains strong.

Julian M. Sturtevant, the first instructor, became Professor of Mathematics and Natural Philosophy once it became possible to specialize at the tiny college, leaving those duties to become its president in 1844. Samuel Adams, M.D., served as Professor of Chemistry and Natural History from 1838 to 1877 and was instrumental in establishing the College's excellent but short-lived medical school during the 1840s. Jonathan B. Turner was on the faculty from 1833 to 1848, ostensibly in rhetoric and elocution. Like his colleagues, Turner actually taught in many areas and he acquired his fame through his originally avocational interest in trees. These three remarkable men established a tradition in science and mathematics upon which their successors at the College have built.

In 1852 Illinois College became one of the first midwestern colleges to establish the Bachelor of Science degree in recognition that the strong emphasis on classics in the standard Bachelor of Arts program was not necessary in the college education of persons preparing for careers in technology and business in the expanding nation. A year later Rufus C. Crampton joined the faculty as Professor of Mathematics and Astronomy. He gave the College thirty-five years of outstanding service including six years as Acting President between the Sturtevant and Tanner administrations.

During the Tanner administration, 1882–1892, the College turned the corner in modernizing its science and mathematics curricula. Two Cornell-trained men, Samuel W. Parr and Truman P. Carter in natural sciences, and a Purdue-trained man, James B. Shaw in mathematics, wrought these changes.

In the twentieth century the College has continued to be favored with a dedicated science and mathematics faculty. Willis P. DeRyke with twenty-seven years in biology and Earle B. Miller with thirty-five years in mathematics are two outstanding examples. Today's science and mathematics faculty is fully aware that it walks in the steps of giants in carrying on the tradition of strong programs consistent with a liberal arts environment at Illinois College.

*Crispin Science Hall, 1963*
Named for Dr. Egerton L. Crispin '02, Benefactor

## STATEMENT BY PRESIDENT MUNDINGER

The cynics in the educational establishment have largely written off the small liberal arts colleges. In this age of bigness, many educationalists have decided that education can only occur in a mega environment—that small, intimate, personal, and informal colleges cannot sustain educational quality.

Other "doom-sayers" dismiss the liberal arts college for other reasons. Demographics mean fewer students in the future. Inflation continues to ravage salaries, budgets, and endowment. The graduate schools ride roughshod over the collegiate curriculum.

Despite the problems the liberal arts colleges face and which also test Illinois College, I remain optimistic about the future. We do true education. We put fine young people into the hands of a fine scholarly faculty and good things invariably happen. The master craftsman brings along his apprentice. A love and a respect for scholarly work grows. The young learn from master teachers. The young learn a craft, the importance of service in life.

This morning the College pauses to celebrate its 150th Anniversary. We center our attention on the natural sciences, to learn from them and to measure their contribution to our mission.

I am pleased that we start the 151st academic year with the natural sciences. The four departments—Biology, Chemistry, Mathematics, and Physics—comprise our work in the natural sciences. They are an essential and an exciting element in our curriculum. The faculty in this division and those who have gone before have strived to be liberal educators—gifted professors highly trained in a scientific discipline, with an interest in the other scholarly areas and culture. The glory of this college is the community of scholars—in our case, some two score and ten strong, who exchange ideas about their profession and their community.

A decade ago, C. P. Snow wrote about two cultures and the dangers of scientific illiteracy. Recently a *Washington Post* columnist, Daniel S. Greenberg, reiterated the danger of scientific illiteracy, especially among college students.

This danger exists on this campus. Scientific advances are esoteric and complex. The application of science, that is, technology, profoundly influences our lives. As educated citizens, we have no choice but to seek to understand.

In a quiet moment, I thought of T. S. Eliot's lines:

We shall not cease from exploration
And the end of all our exploring
Will be to arrive where we started
And know the place for the first time.[1]

We are fortunate this morning that our speaker, Professor Kip Thorne, will lead us in our exploration. We are fortunate because he is bright and articulate. We are fortunate because he will interpret the importance of scientific discovery. As we explore with him and return to the place where we started, we shall know—know our college more fully.

Ladies and Gentlemen: Professor Kip Thorne.

---

## THE SEARCH FOR A BLACK HOLE IN SPACE
### DR. KIP S. THORNE
#### PROFESSOR OF THEORETICAL PHYSICS
#### CALIFORNIA INSTITUTE OF TECHNOLOGY

When we ask, "What is our greatest cultural heritage from the Renaissance?" the answer is obvious: the paintings of da Vinci, Michelangelo, and others. What, by analogy, will people of the twenty-second century regard as their cultural heritage from our time? Perhaps they will cite the operas of Gilbert and Sullivan, rock music, the majestic arcs of freeway interchanges. But whatever else they may cite, they surely will include the discovery of the nature of the Universe around us.

The quest for an understanding of the Universe first became a part of popular culture in the 1920s, when Albert Einstein was a folk hero and his theories of relativity were expounded in frontpage news-

1. T. S. Eliot, *Four Quartets: Little Gidding*, V, in *Collected Poems, 1909–1962* (New York: Harcourt, Brace and World, n.d.), p. 208.

paper stories and in literary-club presentations. The year 1979 is not only the Sesquicentennial of Illinois College but also the Centennial of Einstein's birth. Therefore it perhaps is fitting, on this occasion, to trace the impact of Einstein's ideas on science and on the culture of our time.

Einstein's greatest contribution to science was his 1915 general theory of relativity. General relativity is a theory of gravity. It describes how gravity, which holds us down to Earth and drives the planets in their orbits, arises from the "curvature of space-time." Einstein gave us a single mathematical equation, the "Einstein field equation," which governs gravity. By mathematical studies of that equation one can learn everything there is to know about gravity.

One great prediction of Einstein's equation was the expansion of the Universe. Einstein himself discovered this prediction in 1917. His mathematics told him that the Universe cannot be quiescent. It must have been created in a "big-bang" explosion and must now be expanding out from that explosion or perhaps might be recontracting if gravity by now has halted the expansion and reversed it. This prediction was too bizarre for Einstein to accept. He was imbued with the philosophy of the nineteenth century—a philosophy which regarded the stars as forever shining, unchanging, eternal. Einstein was so upset by the prediction of his field equation that he changed the equation and his general relativity theory—changed them in an aesthetically ugly way—to save them from predicting the expansion of the Universe.

A decade later the world's newspapers carried headline stories: EXPANSION OF UNIVERSE DISCOVERED. Edwin Hubble, working with the new 100-inch telescope atop Mount Wilson in Southern California, had discovered that distant galaxies (great star clusters) are moving away from Earth. The farther a galaxy is from us, the faster it moves away. Hubble and other astronomers, by measuring this motion, concluded that about ten billion years ago all the matter in the Universe was squeezed down into a tiny volume, from which it came flying out in the "big-bang" explosion predicted by Einstein's original equation. Einstein retracted his ugly equation, resurrected the original beautiful one, and said his failure to believe his original prediction was "the biggest blunder of my life."

A second prediction of Einstein's relativity equation is the "black hole." It was not Einstein who discovered this prediction in his mathematics. Rather, it was J. Robert Oppenheimer, the University of California physicist who later went on to lead the atomic bomb project. In 1939 Oppenheimer and his student Hartland Snyder used Einstein's equation to compute the fate of a star that has exhausted all its nuclear fuel. They found that the star—a great fiery ball of gas a million miles in size—can no longer support itself against the inward pull of its own gravity. With its nuclear fires extinguished, its gravity pulls the star inward upon itself. The star shrinks in size, catastrophically, until it becomes so small and its gravity becomes so strong that light can no longer escape from it. Where the star once was there now remains only a gaping black hole in space—a hole down which matter can fall, but out of which nothing can ever come.

This autumn Walt Disney Studios will inject the story of the black hole into popular culture. The Disney producers have spent fifteen million dollars to create a movie about the black hole—more money than the world has spent on scientific research on black holes from the days of Oppenheimer until now!

Perhaps the clearest way to understand black holes is by the following parable. Imagine the time, three centuries hence, when man has achieved interplanetary travel and has populated the galaxy with spacecraft and planetary colonies. A particular star has been pinpointed. We know that this star will soon exhaust its nuclear fuel and will shrink to become a black hole. We wish to study the birth of the black hole by means of a practical rocketship experiment. On the fiery surface of the star we place a number of asbestos launching pads, and on each pad we place a rocketship. Now when NASA launches a rocket off the surface of the earth the engine must drive the rocket to a speed of seven miles per second in order that the rocket may escape from the Earth's gravitational pull. We say that the Earth's "escape velocity" is seven miles per second. The objective of the rocket ship experiment is to measure the escape velocity from the surface of the star as the star shrinks. The first rocket is launched shortly before the shrinking begins. The rocket flies up and away from the star, and in order to escape it must achieve a speed of at least one hundred miles per second. The star then begins to shrink. When its circumference has been reduced from forty million miles to ten million miles, a second rocket is launched. The gravitational pull which this rocket must fight is stronger than that fought by the first rocket, because this rocket begins closer to the star's center—four times closer. (Newton's theory of gravity, and also Einstein's, says that the gravitational pull is inversely proportional to the square of the distance from the center of the star.) Because the pull of gravity is greater, this rocket must fight harder to escape; its escape velocity is 200 miles per second rather than 100. The star continues to shrink. One rocket after another is launched. Ultimately the star is so small—approximately fifty miles in circumference—that the escape velocity has reached 186,000 miles per second, the speed of light. Now we all know that nothing can move faster than the speed of light; not rocketships, not subatomic particles, and not light itself. At this point the star squeezes itself off from the external Universe. It can no longer communicate with us. It cannot send us rocketships, particles, light, radio waves, or any form of communication whatsoever. It leaves behind only a gaping black hole in space—a veritable edge of our Universe not unlike the sharp edge of the earth which medieval people believed a ship would encounter if it sailed out from land too far.

During the past decade theoretical physicists have worked hard on mathematical analyses of Einstein's equation. From these analyses they have learned a lot about how black holes should behave. The leader in this mathematical research has been a thirty-seven-year-old man in Cambridge, England, named Stephen Hawking.

Stephen is a close friend of mine. He is also a complete cripple. When he was a young student he contracted a rare variant of a rare disease called atypical amyotrophic lateral sclerosis. The doctors gave him only a few years to live. Since then he has fought a valiant battle against death—a battle which so far has been successful, but cannot be successful for many more years. This battle has left his body wasted away; he weighs only about eighty pounds, but standing erect (if he *could* stand) he would be nearly as tall as I. Stephen has lost the use of his hands; he can no longer feed himself. His neck muscles can no longer hold his head up. And he speaks with such great effort and with such distortion of sound that nobody but his closest friends and family can understand him. Nevertheless, his mind is clear; extremely clear. He is the most brilliant scientist I know. When I am with him I forget that he is crippled. He and his wife have three children, one born only a few months ago. They maintain a normal family life. When they were in Pasadena with my research group for a year, five years ago, they often gave parties for the students and faculty. I recall standing beside Stephen at one party. His body was curled up onto itself so that his head rested in his lap; and he was motionless. I was speaking with somebody else. At that moment Jane, his wife, walked up to him and spoke in a sharp tone of voice, "Stephen! Straighten up! The people at our party look at you and think you are in pain. But *I* know that you are sitting there happily thinking about physics. It's not fair. Straighten up and talk with your guests!"

One of the great predictions about black holes which Stephen Hawking has milked out of Einstein's mathematics is the "second law of black-hole mechanics." This law says that if you have a black hole here in this room (and this room is floating in outer space so that the hole will not fall down through the earth, eating up matter as it falls!), and if you measure the surface area of the hole, that surface area will never decrease. Moreover, every time something falls into the hole, the surface area grows larger. And every time you wave your fist at the hole, your fist raises a small tide on the surface of the hole much like the tide which the moon raises on the Earth's oceans. That tide, moving up and down, exerts a gravitational pull back on your fist and in the process extracts energy from your muscles. This energy, going down the hole, makes the hole grow larger. Its surface area has increased. If you have two black holes in this room, and if they collide and coalesce to form one black hole, then the surface area of the new black hole will be larger than the sum of the surface areas of the original black holes.

If black holes always grow larger, then is there a danger that they will eat up the entire Universe? No; fortunately not. They simply do not grow fast enough. If the sun were to turn into a black hole tomorrow, then its circumference instead of being four million miles would become only ten miles. A ten-mile black hole, wandering through the vast reaches of outer space, cannot eat matter very fast.

For several decades after Oppenheimer's first black-hole prediction, astronomers and physicists did not take the prediction very seriously. It was too bizarre! Even Oppenheimer himself found the prediction hard to believe. Then in the 1960s astronomers began to realize how truly bizarre the Universe really is; one after another were discovered quasars, pulsars, fireball radiation left over from the big-bang, organic molecules in outer space. Now the black-hole prediction seemed less bizarre. Astronomers began to ask themselves how they might test this prediction. Could they in any way discover black holes in outer space?

It was Yakov Borisovich Zel'dovich in Moscow, Russia, who first proposed a promising method for the search for a black hole.

Zel'dovich has a fascinating history. If you go to the Museum of Atomic Energy in the Park of Rest and Culture in Moscow, Russia, you discover that Zel'dovich was responsible for the first Russian work on nuclear energy. He did pioneering research on nuclear chain reactions in 1938. Later he went on to play a key role in the development of the Russian atomic bomb and hydrogen bomb. Then, in 1962 when he was approximately fifty years old, he turned his attention to astrophysics. Suddenly he became accessible to Western scientists. Since then we have been able to discuss science with him freely, working together with him on the mysteries of black holes and other strange phenomena in the distant Universe. He is not allowed to travel to the West; he knows too much about Soviet nuclear weapons, and in addition he is Jewish. However, when American scientists visit Russia they are perfectly free to talk with Zel'dovich about astrophysics and to carry out research jointly with him.

In 1963 Zel'dovich proposed his method for searching for a black hole in outer space. He knew that it was hopeless to point a telescope into the sky and see a patch of darkness where the black hole is blotting out light from behind. This is hopeless because the black hole is so small (fifty miles in circumference) and so far away (many trillions of miles) that its blotting-out effects are too minuscule to be seen even with the world's largest telescopes. But Zel'dovich had an alternative idea. Many black holes, he reasoned, should be in orbit around normal stars—in much the same way as the moon is in orbit around the earth. Moreover, if the black hole is close enough to its companion star, the hole's gravity will pull gas off the surrounding star and suck it down toward the edge of the hole. The infalling, swirling gas will be heated up, Zel'dovich computed, until it reaches a temperature of ten million degrees. At such a high temperature the gas will emit not light but X-rays. Therefore, Zel'dovich proposed, to discover a black hole you should point an X-ray telescope at the sky, find an X-ray emitting star, and then look with a normal optical telescope to see whether the X-ray star is in orbit around a normal star. If so, then one has a good black-hole candidate. And how can one be sure that this is a black hole? The answer is a bit indirect. In such a "binary system," gas being pulled off the normal star can also be heated to produce X-rays if the pulling object is a "neutron star" or "white dwarf." They can do the job just as effectively as a black hole. But nothing else that we know of can do the job. Now it is a remarkable fact, which has been proved by mathematical calculations with the laws of physics, that white dwarfs and neutron stars can never be heavier than three times the weight of the sun. Therefore, Zel'dovich reasoned, when one has found a black-hole candidate, one should weigh it. If it is much heavier than three times the weight of the sun, then it cannot be a white dwarf or a neutron star; it must be a black hole.

But how can the weighing be done? Remarkably easily in principle—though not in practice. The black hole and its companion star are actually in orbit around each other. The heavier the hole is, the harder its gravity pulls on its companion and the faster its companion must move in its orbit in order to escape falling into the hole. Thus, to weigh the hole, one need only measure the speed of its companion in its orbit. This can be done by carefully monitoring the color of the companion's light. As the companion moves toward us in its orbit, its light gets shifted to the blue; as it moves away, its light gets shifted to the red. This is the "Doppler shift"—analogous to the shifting of the pitch of a train whistle which is higher as the train approaches us and lower as it recedes from us. The actual weighing requires much more than simply measuring this Doppler shift; but the Doppler shift is the key.

In 1971 the world's first X-ray telescope observatory was flown by NASA in a satellite above the surface of the earth. (X-rays cannot penetrate through the earth's atmosphere, so an earth-orbiting observatory is needed.) This telescope pinpointed a source of X-rays called "Cygnus X–1." When astronomers turned their optical telescopes onto this object, they discovered that it had a companion star which orbits around it in just the manner suggested by Zel'dovich. The weighing of the black-hole candidate then began. This was an arduous and complicated task. It required the gathering of huge amounts of astronomical data by roughly one-hundred-fifty astronomers using roughly twenty-five telescopes scattered around the world. The weighing required several years. But finally the answer came in: Cygnus X–1 weighs somewhere between eight and twelve times what the sun weighs—so much that it cannot be a white dwarf or a neutron star; it can only be a black hole, or something which theoretical physicists have not yet conceived of.

We have been burned before. All too often we think we have firmly understood something in outer space, and new data coming in prove us wrong. Therefore, although the case for a black hole in Cygnus X–1 looks airtight, I am not fully convinced. I would give it only 80 percent odds. The remaining 20 percent I reserve for the possibility that we are more ignorant than we believe. However, as the next few years pass and we obtain more and more observational data about this bizarre object in Cygnus X–1, we can hope for our confidence in the black-hole discovery to be firmed up.

During the past three years the search for black holes has been extended in a new direction. The holes of which I have spoken so far typically weigh several times what the sun weighs and are created by the death of a normal star. For some years theoretical astrophysicists have speculated that much heavier black holes might reside in the centers of galaxies. These holes might weigh between one-hundred-thousand and ten-billion times the sun's weight. Two years ago a graduate student at Caltech named Peter Young had an idea as to how one might search for such huge holes in centers of galaxies. His idea involved taking new television-camera-type devices and placing them on the back end of the world's largest telescopes. The telescopes would then be trained on the centers of nearby galaxies and the colors and intensities of the light would be measured in the vicinities of the very centers of the galaxies. By a very special and clever set of measurements one might be able to discern the gravitational pull of the giant black hole on stars residing near it. Peter gathered together several of his professors at Caltech and convinced them that the idea was a good one. Together they made the observations, and from their data they discerned strong evidence for a five-billion solar mass black hole in the center of a galaxy named M87. The evidence is not conclusive, but it becomes stronger with each observing season.

And what of the future? To me the most exciting prospect for the future is the attempt to watch a black hole be born. The birth of a black hole will generally occur deep in the interior of a dying star. Surrounding the newborn hole will be the outer layers of the star, which obscure the details of the birth from our view. Light cannot escape through the dense layers of stellar gas, nor can X-rays or radio waves or any other normal type of radiation. However, there is a new type of radiation predicted to exist by Einstein, a radiation which should be produced prolifically by the birth of the hole and which can penetrate with impunity through the surrounding layers of gas and dust. This is gravitational radiation, waves of gravity analogous to electromagnetic radiation. These waves of gravity can propagate from the newly created hole to Earth, where astronomers hope to detect them and use them to watch the birth of the hole.

At Caltech Professor Ronald Drever, a Scotsman, is now embarking on the development of a new kind of telescope designed to detect and measure waves of gravity. Similar efforts are being pursued elsewhere. Drever's telescope will involve massive mirrors suspended as pendula from overhead supports and separated by distances of several miles. The distances between the swinging mirrors will be measured using a laser beam bouncing off them. When a gravitational wave from a black-hole birth flies past this apparatus, it should swing the mirrors slightly closer together or farther apart. The laser beam will be used to search for such sudden swinging. It is necessary to measure the mirror separation to a precision of one one-hundredth the diameter of the nucleus of an atom—although the mirrors are separated by distances of several miles. This is a fantastic technological task; nevertheless, it looks feasible. And if it succeeds, it will give us a completely new kind of window onto the Universe!

As you can see from these remarks I am very excited not only about the past but also about the future. This, the Sesquicentennial year of Illinois College and the Centenary of Einstein's birth, is a very special time in the development of our knowledge about the distant Universe. We are rapidly gathering the new insights which will be the foundations for some of the great cultural contributions of our era.

# 7

## *The Convocation on the Humanities*
## *October 24, 1979*

The Humanities Convocation was the second in the fall series oriented to the three major curricular divisions of the College. The formal convocation included the usual academic procession and music
by the College Choir. The hymn selected by Organist-Choir Director Rick L. Erickson was chosen because it had been sung at the
dedication of Tanner Library on October 13, 1929, during the Centennial Celebration. The hymn was "Awake, My Soul, Stretch
Every Nerve," with words by Philip Doddridge sung to the tune
*Christmas*, by Handel. The proceedings followed the now customary
pattern, with remarks by the President, the address by the guest
speaker, and the awarding of honorary degrees to the speaker and to
several alumni. Once again the College community was to enjoy a
delightful combination of festivity, intellectual stimulation, and the
renewal of ties with graduates of earlier student generations.

Dr. John W. Kronik, Professor of Romance Studies at Cornell
University, was invited to address the faculty, students, and guests
who were present at the Humanities Convocation. Dr. Kronik's title
for his address was both playful and serious: "The Mouse and the
Butterfly: Space, Language, and Society in the Modern Spanish
Novel." The address had light moments adorned with urbane wit
and good humor; overall, it was a scholarly analysis of the manner
in which literature both reflects and illuminates culture and provides
the reader with insight as well as entertainment. Dr. Kronik, a native
of Vienna, was educated in the United States and was elected to Phi
Beta Kappa by his undergraduate Alma Mater, Queens College. He

earned the Ph.D. degree at Wisconsin and had taught at Hamilton College and the University of Illinois before accepting his present appointment. He is the author of a book and of numerous articles and has held both Danforth and Fulbright Fellowships. Arrangements for Dr. Kronik's visit to the campus were made by Dr. Lynette H. Seator, Professor of Modern Languages (Spanish). Dr. Seator presented Dr. Kronik when the honorary degree of Doctor of Humane Letters was conferred upon him by Dr. Mundinger.

Three alumni were also awarded the L.H.D. degree. Mr. Rainer (Ray) Lothar Broekel, a native of Germany, had enrolled in Illinois College in 1941, his studies being interrupted by a period of military service in the Pacific Theatre. Afterwards he returned to the College and, having taken some science courses along with his concentration in modern languages, he graduated in 1947. As a student he had won the Smith Prize in English, joined Gamma Nu, and played in intramural sports. Mr. Broekel's professional career began with several years as science teacher at Jacksonville's Jonathan Baldwin Turner Junior High School, which stands at the foot of the College's hill. He then was science editor and supervisor for *My Weekly Reader*, a publication with a readership numbering millions of school children. He has written and edited scores of books and hundreds of articles and short stories for children in the field of science. Mr. Broekel was presented for the honorary degree by Associate Professor Erwin C. Bleckley (Modern Languages—French).

The Reverend William Neill Malottke had graduated with the Class of 1955, majoring in English and achieving election to Phi Beta Kappa. As a student he was a member of Sigma Pi, was active in the Forum, served as student chairman of the 125th Anniversary Committee, and was student marshal. Earning both the M.A. and B.D. degrees, he was ordained to the Episcopal priesthood. Father Malottke served churches in Illinois and Michigan prior to becoming Rector of Jacksonville's Trinity Episcopal Church in 1970. He has sung major roles in both sacred and secular music and has ably assisted Illinois College at various times by teaching in the English Department and directing the Choir. The citation for Father Malottke was read by Associate Professor George William Horton, Jr.

Miss Gwendolyn Ellen Staniforth, Class of 1954, also majored in English and she also was elected to membership in Phi Beta Kappa. As an undergraduate she had won the Smith Prize in English and had edited the *Rig Veda*. Her graduate studies, which culminated in the Ph.D. degree, were completed in California, where she remained and for a time served as a researcher before accepting her first teaching appointment. She is now on the faculty of California State University at Hayward. Her teaching fields are Shakespeare, Renaissance Humanism and Drama, Poetry, and Composition, and she has done advanced research on John Donne. Dr. Carey H. Kirk, Associate Professor of English, presented Dr. Staniforth in the honorary degree ceremony.

Immediately following the convocation many persons from the College community and the Jacksonville area greeted the honored

*Tanner Hall: The Centennial Building, 1929*
Remodeled, 1977
Named for Edward Allen Tanner, President, 1882–92

guests at a reception in Schewe Library. Among them were the Malottke and Horton families, including the children who were allowed
the morning off from school.

On the evening prior to the convocation the various guests who
were to be honored had dinner at Barnes House with the Mundingers. Later in the evening Dr. Kronik joined several faculty members
in a seminar on the Spanish author and philosopher, Jose Ortega y
Gasset. Dr. Lynette Seator had done the planning and had arranged
for interested faculty to prepare for the discussion by reading some
of Ortega's works.

The faculty essay on the history of the humanities at Illinois College was prepared for the printed program by Miss Ruth E. F.
Bump, Associate Professor of English. The essay, President Mundinger's remarks, and Dr. Kronik's address, are included in this chapter. Dr. Kronik's paper has been abridged somewhat; the places at
which omissions have been made are appropriately indicated.

---

### THE HUMANITIES AT ILLINOIS COLLEGE
### MISS RUTH E. F. BUMP
### ASSOCIATE PROFESSOR OF ENGLISH

The story of language and literature at Illinois College is long and
difficult to relate and to follow. Rammelkamp's *Centennial History*
tells us that rhetoric and the ancient classics were to constitute a part
of the curriculum from the earliest times.

The modern languages and literature, including the English, per
se, did not appear in the college catalog as distinct departments until
1864–1865 when French and German were to be offered if there was
sufficient demand for either or both. Spanish did not get into the
catalog until 1919 when changing world conditions and attitudes and
educational responsibility suggested that the college was really an
integral part of the community and should, in fact, prepare students
to take their places as quickly as possible and efficiently in a world
closely knit by the new and ever-expanding inventions of the first
quarter of the nineteenth century and on.

All this is to say that Illinois College has through its entire history been aware that true learning in language and literature of whatever nation or period leads to communication and ultimately to understanding among men of "good will."

Through the years since the founding of Illinois College there have been men and women who have left a deep impression on the College and on the students who sat in their classes. One cannot name them all, and perhaps the readers of this brief sketch would name others and legitimately so, but here are just a few who are remembered: in the classics, T. M. Post, Edward Capps, H. W. Johnston, Raymond H. Lacey; in modern languages, Mary Louise Strong, Robert Busey, Leonora Tomlinson, Stella L. Cole; in English, Jonathan Baldwin Turner, John G. Ames, Charles E. Frank, Ethel Seybold.

That the humanities have played a significant role in this college is evident in recent activities of the departments concerned. One does not forget the student tours of Spain, England, and Germany, led by faculty members; equally memorable are such foreign language films as *Don Quijote de la Mancha* and the *Umbrellas of Cherbourg*. An almost yearly presentation of one of Shakespeare's plays, such as *Henry V*, has made the master playwright from Stratford live again. The German department has sponsored *Oktoberfest* and Christmas caroling.

Illinois College is fortunate to be included in the Visiting Scholar program of Phi Beta Kappa, which has brought such outstanding scholars from leading universities as Dr. Eugene Vinaver (Wisconsin), French and English; Dr. Hazel Barnes (Colorado), Philosophy and Classics; and (from Stanford) Dr. Virgil Whitaker, English Literature.

Through gifts made by Paul E. Clavey '51, the Claridge Lectureship in English was established in 1976. Earlier his gifts had made possible campus visits by men and women of letters such as Paul Engle, Leonie Adams, and Harry Mark Petrakis. Then the Claridge Lectureship brought distinguished Oxford Scholar, Jonathan Wordsworth; Howard Nemerov, Pulitzer Prize Poet for 1978; and as a fitting 150th Illinois College Anniversary Year event, Ethel Seybold, Thoreau authority and graduate from Illinois College with the Centennial Class of 1929.

All in all one observes with pride that Illinois College, indeed, has carried out its mission to provide, in the words of the Charter, for "the promotion of the general interests of education, and to qualify young men [and women] to engage in the several employments and professions of society, and to discharge honorably and usefully the various duties of life."[1]

------

### STATEMENT BY PRESIDENT MUNDINGER

Over the past two years, the 150th Anniversary Committee has worked on the observance of the Sesquicentennial of Illinois College. The jubilee events have been carefully planned. The programs are part of a sequence designed through the participation of gifted and strong-minded people.

This semester, we have planned convocations to recognize the contributions of the three college divisions and of their graduates. Today's convocation, therefore, is not a separate isolated event. The context in which this program occurs is important. In a sense, this morning's convocation was anticipated in the March, 1976, dedication of the Schewe Library. You will recall the stirring address of Dr. Martin Marty, who spoke about the importance of books in a liberal education. The Schewe Library is the centerpiece of the Sesquicentennial Plan—a plan to which many of you contributed so much.

This convocation also looks to the future. This spring, the 150th Anniversary Committee will, with the assistance of several departments, plan for the dedication of the Fine Arts Center. I see in the address this morning by Professor Kronik a bridge—a bridge that will build understanding and continuity. A bridge between and among disciplines, especially as they exist at Illinois College.

A fortnight ago the freshmen in the Interdisciplinary Studies course were asked to read a paper by President Samuel A. Banks of Dickison College. The Banks thesis is that a true higher education is a creative *unlearning* process. Our freshmen are "unlearning" some

------

1. *Charter of Illinois College*, sec. 5. Printed in Charles Henry Rammelkamp, *Illinois College: A Centennial History, 1829–1929* (New Haven: Published for Illinois College by Yale Univ. Press, 1928), p. 543.

of their past and are beginning to learn about collegiate education and some of the important elements of liberal learning.

Today, I want to stress the importance of "unlearning" some of our past. Neil Postman was a radical educator some ten years ago. His early book was *Teaching As a Subversive Activity*. He recently underwent a conversion. His new book is called *Teaching As a Conserving Activity*.

Postman points out that from the ages of five to fifteen the average American child spends approximately twenty thousand hours with television, radio, records, and movies—twice the time he spends in school. Schools are conducted in the medium of language to promote the rational, critical, coherent, and cooperative faculties. Postman points out that television, as a medium, is biased toward the emotional, discontinuous, isolated, and present-centered experience. The television program is really a miniparable—a quick fix for a complicated human experience. What's more, television is authoritarian and permits no opposition. It subverts all authority outside itself.

I am not a Luddite. I do not turn my back on progress nor do I desire to destroy technology. But, I am committed to the rational, critical, coherent, and cooperative faculties of the mind. I am committed to fostering humane values—especially the authority of learning over ignorance and of the educated over the not yet educated.

Postman urges the colleges to impart the virtues of intellectual inquiry and the vigorous and subtle use of language to what he calls the "continuity of human enterprise"[2]—the arts, science, and religion. I applaud this.

I see in the work of the Sesquicentennial Committee a commitment to a similar end. More specifically, I see in today's Humanities Convocation a speaker who has placed himself under the discipline of the rational, critical, coherent, and cooperative faculties. I look forward to his analysis of space, language, and society in the modern Spanish novel under the title "The Mouse and The Butterfly."

Ladies and Gentlemen: Dr. John W. Kronik.

2. Neil Postman, *Teaching As a Conserving Activity* (New York: Delacorte Press, 1979), p. 136.

THE MOUSE AND THE BUTTERFLY:
SPACE, LANGUAGE, AND SOCIETY IN THE MODERN
SPANISH NOVEL
DR. JOHN W. KRONIK
PROFESSOR OF ROMANCE STUDIES
CORNELL UNIVERSITY

President Mundinger, Dean Jamison, Professor Yeager, Professor Seator, distinguished guests, my friends—old and new—at Illinois College: Happy Birthday to you! This is only the second time that I have been at a 150th birthday party. The first such occasion was at Hamilton College, an institution which is just a few years older than you, where I spent the first years of my career, and where I came to know, to appreciate, and to love a small liberal arts college. My congratulations to you on your survival through good times and hard, and for bearing the burdens of your age with such grace and distinction.

A real source of pleasure for me on this visit is to be here as a representative of the humanities. Because humanity—and so the humanities—are what a place like Illinois College is all about. Of course, the world is not exactly dancing a jig around the humanities these days, and devotion to humanistic endeavor admittedly is not the quickest way to fill your pocketbook, private or institutional. But that's an old story, isn't it? The physical and biological scientists get the money; the social scientists get the power; and we humanists get all the inferiority complexes. Well, so be it: those complexes keep us from getting smug; and they stimulate us to raise our voices in order to remind our fellows that the humanities are the conscience, the soul, and the finest expression of society.

This morning I would like to tell you something, briefly and summarily, about the modern Spanish novel. Spanish, because that is my field of special interest. Briefly, because I have been threatened with mayhem if I exceed my time. But I would also like to give you a demonstration in method. I propose to show you that two types of humanists—the novelist and the literary critic—are *not* working on the other side of what really matters, that they *do* make significant statements of social import, and that they can do so without sacrificing their integrity as humanists.

Now, the study of literature these days is usually grounded on a single basic assumption: namely, that man is a function of his social and historical circumstance. In modern times, the biological sciences, behavioral psychology, and Karl Marx have teamed up to confirm that fact as an obvious truth. The creative artist, as a private individual, as a man or a woman, is subject to the same influences as anyone else, and therefore is a social creature. On the other hand, by virtue of his or her special sensitivities, the artist is entrusted with the fabrication of some of society's most treasured belongings. The literary artist, the writer, who wields society's own vehicle of communication, the word, is perhaps even more directly tied to his vital context than is the artist who expresses himself through color, shape, or sound. So, it is natural that the literary critic should feel the urge to discover the links that exist between the literary artist and society; and to do that, we have two options: we can turn to the writer, or we can turn to his art.

First, though, we should point out a fact about modern Spain. If we see a relationship between the artist and his circumstance, then we must concede that the contemporary Spanish writer has lived and survived a particularly adverse and trying circumstance. How can a writer experience a devastating Civil War and not be marked by it forever in his writings? Does it seem possible that anyone should live through the War's brutal aftermath, the four decades of Franco dictatorship, and not react? True, there were those who turned their backs on these events and escaped into fantasy or humor. But Sartre once made the point well when he said that he who chooses not to choose has made a choice. The fact is that many young Spaniards, most of those whom we read today, did make a choice. They became the repressed opposition, the enemy of the political order. Some fled into exile and dramatized their hostility through that personal act and in what they wrote abroad. Those who stayed gave vent to their inconformity in one manner or another, to one degree or another, to the extent that censorship allowed.

Mind you, we are talking about a generation here that rejected García Lorca while the rest of the world fawned on the Spanish poet.

They certainly embraced him as a symbol of victimized innocence, and they recognized his singular poetic genius. But, they asked, what's the point in carrying on about some country girl's virginity when political prisoners are rotting in jails? What's this business of the Moon and Death prancing about on stage when a whole country is demoralized, oppressed, and hungry? The serious artist that emerged after the Civil War was not only a product of his circumstance and engaged by it; he was outraged by it. In fact, his outrage was so intense that we cannot simply say: "Well, you know what artists are like; they're in a congenital state of social and existential anguish." The critical attitude is of course understandable in those who were on the side of the defeated in the Civil War or who grew up in the shadow of Franco as angry young men and women. But interestingly, the tension of intellectual resistance also reached those who were not from the start the political enemies of the regime. Also, I should stress that I am referring here to poets, playwrights, novelists, and essayists alike. I intend to isolate the novel this morning only for reasons of economy and because as a genre it is a ready mirror of society.

To pinpoint and define the tensions that have existed between modern Spanish writers and the society that spawned them, we could go, as I said, to the writers themselves. Practically all of them have written newspaper articles or essays, or they have given interviews in which they fulminate against every aspect of the Spanish scene, from God to Coca-Cola and from censorship to soccer. I for one find that option much less interesting and critically less worth while than the exercise of extracting these postures from their creative writings. D. H. Lawrence put it nicely when he said, trust not the author; trust the tale.

Heeding that advice, the literary critic who is still burdened by his sense of social obligation tends to look at a novel as a historical document. He examines its thematic content, extracts an ideology from it, and decides what the author has said. That is a useful undertaking, but I don't think that looking for the expression of history within the fiction is necessarily the richest path for the literary critic. Rather, it behooves us to keep in mind that the novel is different from a social or historical document, that it is a special sort of humanistic expression, that it builds its meaning on a unique set of structural and linguistic codes. A novel is, after all, a metaphor. Its prose speaks to us in poetic terms. If I go straight to a novel's ideas, I am forgetting the peculiar mode in which these ideas have been dressed. If I turn sociologist, I am not only usurping somebody else's trade; I am also proceeding at the expense of the object that means to be a work of art.

So, in today's flight across the modern novel in Spain, I am going to try to do the following. First, I will draw your attention to the initial group of novels written soon after the Civil War ended, and I will extract from them the dominant metaphor that appears to govern them structurally. It so happens that this structuring metaphor is a spatial one. I will give you examples of these units of space, and I will try to show you how they function. That should lead us to a statement about their significance. In other words, I believe that by zeroing in on these novels' arrangement of their fictional space, we can uncover the authors' view of their society and of society as a whole. After that, I would like to take a quick look at the manipulation of language in the novels of the past fifteen years or so. In these novels the authors have taken a direct and burning interest in the language they use. It is as if language had become an end in itself instead of a vehicle of expression. Again, we shall discover that this peculiar linguistic treatment constitutes a social statement on the artist's part. Finally, putting together this manipulation of space and of language, we should be able to draw some conclusions about the artist's view of society in Franco Spain and about his sense of existence in the mid-twentieth century. And if there is an escape for the artist who feels himself in a bind, we should be able to discover that too. (If you're wondering when my mouse and butterfly will make their entrance, you'll just have to be patient. They're waiting in the wings!)

The first thing to recall is that space in the novel is not merely an accessory element, not merely the setting or locale in which characters and action are deployed. The work's spatial construction is likely to have a metaphoric value, that is, a meaning in itself beyond its required background function. That metaphoric potential of space harks all the way back to Plato's Cave; it is so prevalent in the romantic period that a book has recently been written on the subject (I am referring to Victor Brombert's *The Romantic Prison*); and in the twentieth century it has taken on vast dimensions and become a constant of both the novel and the theater. Meursault in Camus' *The Stranger* lives out his final days in a jail cell that signals his separation from the world and from himself. Proust flees into the protective isolation of his four walls; and in Kafka space threatens, transforms, and suffocates his characters. Sartre has spoken as loudly as anyone else through the enclosures that trap and nauseate his characters, for example, in his short story appropriately titled "The Room" and in his well-known play *No Exit*. On the Latin American scene, Borges' *Labyrinths* are fun and games, but they are also a menace. And the village of Macondo in García Márquez's *One Hundred Years of Solitude* is at the same time an enclosed space and a space that encloses. Lorca's *The House of Bernarda Alba* has already become a classic illustration of enclosure dramatized. The list of works in which space, and concretely a bound space, has become the basic unit of meaning is endless.

The first serious novel to come out of Spain after the Civil War is dependent in every respect on structures of confinement. I am referring to Camilo José Cela's *The Family of Pascual Duarte*, which appeared in 1942, exactly at the same time as *The Stranger*. It consists of the memoirs of a Spanish peasant who, it would seem, has been victimized by an adverse circumstance. He has committed a series of murders, from his dog to his mother, and he is now in prison awaiting his execution. Not a pretty story.

It is evident immediately that the entire novel is generated by Pascual's cell. The cell becomes the catalyst for the act of writing and for the creation of Pascual Duarte as a literary figure. That cell space is also the novel's marker of time. It is the narrative present of a first-person story—the novel's and the character's only reality. The imprisonment and condemnation of Pascual, not for the murder of his mother, but for a crime against society, separates the individual from that society. It establishes a difference and a barrier between inside and outside. To be inside a cell is to be outside of society. But that formula does not work in reverse, because society is not the liberating outside from the vantage point of the prisoner. Society is simply another form of incarceration. The choice lies between a unique imprisonment—the cell, and a communal one—society. That is a depressing state of affairs.

On a more profound and personal level, the memoirs spawned by that sequestration signal the individual's introspective act of splitting himself. When I write in my diary, I am creating another version of me; I become the protagonist of my literary creation: voluntary schizophrenia. I remove myself into the enclosure of my inner world. Such a withdrawal can be voluntary, as it is in the case of most of the modern existentially anguished heirs of Dostoevski's underground man, or it can be imposed, as with Pascual. In either case, whether we are dealing with an exile or a self-exile, the withdrawal occasions a separation of the self-that-exists from the self-that-has-existed: that is, a painful private alienation on top of the social one.

The cell is not this novel's only metaphor of enclosure. We find several others in Pascual's narration of his past. The house in which he grew up was a miserable hovel befitting his social station. The reader cannot fail to see it as a forming and deforming structure. The village in which he lives also swallows him up in its insignificance and marginality. This village is the lowliest unit in an ever-expanding series of larger geographical sectors. It is two leagues from a slightly bigger town, which in turn is a few miles from a provincial capital, and all are situated inside the most desolate region of the country. We have a series of Japanese boxes—only in this case the boxes are Spanish: the expanding succession of enclosing boundaries ultimately points at Spain, at that time shut off from the world in its deplorable state. . . .

I said before that the critic should look closely at how the book is made. The spaces that asphyxiate the characters inside this novel by Cela find an echo in the physical structuring of the text itself. First of all, we notice that the book is so divided up between narration of memoirs and present thoughts in jail that each third of the text is the fiction of the past imprisoned in the reality of the present. The prison scenes themselves are encased in the surrounding text. On a more obvious scale, the body of Pascual's confessions is framed by a transcriber's opening and closing notes and by other texts that have disturbed some critics. In a more traditional novel this device could be shrugged off as a time-worn attempt at the illusion of historicity. Here the effect is different: we are informed that Pascual's manuscript was found in a pharmacy, neatly tied into a bundle with twine. Notice the literal enclosure of literature. On the other hand, Pascual's autobiographical narration is boxed in by the commenting frame. The written object itself, the word, has been made to suffer enclosure. The dialectics of freedom versus entrapment could not have been more effectively dramatized. . . .

I could multiply examples for you for the rest of the morning—don't worry, I won't!—and I could show you how each succeeding novel is a variation on the theme of enclosure. The figure of confinement never disappears from the postwar novel. But as we proceed through the years, we find that it does relinquish its primacy as it gives way to a new focus on language. A transitional novel dating from 1956 and named after a river near Madrid, *El Jarama*, is an impressive tour de force that purposely limits and truncates its language in order to dramatize the narrowness and insignificance of its speakers' lives. In the following decade we then witness a frontal attack on language, semantically and syntactically. The tradition of Virginia Woolf, Joyce, and Faulkner is prolonged and intensified.

When we consider this brutalization of language, we have to keep one thing in mind: when language is radicalized, so is the novel—because the novel *is* language. Let me put it to you in terms superficially borrowed from the French critic Roland Barthes. The literary text is comprised of units, each of which is a structure that signals the whole, elements of an internal code that leads to understanding. The meaning that we derive from a given segment is ultimately the meaning of the totality. We are talking, in that case, of a metaphoric process where A, the part, equals B, the whole. A particular spatial unit of the sort we talked about is such a structure with signifying importance. The linguistic unit, the word, is of course fundamental to the literary enterprise. But not only is language itself literature's technical vehicle for meaning; what is *done* to language can become the code for the apprehension of meaning. A traffic sign that is willfully mutilated or knocked down continues to bear on its face the meaning that was imprinted on it. But also, the act of violence perpetrated on the sign carries its own significance.

One of the most important novels of the period, Martín-Santos' *Time of Silence*, published in 1966, still relies heavily on the enclosing space. But the title of the novel, with its invocation of silence, adduces an absence: the absence, that is, the meaninglessness or futility of language. Man, or society, is of course responsible for the debasement of language. But the literary text, in order to engage in the constructive process of reflecting that deterioration, must itself participate as a degrading agent. What I am saying is that the text must do to language the very thing that it tells us has happened to language. Martín-Santos' favorite instrument for this purpose is parody of every imaginable linguistic code. In *Time of Silence* there is parody of exalted official rhetoric and of lower-class argot; there is abuse of the language of love and of the language of science. Every imaginable literary style, from romanticism to realism to modernism to surrealism, is laughed at. Not Cervantes, not Proust, not Joyce, nor any of their lesser colleagues, come out unscathed. The literary tradition and the act of writing are subjected to violence. In the hands of Martín-Santos and others, language becomes a lie and literature a subversion. In the end, the text that parodies language and literature rebukes its own raw material and becomes a self-parody. The novel becomes an antinovel.

Besides parody, the other option available to the novelist is an outright onslaught on language. In Martín-Santos' novel we find absurd repetitions, random lists, ludicrous juxtapositions, recondite vocabulary, sentences that run for several pages, adjectives that annihilate the noun they accompany. In the most recent novels, that ferocity directed against language has become ever more strident. . . .

The last two novels of Juan Goytisolo, *Count Julian* and *John the Landless*, which date from 1970 and 1975 respectively, carry the attack to its extreme. Probably the most radical of Spain's new novelists, the one most closely tied to the recent Latin American literary boom and to the critical circles of Paris, Goytisolo is bent on destruction—at least on the destruction that has to precede a reconstruction. The parody and the subversion of language, from typography to vocabulary to structure to meaning, are relentless. At the end of *John the Landless*, the text dissolves into gibberish and finally into Arabic script. Note the irony: a return to the language once spoken on the

Iberian peninsula is incomprehensible to the modern Spaniard. . . .
Spain has been removed from the map and deprived of its historical
existence. . . .

What do we make of all this? Every social order has its language,
and that order can be undermined only as its language is accosted.
The word is a symbol, and language is a symbolic system that signals
structures beyond it. An assault on language that ridicules it, cor-
rupts it, emasculates it by divesting it of its traditional signifying
power—that assault is an aggression against the structures that language denominates. Fractured language that loses its traditional
symbology becomes automatically discourse about discourse: that
is, it draws attention to itself. In that way, it turns into criticism:
both criticism of literature and criticism of the world that lies beyond
literature.

Thus, whether we are dealing with the metaphor of enclosure or
with the subversion of language, we find in either case a symptom
of the writer's disconformity and pain. Three decades and a half of
novelistic production in Spain have witnessed an evolution in styles,
but the anguish has endured.

So it is that man has been *shut up*. In both senses of that term. And
yet, a text remains.

Let me draw your attention to a portion of the text that Pascual
Duarte narrates from his cell: "From my window," he says, "I can
see a small garden. . . . I see a butterfly, all splashed with color,
wheeling around the sunflowers. It flutters into the cell, takes a couple of turns about, and goes out, because they've got nothing against
it. Maybe it will fly on and land on the warden's pillow. . . . I grab
my cap and catch the mouse that was nibbling away at what I'd left.
I look at it and then I let it go—I've got no charge to hold it on—
and I watch it scurry off in its mincing way to its hole where it hides,
that hole from which it comes out to eat the stranger's food, the
leftovers of a stranger who stays in the cell only a short while before
he quits the place, most often headed for hell."[3]

One can grasp quite readily that the pretty butterfly represents the
freedom that Pascual lacks, while the mouse in the hole in the prison

3. Camilo José Cela, *The Family of Pascual Duarte, Obra completa*, vol. 1 (Barcelona: Edi-
ciones Destino, 1962), p. 97. (Passage tr. by John W. Kronik.)

is the appropriate companion to his confinement. Stretching the metaphor a bit, one might see in the butterfly flights of the imagination, art and beauty; and in the mouse the gray vision of filth and stealth in contemporary society. Maybe so.

But the ultimate release from the dilemma of the artist's existence in society rests not with the butterfly, but with both the mouse and the butterfly. The very creation of the two creatures and their coexistence in metaphoric juxtaposition is an act of faith on the part of the artist. In a novelistic context, the mouse and the butterfly are equal in their constitution and function as language. If the writer cannot escape his sense of confinement, then his imaginative projection of that sentiment through the word is a solution. Perhaps even a better solution than escape. If voluntary or forced removal is an expression of alienation, the act of writing is an expression of the conquest of alienation.

By the same token, the destruction of language is brought about—can be brought about—only through language. The word that bears the brunt of the assault also serves to launch the attack. The desire to destroy through creation produces a work of art. As long as the writer writes, there is hope, for there is something to read. And there will be something to lecture about at your bicentennial celebration.

# 8

*The Convocation on the Social Sciences*
*December 5, 1979*

The third of the fall semester convocations in the Sesquicentennial series was planned to highlight the Social Science Division and to recognize distinguished alumni selected as representative of the many graduates who have majored in the departments gathered under that rather large umbrella. Certain disciplines such as philosophy and religion, which elsewhere might be included with the humanities, and psychology, which sometimes is grouped with science, have long been a part of the social sciences (earlier called the social studies) at Illinois College. Each of the College's more than twenty departments must have a home in some one of only three divisions, and because the boundaries of the other two are rather clearly demarcated, Division III encompasses a wide range of subjects. Because of the number and diversity of these departments it was decided that this Convocation should not be oriented toward a single representative discipline but should celebrate the College's role in the cause of human freedom and direct our concern to justice in the present-day world.

The early December weather was quite favorable and despite the pressures of approaching final examinations and imminent due dates for term papers, the College community participated fully in the various activities. The now-standard order was followed in the program. The students in the Concert Choir sang gloriously, presenting Handel's "Lift Up Your Heads," a portion of the *Messiah* based upon Psalm 24. The hymn chosen for the audience to sing was the "Illinois College Centennial Hymn," written a half-century before by William D. MacClintock, then acting Professor of English. (It had been sung at the Centennial Convocation on October 15, 1929, and since has been used frequently at Commencement time.) President Mundinger in his remarks made some observations about the theme of the program and introduced the speaker.

Dr. Samuel DuBois Cook, President of Dillard University in New Orleans, delivered the major address. His subject was "Human Rights, Social Justice, and the Beloved Community," a comprehensive title which brought together concerns of both historic and contemporary significance to the Illinois College community. Dr. Cook was well-qualified both personally and professionally to address the convocation audience on this theme. Awarded the Doctor's degree in political science by Ohio State University, Dr. Cook had taught in that discipline at Atlanta University and then at Duke, where he was the first Black professor. His many honors include election to Phi Beta Kappa and fellowships from the Ford and Rockefeller Foundations. He has been a member of many regional and national commissions and is a trustee of the Martin Luther King, Jr. Center for Social Change. Dr. Cook was then in his fifth year as President of Dillard University, which is a sister college of I.C. (because both are related to the United Church of Christ). In the concluding ceremonies of the convocation Dr. Cook was awarded the honorary degree of Doctor of Laws. He was presented by Dr. Laurence C. Judd, Associate Professor of Sociology.

In these same ceremonies four alumni who had majored in the social sciences were honored by their Alma Mater for their achievements. The conferring of four honorary degrees (instead of three, as at the two preceding convocations), was justified by the very large proportion of alumni who in recent decades took majors in the departments of the Social Sciences Division. Two of these alumni were chosen from academic life—one a college president, the other a college professor. The other two were selected as representatives of alumni in government and in international service.

The Reverend John Frederick Burhorn '48 had majored in history, serving as a student assistant in that department, and was elected to Phi Beta Kappa. He was president of Phi Alpha and a charter member of Pi Kappa Delta national forensics fraternity.

Earning Master's degrees in both theology and political science, the Reverend Mr. Burhorn has been a Presbyterian pastor and a professor of religion and political science. His first college administrative post was that of dean, and just recently he had assumed the presidency of the College of the Ozarks. Dr. Burhorn was presented for the L.H.D. degree by his close friend of college days, Associate Professor Richard L. Pratt '49, Librarian of Illinois College.

Dr. Julian Sturtevant Rammelkamp is doubly a son of Illinois College, having lived in Barnes House when his father was president and later enrolling as a student and graduating with the Class of 1939. His field of concentration was history and political science. He edited the *Rambler*, held office in Sigma Pi, and was chosen student marshal. Earning a Ph.D. degree at Harvard, Dr. Rammelkamp had taught history at Albion College for twenty-five years and became department chairman in 1975. He has specialized in the history of journalism and is the author of *Pulitzer's Post-Dispatch, 1878–1883*. In 1978 he was invited to give the annual Joe Patterson Smith Lecture on the I.C. campus. In his address he considered the Constitutional rights to freedom of speech and of the press and in answer to his own question, "Did the Founding Fathers Make a Mistake?" made an excellent case for the contributions the press has made for the protection and strengthening of our liberty. Associate Professor

*Schewe Library, 1976*
Named for Karl and Louise Schewe, Benefactors

Richard T. Fry presented Dr. Rammelkamp as a candidate for the Doctor of Letters degree.

Mr. Joel Wolfe Scarborough '48 had included course work in economics and French along with a concentration in history in his undergraduate course of study. He was a member of Phi Alpha. After earning the M.A. in American History and later studying Asian History, Mr. Scarborough joined the Asia Foundation and for more than twenty years has worked to develop international understanding in Thailand, East Pakistan, Pakistan, and most recently, in Afghanistan. Increasing political unrest in that nation had necessitated the recall of American personnel and he had returned to the United States the previous September (thus solving the Committee's problem of how to arrange for him to be present for the convocation). Overseas Mr. Scarborough was a leader not only in education but also in music and ornithological studies and was also an active churchman. Currently he was assigned to the San Francisco office of the Asia Foundation. Associate Professor Carole M. Ryan '59 (Modern Languages—French) presented him for the L.H.D. degree.

Born in Jacksonville and a graduate of Jacksonville High School, Mr. Paul Williams, like many of his generation, saw military service before completing college. His major field of study was economics. He participated in the Forum, Alpha Phi Omega national service fraternity, the Veterans' Club, and the Econ Club. He served Phi Alpha Literary Society both as secretary and president. Following his graduation in 1956 he completed graduate courses in management and labor relations and, after some years in Chicago's Department of Urban Renewal, he entered federal service in Washington, D.C. There he has been in the Departments of State and Housing and Urban Development and currently was Director of the Office of Management of H.U.D. Dr. Wilbur Chien, Professor of Economics, read the citation recommending Mr. Williams for the L.H.D. degree.

Most of the honored guests were present at a coffee hour and informal reception late on Tuesday afternoon, the day preceding the convocation. Department chairmen in the division had been asked to invite several upperclassmen majoring in their departments to meet and talk with Dr. and Mrs. Cook and the alumni honorees and their families. Other members of the faculty and student body were also invited. That evening the special guests and their spouses were entertained at dinner at Barnes House. Following the convocation on Wednesday morning there was the usual reception in Schewe Library.

Following are the texts of the faculty essay, written by Associate Professor Richard T. Fry for inclusion on the printed program, and the remarks by President Mundinger and the address by Dr. Cook.

---

## THE SOCIAL SCIENCES AT ILLINOIS COLLEGE
### DR. RICHARD T. FRY
#### ASSOCIATE PROFESSOR OF HISTORY AND POLITICAL SCIENCE

It is not unfitting that the social sciences should be the last to be honored in these special academic convocations marking Illinois College's Sesquicentennial year. Mathematics and the classics were considered the rudiments of liberal education when the College was founded, and the sciences and humanities have been at the conservative core of our curriculum ever since.

In the early history of the College it was not until the junior year that one was required to read "outlines of ancient and modern history," and it was only as a senior, Rammelkamp tells us, that one studied "intellectual and moral philosophy, logic, natural theology and evidences of Christianity, . . . political economy (such as it was), American law and rhetoric."[1] Instruction in such matters was for a long time the responsibility of the College president. Edward Beecher, for example, was not merely president, but "Professor of Moral, and Intellectual Philosophy, Political Economy, and History."[2] Sturtevant, who began here as a lecturer in science, became "Professor of Mental Science and Science of Government, and In-

1. Charles Henry Rammelkamp, *Illinois College: A Centennial History, 1829–1929* (New Haven: Published for Illinois College by Yale Univ. Press), p. 54.
2. *Catalogue of the Officers and Students of Illinois College, 1839–40* (Jacksonville, IL: Goudy's Job Office, 1840), n.p.

structor in Political Economy, Moral Philosophy, and Evidences of Christianity."[3]

It is not surprising that the social sciences (or really the social studies) were presented within a self-consciously moral and even theological context throughout most of the nineteenth century. One learned from the college catalog of 1888–89, for example, that "Duties to God, Reverence, Obedience, Prayer, and the observance of the Sabbath" were the first concerns of a course on practical ethics, that "God's laws—which are the thoughts of God—are the principles of history," and that "economics is the application of God's laws to the production, the distribution, the exchange and consumption of wealth." It was only with the passing of President Tanner, who in a sense was the last direct descendant of the Yale Band, that such justifications of the social sciences were dropped.

The variety of College offerings in the social sciences has remained fairly constant over the past eighty years, and some courses have been taught since the beginning. But alliance systems in the catalog have been reshaped fairly often. There was once a Department of Psychology, Ethics, and Philosophy, for example, and for a time courses in economics, political science, and sociology were taught as offerings of the History Department. Courses in pedagogy and physical training have been taught since the 1890s, but there were no majors in those fields until recent years.

Although our programs have always depended upon the interests and strengths of individual faculty members at a given time, they also reflect the influence and often heroic labors of great professors of the past. Especially notable have been the contributions of Charles Henry Rammelkamp, Joe Patterson Smith, and Ernest G. Hildner, Jr., in the Department of History, Political Science (Government), and Geography; of H. John Stratton in Economics and Business; of Eleanor O. Miller in Psychology and Education; of Frederick B. Oxtoby and Malcolm F. Stewart in Philosophy and Religion; and of Severyn T. Bruyn in Sociology. E. Joseph Brooks, chairman of the Department of Physical Education, Director of Athletics, and now

3. Ibid., *1880–81* (Printed at the *Daily Journal*, 1881), n.p.

the senior member of the faculty, began his years of service to Illinois College in 1947.

There is a long-standing commitment within the Social Sciences Division to preparing students for public service and the professions, and a growing number of practical courses and internships offer balance to courses in theory. In the last two decades our largest growth has been in psychology, sociology, teacher preparation, physical education, and especially business administration. The Joe Patterson Smith lectureship, established in 1962, brings outstanding public figures or historians to campus each year. New programs have been created in Asian Studies and Religious Studies and as Interdisciplinary majors. The social sciences have been a liberalizing element within our liberal arts program, one contributing to the ongoing responsiveness of Illinois College to the demands of its time.

---

## STATEMENT BY PRESIDENT MUNDINGER

To the east and a little to the south of Beecher Hall, near the tennis courts, there is a bronze tablet which reads: "To the loyal students of Illinois College whose 'Lovejoy Protest Meeting' held near this spot did much to create widespread sentiment against slavery. Erected by the Department of Illinois Women's Relief Corps, Auxiliary to the Grand Army of the Republic, June 5, 1933."

Edward Beecher, our first president, was a close friend of Elijah P. Lovejoy, and was with him just prior to the Alton riots. In the 1850s, Professor Jonathan Baldwin Turner was "helping runaway slaves on the Underground Railway." Professor Sanders, according to the *Illinois State Register* of Springfield, was a "freedom-shrieking tool of abolitionism." The *Register*, on April 16, 1857, called Illinois College "the fountain and hot-bed of ultra abolitionism."[4]

Illinois College was in the vanguard of human freedom. Our people were in the struggle when it meant personal vilification and danger. Blacks were welcomed and made part of the College. Not for a moment do I think that we have done enough for blacks and others in need within our society. While past wrongs, in a sense, are

---

4. Rammelkamp, *Centennial History*, pp. 200–01.

irreparable and cannot be compensated, our history has been one of helping those in need.

On Thursday, November 29, 1979, Linda Brown Smith asked the Federal District Court in Wichita, Kansas, to reopen the case of *Brown vs. The Board of Education* (1954). It has been twenty-five years since the Supreme Court struck down the separate, but equal, doctrine—thus making segregation illegal. Linda Brown Smith was the Linda Brown in the original case. She is now married and a mother, and she is suing to right the wrongs she suffered so that her daughter will not, in 1979, suffer the same injustices.

Illinois College is open to all students—men, women, blacks, and whites. We must go beyond the law; we must strive to become more open and accessible—a more open college, a more open nation.

This morning, U.S. hostages continue to be held in Teheran. Their lives are in grave danger. I compliment your wisdom and intelligence; you have treated our Iranian students with respect and understanding, which they have earned. The crimes of others must not be laid at their feet. I am proud of each of you—you have not fallen into the trap of national xenophobia and jingoism.

Our speaker this morning—President Samuel DuBois Cook of Dillard University—a distinguished educator, a colleague as president of a sister United Church of Christ college, a fellow political scientist—will speak about human freedom and the liberal arts. If there is an institution which is vital to human freedom, it is the liberal arts college—an institution dedicated to knowledge and truth in the battle against ignorance, superstition, and fear.

Ladies and Gentlemen: President Cook.

---

HUMAN RIGHTS, SOCIAL JUSTICE, AND THE BELOVED COMMUNITY
DR. SAMUEL DUBOIS COOK
PRESIDENT, DILLARD UNIVERSITY

President Mundinger, Dr. Yeager, members of the faculty, students, alumni, and friends of historic Illinois College: I am indeed delighted and honored to be with you today. You are celebrating your Sesquicentennial. You have much to celebrate and to be proud of.

Since 1829, Illinois College has stood for more than high academic standards in the classic liberal arts tradition of idealism, humanism, and rationalism. As an enlightened church-related institution of higher learning, it has also embodied the blessed union of the love of knowledge and the vision of the Kingdom of God, learning and faith, religious ideals and critical inquiry, meaning and mystery, the reach for the divine and sacred and preparation for human vocation and the market place. Perhaps even more compelling, precious, and rare, Illinois College has been a symbol and oasis of human decency, civilization, hope, and our common humanity. During much of your early and fledgling history, Illinois College was on the cutting edge of the Divine struggle for social justice, human equality and dignity, and the Beloved Community beyond race and color. You do indeed have a "Proud Heritage" and a "Promising Future."

My subject is "Human Rights, Social Justice, and the Beloved Community." My subject was dictated, in no small measure, by the logic and morality of the early history of Illinois College and its contribution to the nobility and creativity of the abolitionist movement. It is also commanded, of course, by certain existential considerations and imperatives.

In a letter of October 17 to me, Dr. Yeager informed me of the following: "In its early years Illinois College and its faculty were actively involved in the abolition movement. President Edward Beecher, Professor Jonathan Baldwin Turner, and later Professor (and then President) Julian Sturtevant were leaders in that cause in Illinois."

Dr. Yeager's concluding sentence in the paragraph is prophetic and timely. "But," he stated, "we cannot rest simply on that early proud history." How true! What happened between the early years, prior to the Civil War, and the present? Has the moral and social vision of this distinguished institution been prematurely arrested, stunted, or exhausted?

If human history teaches any lessons, one of the most significant is that the struggle for human decency, social justice, and a more humane civilization and culture is never-ending. It is never complete, never finished. Because of the perennial defects, shortcomings, and imperfections of the social order, political system, and economic structure, the challenge of the ideal is always there. The opportunity forever beckons. The moral need and urgency are always crying out for betterment, enrichment, improvement. A mark of what it means to be truly civilized and human is the sense of moral outrage at injustice and inhumanity. We are continually called upon by the ideal and by God Almighty to chase the higher possibilities of history, reach for the unattainable ideal, and "Dream the Impossible Dream."

Whatever else may be said about man, there is one thing beyond dispute, argumentation, and refutation: Man was made for the highest, the noblest, the best. Whatever his failures and shortcomings, man was made for the highest. We must be creatively restless in search of a better world. The core of the ethical consciousness is the bitter cry and the deep hunger of the heart for something better, richer, fuller, nobler, higher. We must always seek to raise the level of human civilization. God wills the betterment of the human condition.

The common element of human rights, social justice, and the beloved community of all mankind is the ancient doctrine of the intrinsic dignity, worth, and value of all of God's children beyond race, creed, class, culture, religion, ethnicity, nationality, gender, or other boundaries that separate man from man and hence man from God. For whatever separates man from man inevitably separates man from God.

The doctrine of human dignity is essential to civilization, human progress, and human decency. It is indispensable in the recognition and affirmation of our common humanity.

Whatever his station in life, background, or external credentials or symbols, each individual, person, or human personality is a center and bearer of infinite meaning, value, dignity, beauty, and significance.

Although the doctrines of human dignity and worth, of the rights of the human person, and of the nobility of personhood have been affirmed by various philosophical and religious systems in the history of ideals and ideas, I believe that its most compelling ground is the Christian faith. According to the Christian faith, human dignity and worth are rooted in the creative and redemptive love of God. Involved is the doctrine of *imago Dei*—man being created in the image of God. Thus man is a child of God; his dignity and value are bestowed by God. Man has a special and unique functional and creative relationship to God. Man was made by God and for God.

Human dignity and worth are, therefore, inviolable, indestructible, inexpugnable, irreducible, and indissoluble. The dignity and value of the human person have an island of security and stability against all the powers of darkness and forces of evil of this world. There is an ultimate value and dignity about each of us that nothing can ever destroy, diminish, or even tarnish.

Human dignity is anterior to and independent of the historical, social, and political process. It is anchored in a dimension and realm of meaning and significance beyond the space-time continuum.

My friends, one of the greatest tragedies of human history is that man is never far from barbarism, as is demonstrated by the holding of Americans as hostages in our embassy in Teheran and subjecting them to cruel, degrading, and inhuman treatment. There are other daily reminders of the frailty of civilization and the depth, power, and persistence of barbarism in modern life and culture. Worthy of special note are the rise and escalation of political terrorism, particularly in Italy, France, Turkey, Spain, West Germany, and elsewhere. Terrorism is the chief method of the Palestine Liberation Organization. Involving kidnapping, torture, fear, murder, physical mutilation; psychological, emotional, and spiritual violence; "blackmail," extortion, and other acts of human destruction and savagery—political terrorism is a deadly menace to civilization and human decency. It must not be tolerated. Terrorism is a rebellion against, and a negation of, civilization itself. Civilization is never secure. It cannot be taken for granted. Civilization is a fragile flower.

Recognition of the fragility of civilization is essential to its preservation, advancement, and enhancement. We can never take human civilization for granted. Forces are always at work seeking to destroy it; the dark forces of human nature, the demonic impulses of various groups, are always lurking and plotting against civilization. The children of darkness seem never to sleep. I do not know why, but the children of darkness always seem to be more active, more alert, and more ready and eager to do battle than the children of light.

My message to you today is that we must desperately cling to the great achievements of civilization—achievements which are the product of centuries of struggle, toil, and tears. They represent the hard-won victories of the human mind and spirit, human vision, creativity, sensitivities, wonder, and man's deepest aspirations over against their counterparts.

Foremost among the great achievements of civilization are these: the belief in the intrinsic dignity and worth of every human being—all of God's children; certain substantive and procedural rights and safeguards such as our bill of rights, the democratic process, constitutionalism, pluralism, the rule of law; the primacy and glory of reason, nonviolence and the peaceful settlement of disputes, tolerance; ideals like justice and equality; principles of international law such as the security and sanctity of embassies, diplomatic immunity, and the right of political asylum; and the ideals of civility and human decency. These ideals and achievements are indeed frail and insecure, but they are of supreme significance and meaning in the human pilgrimage—in the progress and hope of human civilization. They separate us from barbarism and animal brutality—the life of the beast. Let us cherish, nurture, defend, and support them at all cost and against all foes, whether of the right or left, the superpowers or petty tyrants, the technologically advanced or the technologically backward. Remember that the cause is man, civilization, and decency.

Man is never far from barbarism. There is always a drive, an urge or impulse in man toward barbarism. In man individually but especially in his collective relationships, there is a perennial civil war between the forces of barbarism and the forces of civilization. Under certain conditions, the collective egoism of man is completely devoid of the restraints of civilization, morality, or rationality. It represents and expresses demonic fury.

The holding of hostages in Iran wrings the heart and makes the soul cry with sickness and sadness. It is a radical violation and defamation of international law, human dignity, civilization, the beloved community, human decency, the rule of law, and the right of reason.

Ayatollah Ruhollah Khomeini has confused, perverted, and corrupted the sanctities of faith, the ambiguities of politics, the complexities of diplomacy, and the frailties of international law and morality. What makes his behavior so infinitely evil, destructive, and terrible are his radical, militant, and fanatical moral and religious perversion and corruption. He unites moralistic nationalism, religious fanaticism, and militaristic tribalism.

In the name of God and religion, Ayatollah Khomeini degrades humanity and flagrantly violates the most elementary rights of the hostages and the most basic obligations of international law and morality. In the name of God and religion, he spreads hate, illwill, tensions, violence, animosity, darkness, and poison. In the name of God and religion, he opens the floodgates of retaliation and vengeance and invites war with a martyrdom complex and apocalyptic syndrome. In the name of God and religion, he inflames the terribly destructive and uncontrollable passions of the mob which will destroy human life as an act of holiness and obedience to the will of God.

God must be sad—infinitely sad. The worst evil is that committed in the name and under the alleged authority of the good. The philosopher William Ernest Hocking stated an awesome truth when he asserted: "Religion, as the highest effort of human nature, is of all things most subject to decay and abuse. The corruption of the best is the worst."[5]

But in spite of our righteous indignation, justifiable anger, and inescapable moral outrage, Americans must respond to Iranian irresponsibility and madness with restraint, cool rationality, caution, moderation, and a heightened sense of responsibility. Our response, despite grave provocation, must be in terms of the best, not the worst, of the American tradition, ethics, and spirit. In particular, it is imperative that we avoid violating the constitutional and moral rights of Iranians in this country. After all, the American republic is informed and inspired by the ideals and presuppositions of a free and open society.

5. William Ernest Hocking, *Man and the State* (New Haven: Yale Univ. Press, 1926), p. 441.

Hate begets hate. Violence begets violence. Barbarism begets barbarism. Betrayal of human decency begets betrayal of human decency. Anti-Americanism begets antiforeignism, nativism, false patriotism, and vulgar nationalism. Incivility begets incivility. Irrationalism and fanaticism beget irrationalism and fanaticism.

Violence is indeed destructive of the creative dimensions of life and experience. As Martin Luther King, Jr., asserted: "The ultimate weakness of violence is that it is a descending spiral, begetting the very thing it seeks to destroy. Instead of diminishing evil, it multiplies it. . . . Violence merely increases hate. So it goes. Returning violence for violence multiplies violence, adding deeper darkness to a night already devoid of stars. Darkness cannot drive out darkness: only light can do that. Hate cannot drive out hate: only love can do that."[6]

In our Divine quest for a better, more humane, just, and decent world, we must appeal to the best, not the worst, of human nature and collective behavior. It is imperative that we recognize the unity and continuity of means and ends, the way and the goal. Noble, rational, moral, and excellent means are the only way of achieving noble, rational, moral, and excellent ends.

I believe that man was made for the highest, the noblest, the best: love, justice, peace, forgiveness, reconciliation, truth, goodness, decency, nonviolence, dignity, community, civilization, and beauty. I believe in the unity of the human family, the solidarity of all mankind, the brotherhood of man, the intrinsic dignity, worth, and value of all God's children.

I believe that man belongs to man. We all belong to each other—whoever we are and whatever we do. I believe that love and justice cannot be separated. I believe, with all my heart, mind, and soul in the beloved community of all humanity—white and black, Jew and Gentile, Protestant and Catholic, Oriental and Occidental, rich and poor, Hindu and Moslem.

I believe with Martin Luther King, Jr., that "injustice anywhere is a threat to justice everywhere. We are caught in an inescapable net-

6. Martin Luther King, Jr., *Where Do We Go from Here: Chaos or Community?* (Boston: Beacon Press, 1968), pp. 62–63.

work of mutuality, tied in a single garment of destiny. Whatever affects one directly, affects all indirectly."[7]

I believe with Martin Buber that "only men who are capable of truly saying *Thou* to one another can truly say *We* with one another."[8] Or again, I believe with Buber that "love is responsibility of an *I* for a *Thou*."[9]

I believe with Jesus of Nazareth that "inasmuch as ye have done *it* unto one of the least of these my brethren, ye have done *it* unto me."[10]

---

7. Martin Luther King, Jr., *Why We Can't Wait* (New York: New American Library, 1963), p. 77.

8. Martin Buber, *Between Man and Man*, Second Edition (New York: Macmillan Co., 1965), p. 176.

9. Martin Buber, *I and Thou* (New York: Charles Scribner's Sons, 1958), p. 15.

10. Matt. 25:40(AV).

# 9

## Commemoration of the First Classes, and Panel Discussion on Illinois College in the Next Decade
## February 4, 1980

This was to be the last in the series of special convocations except for the dedication of the new Fine Arts Center later on in the semester. It was appropriate near the end of the Sesquicentennial celebration to review and sum up the three-fold purpose stated by the 150th Anniversary Committee in 1977: to recall and celebrate significant events of the past, to take stock of the College in the present, and to consider the direction the College should take in beginning its fourth half-century. This convocation was planned therefore as a kind of wrapping-up session and was intended to remind the College community that the real value in looking to the past would be expressed in the wisdom and vigor with which we continued the College's purposes into the future. Arrangements were made by the Committee for a panel discussion of the prospects and plans of the College in entering upon the new decade of the eighties—and the sixteenth decade of its own existence.

The format for the day's program was simple; there was no academic procession, nor an out-of-town speaker, nor an honorary-degree ceremony. The convocation began with the singing of the *Alma Mater*, following which Dean Wallace N. Jamison gave official recognition of that fact that it had been 150 years ago that the very first classes had met on the campus in Beecher Hall. He reminded the audience that it was a very small group of students who had met with the one instructor and that they had gathered in a still-unfinished room; only a small library collection was on hand. In the ensuing decades the College was to be in jeopardy many times because of successive depressions, the impact of the Civil War and later wars, and its own internal difficulties. But the College did survive—and proudly.

The printed program included the description of that first day of classes—January 4, 1830—which had been given by President Julian M. Sturtevant in his "Historical Discourse" at the Quarter Century Celebration in 1855. This statement, similar to the better-known account printed in Rammelkamp's *Centennial History*, is not readily available and so is included here.

When the day appointed arrived, we repaired to the still unfinished edifice, then a full mile distant from Jacksonville, where we found the room which has ever since been used as a chapel, finished, lacking the desk, the lathing and plastering, and for the most part the seating. The rest of the building was in a still more unfinished condition. . . . Nine pupils presented themselves on that day. . . . The pupils were called together, a portion of Scripture was read, a few remarks were made on the magnitude of the errand which had brought us there. It was said that we were that day to open a fountain, for coming generations to drink at. Prayer was offered to Almighty God. After this, instruction was commenced.

Notes in the printed program provided information about the early students and faculty and the course of instruction.

Sturtevant himself was the only teacher for a time, and because none of his students had ever studied English grammar and only a few knew the ground rules of arithmetic, the first classes were strictly preparatory. William Kirby came in 1831 to be a tutor and in that year the first collegiate courses (Latin, Greek, and mathematics) were taught. Of the original nine pupils four graduated from the College: Charles Barton, Alvin Dixon, and James Stewart in 1836 (the second graduating class) and Rollin Mears in 1838. All four became clergymen, and three of the four were awarded master's degrees a few years later—the requirement then being the completion of three years of teaching or further study.

The room where the classes met was the lower floor of the "College Building," the south half of what is now known as Beecher Hall. The students lived in eight small rooms upstairs. The north half of Beecher was built a few months later (in 1830) to provide rooms for twenty-five more students.

A program later in the spring semester would honor the memory of the College's first two graduates; interestingly, neither of the members of the Class of 1835 was among the group who entered as preparatory students in 1830. A later chapter will describe that memorial program for Jonathan E. Spilman and Richard Yates.

Other material on the printed program included a brief essay by Dean Jamison and a list of the faculty members who have been recipients of the Harry J. Dunbaugh Distinguished Professor Award. The latter list may by found in Appendix E. Dean Jamison's statement is included here.

---

## LEADERSHIP AND THE LIBERAL ARTS
### DR. WALLACE N. JAMISON
### DEAN OF THE COLLEGE AND PROFESSOR OF HISTORY

The most important long-range task of any society is the selection and training of its future leaders. This process in large measure determines whether a society flourishes or perishes. Through most of

*Beecher Hall, 1829 and 1830*
Remodeled, 1950
Named for Edward Beecher, President, 1830–44

recorded history, the selection process was chiefly a matter of heredity: the sons of kings succeeded them; rulers were drawn from the nobility or landed gentry whose sons in turn became the next generation of leaders. The training process was often more haphazard, though in the Middle Ages the sons of leaders were educated either at court or in the great universities such as Oxford, Paris, and Bologna. There the curriculum was a form of what we now call the liberal arts.

When the American colonists of the eighteenth century decided to establish a government independent of England or Europe, they disagreed on many things, but one conviction had their whole-hearted support; there would be no hereditary nobility or monarchy over here. Leadership would be based on ability and education alone. But the training of the nation's leaders would be in colleges or universities such as obtained abroad. Illinois College was founded according to this pattern, and to a large extent follows it still. Students who came here then came not just to find jobs but to prepare for leadership roles in society. They still do. Leadership in our society is not automatic; it does not come free. Rather it is bestowed on those who have the capacity and discipline to earn it. We are an elite, an elite not of wealth or heredity, but an elite of leadership based on critical thinking, mastery of a field of knowledge, skills in communication, and moral integrity.

Thousands of alumni have earned these qualities by their study here and have moved into places of leadership throughout our state and nation. Those of us who are privileged to be part of what Arnold Toynbee liked to call the "creative minority" of society have the responsibility not just to get through our studies as painlessly as possible, but to use every means at our disposal to cultivate those special skills which will enable us to be leaders in whatever vocation we enter. The liberal arts are the age-old disciplines which prepare us for this demanding role. Not only our success but cumulatively the success of our nation will depend in large part on how well we master the humanistic studies and the natural and social sciences which are the core of our common endeavor. The liberal arts are cogent testimony that only the disciplined are truly free. And only the truly free deserve to lead.

The main feature of the convocation was a panel discussion on the subject, "Illinois College in the Next Decade." The moderator was Dr. Don P. Filson, Strawn Professor of Chemistry and the faculty marshal. The members of the panel represented the major elements of the campus: Mrs. Carole M. Ryan '59, Associate Professor of Modern Languages (French); Mr. John Mark Althoff '80, President of the Student Forum; and President Donald C. Mundinger. The statements reprinted here were prepared by the panelists and were presented in substantially this form during the first part of the discussion, although none of them was given verbatim. The summary of the questions and answers at the end was prepared from a tape recording of the discussion.

PANEL DISCUSSION:
ILLINOIS COLLEGE IN THE NEXT DECADE
PROFESSOR DON P. FILSON, MODERATOR

*Mrs. Carole M. Ryan '59*
*Associate Professor of Modern Languages (French)*

Dr. Harold Gibson's recent account of the early history of Illinois College heralds the *Yale Report of 1828*, with its defense of the classical curriculum of Yale College, as the cornerstone for this College on the prairies of Illinois. According to Dr. Gibson the *Report* stated that "the fundamental purpose of [Yale College] was to lay the foundation of a superior education rather than to train with special reference to future professional pursuits. Yale's President Day maintained the purpose of an education was to provide 'discipline and furniture of the mind'." In the oldest catalog of Illinois College, for the year 1832–33, "we find the freshmen spent most of their time studying ancient languages and some algebra. The same is true for sophomores, except the mathematics was trigonometry with some surveying provided. In the junior year still more languages with advanced courses in mathematics." In the senior year, said Dr. Gibson, "the study of languages was greatly reduced. . . . Senior courses

were listed as logic, intellectual philosophy, moral philosophy, political economy and the federal constitution."[1]

At the threshold of 1980 the Illinois College curriculum and faculty are still as strongly committed as ever to the classical ideals of
"discipline and furniture of the mind." But we are also seeking to
respond to the needs of the student of the eighties who feels greater
pressure than ever before to be career-oriented. At the heart of this
challenge of the eighties is the need to develop citizens of the world!
The importance of a global perspective in the curriculum was emphasized two weeks ago by Dr. Donald Tracey in his convocation
address on Islam in historical perspective.

Spurred by Illinois Congressman Paul Simon's study of the Hel-
sinki Agreement, President Carter formed a President's Commission
on Foreign Language and International Studies. The Commission's
report was received this past November. I am a member of the Illinois Task Force on Foreign Language and International Studies,
which issued a report in June that is already being acted upon, thanks
to the support of our Illinois State Superintendent of Education, Dr.
Joseph Cronin, and Dr. Paul Griffith, Educational Consultant in Program Planning and Development of the Illinois State Board of Education.

Both reports are explicit in recommending foreign language and
international studies, beginning at the elementary level and continuing throughout the entire educational program. There will be no
return to the language-laden curriculum of the 1830s cited in my
opening remarks, but language study will be revitalized because the
classical disciplinary content is now enhanced by the contemporary
need for a global citizenry. What is needed is such a citizenry which
can understand and appreciate other cultures and whose members
can undertake business discussions and political debates in the native
tongues of others. Illinois College in the eighties should therefore
seek an international perspective in the current curriculum. This will
involve an expansion of the already viable faculty-sponsored travel

1. Harold E. Gibson, "An Account of the Early History of IC [Illinois College]," an address
to the Morgan County Historical Society, November 8, 1979; printed in the *Jacksonville Journal
Courier*, January 27, 1980.

programs, a reenforcement of languages currently offered, and the addition of other languages such as Japanese, Russian, and Arabic.

The crucial importance of language for the business and political world leads to my second point, the relationship of the liberal arts and vocational concerns. The 1980 spring semester opened with a faculty workshop on liberal arts and vocational needs. Such a project was in part a response to a "Services Needs Inventory" which indicated that a large percentage of students wanted help with career-planning. Mr. Ed Watkins of Doane College in Nebraska emphasized that relating liberal arts to vocational interests does not mean changing the curriculum or softening the academic rigor of the classroom but rather extending its basic goals and objectives.

This decade opens with a curriculum basically the same as it was when I graduated two decades ago. However, within this basic curriculum there is renewed emphasis on quality and on extended opportunities for experience. For example, the curriculum for the Teacher Preparation Program now includes 100 hours of clinical experience prior to student teaching, yet the new degree in elementary education has stringent academic requirements. An example of the increased emphasis on quality is the addition of comprehensive examinations as part of the graduation requirements for several majors such as history and English. The internship program for political science students who work with leaders in state government is outstandingly successful. Academic credit is now being granted for work on campus publications. The Departments of Economics and Business Administration, Psychology, and Sociology now profit more fully from the community's resources, continuing to develop programs which offer field experiences for their majors. The registration in Dr. Cross's relatively new course entitled "Careers" continues to overflow. Guests from the professional world talk informally with students, and formal job interviews are simulated. Mrs. Lois Hughes finds that every available minute (beyond the demands of her position as Director of Student Financial Assistance) is filled with students seeking professional advice and guidance, that is, with career counseling.

The College has been fortunate to have the Helena Rubinstein

Grant renewed for three more years for the continuation of the Women's Collegium. The new proposal will make available programs which will prepare the liberal arts college graduate—the non-vocational student—for entry into the contemporary world and do so with regard to both personal and professional qualifications. The Collegium is now sponsoring a student-developed and student-maintained peer counseling service entitled "Planning for Career Options." The primary goal of this is to know oneself first. We are initiating World Work experiences via "mini-internship" programs with College alums and others for women and men in as many fields as possible. We continue to support programs with a strong liberal arts inspiration, such as a visit to the campus by Gwendolyn Brooks for a program sponsored by Minority Students for Cultural Advancement, and a guest scholar and a guest artist for Dr. Seator's literature course, "Fabulous Images of Women."

Illinois College in the eighties should continue to demand quality academic achievement and to expand professionally-related experiences, but it should not replace the academic with the experiential. Examples of the appropriate kind of experiences are the Collegium, the development of career counseling services provided by some faculty and administrators, and the expansion of the professional career counseling programs. These are significant measures for the eighties.

Finally, as Illinois College moves into the eighties we see still another illustration of the desirable combination of contemporary and classic elements of higher education. Illinois College's computer terminal is at capacity usage because various departments take advantage of this facility to prepare students for the technological dimension of a computerized world. At the same time the liberal arts dimension of campus facilities has been greatly expanded with the acquisition of the magnificent Holtkamp pipe organ and the addition of the McGaw Fine Arts Center. The College's commitment to quality in all academic areas is reflected in our still-new Schewe Library. With such physical equipment, the curriculum of the eighties at Illinois College will see continued endorsement of the latest technical and scientific advances; an expansion of the opportunities in the fine arts—in art, music, and drama; and a renewed support for the classic—yet contemporary—core curriculum.

The challenge to the faculty is to prepare students to be responsible world-citizens via a quality liberal arts background and the development of the necessary self-confidence to enter the world which lies beyond the baccalaureate degree and therein develop their full self-potential, both personally and professionally. Cannot we continue to provide "discipline and furniture of the mind" while responding to the changing needs of students in a changing society? Cannot we be flexible with the *body* of the liberal arts curriculum without destroying its *soul*? Can we afford not to, either as supporters of the liberal arts or as responsible citizens of the eighties?

*Mr. Jon Mark Althoff*
*President of the Student Forum*

I see the 1980s as a turning point for Illinois College and its students. Illinois College's response to the 1980s will be crucial, as well as the students' willingness to prepare.

Student attitudes have gone through a pendulum motion. The sixties were a period of societal concerns (for the environment; expressions of antimaterialism; and antiwar protests). In the seventies the pendulum swung completely opposite, to the "me" orientation. The concern was for one's personal future, one's job. In the eighties the pendulum will swing back to the middle, including concern for society *and* concern for self.

I.C.'s curriculum must prepare us for roles which embody this dual concern. Liberal education in the broadest sense must be continued. And we students must do what we can to see that it is. This is of utmost importance due to the fact that we are entering into a period when the globe is shrinking.

No longer is the United States an island which can stand alone. There is more interaction and communication, and greater need for that, than ever before. What happens in Iran or Afghanistan affects us all, even though they are on the other side of the globe.

Due to the shrinking of our world and the increasing interaction of its peoples, it is up to us students to learn:

1. The most basic ability: to understand the words and thoughts of

other peoples—which emphasizes the importance of the foreign languages at Illinois College;
2. To relate to other cultures—sociology;
3. To understand our thoughts and feelings—psychology;
4. To understand our inner selves—religion and philosophy;
5. To understand government—political science, history;
6. To understand our physical environment and improve our personal health—biology, chemistry, physics, and physical education (for our bodies as well as for our minds);
7. To become more human and deepen our understanding—art, music, speech, drama, and the literary societies; these help to humanize us;
8. To provide what we need in proper amounts—business and economics;
9. To teach all these understandings—the teacher preparation program.

No longer can we have a pure scientist or *un*cosmopolitan populace. We will need scientists with compassion and masses with sharp minds capable of separating the wheat of truth from the chaff of falsehood. We need a citizenry open-minded enough to be able to fit comfortably into the new roles and positions which will be created by the process of relating to different cultures.

These goals are what Illinois College stands for and must continue to stand for. "We will make you a better-rounded person" is a statement we often hear although the "medicine" to accomplish that may not always be pleasant. Convocations, the free chapel period, requirements for courses from different major fields, and encouragement to take nonmajor electives are all important features in achieving well-rounded personality. We as students must accept these and improve upon them.

*Knowledge or Certainty* was the title of Jacob Bronowski's film which was shown in the Interdisciplinary Studies course. It exemplified the importance of seeing things from all angles and being open to new ideas. I can remember the feeling of thinking that I had it all straight in my mind before the big Interdisciplinary Studies test. Then a chemistry major and a speech major presented their views, and mine didn't look so good any more. There are many points of view to weigh and we must always be open to the possibility that

"I may be wrong." We must be open to other views, especially as our world grows smaller and we come into contact with different ideas.

Another benefit of a small, concerned campus is that you don't have the "privilege" of becoming lost in the crowd and escape having to stand up for your ideas, as happens at a bigger or less-caring college or university. I'm wearing a "Reagan for President in 1980" button. Each day I have to defend my stance. By election day, I may not even vote for Reagan; I may bow to other people's views and ideas.

I would be remiss if I did not mention the important role of the Forum. We are in a time unlike any previous time. We must continue to provide relaxation and fun in large-enough quantities to lessen stress; in this regard the Student Activities Board has a very important function. We must continue to uphold the quality of students' expression and their right to communicate freely in the darkroom, *Forte*, the *Rambler*, the *Rig Veda*, WILC [the campus radio station], and the Hilltoppers.

It is the responsibility of us, the students, to make certain that the Sturtevant "fountain" does not run dry. Perhaps the most important function of the Forum will be the work of the Student Educational Policies Committee in its joint deliberations with the Faculty Educational Policies Committee. The upcoming period of unstable economic conditions and declining enrollments may mean compromises. We must see to it that Illinois College does not forfeit its destined objective of providing a truly broad liberal arts education, with uncompromised academic and admission standards. We students must keep the College honest. Our current ACT scores of newly admitted students are growing steadily higher. Our curriculum is expanding and our liberal arts commitment is deepening. These things must not be compromised.

---

*President Donald C. Mundinger*

In idle moments during the Sesquicentennial Year, I have often wondered what Sturtevant—the first teacher at Illinois College—would say about the Illinois College of 1980.

Sturtevant would say a number of things, I think. The purpose of the founders has been translated into a contemporary idiom. Today's interest in higher learning and humane values as preparation for life and work is as strong as in the early days of our College. He would be pleased—very pleased—with the College, especially with the faculty, that is, preparation, teaching ability, and commitment.

Sturtevant would say the same about the students—bright, teachable, and enthusiastic. And, as he compared the physical campus of today with the primitive conditions of the frontier, he would be pleased with the beauty, ambience, and utility of our buildings. In brief, I believe he would say "well done" to his successors.

Sturtevant would make a second series of judgments. He would, I think, take serious notice of the problems we face in the 1980s and he would also emphasize the opportunities inherent in our future.

The problems are present. The problems are serious and will certainly change the character and life of the College. Inflation is the most devilish problem. A highly industrialized society cannot long tolerate a 13.3% annual rate of inflation. The fabric of the social democracy begins to rot and incentives wither. But this is what we have had and what we face in the future—especially in the cost of energy. Inflation is causing the College—faculty and students—to suffer.

The decline in student enrollment is a second major problem, one which most independent colleges have suffered this past decade. Most of us are smaller now than we were in 1970. In relative terms the decline is also sharp. After World War II, private colleges educated about 65 percent of university students and now it is barely 20 percent. The irony is that inflation leverages and exaggerates the problem of declining enrollment because it is at public universities where students find a haven from inflation.

The number and complexity of government controls is a third problem. The invidious thing is that they compound cost and thus fuel inflation. Colleges, in plain language, use money which should go into teaching (people, offices, and materials) to keep records and make reports. While important social goals are served, expenses mount—and who is to pay? The students, of course.

Finally, in the coming decade we face the challenge of maintaining the liberal arts. A decade ago this problem did not seem to exist, for that was a time when there was a shortage of workers and industry would take, and eagerly, graduates from all institutions. The calculus of competition has changed dramatically—now industry picks and chooses and demands narrow technological skills to fuel the energies of industry and pays such graduates well. The arts and science people must settle for what President Bok of Harvard calls more modest expectations.

We must find the way to educate for productive and responsible adult life. But, thinking with power, understanding with discernment, and caring for humans with compassion and love must grow in a parallel development with the preparation of work skills.

It is this decade—the sixteenth decade—which I find so exciting. The elements are present and in abundance for this College to do a better job in 1990 than in 1980.

Our most precious possession is our integrity of purpose. There is an enthusiasm—a spirit—which marks the College. Good people— men and women, students and professors—are working and improving the College so that the education we provide does, indeed, liberate—freeing men and women through education to become courageous, to soar with the angels, and to be free from the crippling power of ignorance, superstition, and fear.

The College is strong as it begins its sixteenth decade. The new McGaw Fine Arts Center will give our people the place, the tools, and the power to strengthen the arts. The visual arts will have the equipment to provide fuller offerings in the practice, history, and theory of art. Introductory work in television will take our students into a medium which has helped shape our world into a community. Music will be served with areas for instruction, practice, and teaching. Finally, the Sibert Theatre helps us understand the wisdom of an art form which predates the Greeks—all designed to contribute strength to an existing program, and to make us demonstrably stronger. As the decade unfolds, the College must define its program to do theory, history, and values and also to help its graduates live a full life including productive work in scholarship, industry, and the professions. This development will continue to require our energy as we strive to become a stronger college. Now, as we come together—to learn and to work—our strengths in mission, people, and facilities prepare us well for the opportunities that lie ahead. Paul Tillich introduced me to the importance of the word *enthusiasm*, meaning the God within. As Illinois College begins its sixteenth decade, may the power of that idea intensify in us the will to move Illinois College to a new level of achievement and an ever-widening circle of recognition.

---

*Summary of Questions from the Audience and*
*Responses by the Panel*

Professor Filson had announced previously that there would be an opportunity for the audience to participate in the discussion after the presentations by the panel members. He had invited students to submit written questions and comments and the ushers collected these at the conclusion of President Mundinger's statement. While the questions were being brought to the platform Dr. Filson made some comments. He spoke enthusiastically about the fine pipe organ in the chancel behind the panelists, and he praised the College's increased commitment to the fine arts which the organ and the McGaw Center represented. Professor Ryan, speaking as an alumna, also endorsed the addition of courses in art and music, noting favorably the considerable expansion of these departments since her own student days.

The first question read by the moderator was an inquiry about Jones Memorial Hall: Why can't the building be repaired and maintained for continuing use? President Mundinger responded by summarizing the Sesquicentennial Plan of 1971–72 when all elements of the College were invited to comment on the College's future development and to recommend specific plans. He noted that all the major new facilities which were proposed in that plan were now complete or well underway: the new library, the remodeling of Tanner, the completion of the gymnasium, and the construction of a fine arts center. The trustees had decided in the earlier years to raze Jones Hall, when the new facilities were ready for use, because of the high cost of rehabilitating the building and maintaining and heating it; that decision had been reviewed periodically—and each time, it had been reaffirmed.

The second questioner asked if there would be a return to "the days of Sturtevant" when prayer and scripture reading were a part of the required program of the College. Dr. Filson suggested that in discussing this subject the panelists might wish to include reference to the broader topic of the College as a church-related institution. In his comments President Mundinger declared that he would oppose any plan to restore compulsory chapel. He affirmed his own commitment to the principle of Christian liberty whereby each person is free to follow the dictates of his own conscience in fostering his own spiritual growth. The thrust of the College, he remarked, derives from the Presbyterian and the United Church of Christ—Congregational—churches and their tenets should continue to inform our work. Mr. Althoff stated his agreement with the President's views and reported accounts he had heard of the student protests in the seventies; he added that he believed these were directed primarily against the compulsory aspect of chapel and were not a rejection of the importance of worship. Mrs. Ryan said that the Christian aspect of the College does not require formal prayer by the whole community but is expressed in the environment of the campus—especially in the respect which faculty and students show to each other.

Jon Althoff replied to a question about the prospective role of the literary societies. Stating that he himself was not in a society, he acknowledged that such membership is very important to a great many students and predicted that the societies will remain strong. He spoke of the close friendships which develop among members and said that the communication skills fostered by the societies in their programs will be of increasing importance in a world which continually grows smaller.

All the panelists discussed the final topic, the subject of several of the questions from the audience: the Interdisciplinary Studies course. Mrs. Ryan noted that the course (which had been adopted in 1970 and was required of all freshmen) was on the agenda for the faculty's monthly meeting scheduled for later that day. She explained that the faculty had been carefully reviewing the program and had sought information from students regarding their views. President Mundinger remarked that the real issue is "general education" and declared that the College must not abandon its essential purpose of providing liberal education for all its students. Such education will be more important in 1990 than it was even in 1970. Whether they are accomplished through the present course or in other courses, the development of critical thinking and participation in a broad cultural range of reading are essential elements in liberal learning. Mr. Althoff spoke very favorably regarding the Interdisciplinary Studies course, stating that it had provided one of the few opportunities for serious discussion of basic ideas with students and faculty from a variety of fields. Through the course he had been introduced to new ideas and as a result of hearing various faculty members lecture in the program he had revised his subsequent course schedule to take classes from them. He too emphasized the importance of that kind of course, whatever name it may have.

At this point in the discussion the moderator announced that the allotted time had come to an end and that the meeting would be adjourned. In closing, he invited those students whose questions had not been discussed to come forward to speak to members of the panel.

The panel members had presented a lively discussion; dealt with basic issues of curriculum, facilities, and finances; and recognized both opportunities and difficulties in the years ahead. Important questions came from the audience and were discussed with candor. Both the content of the discussion and the general spirit of the day gave good reason for optimism about the College's prospects for successfully meeting the issues of the coming decade and beyond.

# IO

# The Dedication of The McGaw Fine Arts Center: The Sesquicentennial Building April 30, 1980

The convocation for dedicating the McGaw Fine Arts Center marked the culmination of years of dreaming and planning and fund raising, and as a consequence this was an especially joyous occasion. The schedule for this event was necessarily more complex than for the other convocations because the main part of the program was held in Rammelkamp Chapel and then the participants and audience moved to McGaw for the final ceremonies.

At 10:00 A.M. on Wednesday, April 30, 1980, the faculty and platform party began the processional down the aisle of Rammelkamp Chapel. When all had taken their places, Dean Wallace N. Jamison welcomed the assembled students and guests, and Chaplain John N. Langfitt read Psalm 145 and offered the prayer of praise. The College Choir, directed by Mr. Rick L. Erickson, sang the anthem, "Christ Is Made the Sure Foundation."

President Mundinger then introduced the speaker, Mr. Croft Hangartner, Vice President, Mobil Chemical Company and General Manager, Plastics Division, Macedon, New York. Mr. Hangartner addressed the audience on the subject, "Challenges and Opportunities in the Eighties." A prominent theme in his remarks was the important contribution of businesses, such as the firm he represented, to the support of the performing arts. Mobil Chemical Company has contributed generously to various projects in this field nationally and in the Jacksonville community. Mr. Hangartner's address is printed in the latter part of this chapter.

The honorary degree of Doctor of Humane Letters was conferred by President Mundinger upon Mr. Hangartner and two other special guests, President John Edward Horner of Hanover College in Indiana and Dr. Donald Elmer Polzin '51, Professor of Theatre Arts at Northern Illinois University, DeKalb. Mr. Hangartner had earned the bachelor's degree in marketing from the University of Washington and began his business career in sales and marketing. Joining Mobil Chemical Company in 1958, he was appointed to his present position in 1976. He has been an active member of various trade organizations and is a member of the Board of Directors of the Rochester Industrial Management Council. Associate Professor Raymond Ford (Speech and Debate) presented Mr. Hangartner.

Dr. John Edward Horner became President of Hanover College in 1958. He is an honor graduate of Drew University, where he was named Honorable Mention All-American in basketball. His academic field is the classics and he earned the M.A. degree from Columbia University and the Ph.D. from Ohio State University. He has taught Latin and English and was a Fulbright Teacher-Scholar in Europe. Under his leadership Hanover College has achieved a high reputation for excellence. President Horner has been prominent in state and national organizations in higher education and has been outstanding as a leader among the Presbyterian colleges. Dr. John N. Langfitt, Associate Professor of Religion and Chaplain of the College, read the citation for President Horner.

Miss Geraldine Staley, Associate Professor of Speech and Director of Drama, presented Dr. Donald Elmer Polzin '51 as a candidate for the honorary L.H.D. degree. As an undergraduate at Illinois College, Dr. Polzin had majored in speech and drama and was active in the Hilltop Players, with several leading roles to his credit. He was on the varsity debate team, worked on the *Rambler*, directed the Radio Forum, joined Phi Alpha, and played on the intramural athletic teams. He was elected to Phi Beta Kappa. His M.A. degree is from the University of Illinois and his Ph.D. degree from the University of Iowa. Dr. Polzin was a member of the I.C. faculty for two years in the middle fifties and has been at Northern since 1962.

Following the conferring of degrees, President Mundinger made the official statement of dedication for the McGaw Fine Arts Center. Responses were given by three representatives of the College community: Mr. Bradley Bartholomew '81, president of the Student Forum; Professor Iver F. Yeager; and Mr. William N. Clark '40, chairman of the Board of Trustees. Dr. Mundinger's statement and the three responses are included in this chapter.

President Mundinger and the platform party, followed by the faculty and then by the audience, proceeded to the main entrance of the McGaw Fine Arts Center on the west side of the campus. There was appropriate music to accompany the processional. While the people were leaving Rammelkamp, Mr. Erickson played Bach's "Fugue in C Minor" on the Hart Sesquicentennial Pipe Organ; while they were walking across the center of the campus the chimes of the Ruth Leach Robinson Memorial Carillon sounded Bach's "Minuet, March, and Minuet." As the people gathered at the main entrance to McGaw, the Illinois College Band, directed by Mr. Leslie E. Fonza, played "The Sinfonians" by Clifton Williams.

The prayer of dedication for the new Sesquicentennial Building was given by Chaplain Langfitt. The key to the building was then presented to President Mundinger by Mr. Eric W. Smith, Jr., whose architectural firm had designed and supervised the construction of McGaw Center. The audience, led by the Choir, sang the Illinois

*McGaw Fine Arts Center, 1980*
Named for Foster G. and Mary W. McGaw, Benefactors
*With the Sibert Theatre*
Named for L. D. Sibert and Robert F. Sibert '36 and Family
*And the Blum Music Wing*
Named for Fred Blum '18 and Alma Blum

College *Alma Mater*. Dr. Mundinger officially opened the building and invited all present to enter.

The faculty and students of the various Departments now housed in the new building—Art, Music, and Speech and Drama—served as hosts and tour guides. The McGaw Fine Arts Center is a very handsome and very useful facility, and the large group attending the ceremonies enjoyed exploring every aspect of the structure. The architects had succeeded well in satisfying the "two masters: Form and Function," as Mr. Smith had earlier described their task. "The design must satisfy the user's needs, it must truly reflect the technology of our times, and it must sit comfortably amid its surroundings."[1] The achievement of these objectives was not a simple matter. McGaw is unique in being a unified building housing the major performing arts in a single structure; the usual approach is to have separate buildings, perhaps connected by a central atrium. The unified form was deemed most suitable for the needs of the College and also for expressing the unity of the arts in the College's curriculum. An additional advantage is the efficiency gained in heating and cooling a square building. The location of the building, on the northwest corner of the campus, serves to fill out the campus and also places the Sesquicentennial Building—the College's newest facility, very close to Beecher Hall—the original "College Building," as it was known in the early days.

The center of the structure houses the beautiful Sibert Theatre, named for Mr. L. D. Sibert and the Robert F. Sibert family, whose contribution of half a million dollars has provided an endowment for the support of the Center and its programs. The theater's continental seating accommodates 250 persons in comfort and allows ample room between rows for people to reach their seats. The large thrust stage is fully-equipped and has electronic and hydraulic controls; the lighting system features the latest state of the art in equipment and the control board. Dressing rooms, a scene shop, and storage areas are near by.

The Blum Music Wing is named in honor of Mr. Fred Blum '18 and his wife, Alma, whose benefactions have provided individual

1. Eric W. Smith, Jr., quoted in "Illinois College 150th Anniversary Challenge," no. 3, October, 1978, pp. 2–3.

practice rooms, studios for faculty, and a large, high-ceilinged practice room for the Band and the Choir. This room is sound proofed so effectively that rehearsals can be held simultaneously in it and in the adjacent Sibert Theatre. The facilities for music are in the southeast and east parts of the building.

The Art Department occupies much of the south and southwest areas of the McGaw Fine Arts Center. There is a huge studio with natural and variably controlled artificial lighting, a darkroom, a kiln room, and facilities for printmaking. Provisions have been made in the main lobby for exhibiting works of art.

The quarters for the Speech Department include a classroom and adjacent control room for basic instruction in television. Also provided are extensive shelves for the large collection of debate trophies which the College's forensic teams have accumulated over many decades. A ticket office, cloak room, and snack bar for public functions all open onto the lobby. A large multipurpose classroom is located in the northwest corner of the building. Offices for the faculty members of these various departments are located conveniently.

The people whose gift of one million dollars made it possible to construct this superb facility are Mary W. and Foster G. McGaw of Evanston, Illinois, and the building has been named in their honor. The McGaws are devout Christians and staunch friends of higher education. Fortunately for Illinois College in its Sesquicentennial advancement the McGaws have chosen to distribute their wealth during their lifetimes. Mr. McGaw was for many years the chief executive officer of The American Hospital Supply Corporation and currently is chairman of the board. It was the McGaws' generosity which stimulated the plans and campaign to raise the additional funds which have provided not only the Sesquicentennial Building but many other improvements in the fine arts and in other aspects of the College's plant and program. The McGaws had come to know about Illinois College through the work of Mr. William N. Clark '40, chairman of the Board of Trustees of Illinois College and for many years Financial Editor of the *Chicago Tribune* before accepting his present position with the Robert R. McCormick Charitable Trust.

The printed program for the dedication ceremonies included a

statement acknowledging the significant contributions of the Mc-
Gaws, Siberts, and Blums, the Kresge Foundation, and others
whose generosity has provided so much support for the College.
Appreciation was expressed also to the architectural firm of Smith
and Entzeroth of St. Louis and to the general contractors, Neff-Col-
vin, Inc., of Jacksonville.

Other items of interest in the printed program were the biographical sketches of the honorary degree candidates and Professor Charles
E. Frank's essay on the history of the performing arts at Illinois College. An insert in the program listed the established scholarships,
prizes, and awards for student achievement in the performing arts.
The first such awards had been made in the 1850s when Professor
William D. Sanders organized contests in oratory; his name has since
been given to these awards which are still presented each year. The
Thomas Smith Prizes in Speech and the H. H. Hall Prize in Oratory
were established in 1871. Various awards for excellence in debate
were first given in the 1920s and 1930s. Awards in other areas of the
performing arts are of more recent origin. The Mary C. Stetson
Scholarship has been granted annually since 1965 for outstanding
participation in music activities. Friends of Dennis J. Ryan '67 established, in 1969, a Memorial Drama Award in his name to be given
for the single outstanding performance in theater. The Elizabeth
Caine Art Award was provided in 1973 by friends of Mrs. Caine at
the time of President L. Vernon Caine's retirement from the College;
it is presented to the student showing the most artistic accomplishment and promise. The 1979 recipients of these and other awards in
the arts, as well as all other awards and scholarships given by the
College that year, are listed in Appendix F. The history of the awards
in public speaking and the history of the teaching of speech at Illinois
College have been recounted by Dean Doris B. Hopper in an unpublished monograph, "The Speech Department at Illinois College,
1829–1971."[2]

The following pages contain the texts of Professor Frank's essay,

2. A typewritten copy of research material prepared by Dean Doris B. Hopper has been
placed in the Illinois College Library. The material was compiled by Dean Hopper for use in
writing a master's thesis at Western Illinois University.

the address by Mr. Hangartner, the dedication statement by President Mundinger, and the responses by Mr. Bartholomew, Professor Yeager, and Mr. Clark.

---

## THE PERFORMING ARTS AT ILLINOIS COLLEGE
### DR. CHARLES E. FRANK
### A. BOYD PIXLEY PROFESSOR EMERITUS OF THE HUMANITIES

In 1829 when Illinois College was founded, we Americans did not regard the performing arts as academic disciplines, and it would be many years before we did. On this frontier campus, the first performing arts to develop were the forensic arts; at the beginning they were extracurricular. Debate and oratory were important features of the meetings of Sigma Pi and Phi Alpha in the 1840s. When intercollegiate forensic contests came into being, Illinois College was among the first to compete successfully, with entrants like Richard Yates and William Jennings Bryan. Down to the present day, our debaters have represented Illinois College proudly and with great honor.

Music and art became a part of the program much later, as a result of the 1903 merger of Illinois College with the Jacksonville Female Academy and the Illinois Conservatory of Music. For a quarter of a century after the merger, many courses in music were listed in our catalogs. The program was offered at Academy Hall by a large professional staff under the direction of such artists as William E. Kritch and Edmund Munger. Courses in theory, voice, instrumental music, piano, and organ were given; available to students were two pipe organs, two concert grand pianos, and numerous practice rooms appropriately equipped. The Conservatory was said to be one of the best music schools in the Midwest. However, in 1928 the Illinois Conservatory merged with the College of Music of what is now MacMurray College, so that there would not be two competing schools of music in Jacksonville. Illinois College students continued to take courses at the Conservatory, but the number diminished and interest in music on this campus necessarily declined.

Nonetheless, throughout all this period, our students performed in bands and orchestras, choruses and glee clubs, which gave musical experience to a large number of men and women and listening pleasure to an even larger number. Also during this period, courses in music appreciation and in theory were offered on campus by such fine teachers as Hugh Beggs and Ruth Melville Bellatti. Thus the musical tradition was kept alive at Illinois College. The recent acoustical reconstruction of Rammelkamp Chapel, the acquisition of the Hart Harpsichord and the Class of 1977 Steinway, and the installation of the Hart Sesquicentennial Pipe Organ have given new impetus to musical performance on campus. Now, the dedication of the McGaw Fine Arts Center marks the acceleration of a musical renaissance.

The McGaw Center will not only provide for musical training and performance, but it will give a new, improved setting for the other arts. As was noted above, art became a part of the Illinois College curriculum along with music as a result of the 1903 merger, but it had an even harder struggle for survival; it was usually tucked away in some remote corner of the campus, and more than once it seemed to have winked out altogether. However, after World War II, a mutually happy agreeement was made with the Art Association of Jacksonville, and a series of able and enthusiastic artists taught at Illinois College and directed the activities of the Strawn Gallery. Now, with a splendid permanent home and equipment at McGaw, art too should take on new life on our campus.

A performing theater came into existence with the organization of the Dramatic Club in 1912. Professor John Griffith Ames was the "onlie begetter" of this club and for many years he was its principal director, presenting a series of Shakespeare plays at Commencement. Over the years, the successors to the Dramatic Club, the Hilltop Players, have provided Illinois College with first-rate theater, often under difficult conditions. The new theater in McGaw will provide the Hilltoppers with superior facilities and give drama a great boost.

Now all the arts will be invigorated. Increased emphasis on them will benefit not only those who perform but all those who participate as hearers and viewers. It is fitting that art and music, drama and forensics, should dwell together here and that they should be so

magnificently accommodated as they are in the McGaw Fine Arts
Center.

---

## CHALLENGES AND OPPORTUNITIES IN THE EIGHTIES
### MR. CROFT K. HANGARTNER
### VICE PRESIDENT AND GENERAL MANAGER
### PLASTICS DIVISION
### MOBIL CHEMICAL COMPANY

President Mundinger; students, faculty, and trustees of Illinois
College; Distinguished Guests:

I am pleased to have been invited to take part in the dedication of
this magnificent new Fine Arts Center and to share with you this
occasion of community pride and pleasure. We are here to dedicate
your new Fine Arts Center. It is a handsome addition to the buildings that grace your campus. For my part, in these next few minutes,
I would like to discuss what this new structure stands for in the life
of Illinois College and address some basic challenges which I believe
will confront us in the eighties.

First and foremost, I think that your new Fine Arts Center sym-
bolizes continuity of public service through academic excellence.
That has been a tradition here for 150 years—but tradition is not self-
perpetuating. To continue to be valid and useful as an institution it
is necessary to anticipate and respond to changes in the social environment. With this new Center, and the educational emphasis it implies, it seems to me that Illinois College is embarked on a course of
healthy self-renewal and fruitful growth—a course that is most appropriate for society's present and emerging needs and aspirations.

In the eighties, it is legitimate to ask: what sort of education is
required to prepare tomorrow's leaders in government, industry, and
other institutions to manage the problems that defy our best attempts at resolution? My suggestion is that there must be a renewed
commitment to the kind of undergraduate education that provides a
firmer basis and also serves as a bonding agent among the specialized
disciplines that are needed to make our society work. Support for
this thesis seems to be gaining ground among the leaders of our
more thoughtful business corporations: recognition that it may be

an advantage to hire people with a broad general education and have the corporations themselves supply the specialized training. This means, I think, that business corporations will need people who can command a broader range of skills, especially the ability to solve problems and to communicate effectively.

To those qualities I would add an appreciation for art and culture. The fine arts element in a liberal arts education might be termed the commanding height of excellence in such a curriculum. The fine arts can serve as a stimulant in society. Great music, art, sculpture can serve to ignite our imaginations—to serve as a vital spark for creative and original approaches to the issues of our lives and times. That, I think, is the symbolic meaning of this act of faith and insight, of the physical edifice we are here to dedicate today.

Today American businesses have become major patrons of the arts. Within the past fifteen years, support for cultural endeavors of all kinds, by private enterprise, has risen from roughly $20 million to over $250 million. Even with inflation and possible recession—factors which tend to cut back on the support the arts receive from the traditional sources—there seems to be no significant fall-off in corporate giving to the arts. This is a major change in the perspective of American business. It has been made possible by the strength of our private enterprise system. The preservation of that system is one of the two major challenges that face both business and education in the eighties. The other major challenge facing both business and education is the ever-growing burden of government regulation.

Preservation of the free enterprise system through the encouragement of risk-taking is the most fundamental goal I see as essential to preserving and promoting the quality of life we have become accustomed to enjoying. People, business, and government today, young and old, threaten or impede the free-enterprise system by their shifting social values and expectations. Simply stated, people too frequently expect things that no system can deliver. The respect of past generations for temperance, thrift, and hard work, is daily challenged by the seeming virtues of consumption and leisure. Likewise many businesses seek growth without creativity and profit without risk. These expectations are also unrealistic. As someone noted recently, "Until a product or service is sold, nothing happens. No

wages are paid; no taxes are paid. A household can't function, neither can a government. The clock stops. So does America."[3]

The seventies saw a significantly greater degree of direct government involvement than ever before in individual markets and the
decisions of entrepreneurs and institutions. Government now preempts
private decision-making in a large sector of the economy. The vast
expansion of regulations related to health, safety, pensions, the environment, standards of employment, and the regulation of wages
and working conditions are of a magnitude far beyond previous experience.

There are at least two features of this new government involvement in our lives that deserve attention. First, many new political
and legal centers of decision-making, uncoordinated by market or a
central political force, have created vast uncertainties for the private
sector. Second, government regulation introduces a short-term perspective. Political considerations change frequently. Government
policy officials have short tenure relative to the changes their regulations impose. In addition, conflicting views of the national interest
are often involved. The notion that government can be a single or
coordinated decision-maker defies reality, at least in this country.

The challenge and the opportunity in all this is to find a way to
work with the government to make it more efficient. We must seek
to inform the government so as to moderate oppressive regulation.
Government, I believe, has reached or exceeded the limits of what
can be accomplished by direction in the arena of economic policy.
What is needed now, and in the coming decade, is consensus building. To accomplish this involves the participation and de facto acceptance by major interest groups (including businesses) large and
small, labor, and other affected elements. The skill of consensus
building is potentially more significant to success in the eighties than
analytical expertise. Unfortunately, it is a scarcer talent.

The point of calling attention to the cost, skills, timeliness, appropriateness or lack thereof, of government's role in business is not a
plea necessarily for less government; rather it is a statement of the
background and the challenge facing us today. Business's successful

3. Advertisement by the Wheelabrater-Frye Company, *Wall Street Journal*, April 18, 1980.

handling of the governmental challenge is, in my mind, best handled by developing a consensus approach and eliminating the adversarial approach. Simply stated, business and government need to move from an adversary relationship to one in which they are coparticipants in meeting the challenge of preserving the free enterprise system.

And how shall we prepare to handle the challenges and opportunities of the eighties? Preservation of free enterprise; cooperative efforts between business and government; consensual problem solving. It is not a training job; it is an educational process. That is why business will continue to support higher education and specifically, education in the broader sense.

The company I represent is, of course, a major supporter of the arts. The cultural activity with which Mobil seems to be most closely identified is our support of public broadcasting—particularly Masterpiece Theatre. In fact, we are one of the largest corporate supporters of public television, a commitment we first undertook ten years ago. Although public television represents the prime thrust of our cultural efforts, we have also sought to be identified with quality programming on commercial television.

The effort on a national level is complemented by programs that Mobil Foundation conducts with our field locations around this country. In Jacksonville, as many of you know, this has resulted in grants for the Art Association, the Symphony Society, the Children's Summer Theatre, and the Jacksonville-MacMurray Music Association, as well as for underwriting concerts here at Illinois College last year. If you consider that similar grants are being made in some sixty communities across the United States by Mobil alone—and that dozens of other companies are equally supportive of local arts and cultural organizations—then I think you will agree that business is a potent force for strengthening art and culture at the community level.

Now, in sketching what the Mobil organization does in support of art and cultural activities, I don't want to leave the impression that we are moved solely by lofty altruism. In fact, our motivations go beyond altruism and are based on what we feel must be the proper role of business in our society. As a private business we enjoy no divine right of existence. We exist *within* a society and our very right to exist stems from our value and usefulness to that society. To the extent that we are able to enrich our society and preserve and enhance the best of its values, we help create a better environment for business and our economic system.

This point of view is not confined to Mobil alone. Recently, the chairman of DuPont, Mr. Irving Shapiro, said: "There is not much point in being a businessman if you're not going to accomplish something that benefits society."[4] We in Mobil know what our business role is. Mobil is a major multinational corporation, engaged in the energy business (not only oil and gas, but coal, uranium, and solar energy). We are also a major chemical company, producing consumer, industrial, and agricultural chemicals. We are also in the packaging business, retail business, and land development business. As for our role in society, we are convinced it is our duty as a business to encourage and support the arts and higher education.

Mobil's Chairman, Rawleigh Warner, Jr., recently spoke of the close link, the interrelationship, that exists between our business as a participant in the free enterprise system and our support for higher education and cultural programs. He said: "We believe that Mobil's outspoken support of the American system of democratic capitalism is compatible with our support of higher education and cultural programs. I am convinced that if our economic system is destroyed or fatally weakened by the relatively small numbers of highly articulate elitists who seem bent on doing just that, whether from ignorance or for whatever reason, then our democratic society and our cultural institutions—including higher education—will be imperiled."[5]

Again, I thank you for inviting me to speak on this happy occasion.

---

THE DEDICATION CEREMONIES
STATEMENT OF DEDICATION, BY
PRESIDENT MUNDINGER

The history of the fine arts at Illinois College has had its high and not so high moments. The College has been blessed with some

4. Quoted in *Time*, April 14, 1980, p. 87.

5. Address at Columbia University, April 26, 1978. (Source reported by Mobil Chemical Company officials.)

gifted teachers and students who have done important work in the fine arts—music, drama, and the visual arts. These people suffered the limitations of a lack of facilities and resources.

The College, as college, has recognized the importance of the fine arts to liberal learning. If it is our goal, and it is, to cultivate basic intellectual skills, critical thought, and informed understanding, then the people we touch should indeed be both free and humane citizens. It is imperative that our students not only read Conrad but also learn to "read" Bach, Ibsen, and Michelangelo. I might add, parenthetically—and also understand and appreciate the wizardry of modern electronics and technology in the fine arts.

With the McGaw Fine Arts Center, friends of Illinois College, trustees, faculty, and students now have the opportunity to work in a more comprehensive and more challenging program in the liberal arts. The opportunity—no, the challenge and the responsibility—to excel is now placed upon faculty and students, administration, and all of us. As we study, teach, and work, the recognition and reputation of Illinois College will grow.

In the name of The Trustees of Illinois College, the faculty, students, and generations of loyal graduates and friends, I both accept and dedicate the McGaw Fine Arts Center. I dedicate it to the glory of God and to the ideals of intellectual freedom and artistic excellence. I dedicate this Fine Arts Center to the honor of Foster and Mary McGaw—devout Christians, concerned citizens, visionary philanthropists—good people who love mankind.

May the service that is rendered in the fine arts in and through the McGaw Fine Arts Center serve generations of students and faculty. May this College grow in both excellence and service and justly earn a higher measure of honor, recognition, and esteem.

---

RESPONSES BY REPRESENTATIVES OF THE COLLEGE COMMUNITY
*Mr. Bradley Bartholomew '81, President, Student Forum*

This dedication of the McGaw Fine Arts Center is indeed a great occasion for the Illinois College community. It is a building that incorporates some of the finest facilities available to help students pursue, study, and train in the fine arts. It stands as the newest cornerstone of Illinois College's commitment to the liberal arts.

What students need to make clear, however, is that this building does not represent the end of liberal arts education. It is not even the direct means. This Center, with all its equipment, space, and beauty of design represents only a tool—a tool to be used by administration, faculty, and students.

From the administration, we must demand leadership. These are uncertain times for all people, especially the young, and we require compassionate, wise leadership and not disinterested authority if we are to grow into the "leaders of tomorrow" as many claim us to be.

From faculty, we must demand the invaluable resources of their knowledge, experience, and training. Their presentation must be, not in a routine, dull, and tiring manner, but in an atmosphere of academic excitement and competence.

And from ourselves, we students must demand dedication, maturity, and drive.

Without these, the months of planning and the construction of this building shall have come to nothing; and we shall all be witnesses to the continuing deterioration of the liberal arts ideal.

So we must take this occasion to recommit ourselves to the ideals this institution and building are meant to stand for, in the spirit of cooperation, understanding, and hope.

---

*Dr. Iver F. Yeager, Chairman, 150th Anniversary Committee*

President Mundinger: It is a privilege for me to speak on behalf of the 150th Anniversary Committee and to represent my colleagues on the faculty.

Once again there is excitement on the Illinois College campus as we dedicate still another fine building. We faculty members who are now the "old-timers" have watched the construction of many buildings during the past two decades: Rammelkamp Chapel and new residence halls, Crispin Science Hall and Caine Student Center, expanded facilities for physical education and recreation, Schewe Library—and now the McGaw Fine Arts Center. Our two newest buildings are set like jewels upon the eastern and western boundaries of our beautiful new campus.

For as long as living memory can reach into the past our colleagues and students in the fine arts have accomplished marvelous results:

championship debate teams, sensitive dramatic portrayals of the many moods of the human spirit, beautiful concerts of choral and instrumental music, and the exhibit of remarkable talent in art and crafts. These four departments until now have been scattered about the campus in as many buildings, and now they will be brought together in a very handsome Center which will focus our attention upon them in an appropriate manner. We cannot ask of faculty or students more than they have given in the past; they have always given their best, despite the limitations of facilities and equipment. In their efforts they have always sought to fulfill the highest standards, and often they have achieved remarkable heights of excellence. Now the time and energies of artists and performers and directors can be focused upon the central purposes of their crafts, and their achievements will be stimulated and enhanced by the lovely setting of the new facilities. The McGaw Fine Arts Center marks the beginning of a new era for the arts and therefore for the enhancement of liberal education at Illinois College and the enrichment of the lives of all of us in the Illinois College community.

We rejoice in the possession of this newest addition to our campus, and we look forward to continuing great achievements from colleagues and students in the performing arts in the years ahead.

---

*Mr. William N. Clark '40, Chairman, Board of Trustees*

It's an honor and certainly a pleasure, to respond in behalf of alumni and trustees on this significant date in the history of Illinois College. For alumni, who have experienced fine arts programs conducted in a necessarily fragmented manner because of the absence of an adequate, centralized facility, it is a joy to see such a facility at last in place.

To those alumni becoming sufficiently long in the tooth to remember where the Hilltoppers gave plays forty years ago and more, the theater in the McGaw Center may never have quite the air of the old gym or the Russel House barn, and thank heavens! The air in that old gym and that old barn was terrible. Both structures served gallantly in their time and, thankfully, are long gone.

For the trustees, who are charged with taking the long look ahead, and for all of us who are interested in what is going to happen to Illinois College because we love the place, the Fine Arts Center represents a commitment to the future. We're all proud that Illinois College has lasted more than one hundred fifty years, but survival alone is not a sufficient objective. Illinois College will endure only if it *deserves* to endure because it provides a distinctive, high-quality educational service.

Good physical facilities help. They don't teach. Teachers teach—we know that. But good facilities which bring together student, teacher, and teaching materials in a most congenial atmosphere help. The McGaw Fine Arts Center will help. What will go on there will enrich the lives of Illinois College students for generations to come. The trustees wish me to express their profound gratitude to all who made this day possible with planning, with financial support, or in any other way. It's a very good day indeed for Illinois College.

PART THREE

*Illinois College and the Churches*

It has ever been the intention of the founders and guardians of the college, that its character should be strongly religious, and decidedly evangelical, but that it should rather represent the great essentials of the Gospel than the denominational peculiarities of any sect.

President Julian M. Sturtevant
"Historical Discourse," 1855

The church will regard the colleges and universities as independent corporate institutions. . . . The church will strengthen the work of the colleges and universities through active concern, through a variety of services, and through the sharing of leadership. . . .

Each college or university will provide opportunities for those who teach and those who learn to attain their highest possible level of achievement and . . . by emphasis on human values will encourage each person to seek and reach a significant commitment of the self in service to individuals and society.

A Statement of Mutual Responsibilities (1973)
The United Presbyterian Church U.S.A.

The United Church of Christ's involvement in higher education is long and proud. . . . A prime tenet of the Christian faith is that God is the source of all wisdom and truth. . . . The church is inescapably committed to the free and persistent quest for truth and to the development of the moral, spiritual and intellectual resources of the human family.

Twelfth General Synod (1979)
The United Church of Christ

The Christian faith has had a prominent role in the life of Illinois College from the very beginning. The Reverend John M. Ellis was serving as a Presbyterian minister in Illinois when he began to look for a site for a college, and he proceeded to enlist the support of church people and others to organize the school and raise the needed funds. Seven young men in the Theological Department of Yale College read Ellis's letter outlining the plan and, after receiving his favorable response to their offer, they organized the Illinois Association—later known as the "Yale Band." Some would be instructors in the new college, and the others would preach in the surrounding area while serving as trustees of the school. The Reverends Julian M. Sturtevant and Theron Baldwin were the first to arrive. Although six of the men were affiliated with the Presbyterians in Illinois, many of them were New England Congregationalists.

The Compact which these men had signed at Yale declares that "religion and education must go hand in hand."[1] Both churches and schools were considered essential to a Christian and civilized society and were regarded as mutually supportive. The College would train ministers for the churches and teachers for the schools, while the schools would prepare their pupils for admission to the College and the churches would encourage their young men to attend the College. The whole community would benefit.

1. The original "Compact" is in the archives of Illinois College, in Schewe Library. The text is printed in Charles E. Frank, *Pioneer's Progress: Illinois College, 1829–1979* (Carbondale: Published for Illinois College by Southern Illinois Univ. Press, 1979), p. 16.

Once Illinois College had begun operating, religion continued to have a prominent place in the lives of both faculty and students. The College was to maintain a close relationship with the Presbyterians and the Congregationalists. Both Sturtevant and Baldwin insisted that the College was intended to be Christian but nonsectarian, and they resisted numerous attempts to bring the College under church control.

Unlike many sister colleges, Illinois has not found it necessary to sever its church relationships to protect its integrity. The current catalog states that "Illinois College is a Christian college, related to the United Presbyterian Church in the U.S.A. and the United Church of Christ (Congregational Christian)." There are several expressions currently of this commitment. The College seeks to develop its policies and practices in a manner consistent with the values of the Christian tradition: concern for the whole person; the development of a sense of social responsibility; and respect for persons without regard "to race, religion, sex, handicap, or national origin."[2] The College has a Chaplain and conducts weekly Chapel services (voluntary since 1970); there is a strong Department of Philosophy and Religion, and two courses in religion (one of them in Bible) are required for graduation; and one clergyman from each denomination serves on the Board of Trustees. There is an annual Staley Christian Scholar lectureship on campus, made possible by a gift from the Thomas F. Staley Foundation.

It was appropriate for the 150th Anniversary Committee to include, as one of the "distinctive and essential elements" of Illinois College deserving to be celebrated, the College's relationship to the churches. And it was equally appropriate to include a seminar on this topic in the program for the first day of the Sesquicentennial observance.

2. *Illinois College Bulletin*, 1979–81 [Catalog Number], pp. 15 and 5.

# II

## The Seminars on the Church-Related College in the 1980s
## January 15 and September 23, 1979

The Seminar on "The Church-Related College in the 1980s" was scheduled for Monday, January 15, 1979, on the afternoon of the Convocation on Liberal Learning. The original plan was to have the higher education secretaries of the two national church bodies serve as panelists, with group discussion to follow. The persons invited were Dr. Wesley A. Hotchkiss, General Secretary of the Division of Higher Education, the United Church of Christ, and the Reverend A. Myrvin DeLapp, Associate for Ministries in Education, the Program Agency, the United Presbyterian Church in the U.S.A. Because of the severe winter weather the latter could not be present and so only Dr. Hotchkiss's paper was presented at the scheduled time.

A general invitation to the Seminar was extended to the campus and the larger community. The only obligation involved was for participants to read two statements, one an article on "The Prophetic Academy,"[1] by Dr. Hotchkiss, and the other a report from the Council for Higher Education, entitled "The Case for Church-Related Higher Education."[2] Copies were distributed to all persons who indicated their interest in attending. About thirty-five students, faculty members, and others from the community gathered in the

---

1. Wesley A. Hotchkiss, "The Prophetic Academy: An Historical Perspective on UCC Related Colleges," *Colleges and Academies Related to the United Church of Christ: A Unique Role in a Unique Time*, a special edition of the *Journal of Current Social Issues* (New York: Council for Higher Education, United Church of Christ, n.d.), pp. 4–9.

2. "The Case for Church-Related Higher Education," a statement of the Council for Higher Education of the United Church of Christ, Spring, 1977, ibid., pp. 26–27.

David A. Smith House for the 1:30 P.M. presentation. President
Donald C. Mundinger welcomed those present and introduced Dean
Doris B. Hopper as chairperson; she in turn introduced Dr. Hotchkiss who presented his paper. Dean Wallace N. Jamison served as
commentator and then the meeting was opened to general discussion, which proved to be lively. After the formal adjournment, refreshments were served in the dining room.

The second session of the Seminar was set for September 23, a
date convenient for Dr. A. Myrvin DeLapp and one which seemed
likely to assure good weather (it was in fact delightfully sunny and
warm). The group of about twenty-five faculty, students, and
townspeople met at 2:30 P.M. in the Gallery Lounge of Tanner Hall.
Participants had been asked to read the working papers which had
been distributed for a national conference of church-related colleges
held during the summer.[3] Dr. DeLapp delivered his address, entitled
"An Age of Less: Challenge to Church-Related Higher Education."
Again there was vigorous discussion, and those who had been present for both seminars agreed that it was advantageous to have the
extended time resulting from the double session.

The papers by Dr. Hotchkiss and Dr. DeLapp are printed below.

---

THE CHURCH-RELATED COLLEGE IN THE EIGHTIES
DR. WESLEY A. HOTCHKISS
GENERAL SECRETARY, DIVISION OF HIGHER
EDUCATION
UNITED CHURCH OF CHRIST BOARD FOR HOMELAND
MINISTRIES

The Reverend Julian Monson Sturtevant, of sainted memory in
this place, wrote in his *Autobiography*:

We never sought for Illinois College any ecclesiastical control, and
would never have submitted to it. We always desired to place it in

3. Suzanne Starnes, ed., "An Overview: The Context of Church-Related Colleges and
Universities," a working paper prepared by the staff for participants in the National Congress
of Church-Related Colleges and Universities, the University of Notre Dame, June 21–23,
1979; mimeographed.

the hands of patriotic, religious men, that it might be managed not for a sect in the Church or a party in the State, but to qualify young men for the intelligent and efficient service of God both in the Church and the State. It was never intended to be a Presbyterian or a Congregational institution, but a Christian institution sacredly devoted to the interests of the Christian faith, universal freedom and social order.[4]

For those who know the context of this statement, it must be seen as a response to the considerable controversy going on in the churches about the nature of the church-college relationship. The Congregationalists and the Presbyterians had formed a loose kind of merger at the turn of the century for the purpose of cooperating in the evangelization of the West. This "Plan of Union" eventually foundered over the nature of the college and the church, when the New Haven theology of the Congregationalists clashed with the more orthodox Calvinism (of the John Knox variety) of the Presbyterians. There was no question about where the forthright Mr. Sturtevant stood. But to assume that this controversy had its origins in a factional fight in the 1800s is to misunderstand the profound implications and long history of this dispute. While Mr. Sturtevant was vigorously defending a turf for the College somewhere between the sectarianism of the John Knox Calvinists and the secularist advocates of state-sponsored higher education, he was really reflecting several centuries of controversy about the nature of human nature and its (our) relationship to the world of matter and spirit. Being a Yale man he certainly saw this College in an unbroken line of descent from the schools of the ancient prophets, through the Athenian groves, the court schools of Charlemagne, the universities of Leyden and London, and on to the New World. Through all this history of the intellectual community there is the recurrent theme of the mystery of human existence and the meaning of the cosmic order.

In our spiritual tradition, the prophet first emerged as the person who stood up to both the priest and the king and brought rational, ethical judgment to bear upon their mystical religious excesses. But

4. Quoted in Richard Hofstadter and Wilson Smith, eds., *American Higher Education: A Documentary History*, vol. 1 (Chicago: Univ. of Chicago Press, 1961), p. 242.

this was monotheistic Judaism, whose God was the Creator of the universe, ultimately unknowable by finite persons, who could only be worshipped as the *Mysterium Tremendum*. In the fullness of time this Creator revealed Himself/Herself in the midst of creation as the Christ. This challenged the Greco-Roman assumptions about the cosmos which they considered to be eternal and without origins, undergoing an unending cycle of decay and regeneration. They had no creation myth and therefore no creator, *but* they had Aristotle. It took the Christians about twelve centuries to come to terms with Aristotle, and St. Thomas finally did it by demonstrating how very logical and Aristotelian our Creator really is! But the Christian community was not totally comfortable with St. Thomas's conversion of Aristotle to Christianity. There were some people, like the Bishop of Paris (1277) who thought that St. Thomas, with the help of Aristotle, was trying to set up the rules of logic by which God had to govern himself. This seemed most un-Biblical to the good bishop and seemed to inhibit the role of revelation. In Spain, a bit later (1550) Aristotle got another going over by dear saintly old Las Casas, the Dominican priest who spent most of his life among the Indians of Mexico. The orthodox Aristotelian Catholic position, so eruditely stated in that debate by Father Sepulveda, was that some are born to be masters and some are born to be slaves. The same necessitarian logic determined that it was manifestly impossible to distribute justice equally to those who are inherently unequal. Therefore, a holy war against the savages of the New World was justifiable. Fortunately for all posterity, that ecclesiastical council (the Council on the Indies, Valladolid, 1550) tilted slightly toward Las Casas in its final decisions. Meanwhile, back in our part of the world (the North Atlantic region) the big news was a new kind of piety arising from the central event of the incarnation. Whereas Judaism desacralized nature by worshipping a God above, beyond, and outside nature, the incarnation resacralized the visible world by investing it with sacramental meaning as Lynn White has shown. The conflict with the Greeks finally resulted in a synthesis which seemed to suggest that since we are thinking animals, endowed with the capacity for logical inquiry, we should use these talents to find out how the Creator has ordered this cosmos and discover how it works. We have been going around and around on these arguments ever since. Descartes was so sure of the godlikeness of human intellect that he practically removed us from the natural order with his announcement, "I think, therefore I am," which sounds even more sonorous in Latin! Darwin, on the other hand, was much more Greek with his mechanistic universe which made little distinction between *homo sapiens* and a Galapagos turtle.

All of this is what Whitehead calls the discord between intuition and the mechanism of science—between verifiable knowledge and meaningful existence. I am sure Mr. Sturtevant knew all of this, and his intuitive posture was somewhere between a Cartesian intellectual God and a Galapagos turtle. The important thing was that he steered a precarious course for this College in that crucial time and in the idiom of that academic community.

Mr. Sturtevant was called by a covenant with the Almighty to bring the benefits of Christian civilization to this vast continent. This was his "Manifest Destiny." Today our destiny is not nearly so manifest. His sacred devotion to "universal freedom and social order" was expressed in the midst of unlimited resources and room for everybody. His destiny was born out of the Utopian confidence in rational processes. He was expressing the civil religion that the good society would emerge if people were given the individual freedom to work out their own destiny. This was the idea of the liberal constitutional political order, a social contract flowing from a divine covenant.

The only similarity between our perception of the problem and Mr. Sturtevant's is that the problem *is* a theological one. The crisis of the academy is a crisis of meaning. Never again will we be permitted the easy optimism of his rational liberalism. We know existentially that the crisis is not one of social organization. It is one of discerning meaning beyond the mystery of the irrational and the unexplainable. We are products of the Great Depression, the demonic irrationality of the Holocaust, a senseless war in Southeast Asia which still continues, mindless disorders in our cities and campuses, and an oil embargo. All this has shaken our confidence in the secular mechanism and its ability to produce the good society by its own inherent rationalism.

Mr. Sturtevant placed this College in the midst of this crisis of meaning. Our task for this time is to take advantage of the intellectual and philosophical position of this College to make a new educational statement for our time.

The central task is to deal with that discord which Whitehead describes. Let me begin with a very simple illustration. Not long ago I was on the campus of Northland College, your sister institution in the north country of Wisconsin, and my Alma Mater. Northland is doing some very interesting things in relating the liberal arts to the environment. They have an Environmental Institute alongside the college which works as an outreach to the region on environmental problems. While I was there, they had a fascinating guest lecturer who is probably the world's foremost authority on black bears. It was an intensely interesting evening in which I learned more than I really wanted to know about black bears. In the discussion period after the lecture there were many questions, and finally I asked a question. I said that the lecture was entirely on the analytical reductionist approach to the anatomy and function of bears, providing answers to the question, "How does a bear work?" Now, my question is, "What does a bear mean?" Not "*What* is a bear?" but "*Why* is a bear?" The response by our distinguished guest was the standard academic one: "That is not my field." But one of the American Indian students stood up excitedly and said: "Yes, that's the more important question, only from my cultural perspective, I'd phrase the question a bit differently: not, 'Why is a bear?' but 'Who is a bear?'"

Now, obviously we weren't just talking about bears—we were talking about the nature of the Academy. Does this College have the right to expect that all scholars here, both faculty and students, will deal with both realms of knowing—the intuitive as well as the empirical? My good Congregationalist buddy, Julian Monson Sturtevant, thought so, but in all due respect, Julian, we can't start where you did theologically.

Reformation Theology of the North Atlantic variety was seduced by the empirical. The centerpiece of this theology was a covenant—a verbal, rational, contractual relationship with the Almighty. Once you had the Almighty's signature on the dotted line, there was little need for symbol and ritual. The clergy was no longer keeper of the mysteries; it was executor of the contract. Now I am fully aware that speaking in this way about the covenant in this stronghold of Presbyterianism makes me a theological skunk at this very lovely garden party, and even Mr. Sturtevant probably won't help me much. But I really believe that the survival of our colleges depends upon a reordering of our theological assumptions. Faced with the odds that are stacked against us in these next few years, we are going to need some very powerful reasons for our mission in higher education. Only a religious zeal will sustain us.

The crucial intellectual need of our time is not in the area of empirical knowledge. The secular multiversity can be depended upon to supply that need—given the insatiable appetite of our technology for this kind of information. The critical intellectual work of our time is in the realm of meaning. It is only in colleges like this—small, sufficiently separated from the knowledge industry of the graduate school, concentrating on the maturation of human beings, intimate enough to integrate the disciplines—that this intellectual task can be worked upon purposively and intentionally by the entire institution.

In order to do this our theology must turn from covenant to creation, and this is a *major* turn almost totally neglected up to now. Briefly, this is an outline of the task:

1. God as Creator repositions humanity in the created order. We become creatures among other creatures in the creation. This becomes a philosophy of science capable of opposing the meaninglessness of the secular. It also becomes the basis for the ethics of public policy for natural resources.

2. God as Creator is not a static concept. God is creating. Therefore the nature of the universe is creativity. Descartes should have said: "I create, therefore I am." This becomes the ultimate foundation for aesthetics in the curriculum and method of the college—not just as a cultural decoration but as a basic element in human maturation.

3. As creatures of the divine imagination, we are created with the mysterious ability to receive revelation. This ability is not the result of a contractual relationship between God and his chosen few—it is the universal gift of the cosmic Creator. North Atlantic Theology has never been able to handle this, and our esteemed colleague Sturtevant equated Christianity with religion. This is simply inadequate

for our global community. To be nonsectarian in our time is to move out from the contractual mentality to the cosmic Creator who has endowed every human creature with the capacity to receive revelation. These other revelations simply cannot be considered vain heathen imaginings but must be seen as bearers of salvation. This is the theological and philosophical basis for the study of human societies and has the capability of saving those disciplines from the meaninglessness of empirical sterility.

4. Creation theology would enable us to deal with mystery. One of the major unfinished tasks of both theology and philosophy is to rescue mystery from its empirical seduction. We have allowed the scientific method to define *mystery* as a quantity of missing data. The word must be redefined as a *quality* within the things we "know." It has to do with purpose and meaning rather than with mechanism. Therefore, the Creator is not a contract maker. He/She is the *Mysterium Tremendum* and the only appropriate response is adoration and wonder. This enables us to deal with the numinous mystery of the Holy, in whatever form it appears, and gives us the existential courage to live in the midst of mystery.

As you can see, this is just the scratching of the surface of the task of reorienting our church-related colleges for their crucial educational task. This clarification of theological purpose underlies all the surface problems, such as the "new vocationalism," interdisciplinary studies, core curriculum and general studies, the relationship of faculty to the institution, and many others.

The big question is, do we have the right to expect all our faculty to engage in this kind of theological conversation? Would this not be a sectarian expectation in itself? The answer is that all educational institutions are gathered around a priori assumptions about the nature of the universe, from the most sectarian to the most secular. We have come now to a place where the assumptions need to be stated. Our assumption is that the universe has meaning—that, as Tillich would say, it is not a self-sufficient finitude. That is a universalist declaration, not to be contained totally in any creed, contract, or covenant.

We, in our tradition, have the possibility of stating for Academia a theological posture which is totally compatible with the concept of a free and open intellectual arena. For me, this means that the Creator who revealed Himself/Herself in the Christ event is the *Mysterium Tremendum* who endows all creatures with the ability to perceive the Holy within the finite and to participate in the creation. The college is a created institution and, because of the limitations of finite reason, it must be radically open to all creative inquiry. Its purpose, too, is to participate in the creation and to redeem our society from meaninglessness. This is the kind of nonsectarian religious posture which can only be expressed intentionally, within the total life of the institution, in places like this College. That, I believe, is our calling for the 1980s.

---

AN AGE OF LESS: CHALLENGE TO CHURCH-RELATED
HIGHER EDUCATION
DR. A. MYRVIN DeLAPP
ASSOCIATE FOR MINISTRIES IN EDUCATION
THE PROGRAM AGENCY
THE UNITED PRESBYTERIAN CHURCH IN THE UNITED
STATES OF AMERICA

I have chosen to focus our attention for a brief time today on the challenge of a future dramatically forced into our consciousness by the crisis in the world's oil markets that began in October, 1973. To be sure, during the last decade or more there have been those persons and groups who have sought to remind us that population growth, food distribution, environmental damage, and oil supplies were going to become increasingly problems for the world. C. P. Snow, in his lectures at Westminster College, Missouri, in 1968, predicted that by the end of the century there would be major catastrophies with the rich countries of Western Europe and North America in the midst of famine involving millions of human beings. He was not sanguine about the possibility of avoiding such global catastrophe but few here in the United States were impressed.

For Americans particularly the 1973 oil crisis began to strike home in a new way. That crisis has never completely gone away, and we have developed a constant habit of selective inattention, ignoring the seriousness of the problem. But our attention has been drawn more

forcibly to the matter again since the revolution in Iran. Now we are
in the throes of manifold charges and counter charges about who is
to blame—the oil companies, the government, the communists, and
so on. Solutions to the crisis are proposed and opposed. We do not
seem as a people to be yet ready to entertain the suspicion that we
are moving into an era of scarcity or, another way to put it, that we
are at the end of abundance. The signs, however, are that we have
come to what Professor Leo Sandon calls the "Age of Less."[5] And
the "Age of Less" will require all of us to think soberly about how
we are going to live in that new era.

I was drawn to this topic for several reasons. First, it will soon be
forty years ago that my generation was dramatically confronted with
adjustment to new living conditions for which we were ill-prepared.
In the late 1930s it was possible for us in America to sense that war
was on the horizon but it was war for Europe—for someone else;
there was no enemy at our boundaries. And despite the fact that
some of us said when we were drafted for one year in 1940 that we
would be gone for more than a year, we still weren't really prepared
for the suddenness with which we were caught up in full-scale war
at Pearl Harbor. Life suddenly was different. It required us to think
differently about our lives, *who* we were, what we believed in, futures, jobs, education. I believe that today we are not only in a crisis
of energy but I believe we are on the verge of new requirements for
living for which we are ill-prepared. And we need to be working at
it now.

Secondly, I was drawn to this topic in part by the contents of a
brief article in *Change* magazine written by J. Gordon Parr, Deputy
Minister of Colleges and Universities in Ontario, Canada. The title
of the article is "Prisoners of Inappropriate Technology." Mr. Parr
suggests that "educational institutions are unable to redirect technological projections into a viable future." Education is so closely
tied—prisoner, if you will—to industrial technology that "forging a
technological style for a felicitous habitation of the planet" seems
hopeless. He asks an intriguing question: "If the survival of the spe-

5. Leo Sandon, "1968," a hitherto unpublished address given at a national meeting of the
United Ministries in Education, Seaman's Institute, New York City, May 11, 1979. Quotations
used by permission of Leo Sandon.

cies had to rely upon alternative technologies—technologies in which resources are conserved and where individuals fulfill individual needs rather than those of corporate enterprises—what assistance could be offered by educational institutions? Schools, colleges, and universities do not inevitably or even intentionally set out to provide manpower and morals for the corporate enterprise, although over the years they have grown into the habit. But they are certainly not very promising resources for the encouragement of new styles of technology."[6]

That question needs to be dealt with by people in educational institutions, especially in church-related education. And it may be that the Mr. Parrs of this world need to know that there are institutions of higher education that are free enough to work at developing a style of life suitable for a "felicitous habitation of the planet."

So here we are in a "crisis of passage"—moving from abundance into an age of less. What will it take to live creatively in this new age? What will be required of us? Can we do it? Whatever we may predict about the future, the only certainty is that it will be different from what we expected. Or, as someone has described our situation, there is no tomorrow in the way we've been looking for tomorrow.

In facing this new situation in which we find ourselves we can join the doomsday prophets and spend our lives decrying the bad deal we have been dealt by fate and continue what C. P. Snow calls excessive "enclave-making,"[7] a place to shut out the noise. We can simply turn away from the hard realities, draw the curtains, protect what we've got and make sure we get our share of what's left.

Preference for that style of living will undoubtedly be present if not dominant when the crunch gets more difficult. But I hope that there will be a growing number of persons demonstrating a new sense of community and active in pointing society in new directions. There's still time to do some positive work in this area. At least some people think there is.

In an article on creative adaptation to rising shortages, Professor Amitai Etzioni, of Columbia University, opts for an optimistic view of humanity which he believes will provide a creative response to

6. J. Gordon Parr, "Prisoners of Inappropriate Technology," *Change* 9:4 (April, 1977): 8, 10.

7. C. P. Snow, *The State of Siege* (New York: Charles Scribner's Sons, 1969), p. 9.

the new conditions. He turns to the humanistic psychology of Abraham Maslow for his perspective on our society and its transformation. Maslow sets forth the needs of humans as security and provisions, love, dignity, and self-actualization. These needs are immutable and no system of social control can bring people to accept a world of hatred and constraint. "Sheer survival (Maslow's most basic need) takes precedence over the higher needs [but] this does not mean that people can be made to disregard the claims of their higher selves and achieve satisfaction in a regimented world without dignity and freedom. When the objective situation allows it, their underlying yearning for satisfaction of their full range of needs will assert itself."[8]

Etzioni then goes on to cite certain studies which tend to support the Maslowian thesis that humans do seek higher fulfillment despite the fact that the so-called American way of life seems to provide proof that man is "acquisitive by nature and has insatiable desires for material goods and services." Etzioni sees growing evidence that the pursuit of conspicuous consumption is recognized as not satisfying. He calls on the West "to lead the way to a new civilization based on satisfaction of Maslow's higher needs."[9] Greater emphasis on collective projects and on self-actualization instead of material abundance would enable the West to avoid both shortages and poverty. However, he says, social engineering cannot make people redefine their values, but increasing awareness that materialism cannot satisfy the full range of human needs will encourage a shift in the appropriate direction.

That positive and optimistic note is appreciated. But I'm not at all sanguine about our capacity as a nation at this time to do much about it for two reasons. We Americans have operated so long on the premise that spatial and economic reality is abundant that it will be difficult to overcome that attitude. Professor Leo Sandon says: "Whatever one's status, whatever one's situation, the notion is that there will always be more and that at least whatever one is going to do about economic and distribution problems, the assumption can be that there will be more than plenty. . . . Material abundance, by

---

8. Amitai Etzioni, "A Creative Adaptation to a World of Rising Shortages," *Annals of the American Academy of Political and Social Science* 420 (July, 1975): 101.

9. Ibid., pp. 103, 108.

general consent, has been assumed to be the most basic condition of our lives."[10] The second reason is the belief in the autonomous individual, which has been basic to our frontier experience and certainly to our economic commitment to free enterprise. We have gotten used to the idea of being personally free to pursue our own self-interest with minimum restraint.

When the assumption of economic abundance is combined with the notion of the autonomous individual predisposed toward competitive individualism, then it seems to me that it will be difficult for us to face the conditions required for living in an Age of Less. But face them we must. And unless we redefine human freedom along more communal lines, we are in deep trouble. Hazel Henderson, Codirector of the Princeton Center for Alternative Futures, describes the contemporary situation of mature industrial societies as demanding that we reshape our values. In her view, the conditions of life on this planet push us in the direction of cooperation and sharing and thus lead us toward restructuring our economic system. She calls attention to the tremendous rebirth of the cooperative movement in America and to the several million Americans who have opted out of the industrial rat race for a simpler way of life with greater psychic rewards.

I know that what I have said does not represent an adequate analysis of present conditions. And certainly what might represent the praxis of church-related colleges is not easily developed—especially by someone outside the college experience. But I would like to toss out several things I think our colleges can do which would help move creatively into the future.

1. Most of our colleges understand themselves to be learning communities. Community gets experienced and engaged in a variety of ways in most of our colleges. I would like for us as faculties and students to work at and give greater attention to the kind of learning experience where *cooperation* rather than competition is the hallmark. I have heard of one college where the community is working from that perspective because cooperation is highly valued. Apparently it brings a whole new set of expectations and interrelationships, even

10. Sandon, "1968."

frustrations! I think Hazel Henderson is right; principles of cooperation, honesty, humility, and sharing are essential for human existence. Where better to get help on this than our church-related colleges?

2. Student groups should be encouraged to model different life
styles which may create and/or utilize appropriate technologies. One
college has a group of students living together for a semester in a
seminar called "Facing the Future," trying to see what it might mean
to bring interdisciplinary study together with a community life practice.

3. We should create faculty and student teams, made available to
the churches, which would be aimed at raising consciousness and
teaching how to live in an Age of Less. I believe congregations will
have to find ways to assist people in facing a future with less. Leo
Sandon has reminded us that "holy poverty"[11] is very much a part
of our Christian tradition but it seems to have gotten lost along
the way!

4. We should continually find ways to celebrate the hope we have
in God, the Redeemer. Our Christian tradition has of all things to
offer a word of hope. God is still in charge. And we can act in faith
on that!

11. Ibid.

# 12

## Illinois College and the United Church of Christ

The relationship to the United Church of Christ dates from the origin of the College, because many of the men involved in founding and governing the College were New England Congregationalists. The nature of the relationship is characteristic of Congregationalism, one of the constituents of the United Church of Christ: the Congregational principle of self-government was applied to colleges (and other organizations) which were established to carry out the mission of the churches. Illinois College received help from local churches, church-founded agencies, and individual church members without being under church control. To a considerable extent the personal relationships of College personnel were the basic form of its connections with the churches, and this is the case today.

Members of the College's faculty, administration, and Board of Trustees have continued to play a vital role in the relationship with the denomination. Many have been members of the Congregational Church of Jacksonville, and several have held leadership positions in regional and state organizations as well as in the local church. Among these have been the late Professor Ernest G. Hildner, Jr., for many years Dean of the College, and Professor Iver F. Yeager, an ordained minister of the United Church of Christ. Other present faculty members are long-term members of the local congregation, and a number of students attend the services of worship and some have been choir members. It has been the custom for some years to have an annual College Sunday in April, when the president of the College is invited to speak and student groups provide special music.

The College and the Congregational Church of Jacksonville have jointly hosted regional meetings of the churches from time to time.

President Julian M. Sturtevant was prominent as a national leader and was one of the five key men in organizing the first National Council in 1865; he was chosen as the preacher for that occasion—a signal honor. In recent times also the College has contributed to the national leadership of the denomination. The Reverend Fred Hoskins '26 became chairman of the College's Board of Trustees in 1955, just a year before he was named Minister and General Secretary of the General Council of the Congregational Christian Churches. When these churches merged with the Evangelical and Reformed Church in 1957, thus forming the United Church of Christ, Dr. Hoskins was elected Co-President of the new nation-wide church.

Recent presidents have been active leaders in the Council for Higher Education, which includes thirty colleges associated with the United Church of Christ. The College is a member of the Council, and previous to the merger was a member of the former Congregational Christian College Council.

Financial support is provided for Illinois College, as before, by individual church members, local churches, and church agencies. A few churches contribute directly, but most funds are channeled through such agencies as the Division of Higher Education (national), the Illinois Conference (state), or the Central Association (regional). From time to time special programs for financial support for colleges have been organized on a national scale, such as the Christian Higher Education Fund which in 1962 provided $100,000 toward the construction of Rammelkamp Chapel. The "17/76 Fund" established in the 1970s has provided scholarship money for minority students.

One of the national church agencies, the United Church Board for World Ministries, made it possible to bring a special visitor from India to be at Illinois College during the opening months of the Sesquicentennial celebration. Mr. Devasahayam Yesudhas of the American College in Madurai, a Third World Missioner, lived on the campus from early January until the end of April. He was guest lecturer in a number of classes and spoke informally with many students and faculty. Frequently on weekends he visited churches of the Central

Association, in Jacksonville and many other cities. Mr. Yesudhas appreciated the opportunity to participate in the events of the Sesquicentennial year because his college was soon to observe its own centennial anniversary. And students, faculty, and townspeople enjoyed getting to know a gracious visitor from India.

### The Church and College Project

The Council for Higher Education approved a 1978 proposal from Illinois College which enabled the College and the churches of the Central Association to join in celebrating their common origins. An advisory committee was selected which included ministers and lay people from a number of churches in addition to administrators, faculty, and students from the College. Local members served as an executive committee, with Professor Iver F. Yeager as chairman.

Several specific projects were undertaken. The focus on history led to arrangements for a seminar on preparing local church records and writing church histories; the resulting recommendations were sent to all sixty-nine churches in the Central Association. More than half the churches provided copies of their histories for the archives in Schewe Library. Another historically-oriented project was the commissioning of a dramatic skit "Town Meeting," about the College's role in the abolition movement; this was written, and produced on the campus, by Mrs. Paula Pulliam McNaughton '77, a drama major.

A program of color slides and narration was prepared to tell of the origins (in Illinois) of the various denominations which now constitute the United Church of Christ; primary emphasis, however, was placed upon the founding of Illinois College and the Congregational churches in the area of the present Central Association. The program has been presented at several area churches, three historical societies, and several service clubs, as well as at the annual meetings of the Central Association and the Illinois Conference. Professor Emeritus Malcolm F. Stewart served as coordinator for many of these projects, visiting a number of churches to present the slide program and to obtain historical information.

A large portion of the funds made available by the grant was used to publish a monograph. *Church and College on the Illinois Frontier,*

*1829–1867.*[1] The early chapters describe the Yale Band and the founding of Illinois College, the early Congregational churches, and the organization of the Congregational Association of Illinois. Subsequent chapters describe the early churches of the Christian, Evangelical, and Reformed denominations. The last section of the monograph provides historical and current information about the College and the churches. The booklet was published in 1980 and has been distributed on the campus and to the churches and to interested individuals.

### The 15th Annual Meeting of the Central Association

The most important event arranged with the assistance of the Committee on Church and College was the 15th Annual Meeting of the Central Association, held on April 21, 1979. President Mundinger welcomed the 160 clergy, lay delegates, and visitors who attended the meeting. The Service of Worship included a litany of praise adapted in part from some of President Sturtevant's writings and celebrating the founding of Illinois College and the early churches of the Association. The Illinois College Concert Choir sang two anthems. Dean Colin W. Williams of the Divinity School of Yale University gave an outstanding address: "Historic Roots and Present Tasks: The Church Then and Now." Dean Williams was introduced by the Reverend Robert M. Cassels, Pastor of the Congregational Church of Jacksonville and an alumnus of Yale Divinity School.

The afternoon program began with a much-appreciated recital on the recently dedicated Hart Sesquicentennial Pipe Organ, played by Mr. Rick L. Erickson. Following that, the honorary degree of Doctor of Divinity was conferred upon Dean Williams. Then after some Association business had been completed, the people participated in seven interest groups led by members of the faculty. A panel discussion, reviewing the past and looking to the future, concluded the day.

The granting of an honorary degree to Dr. Colin W. Williams would have been justified simply on the basis of his position as Dean

1. Iver F. Yeager, *Church and College on the Illinois Frontier, 1829–1867* (Jacksonville, IL: Illinois College, 1980; printed for Illinois College by Production Press, Inc.).

of the Divinity School of Yale—which 150 years earlier had sent the first of many of its students to found a college and establish churches in Illinois. The honor was equally deserved by Dr. Williams on personal merit. A native of Australia, Dr. Williams has taught history and historical theology both in his native country and in the United States and was Director of the Doctor of Ministry Program at the University of Chicago for several years. He has held important positions in the National Council of Churches and has been a leader in the ecumenical movement, having participated in the Assemblies of the World Council of Churches at Evanston in 1954, at New Delhi in 1961, and at Uppsala in 1968. He is the author of several books on theology and the church.

The program of the April 21 Association meeting, the service of worship, the statement by President Mundinger, and the text of Dean Williams' address, are included in the following pages.

---

PROGRAM AND SERVICE OF WORSHIP
15TH ANNUAL MEETING OF THE CENTRAL
ASSOCIATION, ILLINOIS CONFERENCE
THE UNITED CHURCH OF CHRIST
SATURDAY, APRIL 21, 1979

MORNING PROGRAM[2]

Registration and Coffee                    Rammelkamp Chapel
Campus Tours—Visit Displays

*Opening Worship*[3]

Organ Prelude: "Fantasie in C"                    César Franck
Mr. Rick L. Erickson, College Organist and Choir Director

2. The members of the Planning Committee for the 15th Annual Meeting were: Chairman, Mr. Carl Andres (Vice-Moderator of the Association); the Reverend Edward Blumenfeld; Mr. William Fine; Mr. and Mrs. William T. Henderson; Mrs. Bea Tholen; Mrs. Lynne Oberlander Walters; Professor Iver F. Yeager; the Reverend J. Robert Sandman, ex officio, and the Reverend C. Thomas Jackson, ex officio. Mrs. Tholen and other members of the Congregational Church of Jacksonville, assisted by Illinois College students, registered the delegates and provided the refreshments.

3. The Service of Worship was prepared by Kathryn Luther Henderson and William T. Henderson of the Community United Church, Champaign.

Introit: "Be Thou My Vision"                          Traditional Irish
            The Illinois College Concert Choir

Call to Worship

   Leader: The Lord is great—He should be praised. He has made
           His wonderful works to be remembered.

   People: Honor and majesty are due to the Lord. We worship Him
           in the beauty and strength of His sanctuary.

   Leader: The Lord is good. He has shown His people the power of
           His works that He may give them the heritage of the na-
           tions.

   People: The steadfast love of the Lord stands forever and ever.
           We give thanks for his love.

   Leader: The Lord sent redemption to His people. His covenant
           shall last forever.

   People: Holy and revered is the name of our Lord. Unto Him be
           glory in His church throughout all the ages.

*Hymn of Praise "Our God, Our Help in Ages Past"      Isaac Watts
            Tune: "St. Anne"—William Croft

*Invocation (in unison)

   Almighty and ever faithful God, we are here as part of your
   church to celebrate the founding of this school and the origin of
   the church in this state. Guide us as we transact our business, and
   inspire us as we work and learn together. Teach us again our oneness as your servant people, gathered in Jesus' name. Amen.

Words of Welcome                               Donald C. Mundinger
                                         President, Illinois College

*A Litany of Remembrance and Thanksgiving[4]

   Leader: Let us join in a litany of grateful remembrance for the "un-
           failing, unflagging purpose which has ever been cherished
           by the religious people of this nation, to disseminate" the
           Good News of "the Gospel."

   People: We give thanks and offer our continued dedication to help
           tell others the Good News.

4. The words and phrases in quotation marks were taken from the Reverend Julian M.
Sturtevant's "Historical Discourse" (pp. 9, 18), delivered at the quarter-century celebration of
the founding of Illinois College, July 11, 1855.

Leader: For the visionary spirit of the Reverend John Millot Ellis who when sent in the fall of 1825 to the prairie state of Illinois by the American Home Missionary Society saw an opportunity to establish "a Christian seminary of learning."

People: We give thanks for the vision of the godly and courageous people who founded this college and for all those who have founded worthwhile societies and institutions in all times and places and for the good that has been fostered by these societies and institutions.

Leader: For the faith of the "seven members of the Theological department of Yale College" who subscribed "their names to a solemn pledge to one another and to God to devote their lives to the cause of Christ in the distant and then wild State of Illinois" and to help found Illinois College.

People: We give thanks for the faith of these and other persons for carrying out good causes throughout the ages. We renew our dedication to carry on the good work wherever we are and whatever may be our Christian vocation.

Leader: For the contribution and influence of all institutions of learning through their leaders, trustees, faculties, staffs, and supporters which in both large and small ways have crossed barriers of distance, custom, and tradition to attempt new modes of service and new means of sharing.

People: We give thanks for the past and pray that we, too, may always be ready to seek new service in our times and in the places where we are; and we pray as Jesus taught his disciples: Our Father, who art in heaven, Hallowed be thy name. Thy Kingdom come, thy will be done on earth as it is in heaven. Give us this day our daily bread, and forgive us our debts as we forgive our debtors. And lead us not into temptation, but deliver us from evil. For thine is the kingdom and the power and glory forever. Amen.

Scripture: Eph. 4:1–16

Anthems: "Old Hundredth"                                     (Psalm 100)
                16th C. Psalm Tune, arr. Ralph Vaughan Williams
    "Lift Up Your Heads"                                 (Ps. 24:7–10)
                George Frederick Handel; from the *Messiah*
                The Illinois College Concert Choir

*Litany for the Church and the Association

    Leader: Let us praise God for the gift of the church. For all those who have given themselves in faithful service, both those who are long remembered by many and those known only to a few.

    People: We praise you, O God, and bless your name.

    Leader: For the Lord of the church, who has called His disciples in many lands and in many times, who has sent them into the world for the healing of the many that they might know God and glorify Him.

    People: We give you thanks, O God.

    Leader: For faithful ministers and teachers who in rightly dividing the word of truth in all seasons and among all peoples have given true testimony to the power and purpose of God.

    People: We would in this day be dedicated to this same truth and would testify to your great deeds and continuing presence among us, O God.

    Leader: We remember the promises of the Lord to be present among us whenever people gather in twos or threes in His name.

    People: We call on His name and glorify Him for His power and presence among us both here in our Association and among the people of whom we are a part.

    All:    Glory to the Father, glory to Jesus Christ, the Son, and to the Holy Spirit. As it was in the beginning, so is it now and ever shall be, forever and ever. Amen.

*Closing Hymn "God of Our Life, Through All the Circling Years"
Hugh T. Kerr

Tune: "Sandon"—Charles H. Purday

*Benediction

*Organ Postlude: Prelude and Fugue in C Minor
Johann Sebastian Bach

    *The people standing.

---

Business Session                      Moderator Everett Seeber
Pastor, Zion Church, Ursa

Call to Order—Minutes—Registration
Report of Nominating Committee—Floor Nominations
Election
Presentation of Printed Reports
Action on Revision of Constitution and Bylaws
Open Forum
Introduction of Keynote Speaker   The Reverend Robert M. Cassels
Pastor, Congregational Church, Jacksonville
Keynote Address                             Dean Colin W. Williams
The Divinity School, Yale University
"Historic Roots and Present Tasks: The Church Then and Now"
Lunch in Baxter Hall          Grace by the Reverend Mr. Cassels

Campus Tours—Visit Displays

AFTERNOON PROGRAM

Organ Recital                             Rammelkamp Chapel
The Hart Sesquicentennial Pipe Organ
Mr. Rick L. Erickson, Illinois College Organist
"Mass for the Parishes"          François Couperin, 1668–1733
"Land of Our Birth," from *Song of Thanksgiving*
Ralph Vaughan Williams, 1872–1958
Fugue in E Flat, BWV 552     Johann Sebastian Bach, 1685–1750
Hymn: "For All the Saints"                Ralph Vaughan Williams
Tune: "Sine Nomine"

Conferring of Honorary Degree, Doctor of Divinity
    Conferrer: President Donald C. Mundinger
    Candidate: Dean Colin W. Williams
    Presenter: Dr. Iver F. Yeager,
                    Professor of Religion and Philosophy
Installation of Area Conference Minister          Moderator Seeber
    Area Conference Minister:     The Reverend C. Thomas Jackson
Installation of Association Officers                Moderator Seeber
Our Christian World Mission Awards to Congregations
                        The Reverend Donald Stoner
    Associate Conference Minister for Stewardship and Interpretation

Interest Groups
    Introduction: Professor Iver F. Yeager
    Skit: "Town Meeting,"                Paula Pulliam McNaughton '77
        Presented by the Illinois College Hilltop Players. Comment by
        Dr. David H. Koss, Associate Professor of Religion
    "Religious Expression in Traditional and Modern Art"
                                                    Mr. Peter Cohan,
                                                    Instructor in Art
    "Glimpses of Life in Early Illinois"           Dr. James E. Davis,
                                    Associate Professor of History
    "The Religious Factor in the Middle East"
                                        Dr. Wallace N. Jamison,
                    Dean of the College and Professor of History
    "The Bible and Archeology"                 Dr. John N. Langfitt,
                    Chaplain and Assistant Professor of Religion
    "Church Records"                       Dr. Malcolm F. Stewart,
                    Professor Emeritus of Philosophy and Religion
    "Problems and Opportunities of the Third World Church"
        Mr. Devasahayam Yesudhas, Chaplain and Assistant Professor
        of English, American College, Madurai, India; Third World
        Missioner to Illinois College and Central Association, spon-
        sored by the Board for World Ministries, United Church of
        Christ
    "Commencement Exercises"                          Interaction
        Dean Colin W. Williams; the Reverend J. Robert Sandman, As-
        sociate Conference Minister; the Reverend C. Thomas Jack-
        son, Area Conference Minister; and the 15th Annual Meeting
Adjournment.
    Snack in Baxter Hall

---

STATEMENT BY PRESIDENT MUNDINGER
What is a Christian college?
Books, articles, and speeches have been written on this topic. The
results have been uneven. While one might say the subject has been
exhausted, there continues to be a gnawing uncertainty as to who
we are, what we are, why we are, indeed, what we propose to be.

One might say that a Christian college is an institution which adheres rigidly to a dogma or creed—that a statement of faith controls and directs the entire life, being, and ethos of the college. A second answer might be that history determines what is a Christian college, that is, whether or not it was begun by a group of people who professed a religious philosophy or a religious purpose for their work. A third response might be that a Christian college is one which derives a substantial amount of financial support from a Christian denomination or Christian individuals. Still another way to approach the Christian college is to determine if Christianity continues to influence the college, especially an influence that flows from and through an ecclesiastical hierarchy or bureaucracy. Course offerings, curriculum, graduation requirements, and chapel—compulsory or voluntary—are also ways to differentiate among institutions of higher learning in America today.

But there is more to this idea of the Christian college than the recitation just offered. By my lights, there are at least three kinds of truths which inform our daily life, our reason for living, and our purpose at this College. There is truth which is scientific—the truth based on observation, testing, validation, and replication or, more simply, empirical truth based on the rules of the scientific method. Moral truth is a second truth—ideas or concepts about the worth of the individual, that is, justice, equity, law, freedom, liberty, and life—all grand concepts, but also essential concepts, which separate us from the beast and the law of the jungle. Finally, a third truth— religious truth, the quest for a higher order of meaning which gives purpose and confidence to our lives. John Gardner, in his thin little volume entitled *Morale*, talks about these three truths. He mentions a friend, a religious man, who justifies the human impulse to seek these three kinds of meaning simply by saying, "that God designed us that way."[5]

As I read the history of this institution, especially as recorded by President Rammelkamp and Dr. Frank, and in my work with alumni, I am persuaded that Illinois College is a Christian institution precisely because there are many of us—faculty, students, and staff—

5. John W. Gardner, *Morale* (New York: W. W. Norton, 1978), p. 118.

who are committed to Christ as Saviour and as the source of hope for personal and world peace.

We claim to be and are a Christian college. Yet, some in our community do not subscribe to a Christian faith. But, this, too, is also an essential part of the Christian college: the freedom, the academic freedom, to search and to teach truth—scientific, moral, and religious.

What then is a Christian college? A Christian college is a people, in the shadow of the Cross living out their lives as colleagues, searching for truth—scientific, moral, and religious—not smugly, not in an exclusionary fashion, but in openness and in the desire to share what we have—knowledge, truth, and the grand mystery of Christian love.

---

HISTORIC ROOTS AND PRESENT TASKS: THE CHURCH
THEN AND NOW
DEAN COLIN W. WILLIAMS
THE DIVINITY SCHOOL, YALE UNIVERSITY

It is a pleasure to be with you and to reflect back over 150 years to the time when my predecessors from Yale came in the cause of Christ to this distant and then wild state of Illinois to establish a Christian seminary of learning and to begin this College. It is interesting to reflect that at that time the church in this young country was undergoing an extraordinary transformation, one which is rather unique in the history of the church and of its relationship to this world in which we serve. The church in New England from which they came, you will remember, had been established by Puritans who had brought with them the vision which they believed could not be fulfilled in the old world of Europe.

They came, they said, to establish a godly commonwealth. But more, they saw their arrival on these new shores as a divine providence in which God was opening a new and final page in history. They certainly were daring in their vision. Let me quote, for example, the well-known words of Governor Winthrop leading the 1630 migration: "We shall find that the God of Israel is among us, . . . when He shall make us a praise and glory, that men shall say of succeeding plantations: 'The Lord make it like that of New England.'" That's why they came here to do just that. "For we must consider that we shall be as a city upon a hill, the eyes of all people are upon us." They were convinced that this was an experiment which God was establishing for all mankind to follow, and therefore in that sense of expectation they were sure that the eyes of the world were now in a future sense set upon this settlement. "So that if we shall deal falsely with our God in this work we have undertaken, and so cause Him to withdraw His present help from us, we shall be made a story and a by-word through the world."[6] That was their daring faith and so they set out to establish a church which would at the same time be a nation and which would show forth to all mankind God's way of life. They had a covenant with their God to establish a holy commonwealth.

But by 1829 a remarkable change occurs. America had undergone the War of Independence and the colonies of New England now faced the task of combining with the colonies of the South to forge a union, and to do that some major changes were necessary— changes of very great moment. The churches of New England, of course, had been state churches; church and state were completely one. But Jefferson and others introduced a remarkable transformation of their understanding by the doctrines of separation of church and state and of toleration on the one hand and on the other by expressing now the divine purpose of America. This was done not so much in terms of the theological language over which the churches were divided but by the use of notions that came from Locke and other thinkers of the enlightenment, which spoke of God's purposes in terms of universal natural rights and liberty and justice for all. And so they began to speak, not of the church as the peculiar providential institution for God in this land, but of the Union, of the nation itself as the community in which God's purpose of liberty and justice for all would be worked out and which all the rest of the world would then be able to follow. And so there was this change: instead of the church being the avenue of God's providence, now the nation was, and the church was given a new and different

6. Quoted from Governor John Winthrop, *A Model of Christian Charity*, in Perry Miller, ed., *The American Puritans: Their Prose and Poetry* (Garden City, NY: Doubleday, 1956), p. 83.

role which remarkably the churches accepted. Their role now was to take care primarily of the private and family lives of the American people, transforming them by the spirit of God so that the springs of moral action would be purified and so that they could be suitable citizens for this holy commonwealth which God was establishing through the Union.

Now it is remarkable also that in the national understanding they took over the Puritan vision of America as a new Israel. In fact they took it one stage further. The Puritans spoke of themselves as coming across the seas, as Israel did across the Red Sea, and coming to this new land; and they saw New England as the new wilderness. That's the way they saw themselves—in training for entrance upon the future promised land. But now with the throwing off of the European yoke, Americans began to say: "The days of wilderness wandering are over. We are entering now the promised land of the new America. The new exodus has been completed." You will remember, for example, that Jefferson in his 1805 inaugural spoke of God as having led our forefathers as Israel of old. You may remember, too, that Jefferson wanted the symbol of America to be the pillar of cloud by day and of fire by night. Apparently from an esthetic point of view that wasn't satisfactory so they changed it, but it indicates the vision of what America was to be.

Now this remarkable sense of the nation as being the community of God's providential purpose for America (and eventually for all mankind) and of the church as being the servant of that purpose through transforming the personal and family life of the people had some remarkable consequences. First of all I think it must be said very clearly that this was responsible for the great success the churches have had in this country ever since. Compare for example the church in this land with Europe, where state churches continued for quite a long time. And rightfully as the world of modern nation states emerged and as the modern industrialized democratic society emerged, the church which represented the past was increasingly rebelled against by the people, so that now in Europe the churches are clearly in the minority situation. But in this country where there was separation of church and state, a modern state was able to emerge and the church was seen as the partner of that development.

And so a remarkable thing has happened. Whenever in this country a national crisis has emerged, whether war or a depression or a moment of terrible crisis like the death of a president—in every one of those cases what happens is that the people then see that as a call to return to the church. If the nation is to fulfill its destiny, the churches also must be asked to fulfill their responsibility of helping us with our spiritual lives, helping us to purify our own vision, in order that we can be proper citizens of this new commonwealth. The great French observer, de Tocqueville, noticed in the 1830s this remarkable change in comparison with Europe. He said here in this land as in Europe the churches disagree with each other on matters of doctrine, but in this land that does not bring division, for all the churches agree upon God's providence for his people in this new commonwealth.

That remarkable achievement therefore made the church relevant to the new age, but it also brought with it major problems. In the Puritans' eyes God's promise to America, his providential purpose for America, was provisional. The people had made a covenant with God as Governor Winthrop said, but if the covenant is to be fulfilled the people must be obedient. And so time after time through Puritan preaching there is constantly a call upon the people to put themselves under the judgment of God in order that the covenant will be kept, and for that reason there was frequent institution of fast days. Every year a major fast was proclaimed by the governor in order that the people in their churches would reexamine themselves and put themselves under the judgment of God, so that God's providential purpose would not be lost. But once there came the separation of church and state and once the state became the bearer of God's promise, that sense of judgment was soon lost and the fast days disappeared in a hurry.

As a matter of fact, just as America saw itself as leaving the new wilderness and entering into the promised land, so its people went even further. They began to speak of America now as the new Eden, going back behind the fall; for having thrown off the old hand of the European past with its sinful accretions, America was now innocent, good, a fit people for God's providential purpose—a theme, by the way, which runs through presidential utterances ever since. Our own Southern Baptist Jimmy Carter, despite the theological convictions of his church which believes strongly in original sin, nevertheless keeps on insisting that Americans are good—something that the rest of the world doesn't seem to understand. So there was cost in this remarkable circumstance, when America began to see itself as a new Adam, innocent, good, a fit instrument for God's providential purpose. That, as we shall see, gave rise to the remarkable American belief in its manifest destiny.

There was, however, one pause along this road of self-confident expansion which America was about to embark upon when this College was founded. That pause came of course with the Civil War, and that pause was given its greatest expression by a son of this state, President Abraham Lincoln. When the Civil War came Lincoln's first and great desire was to save the Union. Why? Because that is what everything depended upon. That's what God had brought forth, this Union, to be a sign to the rest of the world of God's providential purpose. And if that experiment were not to succeed then God's providence would be lost. The nation must be maintained; that was the first task—to save the Union.

As the Civil War wore on he began to say, isn't there something else? Isn't this Civil War to be interpreted as God's hand of judgment upon this nation because of its failure to live up to the covenant? And so Lincoln began to speak of the inner covenant which had to be maintained if the outer covenant was to be continued. Remember, for example, these terrible words from his second inaugural address: "Fondly do we hope, fervently do we pray, that this mighty scourge of war may speedily pass away. Yet, if God wills that it continue until all the wealth piled by the bondsman's two hundred and fifty years of unrequited toil shall be sunk, and until every drop of blood drawn with the lash shall be paid by another drawn with the sword, as was said three thousand years ago, so still it must be said, 'The judgments of the Lord are true and righteous altogether'."[7] Lincoln insisted that the war had to be understood as the judgment of God upon America for its failure to live up to the covenant, particularly in the institution of slavery. And to call Americans back to their

7. Abraham Lincoln, "Second Inaugural Address," March 4, 1865, in Henry Steele Commager, ed., *Living Ideas in America* (New York: Harper and Brothers, 1951), p. 624.

original providential purpose, Lincoln put Thanksgiving Day permanently at the center of the American national calendar—a reminder that Puritan vision was necessary if America was to fulfill its providential purpose. Lincoln also restored with Thanksgiving Day the fast days, but it must be said that they disappeared almost immediately after the Civil War was over.

Reconstruction saw this awareness of the need for Divine judgment quickly diminish and in fact disappear. In 1845 the journalist from St. Louis, John Sullivan, coined the term "manifest destiny," and it was a fateful term. At the time Sullivan saw the annexation of Texas as a foretaste of indefinite expansion. He began to extol the wonderful future which was now opening up America's manifest destiny with the annexation of Texas; indefinite expansion could now be had, with America moving on through Mexico to Latin America and on to the Pacific. And in this way God's purpose for all mankind would soon be realized with the American way of life, with its democratic processes, with its free enterprise and with its Christian virtues being given to all mankind. But notice a difference. The Puritans had seen this way of life (with the exception of the free-enterprise system which had been included in the creed by this time) as a city set on a hill. They were to be a community amongst whom God by his purifying purposes would work out this way of life so that others seeing the light shining forth from the city set on the hill would have one great desire: to follow that way, to accept it for themselves. It was destiny by example. It was to be a new Jerusalem to which the tribes would flow up as in the Biblical vision.

But, Sullivan turned it all around. The tribes were not to flow up to the new Jerusalem. The new Jerusalem was to conquer the rest of the world for God's way of life through the confident, aggressive purpose of manifest destiny. And so America rode on the conquering force of manifest destiny into its triumphant beginning of the twentieth century, through the Spanish War and the annexation of the Hawaiian Islands. That vision did not go unchallenged. To refer to another of the favorite sons of this part of the country, Mark Twain was horrified by it all. Now Mark Twain was hardly a Puritan. His theological vision was scarcely the same as that of Abraham Lincoln. But Mark Twain countered that it's against all our traditions to conquer anybody in the name of God. He wasn't too sure about that name God anyway, but he was sure that whatever the name of God meant it certainly did not mean aggression. It certainly did not mean imposing one's will by violence. Whatever it meant, America meant the example which people could freely follow. But others gave that same protest more theological expression. Perhaps most eloquent at this time was the expression of Henry Van Dyke, whom you may know as the man who wrote "The Other Wise Man." Henry Van Dyke analyzed in a famous Thanksgiving sermon (at the time of the annexation) the Puritan vision and its expression of the way of God as a way to be freely chosen as citizens lived out under the judgment and promises of God, the way of liberty and justice for all—showing through their care for others, their love for others, the desire of God that all should participate in his love and justice. But he said America can once again be the people of God's promise only if they will give up all thought of imposing their will on others and will instead see as God's purpose, the way of service, of serving others in the way of love and justice.

That struggle then entered into the twentieth century and can be rightfully said to be the struggle which still goes on in the soul of the church in our time. This struggle, of course, came clearly out into the open in the 1960s. The beginning of the 1960s saw the return of the civil-rights movement. The sixties of this century became then in an advanced way the replay of the sixties of the nineteenth century in the Civil War. It is interesting to reflect upon Martin Luther King's famous "I Have a Dream" speech and to ask what the central theme was. The central theme was that of promise unfulfilled in the American dream. By no means had he given up on the American dream—the opposite! If there is any country in which this dream is to be fulfilled it is, first of all, America. If there is any country called to be an example to the rest of the world on this great issue of race, it is to be America. For here in the vision of liberty and justice for all, here in the ringing words of an Abraham Lincoln, that vision has been clearly expressed. And now, said King, we have come to claim that inheritance, to bring that vision, that providential purpose to its fulfillment. "I have a dream"—and as he spoke that dream you remember that across the country our hearts resonated to those words. We knew that this was the genuine call of God for repentance, for judgment, for us to face again the judgments expressed to us by Abraham Lincoln, for us to face again the need to struggle within our life for liberty and justice for all.

But we saw something more. We saw that the church was called for special responsibility. Back in the time of the War of Independence the church had perhaps too easily allowed itself to be pushed over into the area of private and family life. The concern for those values was in itself good. One of the great moments was when the church saw that if it would accept responsibility for that private and family life, for training up its children in the way of God, for facing us personally with the need for repentance and transformation, we could be the children of God. Then this nation would have a chance of fulfilling the purposes of God.

But hadn't the church too easily left public matters, such as the institution of slavery, to the state—thus exempting the state and public life from the judgments of God? And so in the sixties the church saw that we had marooned ourselves too often in private life alone, having been led astray by the oldest simple statement that the church must keep out of politics, forgetting that there are two meanings to that term. Certainly the church must keep out of politics in the sense of not again becoming an established church. Certainly the church must keep out of politics in the sense of not again forming itself into a political party trying to seize direct political power. But certainly the church must not keep out of politics—must never keep out of politics—if politics has to do with liberty and justice for all. If politics has to do with the infamous practice of slavery, if politics has to do with a nation which has exempted itself from the judgment of God and under the name of manifest destiny, imposes its way upon others—certainly in that sense the church must relate to the political processes.

And so the church in the sixties faced that struggle—a struggle now going on in the church over the whole question of liberation theology, a question which I do not have the time here this morning to explore but which is certainly very central to the life of our churches now. Whether women's liberation, or liberation of the Third World, or the liberation of minorities in this county, it is the responsibility of the church to represent God's liberating purpose in those areas. In that question the church is struggling to understand itself once more in our own time.

But in the seventies we find ourselves now faced with the question of how we balance these issues. Towards the end of the sixties in our enthusiasm to relate the church to these public issues, very often we found ourselves drawn out into the social struggles of our times in such a way that we were tending again to forget our own spiritual roots. Drawn out into these struggles in such a way too that we began to be over confident about our ability to read the purposes of God and our ability to transform the institutions of this world so that they could become the kingdoms of our Lord Jesus Christ. So the seventies saw us needing once more to regain our sense of modesty under the purposes of God and needing once more also to turn back into ourselves to rediscover our spiritual roots; to rediscover the basic gospel of the need for repentance, of the need to understand ourselves as sinners who by God's grace alone can be turned around so that we can begin humbly to walk with our God on the painful road of struggling on towards liberty and justice for all. So in our time the church is facing the struggle to bring these two necessary sides of the mission of the church into balance, to redress somewhat the balance of these as given in the mission of the church at the time of the War of Independence, but nevertheless to take the remarkably positive aspect of that inheritance which is ours. From that base of the church's role in the private and family life of our people the church is to move out once again to relate the gospel of God's judgment and promise to the public life of this nation.

For surely it is still true that, as Martin Luther King reminded us again and again, this nation was given by God and is still given by God a remarkable opportunity to be an example to others in the struggle towards the vision of liberty and justice for all. We who are being called by the Lord to repentance and new life are also being called together as a community to struggle for the rights of others and so to fulfill the promise given of old by the prophet Micah, a promise that we can do justice and love mercy and walk humbly with our God on this way we have undertaken.

# 13

## Illinois College and the United Presbyterian Church in the U.S.A.

Illinois College since its beginning has had close ties with the denomination presently known as the United Presbyterian Church in the U.S.A. There was a Presbyterian church in Jacksonville two years before the Reverend John M. Ellis organized the founding of the College, and Ellis was serving as its pastor at that time. The College's connections with Presbyterianism have involved every level of the organized church: the local congregation, the presbytery and synod, and the national church and its agencies.

In recent decades faculty members and administrators have frequently been active Presbyterian clergy and laity, and considerable numbers of students have made the First Presbyterian Church, just two blocks from the campus, their college church. The long-continued interest of the First Presbyterian Church in the College and its welfare was expressed (among other ways) in a special Service of Divine Worship, planned during the Sesquicentennial celebration in honor of the College. President Donald C. Mundinger and Jon Mark Althoff, President of the Student Forum, assisted in leading the service. More than half the faculty members were present, wearing their academic robes and hoods, to participate in the processional. The guest preacher for that day was Dr. A. Myrvin DeLapp, Associate for Ministries in Education of the Program Agency, one of the instrumentalities of the national church.

The Great Rivers Presbytery held its regular meeting for September, 1979, on the Illinois College campus, and in this way shared in the College's observance of its 150th Anniversary. Dean Wallace N.

Jamison welcomed the large assembly and several faculty members participated in the program and service of worship. Mr. Rick L. Erickson, College Organist, played the new pipe organ and also directed the choral numbers sung by the Illinois College Concert Choir. The *Minutes* of the Presbytery's meeting record a resolution of congratulations extended by the delegates to the College on the 150th Anniversary of its founding.

The following pages include several items which explain or illustrate the continuing relationship of the College and the United Presbyterian Church. Professor Emeritus Malcolm F. Stewart has written an essay on the historical and contemporary institutional forms of that relationship. Also included are the order of the commemorative service of worship at the First Presbyterian Church, followed by the text of Dr. DeLapp's sermon, and the program and service of worship of the Great Rivers Presbytery meeting.

---

## THE RELATIONSHIP OF THE PRESBYTERIAN CHURCH TO ILLINOIS COLLEGE
### DR. MALCOLM F. STEWART
### PROFESSOR EMERITUS OF RELIGION AND PHILOSOPHY

Education has always been a high priority of Presbyterians. It has been their conviction, as well as that of the Congregationalists, that "religion and education must go hand in hand."[1] Illinois College has the unique distinction of being founded through the cooperative efforts of Presbyterians and Congregationalists. Although the two denominations shared much in common, Congregationalists wanted as much independence as possible. Presbyterians, on the other hand, tended to demand greater control.

It was the spirit of independence which prevailed in the founding of Illinois College. The members of the Yale Band agreed to come to Jacksonville only under the condition that the College would be "independent of any extraneous influence" and that the Board of

1. From the "Compact" of the Illinois Association or "Yale Band." The "Compact" is quoted in full by Charles Henry Rammelkamp, *Illinois College: A Centennial History, 1829–1929* (New Haven: Published for Illinois College by Yale Univ. Press, 1928), pp. 23–24.

Trustees would have "full power to fill their own vacancies."[2] These terms were agreed to. When the charter was issued in 1835 Illinois College was designated as an independent college with a self-perpetuating Board of Trustees.

The presbytery which had jurisdiction over the state of Illinois did not support the founding of Illinois College. There were many Presbyterians, however, who did. The Reverend John M. Ellis, pastor of the First Presbyterian Church of Jacksonville, enlisted the full support of the members of that church as well as of other churches. Four members of the original Board of Trustees, organized to receive donations for the College, were elders in the Jacksonville church.

Although Illinois College was independent by charter, the Presbyterians and the Congregationalists maintained a strong influence both through financial support and through the Board of Trustees. The more conservative of the Presbyterians were fearful of Congregational influence. Efforts were made to insure that a sufficient number of Presbyterians were appointed to the faculty. There were questions concerning the orthodoxy of the members of the faculty. A controversy arose in the 1850s concerning the number of members from each denomination on the Board of Trustees. Again in 1866 a proposal was made to appoint to the Board of Trustees and the faculty an equal number from both denominations. President Sturtevant reacted strongly to any suggestion of control by either denomination, saying privately that if that came about he would resign. It was his conviction that "ecclesiastical control of higher education was as dangerous as political control."[3]

It was not until 1903 that the Synod of Illinois gave Illinois College full recognition as a Presbyterian college. In that year Illinois College became coeducational and the Jacksonville Female Academy, which had the support of the Synod, was merged with Whipple Academy. According to the report of the merger, recorded in the Synod *Minutes* of that year, it was agreed that a majority of the trustees were to be Presbyterian. In addition, to insure its continuation as a Presbyterian college, the sum of $50,000 was set aside to revert to the

2. Rammelkamp, *Centennial History*, p. 28.
3. Ibid., p. 189.

trustees of the JFA if the College ceased to be Presbyterian. Under these terms the Synod gave its full recognition to Illinois College.

Since that time Illinois College has cherished its formal relationship with the Presbyterian church. Even so, some Presbyterians continued to express concern that Illinois College was not tied more closely to the church. In the 1940s some in the Board of Christian Education regarded Illinois College as being on the "outer fringes"[4] of Presbyterianism.

In 1943 a "Set of Standards" was adopted by the Board of Christian Education to provide some uniform requirements to which all Presbyterian-related colleges must adhere in order to continue their relationship. President H. Gary Hudson reacted strongly against the Standards, not solely on account of their content, but because he looked upon them as an attempt to curtail the freedom of the College. Discussion continued between Illinois College and the Board of Christian Education regarding the church-college relationship. In 1953 an agreement was drawn up and approved by both parties. This agreement tacitly recognized that the relationship between Illinois College and the Presbyterian Church in the U.S.A. was a voluntary one, maintained for the mutual benefit of both institutions. It was agreed that the president of the College would always be a person of "strong avowed evangelical Christian faith." It was further agreed that three-fourths of the members of the Board of Trustees would be "persons who are members in good standing of evangelical Christian churches." In addition, consultations would be held by the president and church officials on "matters of mutual interest and advantage." In return the judicatories of the church would "encourage Presbyterians to contribute to the moral and financial support of Illinois College."[5]

By 1973 changes had taken place in the attitude toward church-college relationships. These were made explicit in "A Statement of Mutual Responsibilities" adopted by the Program Agency of the United Presbyterian Church and the Presbyterian College Union. This statement explicitly recognizes the colleges as "independent

4. Charles E. Frank, *Pioneer's Progress: Illinois College, 1829–1979* (Carbondale: Published for Illinois College by Southern Illinois Univ. Press, 1979), p. 236.
5. Ibid., pp. 238–39.

corporate institutions" which are "not under the control of the church," and in which the "responsible exercise of academic freedom" is encouraged. The two institutions supplement each other in their endeavor "to serve society with sensitivity and skill." The colleges can contribute "knowledge, skills, and related educational resources" to the church. The church, in turn, will provide the colleges "financial and other support" and will "encourage such support from individuals, congregations, and other agencies." Both institutions will "share with one another results of research, insights, and experiences" that can be of mutual benefit. Both are committed to "the struggle for full recognition of all persons as children of God."[6]

The relationship between the United Presbyterian Church and Illinois College has been of mutual benefit to both institutions. Through the Presbytery, the Synod, and the General Assembly, there has been continual financial support of the general operation of the College. Contributions have been made from time to time to help finance specific projects, such as the construction of Rammelkamp Chapel. Under formal contract the Board of Christian Education, for many years, gave financial support for the teaching of Bible. Specific grants have been made for special lectures, days of religious emphasis, increases in faculty salaries, and other purposes. Individuals and local churches have been encouraged to support the College. The College is deeply grateful not only for the financial support but also for the advice, the counsel, and the encouragement given by the church.

Illinois College, in its turn, has served the United Presbyterian Church not only through its formal relationship but through individuals who have assumed positions of church leadership. Before the reorganization of the church, Professor Malcolm F. Stewart had served as moderator of the Springfield Presbytery and of the Synod of Illinois. President L. Vernon Caine was formerly active in both Presbytery and Synod, and Dean Wallace N. Jamison has recently completed a term as moderator of the Great Rivers Presbytery. Professors John N. Langfitt and Laurence C. Judd are currently active.

6. "The Church and Related Colleges and Universities: A Statement of Mutual Responsibilities," adopted by the Presbyterian College Union and the Program Agency, the United Presbyterian Church U.S.A., 1973, n.p.

Illinois College has sought to cooperate with the church and support it in every way possible.

Illinois College has always valued its relationship with the United Presbyterian Church and its commitment to higher education within a Christian context. Both church and college have much to contribute to each other in the years ahead as they continue their relationship in the attempt to fulfill their responsibilities within a changing world.

---

## The Service of Divine Worship Celebrating The Illinois College Sesquicentennial First Presbyterian Church Jacksonville, Illinois September 23, 1979, 10:30 a.m.

★Processional: "March in D Major"      Johann Sebastian Bach
Dr. Ralph Robbins, Organist
★Call to Worship      Dr. Dale W. Robb, Pastor
★Hymn: "God of Our Fathers"      Daniel C. Roberts
Tune: "National Anthem"—George W. Warren
★Corporate Confession      President Jon Althoff, Student Forum
Almighty God, in Jesus Christ you called us to love our neighbors as we love ourselves, but we are not always useful in the work you gave us to do. We are often silent when we should speak and motionless when we should act. We avoid the scene of an accident and entertain those who show hospitality to us. Have mercy on us, O God, and empower us to shed the habits which render us useless. Forgive us, free us from sin, and make us new creatures in him whose life is our model of loving service; through Jesus Christ our Lord. Amen.
★Assurance of Pardon
★"Gloria Patri"
Welcome and Announcements
Greetings from Illinois College      President Donald C. Mundinger
First Scripture Lesson: Job 28:20–29
Children's Time

Anthem: "With a Voice of Singing"                    Martin Shaw
            The Chancel Choir: Howard Jarratt, Director
Second Scripture Lesson: Phil. 1:1–12
Sermon: "Love, Knowledge, and Discernment"
                                    Dr. A. Myrvin DeLapp
*Hymn: "Break Forth, O Living Light of God"
                                    Frank von Christierson
            Tune: "St. Peter"—Alexander R. Reinagle
Minute for Mission                    Mrs. Martha Blackwood
Prayers of Intercession        The Reverend Stephen C. Kolderup
                                        Assistant Pastor
*Offering: "Prelude in D Major"                        Bach
*Prayer of Thanksgiving and the Lord's Prayer
*"Doxology"—Presentation of Offerings by the Ushers
*Benediction: "Alta Trinita Beata," from *Laudi Spirituali*
                                        (14th Century)
                The Chancel Choir
Postlude: "Rigaudon"                            André Campra

---

LOVE, KNOWLEDGE, AND DISCERNMENT
DR. A. MYRVIN DELAPP
ASSOCIATE FOR MINISTRIES IN EDUCATION
THE PROGRAM AGENCY
THE UNITED PRESBYTERIAN CHURCH IN THE UNITED
STATES OF AMERICA
*New Testament Lesson: Phil. 1:1–11*

Let me take this opportunity to tell you that I am overwhelmed
by your generous expression of welcome and my inclusion in your
worshipping community. I am grateful to President Mundinger, the
faculty, and the trustees for the honor bestowed upon me last January. I appreciate your invitation to give me a second chance to visit
and to share in the community of which I am now a part.

What I have to say this morning about church-related education is
against the background of Paul's letter to the Philippians which I just
read. Paul's letter to the Philippians is a very personal and pastoral
letter. That's why I like it so much. And the tone for the whole letter

is set in the passage just read. Paul wants his friends to know at the outset that he remembers them with joy, he's grateful for their partnership in the Gospel, and he just plain misses them. These are words from a close friend and a good pastor. Paul follows these opening warm expressions of friendship and Christian love by identifying the substance of his prayer for them and he does so in a *striking* way. Paul wrote: "And it is my prayer that your love may abound more and more, with knowledge and all discernment, so that you may approve what is excellent, and may be pure and blameless for the day of Christ."[7]

I refer to this as striking because in ordinary usage love is seldom linked with knowledge, and discernment seems far removed from love. Too often love is perceived as a mainly sentimental feeling, a romantic impulse of mindless infatuation, having little to do with knowledge. Our tendency is rather to separate the life of the mind from that of emotions or "things of the heart." So the linkage of love, knowledge, and discernment is unusual. It is also important.

For Paul the relationship of love, knowledge, and judgment was a life-and-death matter for the community. The early Christian communities were always on the verge of disruption or destruction. They were often threatened internally by those who wanted to turn the belief and actions of the community to their own ends and were very persuasive about the matter. It was threatened externally by the principalities and powers who often viewed Christians as a threat to the public good and disturbers of the status quo. So Paul's prayer was fervent that their love for Christ would be a growing love for one another and that together they would learn to live in the world for the sake of the world and, in Jesus' words, be "wise as serpents, and harmless as doves."[8] They were to be the shining instruments through which Christ could be seen in his beauty and saving love.

The linkage of love, knowledge, and discernment is important for us, too. Especially so since we live in what is called by some "a lifelong learning society." Knowledge is more than schooling, but with the vastness of our educational enterprise we look to it almost exclusively for the production of knowledge. Often it appears that we

7. Phil. 1:9,10 (RSV).
8. Matt. 10:16 (AV).

have more and more knowledge about ourselves and the cosmos but unfortunately, at times, show less and less evidence that the uses to which we put our knowledge have any relationship to our love for ourselves or for others. For example, our technological development of devastating defoliants and destructive war materials for use against the peoples of Southeast Asia stands in stark contrast to what appears to be the very limited capacity we have demonstrated so far to reach out in love to the victims of the use of that knowledge, many of whom are now known as "the boat people" and even those of our own who are victims of "agent orange."

Love linked with knowledge can deliver love from mindless romanticism, excessive sentimentalism, or head-in-the-sand concern for one's own self alone. Knowledge—learning—can inform love about how the world really is, can open up more and more new vistas for expressions of care and concern in the world, and can even point to how God has acted and continues to act in the world. But knowledge without love can become planned deception—selfish and demonic utilization of knowledge. And on occasion in the midst of all our learning and accumulation of knowledge, however useful and necessary it may be in our technological world or for just plain living, we need to be reminded as Paul reminded some of his friends: knowledge will pass away. That is, we are not saved by right thinking nor by the accumulation of accurate data, nor by right feeling. We are saved by God's grace, and that is not of our doing. But it is love linked with knowledge and discernment that can help us reflect upon our state of grace, to tell about it and to express love and grace, compassion and mercy, for the sake of the world. That's our calling as Christians.

I believe, therefore, that Paul's prayer that love may abound with knowledge and discernment can symbolize what I regard as the heart of education from the Christian Church's perspective: love for others and self, informed by rigorous and honest examination and exploration of the world and its life, action, and promise; and the dedicated application of love and knowledge in wise, compassionate, and humble acts of justice and mercy for the sake of the world.

Education is a tool to help us actualize our potential for service to the world. It is aided by one's experience of learning in community and then, continuing to learn, identifying that portion of the world where one desires to put one's oar in and begin to row.

The colleges established by Christians early in this country's history generally understood their purpose to be educating for service to the commonwealth. Illinois College is such a college. Julian M. Sturtevant wrote about the College: "We never sought for Illinois College any ecclesiastical control, and would never have submitted to it. We always desired to place it in the hands of patriotic, religious men, that it might be managed not for a sect in the Church or a party in the State, but to qualify young men for the intelligent and efficient service of God both in the Church and the State. It was never intended to be a Presbyterian or a Congregational institution, but a Christian institution sacredly devoted to the interests of the Christian faith, universal freedom and social order."[9] That purpose continues to be an intention of the fifty-two colleges related to our church. "A Statement of Mutual Responsibilities" of our church and its colleges reads:

We, The United Presbyterian Church in the U.S.A. and the colleges and universities related to The United Presbyterian Church in the U.S.A., affirm the validity and the value of our historic relationship. These institutions of higher education generally were founded by men and women committed to Jesus Christ as Lord. As participants in the Reformed tradition, their faith called them to establish these colleges and universities that successive generations might discover and appropriate the knowledge found in the many disciplines. We value our common heritage and we pledge our continuing commitment to be involved together in service to God and society through higher education.[10]

The motif of commitment to service in love for the world is essential to a college's church-relatedness. But there is another ingredient also important for the church and its colleges in their role of educating the public. Today, more than ever, it is to maintain and strengthen the colleges' institutional integrity in a time when the

9. Julian M. Sturtevant, *An Autobiography*, ed. J. M. Sturtevant, Jr. (New York: Fleming H. Revell Co., 1896), p. 237.

10. "The Church and Related Colleges and Universities: A Statement of Mutual Responsibilities." (Italicized in the original.)

total higher education milieu is shifting and sliding and being put under all kinds of new pressures. Such integrity involves careful and honest telling of what and who we are when dealing with potential students. It involves maintaining a steady apprehension of our goals and mission when faddism in education programs seems to offer greener pastures.

In a report made public recently the Carnegie Council on Policy Studies in Higher Education expressed concern about matters of unethical conduct ranging from student cheating to misleading advertising by institutions of higher education. The report says:

Fair practice has been a basic and continuing theme of American higher education since the founding of Harvard in 1636. Colleges and universities have taught and practiced moral and civic virtues throughout our national history, have sought to advance the truth, and have been devoted to public service. Their members often have served as the conscience of the nation.[11]

Yet we are concerned [by a] significant and apparently increasing amount of cheating by students in academic assignments; a substantial misuse by students of public financial aid; theft and destruction by students of valuable property, most specifically library books and journals; . . . [and] inflated and misleading advertising by some institutions in the search for students. [And this sad comment.] Most institutions of higher education, to a small or large degree, exhibit one or more of these destructive aspects.[12]

In the face of this social condition we need to encourage and support our colleges in their efforts to convey the importance of an ethical dimension of life and help them to maintain their institutional integrity. We should expect them to do so. For they can be a witness to an integrity that will strengthen the moral fabric of society.

A third element of church-related higher education has to do with its capacity for and its responsibility for *being prophetic in its freedom.*

---

11. Carnegie Council on Policy Studies in Higher Education, *Fair Practices in Higher Education: Rights and Responsibilities of Students and Their Colleges in a Period of Intensified Competition for Enrollments* (San Francisco: Jossey-Bass Publishers, 1979), p. 1.

12. Ibid., p. 3. [The format of the original itemized listing of the negative aspects of the conduct of higher education has been altered to paragraph form, with appropriate punctuation added; no changes have been made in the wording except those indicated by brackets and ellipsis points. Ed.]

A task of the church is to be prophetic! That is, it is to be so aware of and concerned about the destructive forces affecting human welfare that it confronts, challenges, exposes, and seeks to eliminate those forces wherever possible. The church does this because it stands under the judgment of God when it is disobedient and ignores its prophetic role.

A church-related college is also called to be prophetic because it is of the church. Its prophetic task is first to encourage the development of the critical mind. Not simply for the sake of criticism—either higher or lower—but for the possibility of challenging people and society to commitment for change where it is needed. This seems to be especially needed today. Someone has said that our biggest enemy today among young adults is that they think they can't do anything about crucial problems and issues. And if they can't do anything, a kind of cope-less-ness has set in. But I believe our church-related colleges are challenging our young adults to do something, to cope with confidence. That should be the task of all universities and colleges.

I have a colleague who insists that the whole educational system these days has been seduced into using education "to fit" people into the system. At least, she insists, the church-related colleges ought to be most sensitive to their role to develop those who can be intelligently critical and be committed to making those changes required for society's health.

In talking about our colleges we are talking about the "delegated intellect," the instruments the churches have created and continue to want to exist for the sake of the commonwealth. Surely we should expect the church-related colleges to be a part of the critical function required for society's health and also to be the church's critic. In fact, the church-related college in our day, because it is of the church, is the freest institution to be the loving critic of the commonwealth and the church. We need to help keep the colleges free to make an important contribution to the whole of society.

The role of our church in higher education continues to be important. Love, knowledge, and discernment are essential to our life and witness. Our church's participation in higher education will take myriads of forms: through the lively participation of congregations with community colleges as they both seek to serve their communities; through ecumenical ministries at state and private institutions of higher education; and, through those colleges who want to be related to our church as our church says it wants to be related to them. There is a rocky road ahead for many of them. And retrenchment rather than growth may be ahead. But as Dr. Roald Bergethon, President Emeritus of Lafayette College, has said, the crucial challenge facing us will be to maintain the significance of the individual and the integrity of humane values against the vast impersonal forces dominating every aspect of life.

There is great diversity in American higher education which needs to be preserved. Even among the colleges of our denomination there is great diversity. Sheldon Jackson College with its fisheries program is quite different from Knoxville College serving a predominantly black constituency or even from Illinois College serving in the heartland of America. But in the midst of the diversity and varied programs Dr. Garber Drushal, recently retired as president of the College of Wooster, has observed a common basis and a common purpose. He. writes:

There are at least two common denominators, two basic principles, accepted as the reasons for being which give encouragement for a workable common commitment.

First, there is an impact on the student of a place where things of importance to the church matter to real people. Often it is a silent impact of the environment of the campus. It may lie in the concern with the spirit, whether in familiar words of worship or in the everyday interaction of students and faculty. It may reside in expressions of goodwill through social action. It may appear in those moments that come in quiet meditation of a heart in the peace that bespeaks resources of spirit and mind. In any case, it is the influence of intangible informal ties with a campus whose personality is built of people whose actions demonstrate goodwill and concern and an understanding of the Christian life. . . .

Second, if the ministry of the church as a concern for the immediate situation where love is relevant to justice and justice to love is even partially achieved on campuses . . . , the life goals acceptable to students will not be at the lowest level of casual purposeless living, but rather a high commitment in responsible Christian freedom.[13]

Paul's prayer is my prayer, and I hope your prayer, for all those who learn and teach, those who administer and those who raise funds, and those who recruit students in all colleges and universities and our church-related colleges.

My prayer for them is that their love may abound more and more, and discernment also, that they may prove what is excellent and may be pure and blameless in the day of Jesus Christ. Amen.

STATED MEETING OF
THE PRESBYTERY OF GREAT RIVERS
THE SYNOD OF LINCOLN TRAILS
SEPTEMBER 25, 1979
MORNING PROGRAM

Call to Order     Moderator Catherine Freed
Roll Call of Ministers and Ruling Elder Delegates
Welcome     The Reverend Wallace N. Jamison
Dean of the College
Business Meeting
   Adoption of the Docket
   Approval of Minutes
   Report of Stated Clerk
   Report of the Treasurer
Department on Presbytery Ministries
   Workshops on "The Year of the Child"
   Reports of Task Forces on Hunger, Major Mission Fund, Refugee Resettlement, and Interpretation and Stewardship
Department on Congregational Development
   Reports of Task Forces on the Small Church, Local Church Property and Finance, Youth Ministries, and Christian Education
Evaluation and Goals Committee Report
Nominating Committee Report and Recommendations

13. J. Garber Drushal, "The Church and Its Colleges: A Status Report for the United Presbyterian Church in the U.S.A." (New York: The Program Agency, The United Presbyterian Church U.S.A., n.d.), p. v.

*The Service of Worship*

The Reverend John N. Langfitt, Chaplain of the College

Organ Prelude: "Piece Heroique" César Franck

Mr. Rick L. Erickson, College Organist and Choir Director

Introit: "Be Thou My Vision" Traditional Irish

The Illinois College Concert Choir

Call to Worship Moderator Freed

Leader: The Lord is great—and should be praised. And has made wonderful works to be remembered.

People: Honor and majesty are due to the Lord. We worship in the beauty and strength of God's sanctuary.

Leader: The Lord is good. God has shown people the power of divine works that they may receive the heritage of the nations.

People: The steadfast love of the Lord stands forever and ever. We give thanks for God's love.

Leader: The Lord sent redemption to people. God's covenant shall last forever.

People: Holy and revered is the name of our Lord. Unto God be glory in the church throughout all the ages.

★Hymn: "Our God, Our Help in Ages Past" Isaac Watts

Tune: "St. Anne"—William Croft

★Invocation[14] (in unison)

★A Litany of Remembrance and Thanksgiving Dean Jamison

Scripture: Eph. 4:1–16 Dr. Iver F. Yeager, Chairman,

150th Anniversary Committee

Anthems: "Alleluia" Randall Thompson

"O Clap Your Hands" Ralph Vaughan Williams

The Illinois College Concert Choir

★Litany for the Church and the Presbytery Dr. Laurence C. Judd

Coordinator, Asian Studies Program

Leader: Let us praise God for the gift of the church. For all those who have given themselves in faithful service, both those who are long remembered by many and those known only to a few.

14. The Invocation and Litany of Remembrance and Thanksgiving were taken from the Service of Worship used by the Central Association; they are printed in chapter 12.

People: We praise you, O God, and bless your name.

Leader: For the Lord of the church, who has called disciples in many lands and in many times, who has sent them into the world for the healing of the many that they might know God and glorify Him.

People: We give you thanks, O God.

Leader: For faithful ministers and teachers who in rightly dividing the word of truth in all seasons and among all peoples have given true testimony to the power and purpose of God.

People: We would in this day be dedicated to the same truth and would testify to your great deeds and continuing presence among us, O God.

Leader: We remember promises of the Lord to be present among us whenever people gather in twos or threes in His name.

People: We call on and glorify the power and presence of the Lord among us, both here in our Presbytery and among the people of whom we are a part.

All: Glory to the Father; glory to Jesus Christ, the Son; and to the Holy Spirit. As it was in the beginning, so is it now and ever shall be, forever and ever. Amen.

\*Hymn: "Praise to the Lord, the Almighty"  Joachim Neander
Tune: *Lobe den Herren—Stralsund Gesangbuch*, 1665

\*Benediction  Chaplain Langfitt

Postlude: "Prelude and Fugue in C Minor"  Johann Sebastian Bach
    \*The people standing.

### AFTERNOON PROGRAM

Coordinating Council Reports
Department of Ministerial Relations Reports
Concluding Business
Adjournment

---

The program has been condensed from the *Minutes* of the Presbytery for this date.

PART FOUR

*Illinois College's Distinctive Heritage*

A PROUD HERITAGE—A PROMISING FUTURE

[The] two story brick building . . . was far from completion on Monday, the 4th of January, 1830, but [there were] on that morning nine pupils assembled for instruction. It was the day of small things, but its inspiration was drawn from faith in God and the future.

President Julian M. Sturtevant

---

Beecher Hall (1829). Edward Beecher, first president. The classical curriculum, modelled after Yale's. The first baccalaureate degrees in the state (1835). The College's abolitionist stand. Sturtevant's long presidency (1844–76). Curricular additions: modern languages, the social sciences. Crampton Hall (1873). Merger with Jacksonville Female Academy (1903). President Rammelkamp's *Centennial History*. Centennial Buildings: Tanner, Baxter. The Epsilon chapter of Phi Beta Kappa. President Hudson's leadership during the war and postwar years; Memorial Gymnasium. Expanded enrollments in the 1960s and six new buildings, including Rammelkamp Chapel, Crispin Science Hall, and a Student Center named for President L. Vernon Caine. Inauguration of President Donald C. Mundinger; Schewe Library, the McGaw Fine Arts Center. The Women's Collegium. Professor Frank's Sesquicentennial history, *Pioneer's Progress*.

Sesquicentennial Brochure (adapted)

---

During its 150th Anniversary year, Illinois College is examining its past as it charts its future, [serving] young men and women by strengthening their intellectual powers and nurturing their spiritual values. We are committed to a high level of excellence and service.

President Donald C. Mundinger

The definition of a college's uniqueness is a task both simple and complex. It is obvious that no other institution has precisely the same history and location, or the same people and program, as Illinois College. In this sense every college is different, although such uniqueness in itself is not necessarily significant. It is, however, meaningful to indicate some of the features of Illinois College which are distinctive.

Illinois College is distinguished by its impressive list of "firsts": the first baccalaureate degree granted in Illinois, the oldest college building and the first medical school in the state, the oldest women's club in existence, one of the earliest of all alumni associations, and so on. Illinois College's founding occurred at the right time and place to make it a part of the frontier, to involve it in the abolition controversy, and to make it a part of the history of expanding educational opportunity and the transition from classical to contemporary curricula. Moreover, the College is on the original site selected by John M. Ellis and described by him as a "delightful spot." The campus is small but well-planned, with unified yet varied architecture; several of its buildings are of historical significance.

The most significant of all distinguishing elements of Illinois College is its people. The College has been blessed by men and women of ability who have devoted lifetimes of dedicated service. No one is ever likely to match Julian M. Sturtevant's fifty-six years, but several have reached (or surpassed) the Biblical forty years, and a good many have gone beyond thirty. There have been only eleven presidents in more than a century and a half. This continuity of leader-

*Crampton Residence Hall, 1873*
Remodeled, 1954
Named for Rufus C. Crampton, Professor, 1853–88, and Acting President, 1876–82

ship, by presidents and faculty and trustees, extends into the present and has made possible a remarkable consistency of purpose. Added to that is the fact that large numbers of students throughout the College's history have come from west central Illinois. Moreover, many families are represented in the student body by second and third generations; recently a Missouri graduate of the Class of 1970 returned to the campus to bring her father to his fifty-fifth class reunion.

The topics of the concluding section of this volume represent only part of the distinctive facets of Illinois College's proud history, but they are illustrative. The chapters on the first graduates and the Remembrance March highlight the crucial early history of the College. The succeeding chapters on the education of women and on the (men's) literary societies focus attention upon two important features of the College, dating almost from its beginning to the present. The chapter on "Illinois Journey" sets the College's own story in the larger context of the state's history, which it so nearly parallels. Illinois College is not unique in being a Phi Beta Kappa school, but its Epsilon chapter is one of only nine in the state and constitutes one more important mark of distinction. The concluding chapter, about the College's 145th consecutive annual commencement, brings its story up to the present and points to the promising future, with yet another generation of students added to the ranks of the alumni.

The much more complete and systematic story of Illinois College's distinctiveness has been told by President Rammelkamp and Professor Frank. Any greater insight can be gained only by becoming a part of Illinois College itself.

# 14

## *Illinois College's First Graduates, the Class of 1835: A Memorial Program in Honor of Jonathan E. Spilman and Richard Yates April 13, 1980*

The credit for conceiving and arranging a delightful program of nostalgic reminiscence and lovely music belongs to Mr. Howard Jarratt, Director of Development at Illinois College. Mr. Jarratt had learned of the historical research by Judge Earl R. Hoover regarding Jonathan E. Spilman, a member of Illinois College's first graduating class in 1835. Mr. Jarratt also secured from the Library of Congress photocopies of six of the seven songs which Spilman is known to have published between 1838 and 1844, including the popular "Flow Gently, Sweet Afton." From these beginnings Mr. Jarratt proceeded to plan a special memorial program in honor of Spilman and his single classmate, Richard Yates. The 150th Anniversary Committee gave enthusiastic support to the proposal.

The program was held on Sunday evening, April 13, with Mr. Jarratt presiding and introducing the various participants in the program, beginning with President Mundinger who welcomed the many guests. Professor Iver F. Yeager then spoke about the education and career of Richard Yates who, after graduation from Illinois College, returned to his native Kentucky for law studies. Completing his formal training he made his home in Illinois where he had a distinguished record of professional and public service. A summary of that record is presented in Professor Yeager's talk, printed in the latter part of this chapter.

Stephanie Smith-Jarratt then sang three of Spilman's songs. Mrs. Smith-Jarratt's beautiful soprano voice gave full, clear expression to the sentiment of both melody and word. She was accompanied by Johanna Meyer Horton on the new Steinway grand piano. Both women wore evening dresses reminiscent of the styles typical in the earlier days of Illinois College. The songs which were sung by Mrs. Smith-Jarratt were: "I Own the Tear that Steals" (author unknown); "The Star of Eve," with words by Miss Power; and "Leonora," with words by Mrs. Torre Holme.

The next feature of the evening's remembrances was the impressive story of Jonathan E. Spilman's life, told by Judge Earl R. Hoover, retired, of the Common Pleas Court of Cuyahoga County, Ohio. Equally fascinating was Judge Hoover's account of how he eventually learned the identity of "J. E. Spilman," composer of one of America's best-loved melodies. Seeking copies of songs by an Ohio songwriter of the Civil War period, he had visited a Kentucky antique shop whose proprietor remarked that his own great-uncle, the Reverend J. E. Spilman, was a songwriter, too, and had composed the well-known music for Robert Burns's poem, "Sweet Afton." He added that Spilman had been a Presbyterian minister in Kentucky and had married the niece of President Zachary Taylor.

Subsequent efforts by Judge Hoover to learn more about Spilman were frustrated again and again. Major histories and encyclopedias of American music either ignored Spilman or told very little—and often what was reported was in error. None of these sources indicated that J. E. Spilman was a minister, and one authority surmised confidently that the initials actually stood for "Jane Eliza." Judge Hoover determinedly followed up the various clues which were provided by the great-nephew and by Presbyterian Church records of ministers. Eventually he was led to the three sources which enabled him to solve the mystery: the First Presbyterian Church of Maysville, Kentucky; Illinois College; and Spilman's granddaughter, Mrs. Jeanne Anderson of Xenia, Ohio.

The account of Spilman's life which is printed in this chapter has been abridged from Judge Hoover's delightful article in *The Register* of the Kentucky Historical Society. Judge Hoover carefully documented his study in detailed footnotes, which have been omitted here with the exception of one which gives information about Spilman's children. Among the specific sources acknowledged by the author are President H. Gary Hudson, various issues of the *Rambler*, and Rammelkamp's *Centennial History*.

Following the address, President Mundinger presented Judge Hoover with a Presidential Citation of Merit. Judge Hoover was recognized for his "outstanding career in jurisprudence," his "carefully researched legal opinions," and his "interest in the rich lode of literature and local history." Judge Hoover, who had attended Otterbein College, graduated from Harvard Law School. He had engaged in private practice before serving on the Common Pleas Court of Cuyahoga County, Ohio; his legal opinions are widely respected and have been cited frequently. Judge Hoover has been active in many civic organizations and has had a life-long interest in American traditions and history—especially the Civil War and songwriters of the nineteenth century. Acclaimed as a public speaker, he has given more than four thousand addresses.

Mr. Alan Louis Caine was also awarded a Presidential Citation of Merit. The citation refers to his "artistic work which brightens the lives of so many people," his "scholarly and creative writing for the British Broadcasting Company's radio series entitled 'Radio Vision,'" and his "inspired and tireless work with his students." The son of President Emeritus and Mrs. L. Vernon Caine, Mr. Caine is well-known in this area for his paintings and drawings; he is also a gifted writer. A graduate of Macalester College, with majors in art and philosophy, and of Princeton Theological Seminary, Mr. Caine was Design Secretary and Editor for the British Student Christian Movement for several years. Since 1971 he has taught art at the University of Leicester, England. He has lectured at the Tate Gallery and the Royal Academy, London, and has produced programs on religious art for the British schools. His work has been exhibited at the International Festival in Edinburgh and elsewhere. Plans had been made earlier to honor Mr. Caine on his next visit to Jacksonville and happily that coincided with the memorial program for Spilman and Yates. An account of the campus exhibit of some of Mr. Caine's work will be included in a later paragraph.

Two more of Spilman's compositions were sung by Mrs. Smith-Jarratt, again accompanied by Mrs. Horton: first, "Speed Thee

Pearlina Fair," with words by Richard Johns, Esq., and then the song most anticipated by all the audience, "Flow Gently, Sweet Afton," with the words of Robert Burns's poem. A tape recording was made of all the songs so that those inspired moments can be enjoyed again and again. Mrs. Smith-Jarratt received prolonged applause from the appreciative audience for the charm and loveliness of her singing. Speaking on behalf of the audience, President Mundinger expressed grateful appreciation to Mrs. Smith-Jarratt and Mrs. Horton and then invited everyone to come to Barnes House to greet the participants and special guests.

Among those present for that unforgettable evening were numerous descendants of Jonathan E. Spilman—there are four grandsons and four granddaughters still living, although not all were present—and two great-great-granddaughters of Richard Yates. Members of the Spilman (or Spelman) family had come from Arkansas, Colorado, Illinois, Indiana, and Tennessee to attend this special program. One of the families had brought a rocking chair (equipped with a writing tablet) which the Reverend Mr. Spilman had used in his study; this was placed on the stage and, while Spilman's songs were being sung, Judge Hoover occupied the antique chair.

There was an exhibit in Schewe Library of some of Spilman's letters and sermons, several of them brought for that purpose by the family, and some from the College's archives. Also on display were the photocopies of Spilman's published songs (obtained through the courtesy of the Library of Congress) and a copy of *The Register* of the Kentucky Historical Society with Judge Hoover's article. The cover of the journal has a picture, from Judge Hoover's collection, of the Reverend and Mrs. Jonathan E. Spilman and five of their children.

A paragraph in the printed program gave further information about the early years of the College and about its first graduates and is reprinted here.

The first students who enrolled in Illinois College had begun their classes in January, 1830, but because they needed considerable preparatory work none of those nine pupils was to be in the first graduating class in 1835. That honor went to Jonathan E. Spilman, a member of the first collegiate class in 1831, and Richard Yates, who after a year of study at Miami College in Ohio (1830–31) had come to Illinois College in 1832 or 1833. The curriculum these young men completed was patterned after Yale's, and their basic studies were in the Greek and Latin classics and mathematics. Other subjects listed in the 1832–33 College catalog (the oldest one known to exist in pamphlet form) were: astronomy, natural philosophy (physics), moral and intellectual philosophy, evidences of Christianity, political economy, and the Federal Constitution. The first Commencement exercises were held on September 16, 1835. The Bachelor of Arts degrees were conferred by Professor Julian M. Sturtevant, in the absence of President Edward Beecher. Spilman delivered the valedictory address, which he had entitled, "Scepticus." Yates, however, was the first one to receive his diploma (and so was the first college graduate in the State of Illinois). The title of his address was "The Influence of Free Institutions in Moulding National Character."

The printed program also provided further information about the participants in the evening's events. It was noted that Mr. Howard Jarratt had been a performing artist in concert, opera, and oratorio and had starred on Broadway. Later he served as General Manager of the Dallas Symphony and the Kansas City Philharmonic Orchestras. He has been at Illinois College since 1975. Stephanie Smith-Jarratt (Mrs. Howard Jarratt) was graduated from Southern Methodist University with the B.F.A. degree in Music, Drama, and Theatre. She sang with the Dallas Civic Opera and appeared in educational television films with the Dallas Symphony Orchestra. Mrs. Smith-Jarratt has performed frequently as soloist with the Jacksonville Symphony Orchestra and recently had sung the title role in a concert version of Bizet's *Carmen* presented by the Belleville Philharmonic Orchestra. Mrs. Johanna Meyer Horton (Mrs. George William Horton, Jr.) earned the bachelor's degree in music at MacMurray College. She teaches piano and sings in the choir of Trinity Episcopal Church and in the Jacksonville Symphony Chorale.

A notice in the program called attention to the exhibit of Mr. Alan Caine's works which had been on display in Schewe Library that afternoon. Thirty oil paintings, water colors, pencil drawings, etchings, and woodcuts were loaned for the occasion by several Jacksonville residents and by members of the Caine family. Mr. Richard L.

*Sturtevant Hall, 1857*
Remodeled, 1965
Named for Julian M. Sturtevant, Professor, 1830–85, and President, 1844–76

Pratt, Librarian, and Mr. Michael G. Crouse, Instructor in Art, assisted in preparing the exhibit.

Following are the two addresses given at the evening program, the remarks on Yates by Professor Yeager and the talk on Spilman by Judge Hoover.

---

RICHARD YATES: FIRST COLLEGE GRADUATE IN THE
STATE OF ILLINOIS[1]
DR. IVER F. YEAGER
PROFESSOR OF RELIGION AND PHILOSOPHY

When Henry and Millicent Yates were married in 1808 they set out on horseback from her family's home in Virginia to establish a new village in Kentucky. This was to be the birthplace of their eleven children, the fourth being a son whom they named Richard. In 1830 Richard, then fifteen, was sent off to Miami College in Ohio for a year of study, and while there he once walked twelve miles, alone, to hear a speech by Henry Clay. Richard left the college without notice to join his father on a walking trip to Illinois and later helped the family move to a farm in Sangamon County, near Berlin. The father was determined that his son should have a career in law and politics and a year later, in 1832, Richard came to Illinois College to resume his education. In addition to the classics and mathematics, the anchor subjects of the curriculum, Richard studied science and philosophy and Christianity and also political economy and the Federal Constitution.

The first college degree granted by Illinois College—and the first in the state of Illinois, was conferred upon Yates at the first Commencement, September 16, 1835. There were two men in that graduating class and each gave an address; Yates's was entitled, "The Influence of Free Institutions in Moulding National Character."

1. The sources used in the preparation of this address were: Richard Yates (the younger) and Catharine Yates Pickering, *Richard Yates, Civil War Governor*, ed., John H. Krenkel (Danville, IL: Interstate Printers and Publishers, 1966); and the articles on Yates in *Dictionary of American Biography*, 20 (New York: Charles Scribner's Sons, 1936), pp. 599–601, and in Charles Moseley Eames, *Historic Morgan and Classic Jacksonville* (Jacksonville, IL: *Daily Journal*, 1885), pp. 133–35.

While a student Yates had won acclaim for his oratory and subsequently he became a popular speaker in the area, frequently speaking on freedom and proclaiming America's invitation to the poor and oppressed of other nations. He took part in the Lyceum and in the community's debating societies. After a year of law study at Transylvania College in Kentucky, Yates returned to Jacksonville to enter the law office of John J. Hardin, whose public service in the state legislature Yates was to emulate.

The marriage of Richard Yates and Catharine Geers took place in 1839. Catharine, a native of Kentucky, had lived in Jacksonville with her family since she was eight years old and on her wedding day she had not yet reached seventeen. The young couple made their home with the bride's mother for nine years, a period of very limited resources while Richard was establishing his law practice and launching his career in public service. Five children were born, the first dying in childhood and the second soon after birth; three children survived to maturity, Henry, Catharine (later, Mrs. John Pickering), and Richard, born in 1860.

It was not long before Richard Yates set about to fulfill his father's expectations for his career. In 1842 he won election to the Illinois legislature; there he delivered a speech pleading for the establishment of the common schools (one in every valley and on every hilltop) and for government support for those schools and for the colleges which were needed to train good teachers and stimulate the love of learning in the frontier state. Twice he was reelected and then in 1850 he won a seat in the U.S. Congress. Later he said that that campaign was the most exciting of his life. He and his opponent rode horseback from town to town, debating at every stop. Reelected in 1852, he lost the following election largely because of his opposition to the Kansas-Nebraska bill, which rescinded the Missouri Compromise and opened Northern states to slavery.

Almost as soon as he had arrived in Washington, Yates met Susan B. Anthony and Elizabeth Cady Stanton and quickly joined the cause of woman suffrage. Small-town newspapers in his district ridiculed their representative for endorsing what the editors regarded as an absurd proposal. In answer to these attacks Yates was to sponsor a bill for woman suffrage every year during his decade of service in

Washington; the bills never got out of committee, but in 1919 his son Richard, then representing the same district in Congress, voted with the majority to establish the cause his father had advocated nearly seventy years before.

Catharine Yates's health was poor and the climate in Washington was more than she could cope with. She and the children lived in Jacksonville most of the time. Yates wrote frequently to "My dear Katie," describing his activities in Congress and explaining his views on important issues. He declared his support for the Hungarian patriot, Lajos Kossuth, then visiting in the United States. He wrote rather disparagingly about the married daughter of a colleague who wore the Bloomer costume and looked more like a boy than a woman. He described the elegant dinner for eighteen men served by Senator Stephen Douglas who had had prairie chickens and partridges brought from Illinois for his guests' delight. He witnessed the great fire in the Capitol building in 1851 which destroyed thirty-five thousand books and several paintings of early presidents. He remarked about the splendor of the East Room of the White House and its elegant carpet imported from Scotland. Yates also told of introducing Mrs. Edward Beecher, wife of Illinois College's first president, to President Filmore. But along with such reports Yates often expressed his great longing for his wife and children, and again and again he urged her to write more frequently.

Since his college days Yates had recognized the crucial role of good transportation in developing his home state, and as the railroads developed he became intensely interested in them. Returning home after his defeat for a third term, he was met at the depot and told, "You are the president of the Tonica and Petersburg Railroad." Yates's primary task was to speak in every township of the ten counties through which the railroad would pass and urge the sometimes hostile farmers to vote approval for the railroad's bonds. The vote was favorable and the railroad very successful, building one thousand miles of track and acquiring sixteen wood-burning locomotives. The Tonica and Petersburg was the forerunner of the Chicago and Alton Railroad.

Many friends urged Richard Yates to return to public office and in 1860 he carried on a hard campaign, continuing day after day for months, for the Governorship of Illinois. He ran on the ticket with Lincoln. Four years before when the Republican party was being formed, Yates had predicted that it would yet be the ruling party of the nation. Then people had scoffed at him, but in 1860 his prediction proved to be accurate. As Governor, Yates strongly supported Lincoln, whom he had known since 1835, and despite a sometimes hostile legislature he succeeded in bringing Illinois' massive support to the Union cause. Illinois produced so many volunteers that the Army had to ask that some be sent home again. Yates ordered Illinois troops to Cairo to defend that strategic river junction from seizure by the Confederate Army.

In 1862 Governor Yates urged Lincoln to prosecute the war against the Rebels vigorously, and he was one of the first to advocate the emancipation of the slaves. He exercised the Governor's powers of clemency to help six Negro men convicted of violating an Illinois law penalizing any Negro, slave or free, who entered the state with the intent to stay permanently. Yates said he was the only Governor who ever pardoned a man for being black! It was Yates's appointment of Ulysses S. Grant as Colonel of the Twenty-First Regiment that led Grant to march his troops on foot from Springfield to Jacksonville and then to Naples—and it was that march which started Grant on his career of military leadership and victory for the Union cause. There were heartbreaks, too, for the Governor—on those occasions when he visited the battlefields and the hospitals to comfort the wounded and dying. He earned the name "The Soldiers' Friend" for his determination to supply Illinois troops, to care for their personal needs, and to provide for their widows and orphans.

Elected to the Senate in 1864, Richard Yates served as Chairman of the Committee on Territories and in that capacity traveled to Colorado Territory, enjoying the new sleeper cars for the first part of the journey and then completing the trip by riding two and a half days on the stage. As a member of the Committee on Railroads he was invited to witness the driving of the golden spike linking East and West by rail.

The victim of a drinking problem in his later years, Yates struggled to overcome alcoholism and suffered much from illness—all the harder to bear because of the continuing separation from his wife and family. His bid for reelection to the Senate failed, and his final act of public service was as a railroad examiner. On his way home in November, 1873, after completing that assignment, he was stricken in his hotel in St. Louis and died suddenly. Yates was survived by his wife and the three children for whom he had so often expressed his deep affection.

Yates himself considered his advocacy of universal suffrage to be his greatest achievement. His strenuous efforts in the Senate overcame all attempts to impose a literacy requirement for voters. Publicly, Richard Yates's finest hour was his triumphant return home in 1865 upon completing his term as governor nearly nine years before his death. The Great Western Railroad ran a special train to Jacksonville, carrying the Governor and twenty-five legislators and many friends. That evening Strawn's Hall was crowded to the utmost. David A. Smith presided at the meeting and President Julian M. Sturtevant of Illinois College, Yates's former teacher and life-long friend, spoke eloquently to declare the gratitude of the Governor's friends and neighbors and indeed of the whole nation. Sturtevant's own words of reminiscence and high praise will be our own eulogy to Richard Yates. I quote from Sturtevant's address on January 18, 1865:

If there is one here who has watched with friendly interest all your career, and rejoiced with you in all your successes and your honors, I claim to be that one. . . . In your youthful days . . . you were my pupil. You received the first literary honors which our college ever conferred, and the first diploma which this hand ever delivered. . . . Your public life, too, has been eminently true to those principles of liberty, equality and justice on which the foundations of that institution are laid. . . .

We are proud too, of your official career. Perplexed and embarrassed by hostile legislation which would have paralyzed the arm of this great State, and rendered her powerless to aid our dear country in the hour of her peril and her need, your patriotism, courage and wisdom have [placed] her among the foremost of the sisterhood of States in defending national unity and liberty. In the name of our country, and of humanity, we thank you.[2]

2. Springfield, Illinois, *Daily Illinois State Journal*, January 19, 1865.

# JONATHAN E. SPILMAN: FAMOUS ILLINOIS COLLEGE GRADUATE[3]
## JUDGE EARL R. HOOVER

The story begins with pirates and . . . a change of name. The songwriter's first paternal ancestor to step on America was his great-grandfather, Henry Spilman. He came from England and he really wasn't a Spilman, but a Spelman. At sea, pirates murdered his father, also a Henry. Young Henry settled safely in Westmoreland County, Virginia. Due probably to his extreme youth, he started misspelling the name with an "i". Henry's son, James, lived in Culpeper County, Virginia. Among James's eight children was Benjamin Spilman, the songwriter's father, who in 1790 married Nancy Rice. Immediately they plunged to Kentucky. Benjamin was just twenty-three. The songwriter was born on April 15, 1812, at Greenville, seat of Muhlenberg County, Kentucky, the twelfth of their thirteen children. . . .

The hardships of pioneer travel from Virginia to Kentucky did not quell the restless Benjamin Spilman. About 1818, the year young Jonathan became six and Illinois was admitted to the Union, the Spilmans plunged Westward again, settling in White County on the plains of Illinois. There Jonathan grew up.

In 1831 Jonathan entered Illinois College at Jacksonville, whose president was Rev. Edward Beecher, the brother of Henry Ward Beecher and Harriet Beecher Stowe. Their father, Lyman Beecher, later an eminent Cincinnati preacher and president of Cincinnati's Lane Theological Seminary, has been called the "father of more brains than any other man in America."

In time, Illinois College would count among its sons, orator William Jennings Bryan and Lincoln's law partner, William H. Herndon, but now it was so shiny new that Spilman was a member of its first graduating class (1835). He had the honor too, of being valedictorian. Of course, the class had only two graduates, but do not underestimate the competition. Today just a handful of statues stand on the grounds of the Illinois State Capitol. One is that of Kentucky-

3. Abridged from an article by Judge Hoover, "J. E. Spilman: Kentucky's Long-Lost Composer of A World-Famous Melody Rediscovered," in *The Register* of the Kentucky Historical Society, 66 (July, 1968):222–41. The portion included here begins on page 229 and continues to the end of the article with omissions indicated. Used by permission.

born Abraham Lincoln. Another is that of Richard Yates, the Kentucky-born, Civil War governor of Illinois, United States senator and Spilman's classmate. . . .

Spilman now reversed his life plan. Twenty years later he would reverse his reversal and resume his original plan. If he had not shelved his original purpose he might never have written his immortal melody because the stray circumstance that inspired it might never have discovered him elsewhere. Spilman had entered Illinois College to prepare for the ministry. As graduation neared he wavered, doubted his call and tabled it for later consideration.

In the fall of 1836 Spilman and his classmate, Richard Yates, entered Transylvania's law school. There the warm friendship that had grown between them at Illinois College became more firmly cemented. Spilman graduated in 1837, but returned the next year for an extra course of lectures as a resident graduate. After Transylvania the paths of the two classmates separated forever except for one brief moment. Yates, though a native of Kentucky, returned to Illinois for the big role that destiny was saving for him. Spilman remained in Kentucky. They met but once again, for an hour's conversation in Springfield when Yates was Governor.

There in his native Kentucky, destiny singled out Jonathan Spilman to be one of the fortunate few who create something that will live. As the hour approached for him to write a deathless song he was young—only about twenty-five. It was a beautiful 1837 summer day. The young law student was taking advantage of it, too, as he sat in the shade of a tree on the Transylvania campus enjoying a book of Robert Burns's poems.

Musically inclined, he turned over in his mind, one by one, the tunes he knew to which various poems of Burns had been set. He came to those lines to Mary and a river. To his surprise he could think of no music to them. He must be mistaken. That just cannot be. So he read the lines over, then over, then over again. Somewhere there must be music for such words. And suddenly there was! Under the spell of immortal poetry, from some unknown somewhere, there came to Jonathan Spilman the strains of an immortal melody— strains that neither he nor anyone had ever heard—strains that fit into the company and do honor to the lines of a Robert Burns. And

Jonathan Spilman, student of law who had tabled a call to the ministry, jotted them down there that day under a black locust, Transylvania campus tree.

At the house, piano in hand, he worked out the accompaniment. He did not realize what he had created. How could he? He took a copy to his sweetheart. She sang it to friends. They suggested publication. He laughed. They continued urging him. He mailed it to an Eastern publisher frankly admitting that such a thing was out of his line, but saying that if the publisher thought the song worthy he could publish it. Spilman emphasized that he took no responsibility. To his elation he received a laudatory reply and twenty-five printed copies.

This is how it happened that, in 1838, one of the 19th Century's leading publishers, George Willig, of Philadelphia, issued a new song in sheet music by Kentucky's J. E. Spilman entitled "Flow Gently, Sweet Afton":

> "Flow gently, sweet Afton, among thy green braes,
> Flow gently, I'll sing thee a song in thy praise;
> My Mary's asleep by thy murmuring stream,
> Flow gently, sweet Afton, disturb not her dream."

It sold many editions.

You recognize immediately that Spilman's tune is also sung to the words of another old favorite—one of the most loved Christmas songs—sometimes called "Away In a Manger" and sometimes called "Luther's Cradle Hymn":

> "Away in a manger, no crib for his bed,
> The little Lord Jesus lay down his sweet head.
> The stars in the heavens look down where he lay.
> The little Lord Jesus asleep on the hay."

After Transylvania Law School, Spilman practiced law for eighteen grueling years in Kentucky—at Nicholasville from 1838 to 1849, then at Covington until 1856. He was a law partner of Judge Samuel M. Moore, later of Chicago, and of Judge John W. Menzies, later a Congressman.

Grueling years turned into crushing years when Spilman's partner entered politics saddling him with extra heavy legal loads. He broke down. Fearing permanent injury, he sold at great sacrifice. A little place in the country restored him. There he had time to reconsider the matter he had tabled more than twenty years. In 1858, he returned to work and to his original life plan—a Christian minister. He was forty-six years old. For thirty-eight years he preached—mostly in small towns—Covington, Nicholasville and Maysville in Kentucky; Canton in Mississippi; Carmi and Flora in Illinois.

There was romance and heartbreak along the way. In 1840, when almost twenty-eight, at Nicholasville he married Mary B. J. Menefee, daughter of Major John Menefee, of Jessamine County. She died three years later, three days after the birth of their only child. The baby died just nine months later. In 1845, now thirty-three, he married Eliza Sarah Taylor, daughter of Hancock Taylor, of Jefferson County, Kentucky—brother of Zachary Taylor. They had ten children.

The great heartbreak in the Rev. J. E. Spilman's life, I discovered, came when he held the pastorate at Maysville, Kentucky—an almost unbelievable story. [Passage had been arranged for Mrs. Spilman on the *Bostonia No. 3* to Cincinnati, and her family had gathered on the porch of the manse overlooking the Ohio River to wave farewell to her as the steamer passed. Before their eyes the packet was suddenly engulfed in flames and Mrs. Spilman was severely scalded by a broken steam pipe. She was helped ashore and managed to get back to her home but she suffered excruciating pain and died two days later.]

Spilman was fifty-four; Eliza, forty-four. They had been married twenty-one years. About half of their ten children were living including Charles, the oldest, who was nineteen, and Lewis Hopkins, the youngest, who was only six.[4] One daughter, Mrs. Julia Byrd Dewey, of Palm Beach, Florida, a writer, was recognized in *Who's Who In America*. The son, Lewis Hopkins Spilman, a lawyer of

4. Jonathan was born April 15, 1812, at Greenville, seat of Muhlenberg County, Kentucky. Eliza was born June 23, 1822. They were married April 10, 1845, and had ten children, namely: Charles, Anna Louise, Mildred Wilson, Richard Henry, Eliza Allen, William Magill, Julia Bird (also spelled Byrd), Clara Lee, Frances Rice, and Lewis Hopkins. Reports conflict as to whether five or six children survived Eliza.

Knoxville, Tennessee, was also a writer who made *Who's Who*. Spilman lived thirty more years but never remarried. What irony that he should gain fame imploring a river to be gentle! His is the drama of a man in whose life two rivers play—two that flow thousands of miles apart in different hemispheres. One that he never saw, brought immortality; the other, flowing beneath his home, death.

Up the Ohio River about 170 miles from Louisville and 65 from Cincinnati—Maysville is still one of the nation's picturesque river towns. . . .

Though J. E. Spilman is forgotten in Maysville today, downtown there still stands the stately First Presbyterian Church where he preached in the 1860s. Forgotten too, though once the focus of a tragedy that rocked the whole valley, there still stands on the west side of town not far from the river, the house where the Spilmans lived.

In my quest there were years of correspondence to New York, Pennsylvania, District of Columbia, Kentucky, Georgia, Mississippi, Texas, Illinois, and California. I made field trips to Kentucky and Illinois. At Maysville, I beheld the manse from which helpless loved ones once saw Eliza Spilman in distress. The story unfolded in dramatic detail, and I had authority for everything—well, except for one thing.

I was hunting that last link on July 6, 1951, when Mrs. Hoover and I entered the little town of Flora in Southeastern Illinois—population 5250. Knocking on the door of the Presbyterian parsonage, I asked hospitable Rev. F. D. McMartin if he could give me some information about a Rev. J. E. Spilman who wrote "Flow Gently, Sweet Afton" and who, I understood, was once the pastor of his church.

He had never heard of Spilman, but he kindly telephoned Arthur Holt, a church official who had the church's old records. Holt had never heard of Spilman either, but he invited me to go to his home where his wife would show me the records. Gracious Mrs. Holt was waiting for me. Neither had she heard, but soon we were scouring the old "Minutes of the Session of the Presbyterian Church of Flora, Clay County, Illinois." And sure enough, there in these more than a half-century-old handwritten minutes for April 2, 1893, we discovered that "Rev. Jonathan E. Spillman, D.D., was engaged to supply the Pulpit on the Sabbath days when Rev. J. F. Flint would be absent at Odin or elsewhere, which was extended after Mr. Flint's departure."

But was this "Spillman" the "Spilman" who wrote "Flow Gently, Sweet Afton?" The minutes did not say. At this anxious moment we found preserved in the old minute book, a printed program of the 85th anniversary celebration of this church. I perused it and beamed. Eureka! There, in a list of the church's pastors was "J. E. Spillman"; and after mentioning that he preached there until 1895 when physical infirmities compelled him to resign, it continued: "It is with pride that we can inform you that Rev. Spillman was the composer of the music to the beloved ballad, 'Flow Gently, Sweet Afton.'" Yes, this was the right man, and I was near the end of the trail in the search for that last link.

I asked Mrs. Holt if there were any residents old enough to have known Spilman. Yes, there was—a Miss Grace Hundley. Mrs. Holt telephoned her. Miss Hundley had not only known Spilman, they had been near neighbors. That called for the big question—and Mrs. Holt asked it over the telephone—was this last link located in Flora? Yes, it was; and Miss Hundley told her where it was.

By now Mrs. Holt sensed that we were in search of something of historical significance. I did not have to ask her; she volunteered to guide me to it. We drove across town, entered a beautifully landscaped terrain, started hunting—and we found it!

There, in the heart of these United States, in Elmwood Cemetery, on the edge of this little community that did not know he was there, not only lost to Flora but lost to the world, we looked upon the grave of the man who among the world's countless billions had done something immortal—the man whose name is associated with Robert Burns and Martin Luther.

The humble shaft gave no inkling of what he had done, or that here lay buried a world figure. It simply said, "Jonathan E. Spilman, April 15, 1812. May 23, 1896. That they may rest from their labours, And their works do follow them."

Yes, the man of two rivers and two professions who attained fame with his hobby even before starting to work, died in Flora at the age of 84.

We drove to the home of Miss Hundley on the west side of Flora. She still lived in the same house at Number 333 W. North Ave., where she lived in the 1890s when Jonathan Spilman lived diagonally across the street and to the left at Number 418. There the song writer spent his last years. In 1892, at the age of eighty and while preaching at Carmi, Illinois, he was, at his request, retired from active work because of his advancing years and because he wanted to be near relatives. He moved to Flora to be close to his daughter, Clara Lee Spilman Andrews (Mrs. George W.), the mother of Jeanne Andrews Anderson.

He built the little cottage that still stood across from Miss Hundley, and became supply pastor of the Flora church. There he lived with his maiden daughter, Anna Louise, just four feet eleven inches tall, and affectionately known as "Aunt Tantie." The Andrews also lived diagonally across the street from Miss Hundley but a little to the right. So Miss Hundley's eagle eye guarded the short highway path from Jonathan Spilman's to the Andrews'.

Fifty-five years had gone since Miss Hundley had seen Jonathan Spilman on that path. It had grown from a village street to a bustling transcontinental highway. Pointing to the Spilman cottage, she said: "Just as if it were yesterday, I can see him walking up the road from his house to the Andrews'. He was tall, handsome, kindly and slightly stooped, with long white hair and beard, but he looked like an aristocrat. He died at the Andrews' house. When he became sick, the Andrews brought him to their home so they could take care of him. . . ."

Then Mrs. Holt and Miss Hundley took me to the old church building in which Jonathan Spilman had held his last pastorate. To make way for a new church building, it had been moved from its original site at the corner of Second and Locust Streets; and then stood on East Second Street. Neither sermon nor hymn had echoed therein for many years, for it had been devoted to something else. . . .

I left Flora happy that I had found Jonathan Spilman, but puzzled that a world could lose such a man. Perhaps Illinois will make amends. Flora is on Route 50 connecting Washington, D.C., and San Francisco. Spilman's cottage is too. Just as it did for another adopted Kentucky son, Abraham Lincoln, perhaps Illinois will enshrine Jonathan Spilman's grave and home so that a neglectful world may come and pay its overdue homage.

# 15

## *The Remembrance March*
## *April 22, 1979*

At one of the early meetings of the 150th Anniversary Committee, Jon Mark Althoff of the Class of 1980 proposed a remembrance march as one of the Sesquicentennial activities. Representatives of College groups and other interested students and faculty would go to Diamond Grove Cemetery to participate in a commemorative service. They would then decorate the grave sites of founders of the College and of other men and women who have made significant contributions to the College during its 150 years. In 1929, as part of the Centennial celebration, wreaths had been placed at the Ellis monument and upon the graves of three members of the Yale Band: Julian M. Sturtevant, Mason Grosvenor, and William Kirby. The proposal for 1979 was to give recognition to a much larger group and to combine a pleasant outing with the solemn ceremony.

The first announcement to the campus community was made in January, 1979, in a letter sent to various student groups and community organizations. Referring to Thomas Carlyle's statement that the present is the living sum total of the whole past, Jon wrote: "Our century and a half have been rich with a proud tradition of excellence; and . . . it has been this past history that has made our present. . . . We must not fail to hold fast to the inspiration and dedication which was given to us unselfishly by those who have preceded us here at Illinois College." The general plan was outlined: groups would assemble at Sturtevant Hall on a Sunday afternoon in April to walk down Lincoln Avenue to Diamond Grove Cemetery, a mile south of the campus. When people had assembled at the entrance,

*Whipple Hall, 1882*
Remodeled, 1968
Named for Samuel L. Whipple, Benefactor

brief ceremonies would be held and the representative groups would proceed to the selected grave sites to place flowers in honor of the men and women who had been prominent in the College's history. The groups would reassemble for the return trip to the campus in time for the evening meal.

Much detailed work had to be completed before the ceremony. Jon spent hours checking with the City Clerk's office and with alumni and local historians to obtain the names of the founders, trustees, and alumni who have been buried in local cemeteries and to determine the locations of their graves. Associate Professor George William Horton, Jr. -52, gave valuable assistance in this exacting task. The members of Alpha Phi Omega organized work crews to help put the grave sites in good order. The Jacksonville Monument Company and cemetery personnel assisted in straightening and repairing those markers in need of such attention. Then on the day of the March, student volunteers marked each of the designated graves with a small blue-and-white "IC" flag. A map of the cemetery with numbers to indicate the grave sites and a corresponding list of the names had been prepared to guide each group to its proper place.

The careful preparations and almost ideal weather—comfortable temperatures and partly sunny skies—combined to make the occasion both reverent and enjoyable. About one-hundred persons participated, many of them student representatives of campus organizations who were present to honor someone of special significance to their group. The names of these organizations and of the community groups which participated are included in the list accompanying the map which has been reproduced in this chapter. The pastors of the two churches with which the College has long had a special relationship were present: the Reverend Dale W. Robb of the First Presbyterian Church and the Reverend Robert M. Cassels of the Congregational Church. Representatives of the Reverend James Caldwell Chapter of the Daughters of the American Revolution took part in the March also.

The people gathered just inside the entrance to Diamond Grove Cemetery. President Mundinger addressed the group and Chaplain John N. Langfitt offered prayer; the texts have been included in this chapter. The representatives of the various organizations each received a spray of multicolored gladiolas and set out for the designated grave sites. A College van was provided to take students and flowers to Jacksonville East Cemetery and to Memorial Lawn Cemetery, south of the city. The day's activities ended with the buffet supper at Baxter Hall.

As a further expression of appreciation and tribute to the Congregational Church and the First Presbyterian Church for the important role they and their members have had in the life of the College, floral bouquets had been provided for their morning services on the day of the Remembrance March. Thus the larger community as well as students and faculty shared in the significance of the occasion, and the events of that day served to strengthen the loyalties which are the foundation of the future.

---

## STATEMENT BY PRESIDENT MUNDINGER

"O death, where *is* thy sting? O grave, where *is* thy victory?"[1]
In this week following the glorious resurrection of Christ on

1. 1 Cor. 15:55 (AV).

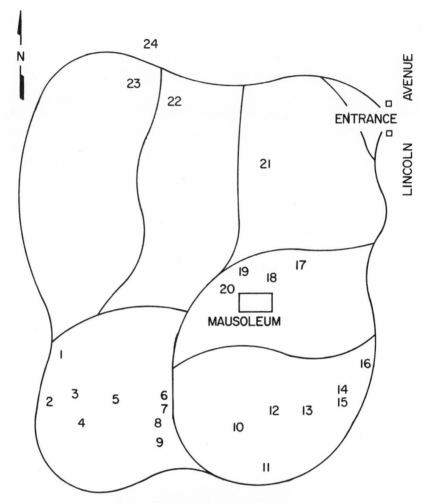

*Map of Diamond Grove Cemetery*
Illinois College Remembrance March
April 22, 1979

Easter Sunday and the first blush of the vernal equinox, both traditional expressions of rebirth and renewal, it is appropriate that we—
at this time, in this place, and with these people—come together to
honor the lives and work of important people in the history of Illinois College.

Whether the name is John M. Ellis, a founder of Illinois College;

REMEMBRANCE MARCH
LIST OF PERSONS HONORED, AND THOSE HONORING THEM
(The year of the person's death is given in parentheses.)

Diamond Grove Cemetery: Key to Map of Grave Sites

| | |
|---|---|
| 1. Mrs. J. M. Ellis (1833) Wife of Founder | Ellis Hall |
| 2. Jonathan B. Turner (1899) Faculty | Turner Hall |
| 3. Gov. Joseph Duncan (1844) Aided College in securing charter | Daughters of American Revolution |
| 4. Wm. Kirby (1851) Yale Band; Trustee | Congregational Church |
| 5. David A. Smith (1865) Trustee | Sigma Phi Epsilon |
| 6. J. M. Sturtevant (1886) Yale Band; First Instructor; President, 1844–76 | President Mundinger |
| 7. Mrs. J. M. Sturtevant (1886) | Fayerweather House |
| 8. Samuel Whipple (1876) Benefactor | Alpha Phi Omega |
| 9. Mason Grosvenor (1886) Yale Band; Faculty | Faculty |
| 10. C. H. Rammelkamp (1932) President, 1905–32 | President Mundinger |
| 11. R. C. Crampton (1888) Faculty; Acting President, 1876–82 | Crampton Hall |
| 12. Arthur J. French (1977) Trustee | Family |
| 13. Hiram K. Jones (1903) Faculty; Benefactor | Hilltoppers |
| 14. Gov. R. Yates, Sr. (1873) Alumnus | Sigma Pi |
| 15. Gov. R. Yates, Jr. (1936) Alumnus | Sigma Pi |
| 16. Miss Ann McCormick (1935) Aided Chi Beta | Chi Beta |
| 17. J. Harker (1938) Principal, Whipple Academy | Faculty |
| 18. Joe Patterson Smith (1963) Faculty | History Students |
| 19. Wm. Cocking (1937) A founder of Gamma Nu | Gamma Nu |
| 20. E. G. Hildner, Sr. (1968) Father of the late Prof. E. G. Hildner, Jr. | History Students |
| 21. Harold Leam (1976) Faculty | Student Forum |
| 22. Miss Stella Cole (1937) Faculty; Founder, Gamma Delta | Gamma Delta |
| 23. E. A. Tanner (1892) President, 1882–92 | President Mundinger |
| 24. Dr. D. Prince (1889) Medical School Faculty | Premedical Students |

Jacksonville East Cemetery

| | |
|---|---|
| Wm. Posey (1849) One of original trustees | Faculty |

Memorial Lawn Cemetery

| | |
|---|---|
| George Wm. Horton, Sr. (1974) Faculty | Phi Alpha |
| John P. Sorenson (1976) Faculty | Music Students |

Charles Henry Rammelkamp, a president; Arthur French, trustee; Stella Cole and John Sorenson, faculty members; Joe Parkinson, a recent student—although they are not with us, yet they live and the lives which they led among us are celebrated and honored today. The spirit of these people and of all individuals who labored to foster and nurture the intellectual and moral climate of Illinois College is recognized this afternoon.

The Christian tradition gives us the grand and noble assurance concerning the purpose and worth of each human life. It is to serve others in love so that future generations will enjoy a fuller and more happy life in service to others.

The people whose names I have just announced have all been very important in the history of this College. They stand symbolically for the hundreds of individuals who have taught, studied, worked, and served Illinois College.

It was William O. Douglas who once said that one should occupy high ground. I use that expression this afternoon not in a physical sense but in the intellectual and spiritual sense. I urge each one of you to renew your pledge to God and man and to work for Illinois College—as student, faculty member, and friend—so that Illinois College will become stronger, so that she may occupy higher ground, so that she may provide a higher level of service now and into the future.

In this very real sense, therefore, people do not die. They live on through their work and through the influence which they pass on spiritually to future generations. As a result, people across the land have been touched, directly and indirectly, by Illinois College. Let this recognition be indelibly written upon our hearts and minds so that we may take inspiration from these souls and have the courage to strive even as they have.

In these days following Easter, let us see in our noble friends the defeat of death and of the grave. On this afternoon early in the spring of 1979, we shall truly become immortal as we work in the cause of Illinois College and all mankind.

## PRAYER AT DIAMOND GROVE CEMETERY
## DR. JOHN N. LANGFITT, CHAPLAIN

"Therefore, since we are surrounded by so great a cloud of witnesses, let us also lay aside every weight, and sin which clings so closely, and let us run with perseverance the race that is set before us, looking to Jesus the pioneer and perfecter of our faith, who . . . endured the cross . . . and is seated at the right hand of the throne of God."[2]

Let us pray.

For all the saints, who from labors of love and duty have now taken their rest, we give thanks and praise. For students who, desiring to learn, gathered on the hilltop campus in response to Your call, showing the way to those of us who study now, we give thanks and praise.

For teachers who, desiring to celebrate You and Your world and advance our knowledge of it, stood ready to receive students on the hilltop, showing the way to those of us who teach now, we give thanks and praise.

For facilitators who, filled with Your Spirit, indeed impelled by Your Spirit, have provided the support of their time, their service, and their creativity for the advancement of our knowledge and learning on the hilltop, we give thanks and praise.

For friends who, in faith and commitment to a vision of Your future, have provided the support of their time, their money, and their prayers, that Illinois College may fulfill its mission, we give thanks and praise.

All praise and thanks are Yours, O God, as we celebrate our past by walking, honoring, talking, or eating today, and as we hope for our future.

In the name of the pioneer of our faith, Amen.

2. Heb. 12:1–2 (RSV).

# 16

## Illinois College and the Education of Women
### A Special Sesquicentennial Program, March 11, 1979

Almost from the beginning of Illinois College the education of women was an important corollary of the education of men, although it was several decades before the two aspects were joined and Illinois College became coeducational. The history of women's education both before and after the merger of Jacksonville Female Academy and Illinois College in 1903 was the topic of a special program on March 11, 1979. The arrangements were made by the Women's Collegium, which had been organized in 1976 to assist in educating women "for Life and Work in the 1980s and Beyond." The Collegium was made possible by a three-year grant, since renewed, from the Helena Rubinstein Foundation. The Director of the program since its inception has been Mrs. Carole M. Ryan '59, Associate Professor of Modern Languages (French).

Dr. Ethel Seybold, Professor Emeritus of English, was invited to give the address, which she entitled, "Illinois College and the Education of Women." As Mrs. Ryan stated in her introduction of the speaker, "No one is better qualified to speak on 'Women and Illinois College' than Dr. Seybold." Miss Seybold was a member of the Centennial Class, earning her B.A. in Classics and graduating with honors. She earned the Ph.D. degree at Yale University and joined the English Department at Illinois College in 1943, serving for many years as Cochairman of the Department prior to her retirement in 1975. During her long and active service on the faculty Dr. Seybold provided strong leadership for the women's literary societies. She had joined Chi Beta as an undergraduate and subsequently, in recognition of her support of the women's societies, Sigma Phi Epsilon and Gamma Delta made her an honorary member. For two decades she was faculty advisor for the freshman women's society, Alpha Eta Pi. She has been chairman of the House Committee of the David A. Smith House Board for more than twenty-five years. Dr. Seybold's address was highly informative and delighted the large audience which met for the evening program in Jones Theatre.

Following the address, Professor Ryan invited the audience to Smith House for a reception, which was hosted both by the Collegium and by the Ladies' Education Society, Mrs. Helen Walton Hackett '27, chairman. The Smith House was a very appropriate place for the reception and provided a lovely setting for it; the house has been beautifully furnished, and it provides excellent facilities for the three women's literary societies. It was especially meaningful to the many women—and numerous men—who were present to visit the various rooms and see the furnishings after they had heard Dr. Seybold's account of the long struggle to provide education for women *and* suitable quarters for their activities. The occasion also provided justly deserved recognition of the Ladies' Education Society, which since its founding has aided more than three-thousand young women in the pursuit of their educational goals. The Society itself is recognized by the General Federation of Women's Clubs as the oldest women's club still in existence in the United States.

---

ILLINOIS COLLEGE AND THE EDUCATION OF WOMEN
DR. ETHEL SEYBOLD '29
PROFESSOR EMERITUS OF ENGLISH

I am truly happy in this year of the Sesquicentennial of Illinois College and under the auspices of the Women's Collegium to have the opportunity of talking to you about women at Illinois College. It enables me to talk about certain subjects in which I have long been interested: the early history of Illinois College, the David A. Smith House, and in lesser degree, the Jacksonville Female Academy, the Ladies' Education Society, and the Young Ladies' Athenaeum.

I am happy also to talk to this particular audience, for I know that no one not interested in my subject would have come out on a Sunday evening at 7 o'clock to hear what I have to say. I am especially glad to talk to the young women of the College; the things I shall be saying are a part of their proper heritage, about which, I suspect, they know very little, a kind of origin and "roots" talk. To my contemporaries and elders—if there be any of the latter—I shall be saying many things that are familiar; I comfort myself that they enjoy, as I do, the retelling of the old familiar stories; but since, as we grow older, we do not always remember the same things the same way, I have chosen for the sake of accuracy not to trust memory or oral reminiscence, but to depend on written records.[1] I hope that I shall be able to add some new and specific information to our body of traditions and to make some significant correlations of facts.

I began my own searching out of facts and my own attempts at correlation as a result of a rather pettish remark made by a casual acquaintance nearly twenty-five years ago. "I don't know why you call Illinois College coeducational," she said. "You've had so few women so short a time." I reminded her that we had then had women on the campus for over fifty years and added that I didn't think the women at Illinois College considered the presence of several men for every woman in the nature of a disadvantage. Then I decided to look more closely into the matter and discovered that Illinois College had to a much greater extent than I had realized been responsible for the establishment of the first institution for the education of women in this area and had maintained a very close spon-

1. Bibliographical Note by Dr. Ethel Seybold: For sources concerning the early education of women in Jacksonville as it was linked with Illinois College, I have used the collected minutes and miscellaneous records of the Ladies' Education Society and such records of the Jacksonville Female Academy, the Athenaeum, and the Illinois Conservatory of Music (catalogs, programs, histories, and so forth) as exist in the Illinois College library. I have also consulted the memoirs concerning these institutions presented at the Centennial celebration of the College. For information concerning the early days of coeducation at Illinois College and for the history of Smith House, I have used the catalogs of the College, the minutes and archives of the Woman's Building Association of Illinois College (the Smith House Board), and the minutes and scrapbooks of the women's literary societies. I have also had recourse to Mrs. Rammelkamp's brief personal memoir of the early days of Smith House and to President Rammelkamp's *Centennial History* of the College. These sources are incomplete and often contradictory; from them I have compiled a history of Smith House containing much of the material in this lecture in considerably greater detail, at considerably greater length, and with greater emphasis on the history of the House. Copies of this paper have been deposited in Schewe Library, where they may be consulted.

sorship and correlation with it for three-quarters of a century until the institutions merged in 1903.

The first step toward an institution of higher education here—for either men or women—was taken in 1827, two years before Illinois College opened its doors, when John M. Ellis, a young Presbyterian minister and missionary to the western wilderness, drew up and published a plan for such an institution. It provided for theological courses (to train ministers), theoretical courses (to train the mind), practical courses such as medicine, agriculture, and woodworking (to provide for the material needs of the community), and, quite astonishingly for the time and place, "a department for female education" until a separate school for females could be established. This may very well have been the first time that the concept of coeducation was advanced in nineteenth-century America, or elsewhere, for that matter.

The idea of a women's department in the College was not, however, put into execution. Illinois College opened in 1829 as a men's college; at approximately the same time, Frances Celeste Brard Ellis, the minister's wife, opened a school for girls in her own home. On September 29 of the next year, the Reverend Mr. Ellis and several other Jacksonville men met at the home of John P. Wilkinson, a trustee of Illinois College, to draft a plan for an educational institution for women to be known as the Jacksonville Female Academy. Among those present were Judge Samuel Lockwood, Chairman of the College Board of Trustees, and Professor Julian M. Sturtevant, a member of the faculty and later President. Less than a week later, on October 4, 1830, these gentlemen met again to choose trustees for the projected academy, which continued to meet in the Ellis home, the first house west of the old Central Presbyterian Church on West State Street, not far from the public square.

It was almost two years later, in August of 1832, that another organization destined to be prominent in the education of women had its beginning. A group of women were invited to meet at the Ellis home for the "special purpose of devising plans for the extension of their usefulness." I do not know what the nucleus of the group was, possibly some church-related missionary group, for it was not entirely local and it had eastern connections. Two of the nonlocal members, teachers themselves, suggested the training of women teachers as a worthwhile project.

Before this group met a second time, Mrs. Ellis died in the cholera epidemic which swept Jacksonville in the summer of 1833, and the Academy had to find other quarters. It opened that fall in a rented building on the southeast corner of State and West Streets with thirty-one students enrolled. Illinois College had an enrollment of sixteen that fall. Miss Sarah Crocker was imported from the East to become the first principal of the Jacksonville Female Academy. This was the first women's seminary in the state of Illinois and the second school for higher education for women west of the Alleghenies.

On October 4 of this same year, 1833, the ladies who had met with Mrs. Ellis the year before to devise plans "for the extension of their usefulness" met with Miss Crocker in her schoolroom and formed a society named "The Ladies' Association for Educating Females."

Thus Illinois College, the Jacksonville Female Academy, and the Ladies' Association for Educating Females were essentially triplets, having the same ancestry, founded at very nearly the same time, by the same or closely associated people, and for closely related purposes.

The stated purpose of the Ladies' Association was "to encourage and assist young ladies to qualify themselves for teaching." There were three basic requirements for the young ladies they assisted: they must show intellectual promise and interest; they must be of good character, not necessarily, but hopefully, Christians; and they must be needy—young women who could not acquire an education without help. The Association was especially interested in orphans and in the daughters of ministers and foreign missionaries. They helped at least two American Indian girls.

In the beginning, they insisted that their protegees should plan to teach. This was probably occasioned by the fact that teachers imported from the East invariably married after a year or two. It seemed that they were really importing wives for western men instead of teachers and that it would be advisable to train their own educators. However, the teaching restriction was abandoned later in favor of the more liberal idea that an educated woman in any sphere was a benefit to society.

The Association was not originally just a local organization, although the nine executive committee members were all Jacksonville residents. All that was necessary to become a member was to contribute not less than fifty cents annually. The membership list was extensive, both numerically and geographically. It grew to include members from all over the state, from most of the states in the Union, and from foreign countries. Groups as well as individuals became supporting members.

The ladies were obviously very careful with their funds. During the first year, they collected $246.40, paid out $29.58, and helped five women students at the Academy. This seems quite incredible, but their aid was not entirely financial. They frequently helped girls to find places to live where they might work two or three hours a day to pay for their room and board while attending school.

The Ladies' Association held a public annual meeting during Commencement Week at Illinois College as a part of the Commencement Week program. They were too modest to appear on a public platform themselves, so they chose male surrogate officers—husbands, relatives, friends—to conduct the meeting and give the reports. The men, too, proposed resolutions of appreciation and encouragement to the Association and often made rather lengthy remarks about what *they* thought the aims of the organization should be. The education of women, one gentleman pronounced, should fit them for domestic duties, should require—I rejoice to learn—severe application of mind, and should enlighten the conscience. Once, the ladies were actually chided for having five hundred dollars in their treasury. Obviously, one gentleman reproved, they were not "doing all they could," if they had so much unspent money.

A year after JFA had opened on West State Street, it had to vacate its quarters and move to Court Street. This caused the trustees to expedite their plans for a building of their own. The reliable John Ellis was among the most energetic in soliciting funds. In 1835, a small building which would eventually become the east wing of a much larger one was nearly completed when "a lady," nameless in the annals of history, discovered to her dismay that this was to be a one-story building only. She begged the authorities for a twelve-hour delay to see what could be done. By the allotted time, the Ladies' Sewing Circle of Jacksonville had pledged four hundred dollars for a second story.

The year 1835 was a good year for the Academy. The building was finished and furnished—with furniture made in the Illinois College workshop—and the school received its charter of incorporation from the state a short time before Illinois College received its charter.

Throughout the rest of the century, Illinois College for men and the Jacksonville Female Academy for women continued to exist as separate, but closely linked institutions. They had separate boards of trustees, but many of the same names were on both lists. They had separate faculties, but again, many faculty members served both institutions. Arrangements were made for JFA girls to attend lectures at the College. Of course, there were also social links, by groups and individually. The men's societies at Illinois College invited the girls for special programs. There would have been more individual links, had the JFA girls not been so well chaperoned. Illinois College men used to say that the initials JFA stood for Jail for Angels.

In 1853, the Ladies' Association for Educating Females changed its character. Whereas it had begun as a kind of central organization in the West, drawing support from the East and extending its influence to far-flung outposts, the situation was now changed. The East no longer felt a missionary responsibility, and what had been frontier outposts were now thriving communities with their own resources. The Association then became the Ladies' Education Society of Jacksonville with only local membership. Later, in 1872, it would incorporate under the new name and limit its membership to a self-perpetuating board of no more than ten, whose task it would be to administer the endowment funds of the Society to help young women secure college educations. It is, incidentally, even now, helping four young women enrolled in Illinois College.

Although the Jacksonville Female Academy was the first institution for female education in Jacksonville with which Illinois College was closely affiliated, it was not the only one. In 1864, William D. Sanders, Professor of Rhetoric at the College, established the Young

Ladies' Athenaeum, which became a very popular and fashionable school. It was located first on the corner of West College and Westminster and later on South Sandy Street, just off the southwest corner of the public square. Its faculty was composed largely of Illinois College professors, among them Rufus C. Crampton, Julian M. Sturtevant, Edward A. Tanner, and, of course, Sanders himself. The Athenaeum was distinguished for its music department, which later became the Illinois Conservatory of Music, also fathered by Professor Sanders. In 1885, when the Athenaeum was discontinued, the Conservatory became part of the Jacksonville Female Academy and was housed there.

After three-quarters of a century of this coordinate kind of education, Illinois College and the Jacksonville Female Academy officially merged in 1903. The alumnae of the Academy, the Athenaeum, and the Conservatory were added to the alumni rolls of the College. The Academy building, called Academy Hall, continued to house the Conservatory and also served as dormitory and dining hall for Illinois College women. When more convenient quarters for women were finally provided nearer the College campus, the site was sold, the building torn down, and the high school gymnasium erected there.

The reasons for the merger were largely financial, and not everyone was happy about it. The College men weren't; apparently they preferred to worship their angels from afar. The parents of the girls must not have been, for few of the JFA girls enrolled at Illinois College when this became possible. Only nine women matriculated at the College in the first year of coeducation.

The young ladies brought with them three of the JFA faculty: Dr. Jane Scherzer, former principal of JFA and Dean of Women; Miss Isabel Smith in Biology, and Miss Stella Cole, who taught French and German. Economy soon forced the elimination of a Dean of Women for so few women. Miss Smith stayed for a quarter of a century to become the beloved "Biddy Smith" of the College; and Miss Stella Cole, from the time of her arrival on the Campus until her death in 1919, was the ardent champion of the girls, their friend and protector.

The women needed someone who was concerned for them. They

walked a mile back and forth between Hall and Campus for classes
and meals. They had no place on Campus to call their own. They
had no organizations comparable to the men's literary societies.
They attempted to maintain an old JFA society, Philomathian, but it
did not survive. Moroeover, the women were hopelessly outnum-
bered by the men; and the College administration, accustomed to
dealing with men only, had little comprehension of or concern for
its new daughters.

It was a man, however, who was responsible—somewhat acciden-
tally—for the formation of the first women's society on the Hill. In
1911, when copy was being prepared for the *Rig Veda*, the male editor suggested that the girls organize and take a name in order to have
a picture in the annual. Discouraged by previous failures, they felt
no great enthusiasm for the project; but, nonetheless, an announcement was sent out that all women interested in forming a society
should meet at an appointed time and place. After the picture was
taken, those girls who were sufficiently interested did organize, and
the first women's literary society, Gamma Delta, was formed at that
time.

Now that the women had an organization, they had a vehicle
through which to plan. At their 1915 Love Feast, Miss Cole presented the electrifying idea of starting a Fund for the Construction
of a Woman's Building on campus as a place "for rest, reading, and
relaxation," with food facilities and meeting places for women's
groups. A Woman's Building Association was promptly formed
with faculty wives and women and town women who had family
ties with the College as sponsors and helpers. Anyone who made a
pledge or donation was counted a member. The sums were small:
one, two, occasionally five dollars a year from the girls; ten, twenty-
five, a rare one-hundred dollars from their older friends. To these
were added proceeds from a variety of interesting, even amusing
projects: dramatic club performances, conservatory concerts, after-
chapel hot dog sales. The girls sold oriental kimonos, realizing $3.50
on each sale. One year at the Osage picnic, they had a melting pot
for old silver, generously giving half the proceeds to the Red Cross
and keeping half for themselves. President Rammelkamp later re-

ferred humorously to these activities as a brave attempt to raise $100,000 by selling sandwiches and candy.

The Fund grew slowly; meanwhile the number of women on campus and their needs kept growing. By 1916, one literary society seemed inadequate for the number of women. Moreover, Gamma Delta, which at its formation had been open to any woman who chose to join, had become selective. Accordingly, a second society, Sigma Phi Epsilon, was formed. This society was quickly followed in 1920 by another, first called Agora and later Chi Beta. So strong a competition for members developed among the societies that, as President Rammelkamp phrased it, "results . . . were not always conducive to the happiness of the girls or the best interests of the College." Faculty women proposed that a special society for freshmen be established to protect entering students from pressure before they could get their bearings and to provide a training ground for membership in the upperclass societies. In 1921, Alpha Eta Pi was established for freshman girls.

There were now four societies and no proper place for any of them to meet. They met in the old Y.M.C.A. room on the second floor of Beecher, in odd corners in Academy Hall, in a small office on the first floor of Whipple. The one place set aside for women generally was a long, narrow room adjacent to the library reading room in Jones Memorial Hall. It was located just about where I am standing now and was called simply "the girls' room."

Between 1915 and 1918, the Woman's Building Association had collected about $2,000. In 1918, they had organized formally with a constitution and a board of directors. They had just started to draft an appeal for funds to the alumnae of the College when the College itself launched a campaign to raise $500,000. Under the circumstances, the women felt it would be improper to go ahead with their campaign; but they were sorely disappointed that after fifteen years, the College had still taken no steps to provide for its women students, and they felt that the matter should be brought firmly to the attention of the trustees.

At this juncture, Rhoda Jeannette Capps Rammelkamp, wife of the president of the College, took the initiative, showing a considerable resourcefulness and diplomacy. Under her leadership, the women sent a message of support to the president and the trustees, stating their decision to discontinue their own fund raising because of the College campaign. At the same time, they expressed their hope that the next College campaign would be for a woman's building, and they called attention to the poor dormitory facilities for women, the inadequate society halls, and the lack of such special courses for women as physical education, domestic science, and the household arts.

It is doubtful that the trustees were much impressed by these needs. They were not much interested in dormitories; most of the men students lived in private homes in town. Everyone walked everywhere; Academy Hall was available, and the College had no money for frills. They may have felt that the four miles of walking which the girls had to do daily substituted for a physical education course; and as for courses in domestic science and the household arts, they might have been a proper education for women when any education for women was a radical idea. But now, when women were coming out of the home, and it was accepted that intellectual capacity was not determined by sex, these ideas were obsolete. If women were to be educated with men, let them study what the men studied. Even in the education of men, Illinois College had moved away from the vocational, abandoning its workshop, its medical school, and its agricultural courses in favor of a purely intellectual, liberal arts curriculum. It was scarcely likely to introduce vocational courses for women.

The idea of a woman's building had been Stella Cole's; the implementation of the idea was very much Jeannette Rammelkamp's. She was a Jacksonville girl; before her marriage she had supervised an elementary physical education program for women on the campus; she knew both the community and the College. Above all, she knew the right people to ask for money, and she could make asking for money seem like conferring a favor. She kept working persistently behind the scenes, giving ground when necessary, but never giving up. It is appropriate that her portrait hangs over the mantel in the south parlor in Smith House.

Suddenly, in the spring of 1921, it came to Mrs. Rammelkamp's attention that one of the finest old homes in Jacksonville, providentially adjacent to the College campus, was about to come on the market. It had been built in 1854 by David A. Smith, a prominent Jacksonville attorney and an early trustee of the College. Seven of his sons and sons-in-law had attended Illinois College, and six daughters had been students at the Jacksonville Female Academy or the Athenaeum. The next-to-last family member had now died, and the last survivor was hospitalized. The house would not, it is true, serve all the purposes the Board had in mind; but it might be within their financial reach, and it would later, after a woman's building was erected on campus, make a lovely home for the literary societies.

Immediately, the Board of the Woman's Building Association appointed a committee to confer with Mr. John Lansden, a Smith family member and their representative, and with the trustees of the College. Mr. Lansden promised to notify the Board when and if the house was for sale. In the fall of the year, the ladies, the trustees, and Mr. Lansden met again. The house had been twice appraised, once at $8,500 and again at $10,000. Our careful ladies offered $7,500; Mr. Lansden named $9,000 as his lowest selling price.

The Board had precisely $3,342.32 in their treasury. They would need nearly $6,000 more to meet the selling price and nearly $2,500 in addition to put the house into usable condition. The College trustees offered to lend the ladies $7,000, taking a mortgage on the house for that amount. They accepted. They had then a little more than $1,000 to spend in conditioning the house.

To acquire both a legal identity for taking title and a tax-free status, they incorporated on a not-for-profit basis. They also rewrote their constitution to create a smaller, firmer, and more manageable structure. The self-perpetuating Board was composed of twenty-four town and gown women, elected theoretically for a term of years, but actually serving until death or resignation. Then they turned their attention to making money and astounded the College by paying $1,000 on the mortgage within six months.

They solicited funds from all the alumnae of the College, all 367 of them. The College had recently appropriated the old "girls' room" in Jones for a chapel annex, thus ousting the Y.W.C.A. chapter; the Board asked for and got a compensation of $250 to help equip the east first-floor parlors in the new house as Y.W.C.A. rooms. The women's societies were asked to make themselves responsible for the $350 annual interest on the mortgage, no small responsibility for a small group of college girls at that time.

So the house was financed, and the girls moved in in the fall of 1924. There was a happy Housewarming in November. No opportunity was lost for making money. Tea was served for a "donation," and craft articles were offered for sale.

But the biggest source of revenue was a plan devised by the Board for naming the house and its rooms. They proposed to name the house for anyone who would contribute $5,000, and a room for anyone who would make a contribution of $500. The Smith family exhibited a cautious interest in having the house named for its builder, but they thought $5,000 too high a price. At the May, 1925, meeting of the Board, a motion was made to reduce it to $2,500. But a cannier judgment prevailed. The Association decided rather to ask the Smith family to make an offer. The family offered $3,000 and asked to have two commemorative tablets put up at their own expense, one inside and one outside the house. There was a good deal of correspondence about this, the family wanting rather larger and longer memorials than the Board thought desirable; but with great tact and amiability, a compromise was reached. The house became officially the David A. Smith House, and the Board applied $2,700 on the mortgage, which was then reduced to $3,300.

Just about a month later, unexpectedly and gloriously, there came enough money to clear the mortgage and endow the House. A trustee of the College and his wife, Mr. and Mrs. Pascal Hatch, anonymously gave $15,000: $5,000 for clearing the mortgage and for whatever immediate expenditures might seem desirable; $5,000 to go to the College Board as endowment for exterior and structural maintenance; and $5,000 for the House Board, to be invested and the income used for interior maintenance.

There were a number of immediate expenditures necessary: sheds had to be torn down, the cistern filled, the basement cleaned and whitewashed. Rats infested the building, and during the winter the House Committee was instructed to "take any measures they thought wise to rid the premises of rats."

With the new source of income, it would no longer be necessary to ask continually for pledges and donations; the women's societies, released from paying the mortgage interest, could pay instead a minuscule rent. Certain public uses of the building were approved and fees set for its use. A part of the second floor was made into a rental apartment. It was the responsibility of the Board to equip the two east parlors on the first floor, used by the Y.W.C.A., along with the dining room, kitchen, and halls. The west parlors on both floors were allocated to the societies, who were expected to finance the furnishing of their own rooms.

Then came still another windfall. The Dwight family gave a gift of $4,500, of which $3,000 was to be used to furnish the Y.W.C.A. rooms, to be known henceforth as the Dwight parlors in memory of Helen McClure Kirby Dwight, a granddaughter of William Kirby of the Yale Compact. The income of the remaining $1,500 was to be used for the maintenance of these rooms.

After years of waiting, scrimping, and begging, the Board had $3,000 to spend for pure pleasure, $3,000 which they were required to spend for pure pleasure. They bought wallpaper, rugs, draperies, and antique furniture. One Board member wrote to an absent friend, "You should see the rugs and furniture the Committee bought for the . . . Dwight rooms! Luscious! We had a regular jollification meeting over them." Most of the furniture now in the Dwight rooms is the furniture bought that year.

It was in that marvelous year of 1925 that Miss Anne Bellatti was elected Chairman of the Smith House Board, a position that she was to fill for fifty years until her death in 1975. If Miss Cole had the idea of a woman's building and Mrs. Rammelkamp the challenging, but joyful task of acquiring Smith House, Miss Bellatti had fifty long years of living with its pleasures and problems. She was patient, fair, and tactful, both with the girls and with her Board of twenty-four strong-minded women. This year, a beautiful console and mirror in her memory have been placed in the front hall of Smith House.

Over the years we have had other gifts and bequests. All the rooms have been named for donors who made the required $500 contribution, and tablets have been placed in the appropriate rooms. We have had two legacies: $1,000 in 1932 from Miss Elizabeth Kirby, and $2,000 in 1940 from Miss Eleanor Moore. Only twice in all these years have we asked for help. In the early fifties, Mrs. Rammelkamp wrote to the Dwight family, asking help in redecorating the Dwight parlors. Mrs. Dwight sent a check for $500, derived from the sale of a first edition of Whitman's *Leaves of Grass*, originally owned by the Beechers. I confess that I had mixed feelings about that. It seemed to me a terrible thing that the Illinois College library should not have had that book, even if the Dwight rooms had to go unfurbished. But, of course, I had nothing to say about it. Again, two years ago, the House Committee initiated a fund raising campaign which resulted in enough money to make some basic improvements, particularly in the entrance hall.

Smith House policies and problems have changed many times in its fifty-odd years. One of the first problems which presented itself and which still persists is a policy for furnishing the House. Well-meaning friends were eager to contribute furniture; the girls had a great deal of enthusiasm for improving their rooms, but not a very well-developed taste. If the House was to be furnished and decorated in proper style, there would have to be some all-over planning. The Board attempted to solve the problem by engaging an interior decorator from Chicago, but her efforts were not entirely satisfactory. She sailed for Europe; and the societies, with hard earned money in their hands and a burning desire to spend it, could do nothing until she returned. When a society asked her to send them a chair for their room, she sent a vase for the mantel; she seemed not to remember the scale of the rooms and sent furniture too small to look well. Finally, she married, the depression came, and the House Committee of the Board was given the task of granting or refusing approval for anything to be brought into the House. This has been a hard task, as I can attest after twenty-six years as Chairman of the House Committee. Sometimes we have to disappoint eager and enthusiastic young women; sometimes we give a reluctant approval under strong pressure and live to regret it. Our work is always complicated by having to do things piecemeal, which makes an all-over harmony difficult to achieve. But it is a pleasure to work with so beautiful a house; the girls have been generally cooperative and careful—I have known upholstery in the House to last for forty years; all of the societies have had helpful alumnae committees; we have gone far beyond simple approval or rejection and have traveled many miles and searched long to find just the right material or the right item for a certain place in the House. Although there is still much to be done, the House develops steadily toward a beautiful, harmonious whole.

With the grounds, we have not been able to accomplish our original, rather grandiose plans for formal gardens to the south. In the beginning, people donated flowering shrubs and plants, and as in the case of furnishing the House, it soon became evident that there would have to be some central authority. In 1925, Dr. Grace Dewey offered to arrange for this at her own expense, and Mrs. Hubbard of Hubbard Woods was engaged to do the planning. But the depression intervened here also, and never again did it seem possible to think in terms of formal gardens. To the Grounds Committee of the Board fell the responsibility for basic landscaping and maintenance. The Board was fortunate in having among its members two women who were expert gardeners, one professional and one amateur, Courtney Crouch Wright and Emma Mae Leonhard, whose names should be added to our list of those who have made special contributions. These two women acted, sometimes alternately and sometimes jointly, as chairmen of the Grounds Committee and produced admirable results over the years. Their efforts had, for reasons of expense, work, and time, to be confined largely to the planting of trees and shrubs. The greater part of the south lawn became and remained for many years a hockey field for the women.

The Board has had some problems with preserving the grounds. Everyone had plans for all that lovely area so near the campus proper. At the time when the property was purchased, the College trustees asked the Board that they "should not at any time consider the sale of any part of the property under consideration without consultation with them." Two years later they asked permission to construct a central heating plant on the southwest corner of the property. In exchange, they would buy for the Board two lots east of the hockey field, behind the house just east of Smith House, cornering with rather than lying behind the House. The Board countered with the suggestion that the College buy a lot to the east and construct their heating plant there "as far east of the boundary line between the two properties as possible." They would then give the College a ten-foot right of way along the east side of their property to provide access from Grove Street to the heating plant, *provided* the plant could be constructed without injury to the property and the hockey field and without expense to the Board. The College came back with the perplexing suggestion that the driveway should come from Park Street across the Smith House lawn, running east and west just south of the House and north of the hockey field. There the matter was dropped.

The City of Jacksonville has also been interested in the property, once when they proposed building an electric power station there, and again when it was planned to enlarge the intersections of Grove, Park, and Mound Streets. In the end, they built the power station on land to the east; and in the second instance, they took most of the ground needed from properties other than Smith House. Recently, the College asked permission to construct tennis courts on the property, and permission was granted for the construction of two courts at the south end, leaving the House itself a still adequate amount of lawn.

When Smith House was acquired, it was still considered possible that a woman's building might be erected on the Campus. This hope, based on the concept of a specialized education for women, vanished with the concept; and Smith House became primarily a home for the literary societies. At that time, however, nearly every Illinois College woman was a member of one of the societies, so that Smith House was truly home to all the campus women. It was used for other purposes also. Certain women's groups from the town were allowed to hold meetings there; the Faculty women, the Faculty as a whole, and various College organizations made use of it. Receptions were held there and distinguished Campus visitors entertained. One year, under necessity, the House was used for the social events of Commencement Week. Students, alumnae, and alumni married in Rammelkamp Chapel held their wedding receptions in Smith House. The Board is happy that the House did and does serve these auxiliary uses. But it regrets that in recent years it has not served as great a proportion of the College women as it once did.

Part of this problem is a matter of size; we have more women than we used to have or than we planned for. But part of it seems to me to be a matter of not caring enough. We used to believe that literary society membership was very valuable for girls and to foster it. The selective system of bidding did not always promote this. Sometimes all the freshman women wanted to join whatever society was largest on the theory that biggest was best; and the resultant crush of members robbed them of their opportunity to participate. At another time, they might all choose to join the smallest society in order to take it over and dominate it. The societies therefore were subject to considerable fluctuation in membership. During World War II, Chi Beta was temporarily inactive, but was successfully reactivated after the War. In a few years, however, Sigma Phi Epsilon, reduced to five members, faced possible extinction. To avoid this and to prevent later recurrences of such problems, the Dean of Women, Genevieve McCracken, who had great influence with the girls, proposed to the societies a system of bidding which matched the preferences of the women and the societies in such a way as to keep the societies approximately the same size and to guarantee all interested women the privilege of society membership. The matching process was so secretly and discreetly done by a disinterested person that no girl ever knew whether she was the first or last choice of her society, and no society ever knew whether a member had chosen it first or last. This operated very successfully for over twenty-five years.

Then in the turbulent 1960s, there began to be leaks in secrecy; dissatisfaction and wrangling grew; pledges were actually traded among the societies. The abolition of Alpha Eta Pi about this time because of the numbers involved and the problem of faculty advisors probably contributed to the unrest. Finally, in the early 1970s, the societies returned to the old system of selective bidding with its divisive tendencies. In addition, the large number of girls on campus deprived them of the feeling of cohesiveness that had once united them, so that interest in the women's societies declined. Smith House is now home to fewer girls than we wish it were.

I do not know what solution there is to these problems. Perhaps we need another Mrs. Rammelkamp to acquire another house for our College women. Perhaps we need another group of town and gown women like that first Board. Perhaps we need other generous benefactors to finance a bigger, better College program for our women. Perhaps I am wishing for something that cannot come again.

But, in any case, it is time for those of us who care for Smith House and take pride in her past to be taking a close look at the present and the future. First and foremost, we must find a better system of financial support. We are going to have to care enough to make a serious contribution. Never has the House been so valuable as a property. Never has it been so valuable in other ways. As many beautiful old houses have been destroyed or fallen into decay, the public has begun to cherish highly those remaining buildings which represent the historic past of the nation. Of these, Smith House is a distinguished example. Illinois College is indeed fortunate to have such a building. I hope it will continue to survive, to be cherished, and to serve worthy needs in the future.

# 17

## *Literary Societies*

Literary societies have a prominent place in the student life of Illinois College. Mention has been made in Chapter 2 of the participation of the societies in various Sesquicentennial events. The address by Professor Seybold, in the preceding chapter, described the important contributions of the women's literary societies in providing for the women students of the College.

Professor George William Horton's essay on "The Literary Society on the American College Campus" has been included in this volume because it describes the historical background of these organizations. Largely because literary societies have disappeared from most if not all other campuses where they had once flourished, few persons even among their own members are knowledgeable about their origins and development and the factors responsible for their nearly universal disappearance; consequently, the societies at Illinois College seem even more unique. Moreover, Professor Horton has gained some insight into the reasons for the survival of these groups on the I.C. campus—the result partly of the men's literary societies which still flourish in the Jacksonville community and thus contribute to an environment sympathetic to their student counterparts. For all these reasons, the essay is included here even though it was not delivered at a Sesquicentennial program. First written in 1966, the essay has been slightly revised and abridged for inclusion in this volume. Appreciation is hereby expressed to Professor Horton for permission to print his account, previously unpublished, in this book. It fills what would otherwise be a serious gap in the portrayal of Illinois College's distinctive heritage.

It is evident from the opening paragraphs of the essay that the author has close ties with Illinois College and with literary societies—and especially Phi Alpha. George William Horton, Jr., is a graduate of Wabash College, where he earned the Phi Beta Kappa key. He enrolled in various classes at Illinois College over a period of years to qualify for teacher certification. His M.S. degree in mathematics education is from Oklahoma A and M University, and he has had additional graduate study in the same field at the University of Oklahoma. He taught mathematics at Upper Iowa University for six years before coming to Illinois College in the fall of 1962. Professor Horton remained for two years, leaving for further graduate study, and then returned to Illinois College in 1968 to become a permanent member of the faculty. He now holds the rank of Associate Professor of Mathematics.

---

## THE LITERARY SOCIETY ON THE AMERICAN COLLEGE CAMPUS
### ASSOCIATE PROFESSOR GEORGE W. HORTON, JR. -52
### DEPARTMENT OF MATHEMATICS

In September, 1946, I embarked on my senior year at Wabash College while my father joined the faculty of Illinois College. The two colleges shared the heritage of being founded by Presbyterian missionaries in the westward surge of college establishment during the first half of the nineteenth century, and for many years they made common cause in the fund raising efforts of the Society for the Promotion of Collegiate and Theological Education at the West.

I quickly noticed two differences in the colleges. First, Illinois was coeducational and Wabash was not. Secondly, there were no fraternities or sororities at Illinois; there, campus society and politics centered on some strange organizations called literary societies.

During the past twenty years I've developed quite a few contacts with Phi Alpha, one of the men's societies at Illinois. My brother joined Phi Alpha as an undergraduate, my father was initiated as an honorary member, my father-in-law was an active member of Phi Alpha as an undergraduate, and finally I was initiated as an honorary member after joining the faculty at Illinois College.

This paper then is the outgrowth of a gnawing interest in the origins and history of the literary society as a campus institution and in discovering why literary societies still flourish at Illinois College.

The American colonial college, as might be expected, was consciously patterned after the English university college. The literary society, however, seems to have been a distinctly American development, appearing on the pre-Revolutionary scene as a result of a "feast of patriotic oratory,"[1] truly "children of the Enlightenment."[2]

The first such societies seem to have appeared at Yale in 1753 with the founding of two competing societies, the Linonian and the Brothers in Unity. At Harvard the Speaking Club and the Mercurian Club were established in 1770. Samuel Eliot Morison credits the College of William and Mary with the origin of the club and fraternity movement, although Phi Beta Kappa, the surviving vestige of the William and Mary clubs, was not established until 1776. A chapter of Phi Beta Kappa was established at Harvard in 1781, with meetings "literary in character, like those of the Speaking Clubs."[3] At Princeton, the fourth permanent college to be chartered in the colonies, the Plain Dealing Club and the Well Meaning Society were founded in 1765, evolving into the American Whig and Cliosophic societies in 1770.

To understand why times were particularly propitious for the literary society movement, it is necessary to realize how different the colonial colleges were from those of a century or so later. The curriculum of the colonial college was a carefully controlled mixture of the Seven Liberal Arts and the Three Philosophies of the medieval universities with the Renaissance-accredited studies of the classical belles-lettres and the learned tongues of Latin and Greek. Campus life was patterned on that of the English residential college. Disci-

---

1. Samuel Eliot Morison, *Three Centuries of Harvard, 1636–1936* (Cambridge: Harvard Univ. Press, 1936), p. 138.

2. Frederick Rudolph, *The American College and University* (New York: Knopf, 1962), p. 137.

3. Morison, p. 181.

pline was rigorous and teaching was emphasized rather than study. Classroom instruction often consisted of little more than rote recitation by the students of the day's assigned reading in the textbook. Under such a system there was little need for a college library, and such libraries as there were primarily contained theological works, "dusty tomes—mostly polemical and controversial,"[4] and student access was strictly limited.

Certainly the formal functions of the colonial college did not include the fostering of a spirit of inquiry among its students. In retrospect it should come as no surprise that a period in American history typified by Thomas Paine, Benjamin Franklin, and Patrick Henry found college students eager to discuss the tumultuous issues of their time. Finding no opportunity to do so within the curricular framework of the colonial college, the students turned to what we would call in today's jargon extracurricular activities.

As the American colleges spread westward, and particularly as they moved into the Middle West following the War of 1812, the literary societies moved with them. This was not in the manner in which the Greek-letter fraternities later "colonized" neighboring campuses; in fact, the history of the literary society movement discloses very little of such activity. Rather, at least two literary societies sprang up on most campuses almost as soon as there were enough students to elect officers. The societies may well have been something less than spontaneous student creations, as many of the new colleges were fashioned by their Eastern-educated presidents and faculties as facsimiles of the colleges from which they had graduated, at least as far as frontier conditions would permit.

Four examples from the Midwest demonstrate the typical development of literary societies on the campus of a new college. Wabash College, founded in 1832, began classes in 1833. In 1834 the Philomathean Society was founded and in 1835 the Western Literary Society was incorporated by the Indiana legislature. In 1838 the latter society reorganized as the Euphronean Literary Society and a subsequent reorganization in 1847 produced the Lyceum and the Calliopean as the two societies at Wabash.

4. E. Shippen, *Notes About Princeton*, MSS, Princeton Library. Quoted in Thomas J. Wertenbaker, *Princeton: 1746–1896* (Princeton: Princeton Univ. Press, 1946), p. 228.

McKendree College and Illinois College were both chartered by the Illinois legislature in 1835, though they had been operating without charters since their establishments (McKendree as a preparatory school in 1828; Illinois College with preparatory classes in 1830 and college-level courses in 1831). Illinois College granted its first baccalaureate degree in 1835, McKendree in 1841.

The Philosophian Society was founded at McKendree in 1837 and the Platonian Society in 1849, although there is some indication that the latter society might have been established two years earlier. There is some evidence that literary societies existed at Illinois College as early as 1836, but they were apparently short-lived. However, Sigma Pi and Phi Alpha, founded in 1843 and 1845, respectively, survived infancy and are flourishing today.

Across town in Jacksonville, the Illinois Conference (Methodist) Female Academy, founded in 1846, became a college in 1851. Its first literary society, Belles Lettres, was founded that fall, admittedly inspired by the example of the men's societies at Illinois College. A second society, Phi Nu, was founded two years later.

It seems almost an anomaly that the literary societies of the first half of the nineteenth century were tolerated by the college presidents and faculties. Some historians have characterized this era as one of a struggle between piety and intellect on the campus. The typical college was primarily concerned with the propagation of that particular Christian dogma of the religious body responsible for its founding and its support. The course of study at such a college was usually topped off by a senior course in moral philosophy taught by the president. This course in metaphysics and ethics naturally was based on the theology of the religious body backing the college and seldom involved any objective philosophical inquiry. Thus the college president often carried the additional title of "professor of moral and mental philosophy" or something similar. So strong was the tradition of this course that David Ross Boyd, who became the first president of the presumably nonsectarian University of Oklahoma in 1892, took the title of professor of mental and moral science.

On the other hand, the literary societies represented a commitment to reason and a faith in intellect that were clearly antithetical to the expressed goals of the colleges themselves. From the very beginning, debate and discussion were the focal points of literary society activities. Public affairs of the day and the fabric of American society, then as now, were an inexhaustible source of topics. At Franklin College, later to become the University of Georgia, the societies debated such questions as: "Which is most to be feared, religious or political fanaticism?" (1829); "Laying aside all scriptural authority could we reasonably conclude that all men were descended from the same pair?" (1836); whether "a system of [free] schools should be established" by the state (1844); and whether "Deseret (Brigham Young's commonwealth) should be admitted into the Union as a state" (1857).[5]

Although literary society meetings, and hence their debates, were clothed in varying degrees of secrecy, there were many ways in which the intellectual purposes of the societies were made clear. At most colleges each society staged an annual public exhibition, or open meeting, in which it featured its best debaters, orators, poets, thespians, and the like. In addition, societies often brought in outside speakers. Ralph Waldo Emerson, the distinguished albeit controversial Concord philosopher, spoke on three occasions at Williams, each time under the auspices of students who were denied the use of college facilities for the presentations. Emerson also spoke twice at Amherst under similar circumstances. At Illinois College Phi Alpha sponsored a lecture by Abraham Lincoln in 1859; the proceeds were insufficient to pay Lincoln's fee and leave anything for the benefit of the society library. Of course, student invitations to controversial figures are not unfamiliar occurrences on today's campuses.

Another manifestation of the intellectual influence of the literary societies was the founding of college literary magazines. Today such magazines, on campuses where they exist, seem to be a function of the English department as it attempts to provide an outlet for student creative writing. But at the old line classical college it was the literary societies that produced the literary magazines, whether the task was undertaken by individual members or sponsored by the organizations themselves. At Cornell the three existing literary societies joined forces in 1873 to publish the *Cornell Review* as a literary maga-

5. E. Merton Coulter, *College Life in the Old South* (New York: Macmillan, 1928), pp. 149, 150, 156, 151.

zine. It "led the hard life of all literary magazines,"[6] through amalgamations and changes of name, until it expired in 1924, long after the literary societies themselves had expired.

During the 1840s the societies at Wabash produced magazines written in longhand. "When these magazines proved too provocative of writer's cramp they were abandoned."[7] For a while student authors had to rely on the local newspapers for publication, but in 1857 the *Wabash Magazine* came on the literary scene. It later became known simply as *The Wabash* and continued publication as a monthly until it folded in 1921. In 1885 squabbling between the two literary societies over its editorial control forced a truce agreement between the two societies concerning the editorial staff. Later the senior class took over the magazine and operated it until its demise.

At Illinois College the *Rambler*, a student newspaper, came into existence in 1877. First a monthly and shortly thereafter a semimonthly, its contents made it clear that its function was essentially the same as that of a literary magazine. The editorial staff was carefully balanced between the two literary societies. President Charles Henry Rammelkamp in 1928 wryly observed that "literary society interests must then, as nearly always in the history of student enterprises, be carefully safeguarded and adequately and *equally* represented."[8] The *Rambler* has continued to the present day, and so also has the necessity for the balance of literary society interests.

One rather curious commentary is that of Morison, who observed that at Harvard "college journalism after 1870 largely took the place of the literary societies of earlier eras."[9] *The Advocate* (1866) was the first Harvard student periodical to survive infancy, and it almost seems that the firm establishment on campus of this aspect of intellect was injurious to the literary societies.

However, it is generally agreed that it is in their libraries that the clearest manifestation of the liberating influence of the literary societies may be seen. As mentioned earlier the college libraries contained

6. Morris Bishop, *A History of Cornell* (Ithaca: Cornell Univ. Press, 1962), p. 299.

7. James I. Osborne and Theodore G. Gronert, *Wabash College: The First Hundred Years, 1832–1932* (Crawfordsville, IN.: R. E. Banta, 1932), p. 96.

8. Charles Henry Rammelkamp, *Illinois College: A Centennial History, 1829–1929* (New Haven: Published for Illinois College by Yale Univ. Press, 1928), p. 291.

9. Morison, p. 429.

highly restricted fare and student access was severely limited. English literature, American fiction, and works of history, politics, and science first appeared on American campuses in the literary society libraries.

At Williams, no fiction was permitted in the college library until Scott and Dickens gained admittance in 1867, but during the period from 1800 to 1859 Williams' two literary societies, Philologian and Philotechnician, acquired 106 of the 140 generally recognized best-sellers. Their two libraries totaled over eight-thousand books in 1861, when the college library contained approximately ten-thousand. Moreover, the society libraries were far more accessible. A similar tale could be related concerning almost every college.

No element of literary society life received greater attention than its library. Societies vied with one another in adding new titles and sponsored lectures to raise funds for that purpose. Books were always an acceptable gift from honorary members in return for the honor bestowed upon them. When in 1861 a fire destroyed the halls of Belles Lettres and Phi Nu at Illinois Conference Female College, the loss of the society libraries was lamented in both the public and church press and fervent requests were made through these media for gifts to rebuild the libraries. The rebuilding was accomplished with the aid, naturally, of the "brother" literary societies at Illinois College. That the society libraries at Illinois College continued to play a large role at that school may be gleaned from the fact that during the month of October, 1887, only ten books were checked out of the College library by students; the two society libraries totaled over three-thousand volumes at that time. No wonder then that the professors at one college were fearful that the society libraries might make teachers unnecessary.

At the typical antebellum college most students belonged to one or another literary society. This did not involve great numbers of students, for most college enrollments were only a few hundred at most. Williams in 1836 had 119 students. It increased to 240 students in 1859 but in the backwash of the Civil War was down to 119 in 1871. This was better than many schools fared; Illinois College had less than 50 students in 1868. Although the Harvard "club" system was atypical, Morison's observation that "it is difficult to see how any student of this period, unless invincibly unsocial in temperament and tastes, could have been wholly unclubbed,"[10] would be generally applicable; belonging to a society was simply the collegiate way. An additional inducement at one college was that the societies began their weekly meetings at 9:00 A.M. Saturday and often ran well into the evening, with appropriate breaks for victuals, while nonmembers were restricted to their rooms until noon before being released to sample what little recreation was proper and available to the collegian in town.

At some schools provision was made by the administration that any student desiring membership in a society would be accepted by one society or another, a system that produced much "horse trading" between societies. In the 1960s a variant of this system was instituted by the women's societies at Illinois College, though not by the men's societies. However, it is true that a male student who has not rendered himself *persona non grata* in some way will usually be accepted by one or another of the societies if he desires membership.

Literary societies also served purposes other than the primary one of providing the intellectual stimulation so lacking in the classroom of the classical college. The antebellum years not only marked the high tide of the establishment of new colleges, primarily in the Midwest, but also marked the fullest flowering of the literary societies in the Eastern colleges. They were also the age of great debaters on the American political scene: Henry Clay, John C. Calhoun, Daniel Webster, Stephen A. Douglas. As a result society meetings featured debates and so provided training for public speaking and thinking on one's feet, training so necessary for the ministry, teaching, and the law—to name three professions that collected many of the college graduates of this era.

Not to be lost sight of is the social function performed by the societies. The classical college felt little positive responsibility for student social life, so it was little wonder that students built a social existence about the literary societies, which were acceptable to the ruling powers. It was not long before the need for space to hold meetings and to house society libraries found the colleges making

10. Ibid., p. 203.

space available for the exclusive use of the societies or permitting the societies to build their own halls on campus. No self-respecting society could feel it was really established until it had quarters of its own. Thus at Franklin College the Demosthenians, acquiring a hall in 1824, were definitely one-up on their rival Phi Kappas until the latter society built a hall in 1836. The twin Ionic temples of Whig and Clio graced the Princeton campus. During my undergraduate days at Wabash (1943–47), the two third-floor rooms of old Center Hall, built in 1856, were still identifiable as the old Lyceum and Calliopean halls. At Illinois College, Phi Alpha and Sigma Pi each occupy a floor of Beecher Hall, the oldest college building in Illinois, under whose roof they have coexisted since 1856. Each of the seven active societies at Illinois College has distinctive on-campus quarters.

Once a society did have a hall of its own, its members had a comfortable club room for study or leisure, aside from its use for regular meetings. Moreover, as the American campus became more worldly, the halls could be used for such pagan purposes as dances. At Illinois College today a considerable part of campus social life is centered about the societies with their fortnightly meetings, date nights, formal dances, rush parties, smokers, and so forth. In fact, to an outsider the College may seem rather sparingly "clubbed," no doubt due to the dominance of the societies.

It should be noted that the literary society was not strictly a campus phenomenon. In many Midwestern towns organized efforts (other than founding a college) were made to propagate literacy and a literary culture. Books occupied a larger place in the interests of frontiersmen than might be supposed. From 1850 onward the most progressive Midwestern towns, culturally speaking, took pride in their literary societies. Following the establishment of the literary societies at Illinois College, men's literary organizations such as The Club, the Literary Union, and the Round Table were established in town, as were women's literary clubs such as Sorosis, Wednesday Class, and College Hill.

What happened to the literary society? During its heyday it was undisputably the preeminent undergraduate extracurricular activity—a resounding answer to the Yale Report of 1828—an institution that caused the faculty at one college to charge "that the duties of college are of little importance in comparison with an attendance on the Societies."[11] Yet today it has disappeared from all but a handful of campuses, and so far as I can determine, only at Illinois College does the literary society still maintain its status as the preeminent extracurricular activity. Literary societies still exist elsewhere, according to the catalogs of MacMurray (formerly Illinois Woman's College, and before that Illinois Female College), McKendree, Dickinson, and Princeton; but in each case it seems clear from the context that their societies have long since lost the dominance they presumably once had.

By the 1870s it was clear that in Eastern colleges the literary societies were no longer the important force they had once been. They were still flourishing, though, in many colleges farther west. Many postmortems have been performed on the literary societies, both at particular colleges and in general. The chief culprits are agreed to have been the fraternity system, intercollegiate athletics, and the all-pervading sense of liberation from the straitjacket of scholasticism in the colleges.

It is in respect to the last-named cause that it might be said that the success of the literary society as a force for intellectualism as against piety contributed mightily to its own downfall. In this context the decline of the society was concurrent with the decline of the old-line classical college. George Schmidt attributes the latter decline to three forces: the new multipurpose western state universities, German scholarship and higher criticism, and the philosophy of evolution. In order to survive the college was forced to broaden its curriculum, make the classroom a place for discussion rather than indoctrination, and move away from piety. To the extent that the college made these changes it absorbed the primary function for which the literary society had been created in the first place.

One concrete manifestation of this loss was the transferral of society libraries to the college library as the latter reflected the changing college. Melville Dewey, as an undergraduate at Amherst, devised his famous decimal system of classification and became college librarian upon his graduation in 1874. He reorganized the library,

11. Quoted in Coulter, p. 164.

opened the stacks to students, and extended the hours. During the next decade the number of new books in theology declined and the number in the sciences and social studies increased. At Yale the two literary societies disbanded in 1871 and presented their libraries, numbering some 13,000 volumes each, to the college library.

This same decade found Wabash remodeling the college library and increasing its size. The society libraries then decreased in significance and the societies soon voluntarily merged their collections with the college library. On the Wabash campus this event seems to have occasioned the recognition that the societies had seen their day. As might be expected the societies at Illinois College held on to their libraries much longer, certainly long after the College library rendered the society libraries virtually useless.

The extent to which the rise of intercollegiate athletics contributed to the decline of the literary society is problematical. In 1859 Amherst defeated Williams in the first intercollegiate baseball game and in 1869 Rutgers defeated Princeton in the first intercollegiate football game. Within ten years President McCosh of Princeton was concerned that "enthusiasm for athletics was beginning to undermine the two literary societies."[12] Princeton historian Thomas J. Wertenbaker seems inclined to label athletics the leading cause of the decline of Whig and Clio during the last quarter of the century. The final passing of the literary society from the Wabash campus in 1917 came during an era when Wabash was producing national-championship basketball teams. Enrollments in the colleges in those days were likely to be under five hundred and, loose eligibility rules notwithstanding, the athletes were usually bona fide fellow students of the nonathletes, rather than the recruited and often cloistered gladiators of today's colleges and universities. Student enthusiasm was genuine, and no doubt some of it was drained off from the literary societies. On the other hand, Belles Lettres and Phi Nu at MacMurray lost most of their preeminence some years ago, and this could hardly be blamed on athletics.

There seems to be a strong feeling that the fraternities brought about the end of the societies. "By the end of the century, the frater-

12. Wertenbaker, p. 329.

nity had definitely displaced the literary society as the central rallying point in American campus life."[13] At the outset the fraternities functioned as literary societies, but this was simply because a literary society structure was acceptable. Once a fraternity was firmly established its literary pretensions soon disappeared.

Why the fraternity system has been so successful in American college life is an oft-analyzed topic. Fraternities offered exclusiveness and the appeal of belonging to an organization with shared secret vows, but so did the literary societies. The fraternity system has also been seen as advancing worldly prowess as a symbol of accomplishment.

This definitely was at variance with the literary societies' primary goal of the promotion of intellect as opposed to antiintellectual piety. Something of a case can be made, then, that the rise of the fraternities represented a return to antiintellectualism in the form of materialism. More practically, by the 1870s the fraternities had begun to acquire off-campus buildings to provide residential quarters in addition to social rooms. It then became possible for like-minded young men to join together and escape both the rigors of dormitory life and the relative isolation of private housing, and then in their joint social activities to express their worldliness.

One gathers the impression that once a student organization acquired a clubhouse which offered at least eating for members, if not lodging, the organization would soon become primarily social— whatever the original purpose may have been. Such was the fate of the Emerson Literary Society at Hamilton College, where the current catalogue lists the society as a social fraternity, and of the Harvard *Lampoon*, where the publication became of secondary interest once its staff built a clubhouse. As primarily social organizations, the fraternities thus deprived the literary societies of the social function they had once served. On another plane the fraternities represented a divisive influence on the literary societies. Almost invariably the fraternity commanded a higher order of loyalty than did the literary society. Society activities and politics were permeated with fraternity rivalries.

13. John S. Brubacher and Willis Rudy, *Higher Education in Transition, An American History: 1636–1936* (New York: Harper and Brothers, 1958), p. 123.

By the turn of the century, about the only function remaining for the literary society was to provide experience in oratory, debate, and parliamentary procedure. In many cases the sinking societies placed considerable emphasis on this function, but this function alone could not save them.

A paternal administration at Princeton built new halls for Whig and Clio in 1890, but the halls were said to be a poor substitute for enthusiasm. Within a few decades the societies were forced to amalgamate for survival. Today the one society exists as a vehicle for speech activities, and it is no longer a potent force on campus. At Wabash, Calliopean and Lyceum were still flourishing in 1908 and were the basis of the college's intercollegiate debate work. They successfully agitated for the establishment of a department of public speaking, only to discover that society debating and classroom debating weren't the same. Deprived of their last function, the societies quickly folded.

In this discussion of the rise and fall of the literary society as an institution on the American campus I have adopted a functional approach. The literary society arose as a student intellectual response in opposition to the official piety of the classical college. It also served to fill a social vacuum and it provided a valuable training ground for public speaking. In fulfilling these functions the literary society became the dominant student extracurricular activity.

During the last half of the nineteenth century, the college moved in to occupy the intellectual ground held by the society. Athletics and the fraternity system drained student enthusiasm from the society and took over its social function. Speech activity, most notably debate, proved insufficient to maintain more than a fragmentary interest in the literary society. When the needs which contributed to the rise of the literary society were met effectively by changing times and more modern means, it withered and passed from the scene.

While factors present in the overall decline of the literary society may be identified, it is risky business to attempt to make each college fit the entire pattern. Hence an analysis of the decline of the societies at any given college must eventually be considered in terms of that college, and conversely, the survival of the societies at Illinois College must eventually be considered in terms of Illinois College.

Let us examine briefly the history of the literary societies at Illinois College. Sigma Pi (1843) and Phi Alpha (1845) were the survivors of the College's early years and still exist today, their fortunes having fluctuated through the years with the fortunes of the College. A chapter of Beta Theta Pi fraternity was established in 1856 but it died out in 1865, having initiated 27 members in its brief existence. No other social fraternity or sorority has ever been established on campus.

Gamma Nu was established in 1897 to meet the demand of an increased enrollment. It ceased operation in 1901 when enrollments were dropping, but it was resuscitated in the 1920s and has been active ever since. A fourth men's society, Pi Pi Rho, led a brief existence in the 1930s and as a result of increased College enrollment was revived in 1966 by students.

The College became coeducational in 1903 through affiliation with the Jacksonville Female Academy. The women brought with them one of their literary societies, Philomathean, but in time it "winked out."[14] Subsequently three women's literary societies were established: Gamma Delta (1911), Sigma Phi Epsilon (1916), and Agora (1920). Agora later became Chi Beta. In 1921 a society for freshman girls, Alpha Eta Pi, was established to alleviate the pressure of rushing activities. The men's societies have no counterpart, but in 1965–66 agreed not to rush until second semester.

Why have the societies continued to flourish at Illinois College? The deleterious influence of the Greeks was absent from the campus, but this absence did not save the societies on other campuses. The intercollegiate athletic history of the College dates back to 1878 and the College has passed through periods of what an outside observer would call overemphasis on athletics, but without any lasting ill effects on the societies. As might be expected of William Jennings Bryan's Alma Mater, the College has a reputation of long standing for its work in speech. However, Wabash has a similar reputation, yet the societies disappeared there fifty years ago.

Nor can a case be made that the College lagged so far behind in swinging from piety to intellect that the societies were necessary for

14. Rammelkamp, p. 524. Rammelkamp places quotation marks around this phrase.

student intellectual activity. In fact quite the opposite is the case. Julian M. Sturtevant, president of the College from 1844 to 1876, became nationally known for his views that a college was primarily an intellectual enterprise, and by 1902 virtually the entire faculty was composed of young Ph.D.'s. On the face of it, then, there does not seem to be any reason within Illinois College itself why the literary society survived on its campus while withering away elsewhere.

It is my hypothesis that the conditions for survival spring from the unusual nature of the community of Jacksonville itself. Jacksonville is one of many communities which lay claim to the title "The Athens of the West." The claim had much to justify it. As mentioned earlier, Jacksonville was the home of many early literary societies. When the city celebrated its centennial in 1925, one observer speculated that there probably was no other community in the Middle West in which clubs with a serious purpose had so grown and flourished. Such societies as The Club (1861) for men and Jacksonville Sorosis (1868) for women still flourish, along with many others patterned after literary societies, particularly for women.

One notable credential for the Athenian claim was the Plato Club of Jacksonville. The founder and moving spirit of the Plato Club was Dr. Hiram K. Jones, an M.D. and a graduate of Illinois College. A philosopher by avocation, he became the leading Platonic teacher in the country. The Plato Club was founded in the late 1860s and in 1883 Jones was instrumental in the founding of the American Akademe, a nationwide philosophical organization based in Jacksonville. Both the Plato Club and the Akademe came to an end in 1892, when Jones's health failed at a time when naturalism was breaking down the sway of Platonism.

One writer, in reviewing the history of the Plato Club, reflected that *both* Jones and Jacksonville were necessary for the existence of the Platonic circle. Not only were the two colleges present, but state institutions for the blind, deaf, and insane were all established in Jacksonville between 1839 and 1848. All these institutions brought to the community a class of people who added much to its cultural life.

Jacksonville never became an industrial community. Its character was primarily determined by the presence of academic and remedial institutions and by its growth as a business and banking center for a rich agricultural area. These conditions provided a uniquely fertile soil for the pursuit of culture.

Another factor in the Jacksonville makeup is a strong consciousness of heritage. One observer phrased it thus: "The bit of New England which those Congregationalist Pilgrims brought to Jacksonville gave the town a Puritan cast which it retains to this day. They stamped these ideals on the community and their descendants adopted them. . . . [Jacksonville's] colleges, charities, and social and cultural spirit have marked it and overshadowed the business of a Main Street."[15]

One last factor to be noted is an outgrowth of the previous two factors. The early citizens of Jacksonville, as educated gentry, sent their children to college and in particular sent their sons to Illinois College. Today both on "Main Street" and in the professions Jacksonville is heavy with Illinois College alumni, and because of the continuing position of the community as an institutional town, the professional element is more populous than in most other communities. These alumni are conscious of the heritage of the literary societies and they want to preserve them. Moreoever there are enough of these alumni in close proximity to the campus to be influential in this respect.

I believe that in this analysis of the community of Jacksonville there lies the secret of the perhaps unique flourishing of the literary societies at Illinois College.

15. Frank J. Heinl, "Congregationalism in Jacksonville and Early Illinois," *Journal of the Illinois State Historical Society* 27 (1934–35): 462.

# 18

## *The Phi Alpha Theta History Lecture*
## *May 15, 1979*

The Illinois College chapter of Phi Alpha Theta, the national history honorary society, was sponsored by the Department of History and was chartered on May 15, 1974. The purpose of the society is to encourage the study of history and to recognize students for outstanding achievement in that field. At the time the chapter was organized, twelve students were initiated. Four faculty members in the Department of History have their names on the charter also: Dean Wallace N. Jamison, Dr. Donald R. Tracey, Dr. Richard T. Fry, and Dr. James E. Davis. The charter has been framed and placed in the Faculty-Trustees Room in Tanner Hall.

The local chapter, in keeping with the Sesquicentennial theme, arranged a special lecture by a man well-qualified to consider both past and present, Dr. Walter Havighurst. Dr. Havighurst has been a member of the English Department of Miami University, Oxford, Ohio, since 1928 and is now Emeritus Research Professor of English. He has stated that during his boyhood he developed "a dual curiosity, wanting to recall the Midwest of past times while trying to understand its present." His interests have ranged widely—over much of America, as a matter of fact—but often his research and writing have focused upon the region between the Great Lakes and the Ohio River. The published result is some twenty books of fiction, biography, and regional history. In addition, he has collaborated with Mrs. Havighurst in writing several historical novels for younger readers. Dr. Havighurst has received numerous awards for his books, and he is the recipient of four honorary degrees. His formal education was received at the University of Denver and Columbia University. He is a member of Phi Beta Kappa, the Society of American Historians, and of several authors' societies.

Dr. Havighurst's visit to Jacksonville had special significance for him personally and also for Illinois College's Sesquicentennial celebration. During his college years he had often visited his family in Jacksonville, where his father was pastor of Grace Methodist Church. And, before beginning his formal address, he reminded his audience that the College's first graduate, Richard Yates, had attended Miami College before coming to Illinois College where he would be a member of the Class of 1835 and the very first person in the state of Illinois to receive a bachelor's degree.

The address by Dr. Havighurst, "Illinois Journey: Past and Present," was given in Crispin Lecture Hall. It proved to be a charming illustration of the speaker's continuing interest in relating the past and the present, the near and the far. Dr. Havighurst was introduced by Dr. James E. Davis, Associate Professor of History and Political Science, who had made the arrangements for his visit. The text of the address is printed below.

---

ILLINOIS JOURNEY: PAST AND PRESENT
DR. WALTER HAVIGHURST
EMERITUS RESEARCH PROFESSOR OF ENGLISH
MIAMI UNIVERSITY

Four hundred years ago, writing an essay on "Age," Francis Bacon said that it appears best in four things: old wood to burn, old wine to drink, old friends to trust, old books to read. We might add another: old colleges to venerate.

I once taught at the University of British Columbia, which began nine years after I was born. I found there a magnificent location, overlooking blue water and snow-capped mountains, and a campus of gleaming glass and steel buildings. But they needed something old. So they erected for a campus gateway a pair of weathered totem poles, brought from an abandoned Indian village, the oldest settlement on Vancouver Island.

Here in Jacksonville you have your own totems and traditions.

Fifty years ago, October 12, 1929, on a bright blue morning after four days of rain, you held the "Parade of a Century." Down elm-shaded, flag-decked College Avenue came the Reverend John M. Ellis, frontier missionary from New England, the Quaker pioneer Thomas Lippincott, and the long-striding young men of the Yale Band. Through shadows of the past appeared the first faculty of Illinois College—Beecher, Sturtevant, Turner, Adams, and Post. They were followed by the pioneer physician Ero Chandler, the rugged circuit rider Peter Cartwright, and Judge Samuel D. Lockwood, first president of the College Trustees.

The oldest settlements of Illinois are river towns along the southern border of the state. Shawneetown and Cairo are the best known and remembered. Near the southernmost point in Illinois is a town so small it shows only on the largest maps. Its name is Future City.

Towboats on the Ohio, pushing long barge trains toward the Mississippi, pass the mouth of the Cache River. That was the old French name, *cache*, meaning Hidden River, but now the name is spelled like the word for money. On the river chart the channel skirts a long, low willow island called Cash Bar—a phrase that has acquired another meaning. At the foot of Cash Bar the pilot fixes course on a beacon flashing green at intervals of two seconds. It is the Future City Light on the Illinois shore at Mile 976 below Pittsburgh.

Future City was plotted on the riverbank in frontier times. If it had a future then, no sign of it remains. Huddled behind a floodwall are 170 inhabitants, a store, a service station, and a one-room schoolhouse now turned into a cash bar.

Traveling through the Midwest in 1842 Charles Dickens referred to certain towns and villages. Then he corrected himself: "I ought to say *city*, every place is a city here."[1] The map of Illinois bears him out. Wayne City, Beecher City, Piper City, Prairie City—all have less than a thousand people. Illinois City, on the Mississippi below Rock Island, has two hundred. So far in its history Future City has never reached two hundred. And it has never had a church.

For a settlement to prosper it must have a church—that is one of the lessons of our history. Pioneer people came with earthly motives;

1. Charles Dickens, *American Notes, 1842* (London: Oxford Univ. Press, 1957), p. 158. (Emphasis added by Professor Havighurst.)

they wanted to own land. They first built barns and houses, but having other needs they raised churches that reached higher than their scattered dwellings. One family could build a crude cabin, but to build a church people had to join together with shared hope and aspiration. The church drew people together and it gave a lift, an upward dimension, to their lives.

How did all that happen? It is a large question, to which I'll try to give a pointed answer.

In the year 1817, in Manchester, England, the Swedenborg Society received a report from the American frontier. "There is in the western country," it said, "a very extraordinary missionary of the New Jerusalem. . . . He goes barefooted, can sleep anywhere, in house or out of house, and live upon the coarsest and most scanty fare."[2] The report also said that he carried in his knapsack a Bible, a book of Emanuel Swedenborg, and a bag of apple seeds, and that in many places in the wilderness he had started apple trees for settlers yet to come.

This young man was Jonathan Chapman, who had come west from Massachusetts in the year 1800. People called him Johnny Appleseed. At twilight he crossed a clearing and stood at a cabin door, saying that he had come with "some news right fresh from heaven."[3] He preached a simple gospel—the oneness of all life, the nearness of God. From his deerhide sack came gifts—a pinch of tea, a sprig of peppermint, a bit of ribbon for a child. After supper was eaten he brought out the gospel tracts, reading by the firelight and tearing off a page to leave behind him. He slept on the floor in the doorway, and at sunrise he was gone.

As well as any land merchant Johnny Appleseed knew where the settlements would grow. When work began on the Ohio Canal he went ahead of the digging; his orchards were bearing when the canal towns came. Then on to the Illinois country; he followed the portage from the Maumee River to the Kankakee, tramping the DesPlaines prairie where surveyors were laying out town sites. As the seasons

2. Robert Price, *Johnny Appleseed: Man and Myth* (Bloomington: Indiana Univ. Press, 1954), p. 120. (Italicized in the original.)

3. W. D. Haley, "Johnny Appleseed—A Pioneer Hero," *Harper's New Monthly* Magazine 43 (November, 1871): 834.

passed he went on across the Mississippi to Iowa and down into Missouri. In his last years he turned back to Indiana. He died in 1845 in a friendly farmhouse two miles from old Fort Wayne, having taken a chill while driving hogs out of his orchards on the St. Joseph River. He was buried the first day of spring under budding apple trees.

Now there are Johnny Appleseed monuments and memorials in various places. The one I like best is the Johnny Appleseed Junior High School in Ashland, Ohio. On its walls are words the children know by heart.

> John Chapman's apple trees produced
> Their rosy fruit and fair.
> John Chapman scattered Bible leaves
> Proclaiming God was there.
>
> Oh green above was the forest roof
> And green below the sod,
> When Chapman walked the wilderness
> In company with God.

John Chapman never built a church. He left no institution. Like John the Baptist he was a forerunner. That homeless prophet had wandered the Judean country, living on locusts and wild honey. He was a voice crying in the wilderness: "Prepare the way of the Lord."[4] So it was with John Chapman. After him came the circuit preachers, men who went out with Bible and hymnbook in their saddle bags, planting the church in the wilderness.

One of them, the Reverend Henry Smith, rode a circuit in a wild Ohio valley. He reported that he had traveled thirty miles in mud and water but despite being wet without he experienced heaven within. With God as his strength and comforter, he overcame three tempters: the devil, the mosquitoes, and his balky horse. In Morgan County, Illinois, the Reverend John Brich, who founded the Presbyterian Church of Jacksonville, was frozen to death while trying to cross the great prairie on horseback in midwinter. Your venerated

4. Mark 1:3 (RSV).

John M. Ellis, missionary to the Illinois settlements, wrote to his Massachusetts kinsmen: "In passing from Springfield to Hillsboro, I swam two creeks with my horse in the winter season."[5] Sleeping in a thicket on a creek bank he dreamed of a seminary of learning, a dream so enduring that we recall it a century and a half later.

In our time the frontier is frequently romanticized, but it was not romantic to its people. They endured hardship, toil, and isolation, and they had dark and silent yearnings. Feuding, drunkenness, gambling, thieving, violence of all kinds were reactions to a hard life in a hard land. The mud-stained preachers called a calloused people from brutishness to trust and aspiration. In those years three church denominations spread through the English settlements: Presbyterian, Methodist, and Baptist.

There was said to be an understanding among the three societies: the Presbyterians would stay in the towns and cities, the Methodists would take the crossroads villages, and the Baptists would work the back roads and creek valleys. In early years the denominations were rivals, sometimes even adversaries. But as time passed they drew together, upholding similar values and striving for common goals.

The Presbyterians were Scotch-Irish, descendants of the God-fearing, Psalm-singing, Bible-quoting Covenanters of Scotland. Their catechism began with a profound philosophy: "God is a Spirit, infinite, eternal." "Man's chief end is to glorify God, and to enjoy him forever."[6] John Knox, the great Scottish reformer, had insisted that the schoolhouse stand beside the church. For Presbyterians religion and learning were inseparable.

It has been said of the determined Scotch-Irish that they kept the Sabbath—and everything else they could put their hands on. Three-hundred years ago a band of exiles left Scotland for a future on the northern shores of Ireland. On the way two rival chieftains agreed that the new land should belong to the clan whose leader first touched that rocky coast. When they drew near, searching for a land-

---

5. Quoted by Charles Henry Rammelkamp, *Illinois College: A Centennial History, 1829–1929* (New Haven: Published for Illinois College by Yale Univ. Press, 1928), p. 8.

6. *The Westminster Shorter Catechism*, Questions 4 and 1, in Philip Schaff, *The Creeds of Christendom* (Grand Rapids, Michigan: Baker Book House, 1966), vol. III, p. 676.

ing place, one chieftain raised his sword, laid his hand on the bowsprit and hacked it off at the wrist. Throwing the hand ashore he cried: "Now it is ours!"

Today in the world's seaports there are cargo ships with a blood-red hand painted on white funnels. The Red Hand of Ulster is the insignia of the Ulster Steamship Company of Belfast. It carries that grim tradition around the world.

In the 1700s Scotch-Irish immigrants crossed the stormy Atlantic and laid their hands on America. Many settled in New Jersey, where they made Princeton the intellectual center of Presbyterianism. As America grew the Princeton Theological Seminary sent trained ministers to new states beyond the mountains. They became leaders in the religious, civic, and educational life of new communities.

Here in Jacksonville the college formed by allied Congregational and Presbyterian leaders in 1829 was logically named Illinois College, being the only college in the state. In this sesquicentennial year you are freshly aware of the College's beginnings. Traveling through Illinois in 1850, the Reverend J. P. Thompson wrote from Jacksonville: "The site selected for the college is . . . most beautiful. . . . Far away from the miasma of rivers, the bustle of commerce, and the wrangle of politics, is this seat of learning and religion. . . . I saw at Jacksonville . . . the *hedge* recently introduced by Mr. Turner, formerly Professor in the College [to meet the need for fencing on the prairies]. Mr. T. experimented with various shrubs for hedging, but without success, until he made trial of the *Osage orange*; this grows rapidly, endures the winter, and is covered with thorns. It has become universally popular, and already stretches across the prairies for hundreds of miles. . . . I may mention that every shade tree in Jacksonville, of which there are hundreds, was set out within the memory of inhabitants not yet gray."[7]

The Methodists were less orthodox than the Presbyterians. They spoke to the heart more than to the mind. John Wesley was a scholar of Oxford University and ordained in the Church of England, but when he heard the fervent gospel of the Moravians he felt his heart "strangely warmed." He then turned to preaching in the open air to

7. Paul M. Angle, ed., *Prairie State: Impressions of Illinois, 1673–1967, By Travelers and Other Observers* (Chicago: Univ. of Chicago Press, 1968), pp. 268–70.

simple, unlearned people. He spoke of faith and salvation as personal experience, an ineffable feeling more than an articulated belief.

In America Wesley's followers carried on a ministry that aroused fervor and enthusiasm. The one we know best is Peter Cartwright. In 1825 he took charge of the huge wild central district of Illinois. Traveling through a region without roads, bridges, or ferries, he brought lonely people together for praise and prayer. His preaching awakened hope and trust in souls that had been torn by greed and rancor. Once while taking dinner with the governor of Illinois, he stopped the meal, saying: "Hold on, Governor, ask the blessing."[8] The governor said he didn't know how. So Cartwright gave thanks at the governor's table.

While Cartwright began riding the Sangamon circuit, a Methodist preacher arrived at Fort Dearborn at the mouth of the Chicago River. In 1831 he organized a Methodist society in a log cabin at Wolfe's Point, where the forks of the river come together. There a Bible study class was begun in the year that Chicago was incorporated as a village. A leading member of that class was Augustus Garrett, who became mayor of Chicago. With his wife Eliza he founded the Garrett Biblical Institute on the empty shore of Lake Michigan. In 1852, when northern Illinois was not in the heart of the nation but in its northwestern quarter, a group of Chicago business men obtained a charter for a college, which they named Northwestern University. Orrington Lunt, the founder of Evanston, waded through a swamp to reach lakefront ridges and hardwood groves that became the campus site. The college opened in 1855 with ten students.

The Baptists in the early years were the sect least burdened with learning. Their belief in total immersion took the place of a catechism. Most of their early preachers were farmers, untrained and unpaid, who on Sunday morning knocked the clods from their boots and rode off to preach in the woods. Yet this unlearned sect produced one of the great writers of our language.

In 17th century England the foremost Baptist was John Bunyan. A tinsmith by trade, he was imprisoned for unorthodox preaching. Instead of stilling his voice, the confinement enlarged it. In a dim cell

8. Carl Sandburg, *Abraham Lincoln: The Prairie Years* (New York: Harcourt, Brace and Co., 1926), vol. I, p. 144.

of the Bedford jail Bunyan wrote the simple story of a man making a journey. But the man was named Pilgrim, his journey was the hard pathway of life, and its goal was the Heavenly City. *The Pilgrim's Progress* became one of the most widely read books of all time. That Christian allegory carried Bunyan's sturdy religion across nations and across centuries.

Here in America as the frontier was settled the Baptists worked zealously for social progress. A century and a third ago the American Baptist Education Society began its work; in 1857 it organized the University of Chicago. For twenty years that was a struggling institution, chiefly concerned with training Baptist ministers. Always short of money, the University closed its doors in 1886. But it was revived ten years later by a man who had money to spare. John D. Rockefeller, prompted by his Baptist minister Frederick Taylor Gates, gave the university twenty-three million dollars. As Rockefeller's benevolence counsellor, Gates became chairman of the General Education Board that helped to shape the development of higher education everywhere.

To look back once more: Our first churches, rude frame buildings with birds nesting in the belfries, were a rallying place for moral standards. Along with spiritual comfort and moral discipline, they provided the first social unit in new communities. The crossroads church was a place where people joined in song and prayer, where they christened their infants and buried their dead, and shared their inmost feelings. In no older country with traditional folkways could the church have such a social role. Here the church bell meant praise and prayer; it also meant community suppers, Christmas and Easter programs, Sunday School parties and picnics. On the frontier worship and fellowship were joined together.

The church bell also meant learning. "You shall know the truth, and the truth shall make you free"[9] was a familiar text in the rough-hewn pulpits. The organizing of schools and their support required groups of people, and the first groups were church congregations. Before a state university was chartered in Ohio, Illinois, and Iowa, those states were dotted with Presbyterian, Methodist, and other

9. John 8:32 (AV). (Adapted)

sectarian colleges. The presidents and professors of the early academies were ordained ministers, their trustees were churchmen, and
church societies raised money to keep the doors open to the young.
William Holmes McGuffey, whose *Eclectic Readers* had the greatest
influence on children in American schools, was a Presbyterian minister as well as a university professor. The America we belong to was
shaped and uplifted by its churches.

The best way to honor the past is to aspire for the future. At
Christmastime two years ago I received a small box labeled "Man of
1776." Inside was a miniature figure of George Washington in boots
and sword and army cloak, his white hair showing under a three-
cornered hat. "Bicentennial," I said. "What will the merchandisers
think of next?" Then, as I turned it over, something caught my eye.
There was a tiny label that started me thinking. It read "Made in
Taiwan."

Last October I was in Taipei for the Taiwan Independence Day,
October 10, the 40th anniversary of Nationalist China. The capitol
city was bright with flags and banners and thronged with people
from all across the country. At noon a crowd gathered on the great
square before the Presidential Palace. There six-thousand children in
red and blue school uniforms marched across the plaza and filled a
grandstand. At a signal they held up color cards that formed the
national flag, while fifty-thousand people cheered. Then, on signal,
their cards formed four Chinese words, each word as big as this
auditorium.

While applause resounded, I tried to guess what ancient Oriental
wisdom those words expressed. In my pocket notebook I wrote:
"venerable ancestors," "honored dead," "national virtue," "guardian
spirit."

Two days later, in Hong Kong, I found in the *South China Post* a
report of the Taiwan celebration with a photograph of the six thousand children and a translation of their slogans. The four words were
"superhighway," "big steel mill," "international airport," "ocean terminal." Instead of the wisdom of the ancient East this forty-year-old
country was reaching for material improvement.

That seemed to me a let-down, a disappointment—until I realized
that it was inevitable in a developing country. Material improvement

was the driving force in frontier America, where people dreamed of bigger fields, better roads, larger houses. That was the motivation of a Swedish immigrant, Lars Bengston, who brought his family to Illinois 120 years ago. In Kane County they cleared a fifteen-acre farm and built a two-room cabin. Every day they walked a mile for drinking water and on Sunday they trudged six miles to the Lutheran Church in Geneva. In 1870, along with two other Swedish families, they organized the Bethany Church in their village of Batavia. When Lars Bengston died in 1900, Batavia was a substantial town surrounded by rich farm lands.

Here in mid-America, with all the material progress that has given us the most abundant life ever known by any people, we still have material dreams: of new technologies that will convert coal into gas, of mass transit lines to serve our cities, of satellite communications that carry sound and picture around the earth, of nuclear research that will bring increasing mastery of nature.

One of the last poems written by Robert Frost was called "In the Clearing." It described a shaggy opening in the woods and the cabin that stood there. But the real matter of the poem is the clearing that human history has made in the wilderness of nature. Nowhere in the world is there a more striking example of that clearing than in the great Illinois Synchrotron near Batavia, where scientists peer into the worlds that exist in the nucleus of the atom—looking into the infinitesimal on the same relative scale that astronomers look into the infinite.

That awesome atomic frontier has a new language: men use their accelerator, their main ring, and their beam lines to explore protons, neutrons, and electrons—the subatomic particles that form the basic structure of all matter. For a dramatic vision of the future there is no place more marvelous than the acres cleared by Lars Bengston and his sons. Their farm now lies under the main ring of the great Fermilab, where silent protons hurl through the accelerator at the speed of light. The 1980s are a frontier of incalculable promise.

Yet we are already an enormously productive nation, and it is not enough to dream of further material progress. We do not need more possessions; we need more wisdom, more compassion and magnanimity. Our future city is not a bigger but a better city—a city of better people living a better life.

On October 10 in Taipei, after the all-day celebration, I went to my small Chinese hotel. The elevator boy, on his low bench, was studying a hand-written page—in English; on the Taiwan Independence Day he was learning our language. It was a slow lift and I was the only passenger; on the way up I looked over his shoulder, wondering what lesson he was learning. It was, to my surprise, a page of poetry. And to my greater surprise the poem was entitled "America the Beautiful."

I had some things to think about as I sat in my hotel window watching the dusk darken that teeming Chinese city. Our country— with all its greed and violence, its oppression and injustice, its distrust and cynicism—our country is still the envy and wonder of the world. "America the Beautiful": "God shed his grace on thee." We are the fortunate people, blessed with a land of plenty, richly endowed by nature, and heroically developed by our forebears. But there was the bottom line of the page that Chinese boy was learning. "And crown thy good with brotherhood / From sea to shining sea."

His language lesson was a lesson for me—the only lesson that can redeem our future from its doubts and fears. The dream is not new; it is as old as the beginnings of human culture and civilization. It is the dream the church and the college brought into the American wilderness, the still-unrealized dream of human brotherhood and the nearness of God. The kingdom of God is in the hearts of people, and all the miracles of technology cannot create it. A better future can only come with a better society.

Fifty years ago, during the Illinois College Centennial in 1929, a speaker declared, "The world is better than it used to be."[10] Will anyone say that in your Sesquicentennial observance of 1979? Our early colleges had a sense of mission. They were designed to prepare an enlightened clergy and high-minded public servants. They gave voice to the nation's hope and trust. Now our huge universities ac-

---

10. *Centennial Celebration of the Founding of Illinois College, October Twelfth, Thirteenth, Fourteenth, and Fifteenth, Nineteen Hundred and Twenty-Nine* (Jacksonville, IL [Chicago: The Lakeside Press, 1930]), p. 77.

cept a lesser role, not to lead and arouse but to keep step with a pragmatic society. They are bent on providing technicians, analysts, accountants, attorneys, advertisers, and marketers for the corporations. Still the sense of mission has survived in places like Jacksonville which aim to educate students with a depth of experience and of conscience, to affirm the great traditions and enduring values. In the Illinois of 1979 that purpose gleams like a lighthouse in a murky night.

# 19

## *The Phi Beta Kappa Banquet and Address*
## *Commencement Week*
## *May 17, 1979*

The initiation of new members by the Epsilon Chapter of Phi Beta Kappa has been a regular event of Commencement Week for many years. The 1979 initiation was the forty-seventh since the chapter was established in 1932 under the leadership of President Charles Henry Rammelkamp and those faculty members who belonged to the oldest, most prestigious national honorary society in America. In recent years the names of seniors who have been newly elected have been announced at the annual Academic Honors Convocation near the end of spring semester classes, and the initiation ceremonies have been held in the Faculty-Trustees Room in Tanner Hall on the Thursday preceding Commencement.

In 1979, as its contribution to the College's Sesquicentennial observance, the campus chapter made arrangements for a banquet in Baxter Hall following the May 17 initiation. The invitation to attend the banquet was extended to the entire campus community, and more than one-hundred alumni, students, and faculty responded. Mrs. Carole M. Ryan '59, Associate Professor of Modern Languages (French), was completing her three-year term as president and presided at the festive occasion. After welcoming the people who had come, Professor Ryan introduced the senior men and women who had just been initiated by the chapter. (The names of the eight students are listed in Appendix F, with the names of others awarded academic honors in 1979.) The officers of the chapter were then introduced: Dr. Richard F. Rogal, Associate Professor of Psychology,

Vice-President, and soon to assume the presidency; and Mrs. Isabelle Boehme, Catalog Librarian, Secretary.

After the dinner, Mrs. Ryan made additional introductions. Alumni in attendance included Mrs. Mary S. Gamon '28, Mr. Bruno H. Ferrari -34, Dr. J. Lee Westrate '44, and Mr. John W. Cully '50. Several emeritus and active faculty members who had been colleagues of the guest speaker were introduced also: Dr. L. Vernon Caine, President Emeritus; Dr. Malcolm F. Stewart, Dr. Charles E. Frank, and Dr. Iver F. Yeager. Many of these alumni and faculty were accompanied by their spouses. Other special guests included Mrs. Joe Patterson Smith and Mrs. Ernest G. Hildner, Jr.

Professor Ryan gave a very warm greeting to the guest speaker, Dr. Eleanor O. Miller, Professor Emeritus of Psychology, and her

*Baxter Hall, 1929*
Remodeled, 1965
Named for Dr. George E. Baxter '96 and Mrs. Baxter, Benefactors

daughter, Mrs. W. B. (Polly) Strobel. In introducing Dr. Miller, Mrs. Ryan recalled that it had been her privilege first to be a student of Dr. Miller's and then a colleague on the faculty. Dr. Miller's remarkable career at Illinois College was summarized: she had come to the College in 1927 on a temporary appointment and then served until 1964 with the exception of a period of leave during World War II when she was a research analyst in Washington, D.C., for the Army's Signal Corps. Dr. Miller had been elected to Phi Beta Kappa as an undergraduate at Northwestern University and later earned the doctorate in psychology at the University of Wisconsin. As a teacher she was respected by her colleagues and her students and was especially admired for her alertness to new developments in the emerging discipline. She published numerous articles in professional and popular journals and wrote a textbook, *Understanding the Handicapped.*

Dr. Miller's delightful address, printed below, combines reminiscences of the College before the Centennial observance with a challenge to the present generation to keep alive the ideals of Phi Beta Kappa in a changing world.

PHI BETA KAPPA IDEALS IN A CHANGING WORLD
DR. ELEANOR O. MILLER
PROFESSOR EMERITUS OF PSYCHOLOGY

It is very pleasant to be here tonight, and it really doesn't seem like nearly fifty years since this chapter was started. It is nice to see the old campus where I spent so many years—and even better to see the beautiful new additions. It is good to see old friends as well as to meet new ones. Of course, I miss those who used to be here. It's not altogether fun to be the "last leaf upon the tree," but it helps to have younger friends. As Ogden Nash puts it:

Senescence begins
And middle age ends
The day your descendants
Outnumber your friends.[1]

1. Ogden Nash, "Crossing the Border," *I Wouldn't Have Missed It: Selected Poems of Ogden Nash* (Boston: Little, Brown and Company, 1975), p. 312.

The subject announced sounds very pretentious: "Phi Beta Kappa Ideals in a Changing World." I am not a learned person, and I have no solution for the many national and international problems that arise as world conditions change. But I've lived a long time and experienced several different life styles. The "changing world" of that title is really my own small world, and the Phi Beta Kappa ideals I refer to are the ones we all share.

What are those ideals? What does Phi Beta Kappa really mean?

I'm sure I didn't think of those questions when I was elected to the Society at Northwestern University, back in 1919. When I started to college my father took out the Phi Beta Kappa key my grandfather and great grandfather had worn at Yale. My father, who had refused to go to college, showed me the key and said, "I hope *you* will be able to wear this."

Frankly, I don't think I was half as gratified at my election as I was at pleasing my father. And all I thought about the ideals of the Society, at that time, was that it took hard work, a little luck, and good grades!

I believe I first appreciated the ideals of Phi Beta Kappa when we came here to Illinois College from the University of Wisconsin. Someone who wrote a letter about my husband when he was applying for the position in mathematics mentioned the fact that I was working toward a doctor's degree in psychology. As it happened, a change was being made here because the chairman of the Department of Psychology and Education would also be dean of the college. Hence, they would need someone to teach a couple of beginning courses. Dr. Rammelkamp wrote to me and asked, if I were interested, to tell him of my background for such teaching. When I wrote back I added a postscript to my letter: "P.S. If it is of any concern to you, I am a member of Phi Beta Kappa."

As it happened, Illinois College was just applying for a charter for a Phi Beta Kappa chapter and needed faculty signatures to the application. I've often wondered if that was why I got the job! But in offering it to me, Dr. Rammelkamp wrote, quite emphatically, "We want you to understand that this is for one year only. It is against the policy of the College to hire two members of the same family."

So I came for one year—and stayed for thirty-seven!

I learned what a chapter of Phi Beta Kappa can mean to a college. It is a stamp of approval of scholarly ideals, primarily in the liberal arts. It means that the students elected to the society would be accepted anywhere as competent persons in their chosen fields. It does not condemn other fields and it recognizes that there are many other kinds of competence, but it is preeminent in its own field.

Phi Beta Kappa stands for excellence in one kind of higher education. That excellence relates to both group and individual achievement. Back in 1961, John W. Gardner, president of the Carnegie Foundation, published a little book called *Excellence*. He admitted that we really cannot define the term. He compared it to the famous Rorschach ink blots in which each person sees something different from what others see. But Gardner could describe many qualities of excellence and how it is attained in any field. "Some people may have greatness thrust upon them," he wrote. "Very few have *excellence* thrust upon them. They achieve it. . . . All excellence involves discipline and tenacity of purpose."[2]

I think I realized that far more by watching my students than I ever realized it in my own efforts of any kind. It is always a joy to hear from former students who have gone on to new heights. It has been quite a thrill to meet, in recent years, those who are now members of the national psychology association, which I still attend occasionally. I went to the meeting in Washington, D.C., a couple of years ago when Rufus Browning, who graduated from Illinois College in 1939, was on the American Psychological Association program. He was chairman of a section on the psychology of humor, and I thought it would be a good joke for me to attend that meeting. I think we both enjoyed that joke. This year I'm planning to go to the New York meeting in September and may find other former students there.

The 1960s were an era of social concern, and Gardner's book carried a subtitle, *Can We Be Equal and Excellent Too?* He was concerned with the social context in which excellence can survive. Not everyone makes Phi Beta Kappa; not everyone wants to! But excellence

2. John W. Gardner, *Excellence: Can We Be Equal and Excellent Too?* (New York: Harper and Brothers, 1961), p. 92. (Emphasis added by Prof. Miller.)

can be experienced at every level and in every serious kind of higher education.

As Gardner says, "there is excellence in art, in music, in craftsmanship, in human relations, in technical work, in leadership, in parental responsibilities. . . . There are types of excellence that involve doing something well and types that involve being a certain kind of person." "But excellence implies more than competence. It implies a striving for the highest standards in every phase of life. We need individual excellence in all its forms—in every kind of creative endeavor, in political life, in education, in industry—in short, universally."[3]

I think I began to realize all that more after I left Illinois College— fifteen years ago. I stayed for two years after my husband died, but I found it difficult to make a life as a single person in the same place where I had been part of a couple. Besides, I realized that if I were ever going to do anything different I had to get started. When I left in 1964 I was already two years past that mystic age of sixty-five when one is supposed to fold his hands, sit in a rocking chair on a screened porch, and rock the rest of his life away. I never was a good prototype of Whistler's mother.

So I went to New York City, found a hotel apartment on lower Fifth Avenue at the edge of Greenwich Village and, among other things, took some courses at the New School for Social Research, just around the corner. I met a number of people, and they asked *me* to teach there the next year. I stayed for five years, and learned about new kinds of excellence.

The New School was, and is, a remarkable place. It is the nation's first university for adults—a privately supported, nonprofit institution. When I was there in the sixties, it enrolled over twenty-thousand students—there are more now! Eighty-five percent of the students were in noncredit courses, and they ranged in age from twenty to eighty, with an average age of thirty-six. They came from New York City and State, from nearby New Jersey, Pennsylvania, and Connecticut.

The school was established in 1919 and later included a small

3. Ibid., pp. 128, 160.

graduate school in the social sciences which attracted famous displaced professors from Europe. It was the larger noncredit student body that interested me most. It, too, had famous teachers as well as many of us who were "also rans." And it was completely different from anything I had ever known before.

Think of it! Classes of twenty-five to thirty, and sometimes much larger. No required attendance, no required assignments, no tests or examinations or grades. I had followed the usual custom at Illinois College. You know—"take the next chapter for Wednesday and we'll have a quiz over the first five chapters on Friday." But now I had to devise different ways for encouraging students to read and study, and both teachers and students established new bases for excellence at the New School.

I was warned when I started that "no teachers over seventy were retained." Since I was already sixty-eight I didn't expect to last long. But nothing more was ever said about age; the contracts arrived promptly each year, and I taught there for five years. I never got tired of the New School, and I'm going back to a reunion luncheon in September. But I did get tired of living in New York City after half a dozen years, so I moved up to Connecticut where my daughter and her family lived at that time.

I think the most memorable compliment I ever received in my life came in a large evening class in human relations at the New School. One of the members of the class, a young and very black preacher from Harlem, stopped on the final evening of the class to thank me and added, "You are a beautiful person." You know, that almost floored me—I was slow to catch on to the new meaning of that word "beautiful."

While I was in New York I investigated another kind of organization, known for its particular kind of excellence. I refer to Mensa—M E N S A—which was started in 1945 in London and had become an international organization of some five-thousand members when I knew it in the late sixties. About one-third of those members were in the United States.

The purpose of Mensa is to form a group of people whose intelligence is higher than that of 98 percent of the general population. And that's fairly high. Admission is by means of a long and involved intelligence test. I took that test as a kind of stunt, and I passed it—and so could all of you.

Having been included in such a group, so what? In a few research studies and samples of opinion, the group has been used to advantage. Otherwise, in New York at least, the members formed small groups for various outings, dances, card playing, and the like. And that was about it, as far as I could discover.

In other words, the group as a whole and the individuals separately possessed one particular talent, or excellence. But mere possession did not imply excellent use of that talent.

Gardner insists that "talent in itself isn't enough. . . . We find ourselves asking 'Talent in the service of what values?' . . . In other words, neither intellect nor talent alone can be the key to a position of leadership in our society. The additional requirement is a commitment to the highest values of the society."[4]

Well, having retired twice I thought I was through, but six months after I had settled down in Lakeville, Connecticut, the psychologist at the local psychiatric center died suddenly, and I was asked to take her place, on a part-time basis. I suppose that illustrates the fact that you never know when something you did long ago proves useful in the here and now.

Back in the 1950s I realized that several of my students were becoming interested in the clinical work of psychology. My own preparation had contained little about clinical procedures. So, to bring myself up to date, I worked for three successive summers in the Jacksonville State Hospital. That was during the time when the hospital was a large and very active institution with many patients of various kinds. Several of our Illinois College students found summer jobs there, mainly in the recreational department. I joined their psychology department of twelve members and was, by far, the oldest and least experienced of them all! During two winters I also worked for half a day a week at the Norbury Sanitorium, a fine private institution that no longer exists. With work in those two places, I obtained a certificate and ultimately an Illinois license as a clinical psy-

4. Ibid., p. 120.

chologist. Now, about twenty years later in Connecticut, I was to put it to use.

I lasted only three years in that job before I retired, permanently. I realized I could no longer endure those long, cold winters and all the ice and snow. So, in 1975, after looking around, weighing pros and cons, I moved to Clearwater, Florida, where I live now and hope to stay for the rest of my life.

There are many arguments, pro and con, about retirement communities. There are advantages and disadvantages. But the aspect of them I would emphasize here is that the concept of excellence exists there, although that excellence is quite different from what we think about it in general.

When I went to the New School I had graduate degrees and years of experience behind me. When I went to Connecticut I had my daughter and her family to cushion the strangeness of a new town. When I went to Clearwater I was alone. In such a community you are a single, separate individual and you rise or fall according to the kind of person you are or could become. Gardner claims that "what we must reach for is a conception of perpetual self-discovery, perpetual reshaping to realize one's best self, to be the person one could be."[5]

Most of the five or six hundred members of my new community come from the Middle West and include retired doctors and teachers and housewives and engineers and writers and ministers and businessmen and nurses and artists and so on and on. What they were is not as important as what they are now as neighbors and possible friends. What they do together implies new goals for everyone. What they do alone may be what they have always done. You never know just what the next year will bring. I expect to discover no new place to live, but I do expect each new year to bring new interests and activities—you never know just what. But you do know that some kind of excellence will lurk within the next twelve months. For instance, I have been asked to start a "discussion group" next fall. Discussing what? I don't know. Nor do I know who will come

5. Ibid., p. 136. (Italicized in the original.)

and what will happen. But it will be interesting, I know. I hope it will be "excellent."

Our Phi Beta Kappa ideal of excellence begins for us in a rather narrow field in our undergraduate years. It can then reach out in many directions, following one experience after another, and we learn to appreciate different kinds of excellence. We ourselves never gain a total gratification even in retirement. There is always something else just ahead. As Gardner puts it, total gratification is "for the cows, possibly for the birds, but not for us."[6]

In spite of all that, however, it is very pleasant to return to this campus kind of excellence. And I am particularly glad to have our daughter with me.

The only idea I have really brought back to you is that there are many kinds of excellence, and I still appreciate what is right here at Illinois College. Lest we get too serious about it, however, let me conclude with another poem by Ogden Nash who expresses my idea better than I do. He calls his verse "The Hippopotamus."

> Behold the hippopotamus!
> We laugh at how he looks to us,
> And yet in moments dank and grim
> I wonder how we look to him.
> Peace, peace, thou hippopotamus!
> We really look all right to us,
> As you no doubt delight the eye
> Of other hippopotami![7]

And that's the way it is!

---

6. Ibid., p. 150.
7. Ogden Nash, "The Hippopotamus," *I Wouldn't Have Missed It*, p. 157.

# 20

## *The Sesquicentennial Class of 1979*
## *and*
## *The 145th Annual Commencement, May 20, 1979*

### THE SESQUICENTENNIAL CLASS OF 1979

Since September, 1835, when Richard Yates and Jonathan E. Spilman were awarded baccalaureate degrees, Illinois College has held an annual commencement, even in the difficult days of financial depressions and civil and world wars. The 1979 Commencement was the 145th in that proud series and the graduates that year were given special recognition as the Sesquicentennial Class. The men and women of the class were well aware of their favored position; indeed, when President Mundinger welcomed them as entering freshmen in the fall of 1975, he informed them that they would be participants in the 150th Anniversary celebration and would graduate in the 150th year of the College. The members of the Class gave to the College several special gifts, which were described in chapter 2 and will be referred to again.

The faculty met on Friday morning, May 18, to take official action recommending the prospective graduates to the Board of Trustees. There were 125 men and women on the list, with 61 A.B. degrees and 66 B.S. degrees to be conferred—two students had qualified for both degrees. The Department of Economics and Business Administration had by far the largest number of majors—55. Other departments with 10 or more graduates were Biology, English, Physical Education, and Sociology. The remaining students had majored in a dozen different fields. Eleven of the seniors, having completed the full requirements of two departments, had "double majors." In addition to those students who were awarded diplomas at the Commencement exercises, there were two who completed their baccalaureate programs during the summer and who have been listed by the Alumni Office, for purposes of class reunions, "as of the Class of 1979." The names of all the graduates and of the officers of the Class of 1979 are listed in Appendix H.

## COMMENCEMENT WEEK ACTIVITIES

The schedule of 1979 Commencement activities was similar to the pattern of recent years, with some additions appropriate to the Sesquicentennial celebration and other anniversaries. The traditional initiation of new members by the Epsilon Chapter of Phi Beta Kappa was held on Thursday evening. This was followed by the special Phi Beta Kappa banquet, which was described in chapter 19. At 9:00 that evening, the Hilltoppers presented the first of two nightly performances of *Sherlock Holmes*.

The arrangements for the Osage Orange picnic were plainly visible on the campus lawn on Friday as the maintenance crew set up the tables for the traditional gathering. Serving tables had been arranged for numerous groups: the College Table (for trustees, faculty, and special guests), Alumni Tables (organized by decades), Parents' and Students' Tables, and individual tables for the Congregational, Episcopal, and Presbyterian Churches. The pleasant weather encouraged a large attendance.

By Saturday a great many of the alumni had returned, and the day was crammed with scheduled activities—not to mention the many unannounced meetings which took place as old friends greeted each other. The Board of Trustees met in Tanner to give final approval to the graduating class and to adopt a resolution acknowledging the many contributions of Professor Charles E. Frank, honoring him upon his retirement and designating him as the A. Boyd Pixley Professor of Humanities Emeritus. They also issued a proclamation to the Class of 1979 in recognition of their pledge of $6,250 to the 150th Anniversary Challenge Fund. Explicit mention was made of the gifts to the College provided by this pledge: the Presidential Chain of Office, the College Flag, and the contribution to the endowment fund. Concurrently the Board of Directors of the Alumni Association held its annual meeting in the Gallery Lounge of Tanner Hall. President Connie B. Pruitt '61 expressed appreciation to the retiring members of the Board. There were reports on the sale of commemorative plates and stationery and other items and regarding the publication schedule of the forthcoming alumni directory; balloting was conducted to elect new officers.

At noon the Golden Anniversary Class of 1929 met for a reunion luncheon, and later that afternoon they assembled once again as guests of honor at a special reception at Caine Student Center. Other special meetings were arranged for Saturday noon, or Sunday, for the Class of 1919 (with the Class of 1918) and the Classes of 1924, 1934, 1939, 1944, 1949, and the Silver Anniversary Class of 1954. More recent "five-year" classes scheduled their reunions to coincide with Homecoming.

Some of the Saturday events, described more fully in chapter 2, need only brief mention here. They included the afternoon reception for emeritus professors and their spouses, which many alumni and friends attended, and the reunion of faculty and students who had participated in the Model Constitutional Convention in 1969.

The Society Love Feasts were held at various locations on Saturday evening. The Pi Pi Rho dinner celebrated the Society's fiftieth anniversary and was the occasion for awarding Presidential Citations to ten alumni, all members of the Class of 1929, in appreciation of their help to Illinois College and their support of Pi Pi Rho. The recipients were: Kenneth A. Danskin, Gerald Downen, Marvin H. Ihne, Richard P. Kennedy, Clifford K. Marshall, Theodore E. Nelson, Ellis H. Reich, Paul L. Sheppard, Harold M. White, and Charles J. Williamson.

Saturday's busy schedule came to a close with an Alumni Mixer, following the Love Feasts. This provided an opportunity for the members of all classes, faculty, and friends, to meet informally.

On Sunday morning, May 20, President and Mrs. Mundinger hosted the graduating seniors and their parents at a coffee hour at Barnes House. The Baccalaureate service in Rammelkamp Chapel began at 10:30, with the seniors and the faculty in academic robes. The order of service had been planned by Chaplain John N. Langfitt and the Class officers, who participated by reading the Scripture and sentences and offering the prayers. The College Choir sang appro-

priate music for the processional and the anthem. The speaker was
Mrs. Patricia Metcalf, Vice-Moderator of the 190th General Assem-
bly of the United Presbyterian Church in the U.S.A. and a Ruling
Elder. Her sermon was entitled "To Reconcile All Things." The at-
tractive printed program for the worship service was designed by
Class President Milan Kruszynski.

Not long after the benediction had been pronounced at Baccalaureate, the alumni gathered at Baxter Hall for the customary
luncheon. The program featured the presentation of Distinguished
Service Citations to nine alumni (their names have been listed in
chapter 2). Special tables were designated for the five-year reunion
classes, and each alumnus who had returned for such a reunion was
presented a picture of a familiar campus scene—the brick pillars at
the northeast entrance to the campus. Each member of
the Golden Anniversary Class also received a special gift from the
Alumni Association. The newly elected officers of the Alumni Association were announced and introduced: President, Dr. Hugo
Stierholz '54; President-elect (to serve as president for 1980–81), Mr.
Jerry Symons '64; Alumni Trustee (to serve a five-year term), Mr.
Conrad Damsgaard, Jr. '57; Alumni Directors (to serve five-year
terms): Mr. Ivan K. Garrison '48, Dr. James L. Green '61, Mr. Elmer
B. Lukeman -40, Mrs. Margaret Deatherage Meyer '43, and Mrs.
Marilyn Shaffner Williamson '52.


## THE 145TH ANNUAL COMMENCEMENT

The weather on Sunday afternoon was bright and sunny, and the
Commencement exercises were held on the lawn to the south of
Tanner Hall. The academic procession was to begin at 3:00 and the
seniors—soon to be graduates—began to assemble early. Members
of the 150th Anniversary Committee presented each of the seniors
with the College gift in honor of the Sesquicentennial—a silver-colored medallion bearing the Seal of the College. The medallions,
hanging from neck ribbons, were worn by the seniors over their
bright blue academic robes.

The faculty marshals and student marshals led the procession and
were followed in turn by the graduating class, the fiftieth anniver-

sary class, the sixtieth anniversary class, the recipients of alumni citations, members of the Board of Trustees, the faculty, and President Mundinger and the platform party. The Illinois College Band, directed by Mr. Leslie Fonza, played the "Trumpet Voluntary" by Jeremiah Clarke. In keeping with custom the invocation was offered by a graduating senior's parent; this time, it was given by a member of the faculty, Dr. William M. Cross, Professor of Sociology, whose son Paul was one of the candidates for the A.B. degree.

President Mundinger introduced the Commencement speaker, Dr. J. W. Peltason, president of the American Council on Education, who addressed the graduating seniors on the subject of "The Company of Educated Men and Women." (More information will be provided about Dr. Peltason with reference to the honorary degree conferred upon him later in the proceedings.) Dr. Wallace N. Jamison, Dean of the College, presented the candidates for the Bachelor of Arts degree, and one by one they filed across the platform as their names were read, to receive their diplomas from President Mundinger. Similarly the candidates for the Bachelor of Science degree were presented by the Dean and were awarded their diplomas.

Honorary degrees were presented to the Commencement speaker and four other persons, two of them alumni of the Class of 1929. Professor Emeritus Charles C. Barlow had graduated from Illinois College in 1929; while an undergraduate he had joined Gamma Nu and was manager of the track team. Later he earned the Master of Letters degree at the University of Pittsburgh and held positions as headmaster of various schools in Illinois, Wisconsin, and Michigan. For several years during the thirties he was on the staff of Illinois College as Assistant to the President, Dean of Men, and Director of Admissions and Public Relations. For twelve years he was employed in public school positions in the Jacksonville area, as superintendent and principal. During this time he was elected president of the I.C. Alumni Association. From 1962 to 1971 Mr. Barlow was Associate Professor of Education and Director of the Placement Bureau of Illinois College. Mr. Barlow was presented for the honorary degree, Doctor of Humane Letters, by Dean of Students Donald R. Eldred.

Mr. Van Cliburn, one of the best-known concert pianists, was presented as a candidate for the Doctor of Humane Letters by Dr. J.

Robert Smith, Professor of Modern Languages (German). Mr. Cliburn had first played in public when only four years of age. When twelve he won the National Music Festival Award and performed in Carnegie Hall in New York City. He graduated from the Juilliard Institute in 1954, with highest honors. He gained international fame and immense personal popularity as winner of Russia's Tschaikovsky Competition in 1958. His career in music is an artistic triumph and manifests a level of achievement made possible only by a rare combination of talent, sensitivity, and discipline.

The Commencement speaker, Dr. J. W. Peltason, holds degrees from the University of Missouri and Princeton University. He has combined in one career teaching, writing, and administration. He has taught political science at Smith College and the University of Illinois, subsequently being appointed Dean of the College of Liberal Arts and Sciences at the University. After several years as Vice-Chancellor of one of the campuses of the University of California, he returned to the University of Illinois to serve as Chancellor for a decade prior to assuming his present post as President of the American Council on Education, in 1977. A member of Phi Beta Kappa and winner of numerous awards, Dr. Peltason is author and coauthor of two widely used texts in political science. Professor Emeritus Elizabeth Zeigler read the citation for Dr. Peltason and President Mundinger conferred the degree of Doctor of Laws upon him.

Professor Emeritus Ethel Seybold was the other member of the Centennial Class to be honored with a doctorate—in her case, the Doctor of Letters. Miss Ruth E. F. Bump, Associate Professor of English and a long-time colleague, made the presentation noting the high points in Dr. Seybold's career as a scholar and teacher. As an undergraduate Dr. Seybold had majored in Classics, had won the Tanner Prize in Latin, and had been elected to Phi Beta Kappa. She was president of Agora (later Chi Beta) Literary Society. Awarded the Master's degree in Classics by the University of Missouri, she taught in the public schools for some years. She earned another master's degree and the Ph.D. degree, in English, at Yale University. Dr. Seybold became a permanent member of the Illinois College faculty in 1946, teaching English and later becoming Professor of English and Cochairman of the Department. She is a recognized authority on Thoreau; her book, *Thoreau, the Quest and the Classics*, was first published in 1951 and has since been reprinted. In addition to teaching and research, Dr. Seybold has been a strong advocate for the women's literary societies and has been an active member of the David A. Smith House Board. Dr. Seybold is expert in the early history of Illinois College, especially regarding the role of women. She was awarded an Alumni Citation in 1975 and is listed in *Who's Who Among American Women*.

President John J. Wittich of MacMurray College was presented for the degree, Doctor of Humane Letters, by Dean Jamison. Like many others in his generation, Dr. Wittich had had his education interrupted by military service during World War II. Subsequently he completed his Ph.D. at Stanford University. He has held numerous important positions in education, serving as Dean of Admissions at DePauw University, his undergraduate Alma Mater, and as director of college and student personnel centers in New York and California. Since becoming president of MacMurray in 1968, Dr. Wittich has been an active leader in the Federation of Independent Illinois Colleges and Universities. He has been a member of several advisory groups of the Illinois Board of Higher Education and belongs to numerous professional organizations. Dr. Wittich is the author of two dozen articles, books, and monographs. He is a lay reader in the Methodist Church.

The Vice-President of the Senior class, Miss Julie Skibiski, had been chosen by the other officers to present the class gift to the College. Addressing President Mundinger, she stated: "Because we are an honored class, graduating on the occasion of this College's 150th Anniversary, we the officers of the Class of 1979 take special pride and personal pleasure in representing this class. We have three gifts we should like to present to Illinois College. First, we pledge our financial support . . . toward the continuing program the College offers. Second, we are proud to acknowledge the Chain of Office which President Mundinger now wears as part of our class gift. . . . [Third] we have made arrangements for a College Flag, now in the process of completion." Miss Skibiski concluded by saying, "We express our thanks and appreciation for everything the College has meant to us these past four years. We would also like to thank the

*Presentation of Senior Gift, Class of 1979*
Judy Goudy, Class Secretary; President Donald C. Mundinger; Julie Skibiski, Class
Vice-President; Mark McNett, Class Treasurer

College for the Sesquicentennial medallions which we wear and will
treasure as a tangible symbol of our part in the 150th Anniversary
celebration of Illinois College."

Mr. William N. Clark '40, chairman of the trustees, expressed the
congratulations of the board to the newly graduated seniors. President Mundinger then made his annual statement, first recognizing
the Sixtieth and Fiftieth Reunion Classes and those individuals given
the Alumni Awards. Mrs. Patricia Q. Lindsay '65 was thanked for
her service during the past five years as an alumni trustee and Mr.
John C. Shepherd -49 was introduced as a newly elected regular
trustee. The President reported on changes in the status of certain
faculty members. He announced that Dr. James E. Davis, Associate
Professor of History, would be on sabbatical leave and leave of absence for the following academic year. Dr. Loren D. Moehn had
been promoted to Professor of Biology and Dr. John N. Langfitt to
Associate Professor of Religion. The Board had granted tenure to
four persons: Dr. William M. Cross, Professor of Sociology; Dr.
Carey H. Kirk, Associate Professor of English; Dr. David H. Koss,

Associate Professor of Religion; and Dr. Donald R. Tracey, Professor of History and Government. By resolution the Board of Trustees had designated Dr. Vidyapati Singh as Dunbaugh Distinguished Professor, Dr. Donald R. Tracey as the William and Charlotte Gardner Professor of History, and Dr. Charles E. Frank as the A. Boyd Pixley Professor of Humanities Emeritus. Dr. Mundinger then spoke in affirmation of the mission of Illinois College as a liberal arts college, noting the expansion of the fine arts curriculum which would be made possible by the remodeling of Rammelkamp Chapel and the new fine arts center presently under construction.

President Mundinger's final words were spoken to the members of the graduating class. He declared the College's pledge to them and their successors: to help students acquire the knowledge needed to function in the waning years of the present century and in the twenty-first century; to help students fight back fear and ignorance and to develop the skills of critical thinking; and always to affirm the importance of persons. "The College pledges," he declared, "to uphold what is true, noble, good, and loving." The President then asked the seniors to stand and face their parents, spouses, guardians, and friends to thank them for making it possible for them to complete their college studies.

The audience stood to sing the Illinois College *Alma Mater*. The Reverend Dr. Harold G. Woodworth, whose son Mark was among the graduates, pronounced the benediction. The marshals and President Mundinger, the platform guests, and the faculty, proceeded down the aisle and were followed by the seniors. The College Band played "Fanfare and Recessional," by James D. Ployhar, and the procession turned to pass around the north section of seats so that the faculty could form a double line and congratulate the seniors as they passed through. Then the seniors assembled on the steps of Rammelkamp Chapel for the class picture, breaking up and forming in family groups for still more pictures. The seniors turned in their blue robes and mortarboards, and within an hour they and their families were gone.

Once more Illinois College had observed an annual Commencement and once more students went forth to jobs and family and further study. But this Commencement in the Sesquicentennial year was one of the very special ones in the life of the College and all who hold it dear. It would be remembered for a long time, and the men and women of the Class of 1979 would leave their impress upon Illinois College always.

## THE COMPANY OF EDUCATED MEN AND WOMEN
### PRESIDENT J. W. PELTASON
### AMERICAN COUNCIL ON EDUCATION

I am honored to share your commencement. It is particularly "your" day. Therein lies the honor of having been invited to address you.

This is a moment in history for your college as well as for you. It is an added honor for me to share the 150th Anniversary celebration with you. Ever since 1829 this College has been part of that treasury of intellectual resource upon which the society so heavily depends.

During its long history, Illinois College has been the site of many significant events and has produced many important contributions to the state and nation. On this campus is the oldest college building in Illinois. Here President Sturtevant, while putting in the stove in that building, made his immortal observation that they had that morning opened "a fountain for future generations to drink at."[1]

Among the members of future generations who have drunk at this fountain of knowledge have been the Class of 1969, who "Saved the Stump"; the Class of 1974, that gave streaking to the world; two U.S. senators; six governors; twenty congressmen; William Jennings Bryan, who was a graduate of the College; Jonathan Baldwin Turner, a faculty member at Illinois College, who was responsible for the Morrill Act—your younger sister institution in Champaign also has a monument in his honor; and Abe Lincoln, who was on campus several times to make speeches. One time Mr. Lincoln came from Springfield to deliver a lecture to raise money for a men's literary

---

1. President Julian M. Sturtevant in a letter to Thomas Lippincott, February 22, 1844. Quoted in Charles Henry Rammelkamp, *Illinois College: A Centennial History, 1829–1929* (New Haven: Published for Illinois College by Yale Univ. Press, 1928), p. 39.

society. The weather was bad and there was a very small turnout. After the speech Lincoln said, "I have not made much money for you tonight. . . . Pay me my railroad fare and 50 cents for my supper at the hotel and we are square."[2] They paid him. They had a few days earlier made him an honorary member of the society—Phi Alpha, which is still in existence today.

I ask that you not fail to acknowledge, today, the debts to those who went before us in this place; those who helped make possible Illinois College's contributions to the commonwealth of men and women everywhere. You may also hope that when your descendants—nine generations from now—are celebrating the 300th anniversary, those who share it will judge you to have been good and faithful stewards of its values in your own time.

Having once "commenced" myself, and having since attended many such occasions, I am aware that the significance of commencement seldom lies in what the speaker has to say. You have earned the significance of this occasion. I can only share it with respect.

Moreover, exposure to commencement rhetoric seldom has pronounced aftereffects. Although I remember every detail about my own graduation—as if it were yesterday!—I confess that the one thing I have no recollection of is who addressed my own rites of passage, nor the slightest idea of what he said. And, I have grown wary over the last decade in particular about anyone attempting to dispense "the wisdom of the elders."

I hope, therefore, that you will be content if I restrict my role to a few observations on matters which seem to me important to the company of educated men and women. Let me first say about this moment that I suspect you may not fully appreciate until you are "down the road a piece" (as they say in New England) how value-freighted has been your life in this place. I don't offer you that hardy commencement cliche, "Now you are about to go out in the world." That, of course, is nonsense. You are well aware that you have long been in it. Instead I would stress that, in part because you have been here at this College, henceforth you will decide how much you

2. Recounted in Rammelkamp, p. 135.

choose to live by the things of the mind and spirit. If my observation and experience can be relied upon, I think I can predict that your choices will not always be easy.

As you do not need me to tell you, yours has been indicted as the "me" generation, self-consumed, with a vision of a world largely or wholly circumscribed by fear, greed, and self-seeking. I don't know whether the considered judgment of history will confirm that indictment. The legacy of this place, however, embraces countervailing values—the true, the good, and the beautiful. If that legacy goes with you, you can more easily live with aspiration and hope. The alternative is despair.

I use the word *aspiration* without apology in our cynical times, but with emphasis on the fact that I do not ask you to ground your aspirations in naivete. The lot of humanity is still too largely characterized by fear and greed. Nevertheless, men and women (particularly one hopes educated men and women) should recognize these characteristics as undesirable or—not to put too fine a point on it—as evil. It seems clear that such a judgment is grounded in values for the most part external to the otherwise compelling presence of the self. In this I take hope for the future, knowing that standards of value have been part of this college's legacy to you.

Let me ask of you, in passing, a brief exercise in retrospection. When you form a judgment about "greatness" in the human condition, what comes most readily to your mind? Is it the very special claim to fame, for example of a Socrates, a Lincoln, or an Einstein—because of how one taught, the other fought, or the third thought—that monopolizes your attention? Or, do you also perhaps remember that they stood out in their times as extraordinarily decent and compassionate human beings?

The true rogues and egomaniacs of history may dominate in their lifetimes. In the end, however, I suspect that their lights will be judged dimmer by far than, say, those of a Francis of Assisi or a Gandhi. As you see I argue, if indirectly, in the humane tradition!

I would ask that you never take lightly your educational inheritance—the injunction, the motivation, and the capacity in all things to make up your own mind, but to do so in awareness that no one lives alone and that one's judgment is always fallible. Whatever has been your academic interest, this College has helped persuade you that your independent judgment is not only precious to you but also a strong asset to the society. It will not be easy, but I hope you will not weary of exercising your own judgments intelligently, decently, humanely, and humbly.

You will be troubled in the doing. An issue is no issue if the truth is self-evident. A problem is no problem if the answer is clear. The truths, and the answers, seldom come in stark blacks and whites. Your education has encouraged the habit of weighing all sides before arriving at judgment. That weighing done, we need only remember that the toil of arriving at personal judgment confers no right to impose it on others.

I would not want you to think that I am either too arcane or too obvious. So, let me ask: How many of us, at this moment, could honestly lay claim to considered, careful judgment, rather than merely response to group pressures, about, for example, such issues as the divestiture of college funds, DNA, nuclear energy, the validity of Proposition 13, consumerism—to note a random few of the knotty issues before us? If you have not individually invested your competence in appraising at least some such matters of public concern we shall be the poorer, and so will society.

Your responsibility to the commonwealth, as mine, is to see to it that judgments about public as well as private matters are thoughtfully considered, that they are not made for us by demagogues, charlatans, and hucksters. Your education should have given you some confidence that you can fulfill this responsibility—and the strong motivation to do so.

I must, however, enter a caveat. There is a price to be paid for the entitlement to independent judgment—and it is that you conceive that you may be wrong, that your judgment is fallible. This is, of course, a conception not wholly congenial to most of us! The history of humankind is strewn with the wreckage from attempts to impose strongly held convictions. The imposition of one's own convinced righteousness on others is unacceptable. Educated men and women must take the greatest care never to impose upon the human dignity and personal integrity of others.

All this said, I do not intend to trot out the old commencement gambit about what a poor job my generation has done—about how bad the world is that we are about to turn over to your generation. For, as Charles Frankel said on a similar occasion, if you think that, you are wrong on three counts. First, if you think this world is a mess, you should have seen the one we took over: a world at war, a world of holocausts, a world in which the burning civil-rights issue of the day was whether we should act to stop lynchings. Second, as a matter of fact, my generation has not done so badly. Third, we are not ready to turn it over to you, yet. We are, however, prepared to share the responsibility with you. We welcome you to partnership with your elders, acknowledging that all wisdom resides in no one generation. Some of our crises are new, some abiding, but the new ones may well become abiding unless we find ways to confront them with all the cultivated intelligence at our disposal.

Two of these special troubles seem to me worth our notice as you celebrate this big day, and as we call on you to make a commitment to use the skills so dearly won during your stay at this institution. First, this country's reluctance to face the world-wide energy crisis is as evident as the crisis itself. There can be little doubt that the social, economic, and political fabric of the world is seriously threatened. The hard alternatives to drift are not obscure. Our apparent inability to pursue these alternatives is founded in part in skepticism, but also I think in the fact that the alternatives carry with them prices that no one wishes to pay.

Or consider the racial crisis, confining our attention to this country. There are few "unreconstructed" among us any more—certainly no governors barring the college door—and there is little or no political profit to be gained by pandering to people's prejudices. The law provides for equity, although we still argue about tactics. But despite the passage of laws and the issuing of court decisions, the number of minorities in segregated schools remains high, and the unemployment among minority youth stubbornly hovers around 40 percent.

The point I make about these crises, and there are many others we could mention—the population crisis, the pollution crisis, the proliferation of nuclear bombs crisis, the safety in the street crisis (you can add to the list)—is that we must recognize that it will take all of the knowledge we have and as much more as we can obtain, plus a willingness to be patient, to work toward their solution or amelioration.

Progress has always been made and will always be made incrementally. Now, incrementalism should not be confused with gradualism. Gradualism has been and remains an excuse to do nothing today, on the grounds that it will be more opportune to do something tomorrow. The trouble with gradualism is that the tomorrow in which such action is possible never comes. Meantime we drift.

Incrementalism, on the other hand, insists that we apply the knowledge we have right now to what needs to be done now, recognizing that tomorrow is getting to be pretty much like today, and that no one law, no one Supreme Court decision, no one school board election, no one president, no one speech by itself, is going to result in the dramatic resolution of any complex problem. To recognize this fact, that progress can be made and has been made by small steps, is to avoid the not-very-useful peaks of euphoria and valleys of despair.

However natural, however fashionable is pessimism, it seems to me peculiarly an evasion of responsibility, especially for the educated among us. Initiative in crisis-solving is unlikely to come from the uninformed and the unsophisticated. Confidence that solutions can be found should mark the well-trained mind, committed to considered judgment.

The bounds of public policy are still ultimately determined by ordinary men and women. Whether those policies will be wise or unwise, just or unjust, will depend heavily upon how considered will be the judgment of the millions who have never walked the halls of Congress nor, apart from television, have ever peered into a corporate board room. Among those millions, surely those responsible for informed opinion are those of us who have enjoyed higher education's benefits.

I would ask you, then, not to wonder overly about those "rights and privileges" which grace your diplomas. Whatever that time-honored expression means, it is not an entitlement to special status in the society. The diploma is not the credit card of an intellectual caste. What I hope it will signify, is an entitlement to a very special responsibility to your fellow men and women. And as you meet your responsibilities as educated men and women:

> May the road rise up to meet you,
> And the wind be always at your back,
> And may the good Lord hold you in the hollow of his
>     hand.

*Appendixes and Index*

# Appendix A
## *Sesquicentennial Committees: Officers[1] and Members[2]*

### 1. THE 150TH ANNIVERSARY COMMITTEE

Mr. Jon Mark Althoff, Class of 1980

Miss Laura E. Armstrong, Class of 1980

Mr. Stanley Lee Bracken, Class of 1980

Mr. Robert E. Chipman '74

Mr. William N. Clark '40, Chairman of the Board of Trustees

Mr. Donald R. Eldred, Dean of Students and Associate Professor of English and Speech

Mr. Edward F. Flynn, Jr., Class of 1979

Miss Judy J. Goudy, Class of 1979; Class Treasurer

Mrs. Mary R. Green '78, Director of Public Information (from January, 1979)

Dr. Robert R. Hartman '35, Secretary of the Board of Trustees

Mrs. Doris B. Hopper '41, Registrar, Associate Dean of Students, and Assistant Professor of Speech

Mr. George William Horton, Jr. -52, Associate Professor of Mathematics

Dr. Wallace N. Jamison, Dean of the College and Professor of History

Mr. Howard M. Jarratt, Director of Development

Mr. Milan A. Kruszynski, Class of 1979; Class President

1. President Donald C. Mundinger is ex officio member of all Committees.

2. Academic ranks and titles are those held at the time of appointment to the given Committee.

Dr. John N. Langfitt, Chaplain and Assistant Professor of Religion
Mrs. Patricia J. Manker '71
Mr. Richard L. Pratt '49, Librarian
Miss Susan L. Pratt, Class of 1980
Mrs. Carole M. Ryan '59, Associate Professor of Modern Languages
    (French), Secretary
Miss Rebecca E. Schutz, Class of 1979
Mr. Mark J. Schwartz '74, Director of Public Information (through
    December, 1978)
Mrs. Martha S. Vache '67, Director of Alumni Affairs and Alumni
    Secretary
Dr. Iver F. Yeager, Scarborough Professor of Religion and Philoso-
    phy, Chairman

### 2. 150TH ANNIVERSARY CHALLENGE FUND COMMITTEE

#### National Committee

Cochairmen
    Mrs. Carol Coultas Lohman '45, Springfield
    Mr. William E. Wilton '39, St. Louis
Vice-Chairmen
    Mr. Walter R. Bellatti '36, Jacksonville (Advance gifts)
    Mrs. Helen C. Foreman '25, Jacksonville
    Dr. A. C. Hart '25, Arenzville
    Mr. Robert F. Sibert '36, Jacksonville (Advance gifts)
    Dr. Frances McReynolds Smith '33, Santa Cruz, California
    Dr. Clarence A. Weber '24, Storrs, Connecticut

#### Regional Committee

Vice-Chairmen
    Mr. Robert M. Bellatti '70, Springfield
    Mrs. Patricia Carlson Damsgaard '53, St. Louis
    Mr. Vernon R. Q. Fernandes, Jacksonville
    Mr. Fred J. Pannwitt '36, Chicago
    Miss Susan Anne Teckenbrock '76, Chicago

## Advisory Members

Dr. L. Vernon Caine, President Emeritus

Mr. William N. Clark '40, Chairman of the Board of Trustees

Mrs. Alma C. Smith, Jacksonville

## Administrative Staff

| | |
|---|---|
| Director | Mr. Howard M. Jarratt |
| Assistant Director | Mr. James L. Dunsworth '77 |
| Public Information | Mr. Mark J. Schwartz '74 (through December, 1978) |
| Public Information | Mrs. Mary Green (from January, 1979) |
| Consultant | Dr. Harold E. Gibson '30, Normal |

### 3. THE FINE ARTS COMMITTEE
#### (THE ADVISORY COMMITTEE FOR THE McGAW FINE ARTS CENTER)

Mr. Brian A. Anstedt '78

Mr. Walter R. Bellatti '36, Trustee

Mr. Peter Cohan, Instructor in Art (1977–79)

Mr. Paul F. Cornelsen, Trustee; Chairman of the Trustees' Committee

Miss Georgia Crawford, Class of 1979

Mr. Michael G. Crouse, Instructor in Art (1979–80)

Mr. Rick L. Erickson, Instructor in Music

Mr. Richard H. Ewert '34, Trustee

Mr. Raymond A. Ford, Associate Professor of Speech and Director of Forensics

Dr. Charles E. Frank, A. Boyd Pixley Professor of Humanities; Chairman

Dr. Robert R. Hartman '35, Trustee

Mr. R. Lokke Heiss '78

Mrs. Doris B. Hopper '41, Registrar, Associate Dean of Students, and Assistant Professor of Speech

Dr. Wallace N. Jamison, Dean of the College and Professor of History

Mr. Howard M. Jarratt, Director of Development

Dr. Royce P. Jones, Assistant Professor of Philosophy

Mr. Bruce Kwiecinski, Class of 1980

Mrs. Anita T. Rundquist, Trustee

Mr. Robert F. Sibert '36, Trustee

Dr. J. Robert Smith, Professor of Modern Languages (German)

Miss Geraldine Staley, Associate Professor of Speech and Director of Drama

Mr. Michael Taylor, Class of 1981

Mr. J. T. Van Horn, Business Manager (through October, 1977)

Mr. Russell H. Walton '50, Business Manager (from November, 1977)

## 4. THE SESQUICENTENNIAL ORGAN COMMITTEE

Mrs. Ruth M. Bellatti, Jacksonville

Mr. Rick L. Erickson, Instructor in Music; Organist and Choir Director

Mr. John Goldsborough '78

Dr. A. C. Hart '25, Trustee Emeritus, Chairman; Arenzville

Mr. Howard M. Jarratt, Director of Development

Mr. Otis Thompson '78

## 5. THE CHURCH AND COLLEGE COMMITTEE[3]

The Reverend Edward M. Blumenfeld, Pastor, United Church of Christ, El Paso

The Reverend Robert M. Cassels, Pastor, Congregational Church, Jacksonville

The Reverend Robert N. Crawford, Pastor, First Congregational Church, Canton

The Reverend William C. Fairbank, Pastor (Interim), Community Church, Morton

Mr. William Fine (Class of 1981), First Congregational Church, Canton

3. All of the churches listed below belong to Central Association, Illinois Conference, the United Church of Christ.

Miss Janice Hagaman (Class of 1981), First Congregational Church, Galva

The Reverend Edward L. Harding, Pastor, Union Church, Brimfield

Mrs. Doris B. Hopper, Registrar, Associate Dean of Students, and Assistant Professor of Speech; Congregational Church, Jacksonville

Miss Barbara Jackson (Class of 1980), Salem Evangelical Church, Quincy

Dr. Wallace N. Jamison, Dean of the College and Professor of History

Dr. John N. Langfitt, Chaplain and Assistant Professor of Religion

Miss Lucinda Reifsteck (Class of 1982), St. John Church, Lincoln

Mr. and Mrs. Howard F. Rissler, First Congregational Church, Springfield

Mrs. Betty Robinson, Secretary of the Congregational Church, Jacksonville

The Reverend J. Robert Sandman, Associate Conference Minister, Illinois Conference of the United Church of Christ, Peoria

Dr. Malcolm F. Stewart, Scarborough Professor Emeritus of Religion and Philosophy; Coordinator of Committee Projects

The Reverend Jonathan Story, Pastor, Congregational Church, Mendon

Mr. Michael Taylor (Class of 1981), Congregational Church, Jacksonville

Mrs. Lynne Oberlander Walters '69, Community Church, Morton

Dr. Iver F. Yeager, Scarborough Professor of Religion and Philosophy, Chairman of the Committee; Congregational Church, Jacksonville

# Appendix B
## Calendar of Sesquicentennial Convocations and Other Major Events Sponsored by or Assisted by the 150th Anniversary Committee

This calendar lists only the convocations and other major events which were sponsored by the 150th Anniversary Committee or given financial or other assistance by the Committee or its members. There were many significant events which were part of the College's overall observance but which were organized by (and supported by) other committees or organizations; information about them is included in chapter 2 and elsewhere in the text.

### 1979

| | |
|---|---|
| January 15 | Convocation: Liberal Learning |
| January 15 | Seminar: The Church-Related College in the 1980s |
| February 14 | Concert: Fresk String Quartet |
| February 20 | Convocation: Public Affairs |
| March 30 | Dedication of the Hart Sesquicentennial Pipe Organ, Dedicatory Recital: Catharine Crozier, Organist |
| April 21 | 15th Annual Meeting, Central Association, Illinois Conference, The United Church of Christ |
| April 22 | Remembrance March |
| April 29 | The *Messiah*: Illinois College Concert Choir and Guest Soloists |
| May 17 | Phi Beta Kappa Banquet |
| May 19 | Reception for Emeriti Professors and Spouses |
| May 20 | Baccalaureate: The 145th Annual Commencement |

1979

August 30        Opening Convocation: The 151st Academic Year
September 23     Illinois College Sesquicentennial Service, First
                 Presbyterian Church
September 23     Seminar: The Church-Related College in the 1980s
September 24     Convocation: Science and Mathematics
September 25     Meeting: The Great Rivers Presbytery, Synod of
                 Lincoln Trails, The United Presbyterian Church
                 in the U.S.A.
October 20       Homecoming
October 20       Cornerstone Ceremonies: McGaw Fine Arts Cen-
                 ter
October 21       Jacksonville Symphony Orchestra: Concert of
                 American Music, in Recognition of the Sesqui-
                 centennial
October 24       Convocation: The Humanities
November 3       Concert: John Walker, Lyric Tenor
November 28      Concert: David Hickman and William Neill, Or-
                 gan-Trumpet Duo
December 5       Convocation: The Social Sciences


1980

February 4       Convocation: Commemoration of the First Classes,
                 and Panel Discussion on Illinois College in the
                 Next Decade
April 13         A Memorial Program in Honor of Illinois Col-
                 lege's First Graduates: Jonathan E. Spilman,
                 Richard Yates
April 30         Convocation: Dedication, the McGaw Fine Arts
                 Center, the Sesquicentennial Building

# *Appendix C*
## *Excerpts from Congratulatory Messages*

Following are excerpts from some of the letters and telegrams of congratulation received by Illinois College as it marked its 150th Anniversary. The statements are presented in the order in which they were received. The paragraphing has been changed in order to combine short sentences, and omissions are appropriately indicated. Some of the messages were addressed to President Mundinger.

### FROM PRESIDENT EMERITUS H. GARY HUDSON AND MRS. HUDSON, MAY 16, 1979

We wish [all our] friends at Illinois College to know that we shall be with you in spirit at this Commencement time which will be a highpoint in our Sesquicentennial celebration. We share with all of you the joy which comes from contemplation of the illustrious past of the College, its present triumphant achievements, and . . . its future prospect of glory.

### FROM PRESIDENT EMERITUS L. VERNON CAINE AND MRS. CAINE, MAY 20, 1979

I see [Illinois College] now as never having been stronger or more highly regarded. My hope is that it will always be true to the vision of the founders who established it as an institution of "Religion and learning." . . . Elizabeth and I who once led this great old College find no better words to express our hopes for its future than those of Ruth and Boyd Pixley:

> May the lamp thy founders lighted
> Lead thee e'er to heights beyond.

## FROM THE HONORABLE ADLAI E. STEVENSON, UNITED STATES SENATOR FROM ILLINOIS MAY 17, 1979

I am pleased to have this opportunity to congratulate the administration, faculty, and students of Illinois College on the 150th Anniversary of this fine institution. This occasion is a fitting tribute to the vitality of Illinois College and its importance to the community of higher education and our state.

## FROM THE HONORABLE CHARLES A. PERCY, UNITED STATES SENATOR FROM ILLINOIS MAY 19, 1979

My congratulations and best wishes as you celebrate the 150th Anniversary of the founding of Illinois College. . . . Illinois College has set a standard of excellence for the entire state.

## FROM PRESIDENT JIMMY CARTER, THE WHITE HOUSE, OCTOBER 17, 1979

I congratulate all those associated with Illinois College as you celebrate the 150th Anniversary of higher education in Illinois. Illinois College is, indeed, a special place. . . . The coming years will see many changes in our institutions of higher learning. But, we shall continue to look for the constant quality exemplified by liberal arts schools like Illinois College to motivate the minds, spirits, and hearts of future generations of our students.

### From the Honorable Paul Findley
### Representative in Congress, October 22, 1979

As Illinois College observes its Sesquicentennial, it is even more rewarding to consider the promise of the future. What a wonderful contribution a college gives to mankind—its teachings multiplied countless times through the learning and the application of that learning by its sons and daughters. Illinois College, may your tribe increase.

### From the Honorable Melvin R. Laird
### Former Secretary of Defense, and
### Son of Melvin Robert Laird '01
### October 24, 1979

On the occasion of the Sesquicentennial observance of Illinois College, I extend my best wishes to you, the Board of Trustees, faculty, and students. . . . One hundred and fifty years of excellent achievement is to be commended. Congratulations!

### From the Honorable Arthur F. Burns
### Former Chairman,
### Board of Governors, Federal Reserve System
### October 31, 1979

Illinois College can be justly proud of its consistent emphasis over the years on ethical values as well as sound scholarship. Under your own sound leadership and that of your . . . trustees, the College can look forward confidently to the future.

# Appendix D
## Recipients of Honorary Degrees Which Were Conferred
## During the Sesquicentennial Observance

Biographical information about each recipient is given in the chapter describing the convocation or program for the date indicated. (See Contents for reference.)

### Honorary Degrees

Charles C. Barlow '29, L.H.D., May 20, 1979
Ruth Melville Bellatti, L.H.D., March 30, 1979
Rainer (Ray) Lothar Broekel '47, L.H.D., October 24, 1979
John Frederick Burhorn '48, L.H.D., December 5, 1979
David Bridgman Capps '48, Sc.D., September 24, 1979
Van Cliburn, L.H.D., May 20, 1979
Samuel DuBois Cook, LL.D., December 5, 1979
Catharine Crozier, L.H.D., March 30, 1979
Mark H. Curtis, L.H.D., January 15, 1979
A. Myrvin DeLapp, L.H.D., January 15, 1979 (*in absentia*)
Alan J. Dixon, LL.D., February 20, 1979
Helen Cleary Foreman '25, LL.D., February 20, 1979
Arthur E. Hallerberg '40, L.H.D., January 15, 1979 (*post obitum*)
Croft K. Hangartner, L.H.D., April 30, 1980
John Edward Horner, L.H.D., April 30, 1980
Wesley A. Hotchkiss, L.H.D., January 15, 1979
John W. Kronik, L.H.D., October 24, 1979
Edward W. Lawless '53, Sc.D., September 24, 1979
William N. Malottke '55, L.H.D., October 24, 1979
J. W. Peltason, LL.D., May 20, 1979

Donald E. Polzin '51, L.H.D., April 30, 1980
Julian S. Rammelkamp '39, Litt.D., December 5, 1979
Joel W. Scarborough '48, L.H.D., December 5, 1979
Harvey D. Scott, Jr. '42, Sc.D., September 24, 1979
Ethel Louise Seybold '29, Litt.D., May 20, 1979
John C. Shepherd -49, LL.D., February 20, 1979
Gwendolyn E. Staniforth '54, L.H.D., October 24, 1979
James R. Thompson, LL.D., February 20, 1979
Kip S. Thorne, Sc.D., September 24, 1979
Colin W. Williams, D.D., April 21, 1979
Paul Williams '56, L.H.D., December 5, 1979
John J. Wittich, L.H.D., May 20, 1979

# Appendix E
## Faculty Members Designated as
## The Harry J. Dunbaugh Distinguished Professor,
## 1970–1981

1970 Dr. Rolf W. Ahlers, Assistant Professor of Religion

1971 Dr. Ernest G. Hildner, Jr., William and Charlotte Gardner Professor of History and Professor of Geography

1972 Dr. Malcolm F. Stewart, Scarborough Professor of Religion and Philosophy

1973 Dr. Charles E. Frank, Professor of English

1974 Mr. Edgar A. Franz, Professor of Mathematics

1975 Mr. Harold S. Leam, Associate Professor of English

1976 Dr. Lynette H. Seator, Associate Professor of Modern Languages (Spanish)

1977 Dr. Iver F. Yeager, Scarborough Professor of Religion and Philosophy

1978 Dr. Loren D. Moehn, Associate Professor of Biology

1979 Dr. Vidyapati Singh, Professor of Economics and Business Administration

1980 Mr. George Mann, Associate Professor of Physics

1981 Dr. James E. Davis, Associate Professor of History and Political Science

# Appendix F
## Honors, Prizes, Awards—1979
### (As listed on the Commencement Program)

### GRADUATION HONORS

#### Summa Cum Laude

Blenda Lavonne Bettis Dennis
Ronald William Doerfler
Nancy Beth Homann
Timothy Eric Jessen
Karen L. Klainsek

Clay Allen Norris
Kent Wayne Savage
Jayne Marie Verticchio
Cynthia Lee Zattich

#### Magna Cum Laude

Sandra Leigh Rogers Anderson
Jane Marie Borrowman
James William Chipman
David Lee Craft
Curtis Dean Kleckler

Christina Lee Morehead
James Dale Ricci
Steven Eugene Ring
Julie Marie Skibiski

#### Cum Laude

Nancy Rae Farmer
June Ann Taylor Pennell
Daniel R. Retzer
Dolores Ann Robinson
Susan Lynn Smith

Lynda Ann Stewart
Debra Marie Williamson
Mark George Woodworth
Kathy Jo Worsley

#### Phi Beta Kappa

Ronald William Doerfler

Nancy Beth Homann

Timothy Eric Jessen                    Kent Wayne Savage
Clay Allen Norris                      Jane Marie Verticchio
James Dale Ricci                       Cynthia Lee Zattich

### Rammelkamp Scholarships
(Awarded to Highest Ranking Student for the Year in Each Class)

Juniors (tie)                          Freshmen (tie)
Nora Jane Davidson                     John Alfred Cross
Melissa Jane Draper                    Jennifer Elaine Filson
David Norbert Kwiecinski               Kathryn Ann Hafer
David Chris Mull                       Steven Curtis Myers

Sophomore
Kent Joseph Siltman

### Faculty Trophies
Faculty Men's Challenge Trophy in Debate              Phi Alpha
Faculty Women's Trophy for Literary Programs        Gamma Delta

### Prizes and Awards
Walter Bellatti Honor Scholar Award             Nancy Beth Homann
Lincoln Academy Scholar                         Douglas Eldon Rupp
Mary Wade Seybold Prize in English              Nancy Beth Homann
Forte Creative Writing Awards
    Poetry                                         Diane Bogosian
    Prose                                     Cynthia Lee Zattich
Forte Cover Design Awards
    First Prize                              Matthew Mundinger
    Second Prize                                Timothy Blesse
Bill Wade Prize in Photo-Journalism
    First Prize                                 Jon Mark Althoff
    Second Prize                                 Barbara Kiebel
    Third Prize                                 Curtis Kleckler
Thomas Smith Prize in Freshman Mathematics          Steven Judd
Thomas Smith Prize in Sophomore Mathematics       Joseph Chapa
Robert Thrall Mathematics Prize                  Ronald Doerfler
Hart Prize in Mathematics                           Ruth Pepper

H. L. Caldwell Prize in Physics
    Ronald Doerfler                              Kent Wayne Savage
    Clay Allen Norris
Chemical Rubber Company Freshman Chemistry Award
                                                      Mark Mann
American Institute of Chemists Outstanding Senior Award
                                                Kent Wayne Savage
Gerald A. Lucas Award in Biology
    Jayne Marie Verticchio                            James Ricci
Lucas Memorial Science Award                       Timothy Jessen
Eleanor O. Miller Award in Psychology        Lori Meyer Elliott
Louis F. Meek Prize in Psychology                   Laura Hajek
Richard McGeath Honor Scholar Award in Psychology
                                                  Steven Vincent
Elizabeth Caine Art Award              Christina Lee Morehead
William Jennings Bryan Prize in Government       Jane Davidson
Fred Kirkman Prize in History                   Martin Schnake
Achievement Award in Biblical Studies             Kent Siltman
Sociology Department Awards for Excellence
    Sue Ann Kallenbach                            Sharon Snider
    Jerri Raye McManus                          Peggy Lee Weber
    Dolores Robinson                  Mark George Woodworth
    Yolanda Sample
Business Department Award for Excellence         Douglas Mills
Wall Street Journal Award                    Susan Lynn Smith
Dennis Ryan Memorial Drama Award             John McCluggage
John Anderson Award in Theatre               Elizabeth Bishop
Gerald and Dorothy Staley Senior Drama Award
                                            Georgia Rae Crawford
Thomas Smith Prize in Declamation             Debra Randall
E. Dwight Smith Endowment for Debate Excellence
    Dennis Graber                              Michael Taylor
George Gridley Wood Prize in Freshman Debate   Santiago Lange
Joe Patterson Smith Scholarship in History        Jon Hensen
Dudley Speech Scholarship                   Bruce Kwiecinski
Mary Stetson Music Scholarship
    J. Connor Haynes                               Cecilia Razo

Cole Yates Rowe Memorial Scholarship — David Kwiecinski
Lt. Charles William Sanders Scholarship — Jane Davidson
Fred Hoskins Christian Influence Award — Julie Marie Skibiski
Norman J. Gore Outstanding Teacher Awards
    Elementary — Sharon Snider
    Secondary — Jane Ann Ralston
Barbara Heintz Albach Memorial Award — Ann Burford
Mae H. and Conrad Noll, Jr., Swimming Award — David Dennler
Conrad Noll III Football Award — Jay F. Wessler
Hansel D. Wilson Track Award — Brian Henry
Al Miller Athletic Academic Awards
    Baseball — Steven Ring
    Basketball — Matthew Duensing
    Football — Neal Michael
    Golf — Lee Bracken
    Swimming — Melissa Scanlon
    Tennis — James William Chipman
    Track — Curtis Kleckler
    Women's Basketball — Bonnie Kellerman
    Women's Softball — Katherine Shea
    Women's Tennis — Kimberly C. Smith
    Women's Track — Jerri Raye McManus
    Women's Volleyball — Julie Marie Skibiski
    Wrestling — Barry Baran

Who's Who Among Students in American
Colleges and Universities

Jane Marie Borrowman — Douglas Rupp
Ann Burford — Linda Schwantz
James William Chipman — Julie Marie Skibiski
Edward Flynn, Jr. — Susan Lynn Smith
Curtis Kleckler — Lynda Stewart
Christina Lee Morehead — Jayne Marie Verticchio
Mary Lou Oriez — Debra Williamson
Cynthia Zattich

Ladies' Education Society Scholarships
Judith Duncan                                        Anita Williams

William D. Sanders Trophies in Oratory
John McCluggage                                   Jennifer Burhorn

Elzie L. Weber Scholarship Awards
For Students Graduated in Fulton County (1978–1979)
Scott Alan Dean                                      Marcus Kuhn

Student Marshals, Class of 1980
Jon Mark Althoff                                      Ann Burford

Harry Joy Dunbaugh Distinguished Professor Award
Dr. Vidyapati Singh, Professor of Economics and Business
                                                   Administration

# Appendix G
## Awards, Athletic Honors Convocation
## May 12, 1979
## ("Annual Intercollegiate Athletic Report, 1978–1979")

(★DESIGNATES CAPTAIN OR COCAPTAIN)

### Football

*Letter Winners*

Joseph Aiello
Richard Bystry
Scott Cantwell
Alan Cessna
Stanley Croenne
Randy Dooley
Rex Ginder
Ronald Graham
Richard Gross
Norman Hairston
Brian Henry
Matt Herzberger
John Jackson
Mark Jiles
Daniel Langan
Michael Long
★John Mangieri
Kevin Martin
Neal Michael
Terrence Moody

Michael Murphy
Lawrence Olliges
David Peck
Reginald Pohlman
Philip Powers
Jeffrey Roberts
Stuart Scheller
Gregory Schone
Mark Shea
Thomas Stehn
Scott Stemm
★Mark Tiemann
Gregory Tobin
Dennis VanBaale
Jay Wessler
Thomas Willett
Travis Wilson
James Woodward
Richard Howe, Manager

*National Association of Intercollegiate Athletics, District 20, Awards*

| | |
|---|---|
| John Mangieri | Mark Tiemann |
| Reginald Pohlman | Jay Wessler (All-American) |

*Conrad Noll III Football Award*                         Jay Wessler
  *(Highest total yards rushing)*

*Most Valuable Player*                                   Jay Wessler

## Basketball (Men's Team)

*Letter Winners*

| | |
|---|---|
| James Bustard | Richard Schone |
| Matthew Duensing | Timothy Smith |
| John Fonke | Daniel Vida |
| *Robert Grimsley | Mark Vortman |
| John Martin | Thomas Wilson |
| Steve Charles Meyer | Milan Kruszynski, |
| Jeffrey Peters | Student Assistant |

*Ernest G. Hildner, Sr., Award (Free throws)*      Steve Charles Meyer
*Bob Hughes Award (Most improved player)*           Jeffrey Peters
*Most Valuable Player*                                  Timothy Smith

## Swimming

*Letter Winners*

| | |
|---|---|
| David Dennler | Melissa Scanlon |
| *Mark Harless | David Winegardner |
| Carter Ransom | |

*Mae H. and Conrad Noll, Jr., Swimming Award*      David Dennler
  *(Most points)*

*Most Valuable Swimmer*                              Mark Harless

## Cheerleaders

| | |
|---|---|
| *Lorene Blette | Carole Pratt |
| Debra Grubb | Mary Rady |
| *Arlee Horton | Melissa Scanlon |
| Connie Powell | Claudia Woodman |

## Pompon Squad

Laura Armstrong
Barbara Jackson
Susan Kindhart
Kirsten Lunde
Juliann Montgomery

Debra Randall
*Laura Soderberg
Lorie Weisman
Kathy Worsley
Penny Young

## Wrestling

*Letter Winners*

Bruce Anderson
Todd Atwell
Barry Baran
Steven Heyen
Richard Kessler
Dietrich Kuhlmann

Richard Milne
Charles Noblitt
Raul Rodriguez
Bernard Schmitt
Byron Schultz

*Most Valuable Wrestler*                    Richard Milne

## Track (Men's Team)

*Letter Winners*

Thomas Baumgartner
Daniel Beasley
John Cummins
John Dye
James French
Steven Hebel
Brian Henry

Ronald Hundley
Curtis Kleckler
Kurt Maaser
Lawrence Olliges
Philip Powers
Dennis VanBaale

*Hansel Dwight Wilson Memorial Award*            Brian Henry
*Most Valuable Track Man*                        Kurt Maaser

## Baseball

*Letter Winners*

Steven Carey
Dennis Franklin
Robert Grimsley
Richard Gross

David Henkel
Mark Jerome
Barry Kellerman
Kevin Kelley

Bruce Mallanik
John Mangieri
Daniel Martin
Joe Meyers
Reginald Pohlman
Steven Ring

*Kenneth Schell
Joe Thompson
Thomas Verticchio
Jeffrey Waggener
Travis Wilson

*Most Valuable Player*                                    Travis Wilson

## Golf

*Letter Winners*
Steven Benoit
*Lee Bracken
John Fonke

Kevin McLaughlin
Douglas Rupp

*NAIA District 20 Awards*
Team: Third Place
Lee Bracken: Sixth Medalist

## Tennis (Men's Team)

*Letter Winners*
James Chipman
Harvey Hessell
Steve Charles Meyer

Timothy Pelton
James Scott
Clifford Williamson

*Most Valuable Player*                                  James Chipman

## Tennis (Women's Team)

*Letter Winners*
Connie Crawford
Kimberly C. Smith

Lorie Weisman

*Most Valuable Player*                              Kimberly C. Smith

## Volleyball

*Letter Winners*
Sherry Baumgarte
Susan Frazier
*Patricia Hanes
*Bonnie Kellerman

Ruth Pepper
Sarah Pratt
Linda Schwantz
Julie Skibiski

Mary Weglarz                      Penny Young
*Most Valuable Player*                 Bonnie Kellerman

### Basketball (Women's Team)

*Letter Winners*
  Andrea Aukamp                   Katherine Shea
  Cynthia Busby                   Dena Traylor
  Karen Kaiser                    Jo Ellen Dunn, Manager
  ★Bonnie Kellerman
*Most Valuable Player*                 Bonnie Kellerman

### Track (Women's Team)

*Letter Winners*
  Cynthia Dixon                   Jan Pohlman
  Jennifer Filson                 Ann Russell
  Karen Kaiser                    ★Melissa Scanlon
  Bonnie Kellerman                Seena Larkins, Manager
  Jerri McManus
*Most Valuable Track Woman*             Melissa Scanlon

### Softball

*Letter Winners*
  Andrea Aukamp                   ★Cynthia Simkins
  Diane Bogosian                  ★Kimberly A. Smith
  ★Arlee Horton                   ★Naydene Tappenbeck
  Mary Ray                        Carole Weimer
  Katherine Shea
*Most Valuable Player*                 Kimberly A. Smith

### Outstanding Athlete Awards, Fall, 1979
(Selected from the "Most Valuable Players" in each sport for 1978–79)

*William J. Downer Award*              Travis Wilson
*Doris B. Hopper Athletic Award*       Bonnie Kellerman

# Appendix H
## Officers and Members of
## The Sesquicentennial Class of 1979

President        Milan Kruszynski
Vice-President    Julie Marie Skibiski
Secretary       Judy Jane Goudy
Treasurer       Mark Clay McNett

*Bachelor of Arts*
William Frank Aeppli
Sandra Leigh Rogers
   Anderson
Jane Marie Borrowman
Kent Ernest Bozarth
William Paul Burger
James William Chipman
Colleen Robin Conrad
Steven Ted Copper
Georgia Rae Crawford
Paul Hartman Cross
Bruce Owen Draper
Douglas Richard Dybdal
Diane Marie Engelsdorfer
Mary Margaret Eppel
Nancy Rae Farmer
Cynthia Kaye Fawkes
Cindy Marie Fortado
Maxine Belle Frost

*Bachelor of Science*
Aderoju Alade Adeniji
Jay Robert Anders
Alan Lewis Arnold
David Charles Arnold
Todd Lauren Atwell
Michael Fredrick Baehr
William Kevin Barker
James Michael Bates
Elizabeth Marie Berning
Cynthia Jean Smith Bliven
Michael Eugene Bourn
Steven Alan Bucy
David Lee Craft
Constance Kay Crawford
Joseph Thomas Delaney
Glenda Lavonne Bettis Dennis
Daniel David Doerfler
Ronald William Doerfler
Douglas Leon Dorsey

Judy Jane Goudy
Ronald Dean Graham
Kathleen Ann Hand
Nancy Jo Henrick
Nancy Beth Homann
Jay Vincent Johnson
Barry Dean Kellerman
John Alden Lashmett
Ronda Lou Love
Madelyn Gail McDade
David Kent Massey
Barbara Ann Millik
Douglas Myron Mills
Joan Ellen Moore
Christina Lee Morehead
Dawn Embleton Murrin
Clay Allen Norris
Carolyn Opferman
Mary Louise Oriez
Gary Pollo
Jane Ann Ralston
Steven Eugene Ring
Dolores Ann Robinson
Kent Wayne Savage
Susan Louise Scheffel
Kathryn Ann Schmidt
Beth Eileen Singer
Julie Marie Skibiski
Kimberly Ann Smith
Sharon Lynn Snider
Kurt Richard Sommers
Lynda Ann Stewart
Cary Christine Tegtmeyer
Shawn Christie Turner
Martha Elizabeth Ward
Peggy Lee Weber
Delores Jane White

Donald Bruce Elliott
Diane Marie Engelsdorfer
Richard Darrel Estabrook
Edward F. Flynn, Jr.
Steven Philip Froelich
Maxine Belle Frost
David Lee Gregory
Robert Leroy Grimsley
Gerald Deen Halligan
Nancy Jane Harrell
Ida Marie House
Timothy Eric Jessen
Nancee Jo Kitchen
Karen L. Klainsek
Curtis Dean Kleckler
Walter Charles Lemmermann, Jr.
David Lee Linback
James Carl Littig
Darryl Ray Long
Mark Clay McNett
Robert Neill Mackey III
Bruce Clark Mallanik
John Anthony Mangieri
Michael Eugene Marks
John Kevin Martin
Thomas Scott Munger
June Ann Taylor Pennell
Charles E. Phebus
Thomas Edward Phillips
Leslie Ann Pierson
Gregory Pohlman
Daniel R. Retzer
James Dale Ricci
Douglas Eldon Rupp
Kenneth Allen Schell
Andrea Leighton Schmidt

Anne Frances Wilkinson
Debra Marie Williamson
Carol Lynn Glasscock
    Woodrum
Mark George Woodworth
Kathy Jo Worsley
Cynthia Lee Zattich

Linda Marlene Schwantz
Susan Lynn Smith
Randall William Spencer
Jeffrey Rich Strothmann
Mark Allen Talkington
Naydene Tappenbeck
Jayne Marie Verticchio
Daniel J. Vida
Roger Allyn Williams
Delbert Ray Williamson
Thomas Brian Wilson

NOTE: The following students completed graduation requirements during the summer and before the opening of the fall semester. They received their diplomas at the 1980 Commencement, but for purposes of alumni reunions they can be considered "as of the Class of 1979." They also received the medallions given to the members of that Class. Both students were awarded the Bachelor of Science degree.

Deborah McLaughlin Scott    Robert Eugene Zirkelbach

# Index

This index includes the names of persons and organizations directly related, in the past and present, to Illinois College. Participants in the Sesquicentennial Anniversary observance are therefore included. Pertinent features of the development and achievements of the College, and the names of College buildings, are also listed. The index does not provide a subject-matter guide; see the contents for the general subjects of the various Sesquicentennial Convocations and other events.